HELL-BENT FOR LEATHER

Postwestern Horizons

General Editor
William R. Handley
University of Southern California

Series Editors
José Aranda
Rice University

Melody Graulich
Utah State University

Thomas King
University of Guelph

Rachel Lee
University of California, Los Angeles

Nathaniel Lewis
Saint Michael's College

Stephen Tatum
University of Utah

HELL-BENT FOR LEATHER

SEX AND SEXUALITY IN THE WEIRD WESTERN

Edited by KERRY FINE,
MICHAEL K. JOHNSON,
REBECCA M. LUSH,
and SARA L. SPURGEON

University of Nebraska Press   Lincoln

© 2025 by the Board of Regents of the University of Nebraska

An earlier version of chapter 8 first appeared as "Come Back, Todd: Rehabilitating *Shane* (George Stevens, 1953) in *Soldier* (Paul W.S. Anderson, 1998)" in *Quarterly Review of Film and Video* (November 2023): 1–19.

All rights reserved

The University of Nebraska Press is part of a land-grant institution with campuses and programs on the past, present, and future homelands of the Pawnee, Ponca, Otoe-Missouria, Omaha, Dakota, Lakota, Kaw, Cheyenne, and Arapaho Peoples, as well as those of the relocated Ho-Chunk, Sac and Fox, and Iowa Peoples.

Library of Congress Cataloging-in-Publication Data
Names: Fine, Kerry, 1974– editor. | Johnson, Michael K. (Michael Kyle), 1963– editor. | Lush, Rebecca M., editor. | Spurgeon, Sara L., editor.
Title: Hell-bent for leather: sex and sexuality in the weird western / edited by Kerry Fine, Michael K. Johnson, Rebecca M. Lush, and Sara L. Spurgeon.
Description: Lincoln: University of Nebraska Press, 2025. | Series: Postwestern horizons | Includes bibliographical references and index.
Identifiers: LCCN 2024012291
ISBN 9781496241542 (hardback)
ISBN 9781496241900 (paperback)
ISBN 9781496241948 (epub)
ISBN 9781496241955 (pdf)
Subjects: LCSH: Western stories—History and criticism. | Motion pictures—United States—History. | Television programs—United States—History. | Sex in literature. | Gender identity in literature. | Sex in motion pictures. | Gender identity in motion pictures. | Sex on television. | Gender identity on television. | BISAC: LITERARY CRITICISM / American / Regional | LITERARY CRITICISM / LGBTQ+ | LCGFT: Literary criticism. | Essays.
Classification: LCC PS374.W4 H45 2025 | DDC 813/.087409—dc23/eng/20240809
LC record available at https://lccn.loc.gov/2024012291

Designed and set in Ehrhardt MT Pro by L. Welch.

Contents

	Introduction MICHAEL K. JOHNSON, REBECCA M. LUSH, AND SARA L. SPURGEON	vii
PART 1	1. The Daddy with No Name: The Kinky Cowboy Aesthetics of *The Mandalorian* JENNESSA HESTER	3
	2. Beyond the Virtual Frontier: New Possibilities of Sex and Desire in *Black Mirror*'s "San Junipero" KATIE GOOGE	22
PART 2	3. Re-creations and Inescapable Repetitions: Sontag's "Pornographic Imagination," Bacigalupi's *The Water Knife*, and the Weird Western MICAH DONOHUE	53
	4. Lost Max: *Mad Max* and the Challenge to Masculine Dominance in 1970s Australia SCOTT PEARCE	75
PART 3	5. "Touch Your Wound, Dear": *Eye Killers* and the Vampire of Manifest Destiny MIRIAM BROWN SPIERS	111
	6. Qweirding the West: Re-forming the Nation in the Novels of C Pam Zhang and Emma Pérez ANNE MAI YEE JANSEN	129
	7. Ishmael Reed Takes on the Weird Western in *Yellow Back Radio Broke-Down* JANA KOEHLER	152

PART 4	8. Coming Back to *Shane* to Redeem the Cyborg in *Soldier* and *Logan* ELIZABETH ABELE	177
	9. Leatherface Families and Final Grandmas: The Reproductive Rites and Slaughterhouse Sexualities in the New "Old West" JOSHUA T. ANDERSON AND REBECCA M. LUSH	198
	10. "What Makes You Worth $100,000?": Heists, the Commodification of Women, and Capitalism Condemned in *The Professionals* and *Army of the Dead* MEREDITH HARVEY	226
PART 5	11. The Woman in Room 237: Western Domesticity and Oedipal Conflict in *The Shining* JEFFREY CHISUM	253
	12. Transgression on the Frontier: The Ludicity of Incest in *Bioshock Infinite* CHRISTINA FAWCETT AND MARC A. OUELLETTE	268
	13. Dead Fathers and Monstrous Daughters in *The Last of Us II* SARA HUMPHREYS	289
	14. "Do I Bring My Own Leash, or Do I Pick One Up at the Door?": Kink, Camp, and Queer Masculinity in CBS's *The Wild Wild West* SARA L. SPURGEON	311
	Contributors	335
	Index	339

Introduction

MICHAEL K. JOHNSON,
REBECCA M. LUSH,
AND SARA L. SPURGEON

When we were working on assembling the manuscript for *Weird Westerns: Race, Gender, Genre* (2020), we had no idea that the book would be launched in the spring of 2020 in the midst of a global pandemic. Although the American West and the western have always been a little weird, we suddenly found ourselves in a world that seemed very strange indeed. We met with our students online via Zoom rather than in person in a classroom. When we did venture out of our homes, we wore masks and dutifully tried to keep six feet of space between ourselves and everyone else. For those of us who live and teach in the American West, we at times felt like we had been dropped into one of the narratives discussed in *Weird Westerns*, a science fiction story or horror tale set in a familiar western place made unfamiliar by the strange circumstances that surrounded us.

Given the sense of isolation that everyone experienced, maybe it's not surprising that we also started to think about sex and sexuality. We weren't alone in doing so. Data from the pornography website Pornhub show "in late March 2020 a 25% increase of total traffic change" as compared to an average day in the four years prior.[1] In *Weird Westerns*, we were interested in exploring issues of race and gender, in looking at the way weird western texts sometimes reinforced traditional depictions of race and gender but also at the way weird westerns sometimes opened up a space within the western genre to challenge those traditional representations. The definition of "weird westerns" that we adopted, and that continues to frame our understanding of the form, is this: "texts that utilize a hybrid genre format, blending canonical elements of the western with science fiction, fantasy, horror, or some other component of speculative literature."[2] All joking about Pornhub traffic aside, in looking back at *Weird Westerns* after its publication, we realized that one of the topics that did not receive enough attention (even if individual chapters touched on it) in the anthology was sex and sexuality. If the tropes of science fiction, fantasy, and the supernatural could "weird" the western, could those speculative genre elements also "queer" the western? If weird westerns could tell us something about our cultural understandings of race and gender, what might they have to say more specifically about sex and sexuality?

As we noted in *Weird Westerns*, sexuality, and a wide variety of sexualities, have always been part of both the classic western and its speculative hybrids: "While the homoerotic elements of westerns have been openly explored in Ang Lee's *Brokeback Mountain* (based on the short story by Annie Proulx) and contemporary weird westerns such as HBO's *Westworld*," such elements "are often barely disguised in earlier texts such as *The Virginian*, *Riders of the Purple Sage*, and *Shane*."[3] Eric Meljac and Alex Hunt's contribution to the volume, "Strange Country: Sexuality and the Feminine in Robert Coover's *Ghost Town*," argues that Coover's postmodern parody "uses literary form as a vehicle for critiquing the oppressive violence that is part and parcel of the myth of the American West, forcing a reckoning with the genre's covert language of desire and sexuality."[4] In *Hell-Bent for Leather*, we posit that in weird westerns the "covert language of desire and sexuality" becomes overt. If the speculative elements introduced into the realist form of the classic western "weirds" the western, those speculative elements may also "queer" the western. Or, to borrow Anne Mai Yee Jansen's coinage from her essay in this volume, many of the weird westerns examined in the anthology participate in "qweirding the West."

In many ways, the western is already qweird, and it is already (even if covertly) invested in the language of desire and sexuality. The western is a deeply sexualized genre where cattle rustling and sexual hustling uncomfortably coexist in a landscape of unspoken (and sometimes illicit) sexual desires. Even in its most traditional and conservative genre forms, the western prominently includes sex workers and fraught homoerotic bonds. In more genre-bending iterations such as the more contemporary weird western, sex and sexuality take on further significance in exploring issues of agency, expression, and possession. If westerns as a general rule enable and perform national mythos about expansion, identity, and desire, weird westerns bring to the surface and make legible otherwise implicit desires. Hybridized genre conventions reframe the western genre's human relationships in stark ways through the incongruence of robots, futuristic technology, or other speculative elements that provide a sense of uncanny resemblance and also uncanny sexualities.

In the classic western, there are few plots more identifiably western than a story of bounty hunters and outlaws. The convention of the pursued and the pursuer can frequently carry sexualized overtones about forbidden desires and unconventional couplings and attachments. When considering the role of sexuality in weird westerns specifically, there are opportunities for exploring the power dynamics of desire and consent, as well as the way sexual relationships can function as metaphors for the sociocultural spaces of the West as both a real and mythic space. Although set in the twenty-second century (in July 2144 to be exact) and involving science fiction tropes such as drug piracy, artificial intelligence, robots, and high-tech science, Annalee Newitz's *Autonomous* (2017) is a western—or weird western—at its core. Bounty hunters Eliasz and Paladin chase outlaw Jack Chen across the deserts, mountains, and plains of the North American West; through a dome-covered climate-controlled Las Vegas, where "the sky rained pixels and market awnings expelled cool mist fine as smoke"; through far northern cities such as Iqaluit and Yellowknife; across the plains of Saskatchewan to a Free Lab located at the University of Saskatoon, where Jack works desperately to find a cure for deadly side effects caused by her own pirated version of a supposedly safe drug.[5]

The hybridized joining of character types from one genre (bounty hunters from the western) to a setting from another (the future of science fiction) makes *Autonomous* easy to classify as a weird western. As Teresa Forde writes, "Both science fiction and Westerns have traditionally encountered borderlines, boundaries, and frontiers," with contemporary hybrid westerns often drawing "upon the notion of the frontier in complex ways" or representing a version of the western's American frontier setting in more abstract or metaphorical ways (the new frontier of unexplored space as traveled by spacecraft, or the new frontier of a previously unknown planetary environment).[6] *Autonomous* describes an identifiably western setting and landscape, a future version of the western United States and Canada, but the frontier is also rendered more abstractly, in the frontiers of scientific research and technology, and also in futuristic cities that replicate the western's untamed frontier towns as outlaw spaces with plenty of substance abuse and carousing, illegal activity (including the buying and selling of humans), and dangerous technology. However, *Autonomous* is most distinctively western in its characters, its rogues and outlaws and those who chase after them; notably, the erotic connection between these western archetypes charges and frames the dynamics of the typical western bounty hunter plot conventions.

A newly booted robot at the beginning of the novel, Paladin is paired with human bounty hunter Eliasz, and the story of their developing bond and erotic partnership is as central to the novel as the chases, shoot-outs, and Jack's outlaw adventures. During a training exercise at a shooting range, Eliasz asks Paladin to carry him on his back and allow him to operate his weapons systems. Resting his hands on the guns that protrude from Paladin's chest, "Eliasz' right hand began to move slowly, getting to know the whole barrel by feel." With his lips pressed against the metal carapace that covers Paladin's back, Eliasz whispers instructions as he "continued to touch the exposed metal of Paladin's guns, fingers wrapped around each slim barrel for a few seconds until they became too hot. . . . Paladin had a lot of ammo to burn, and he took his time."[7] Paladin observes, "Eliasz' heart was beating fast, his skin slightly damp. The man's reproductive organ, whose functioning Paladin understood only from military anatomy training, was engorged with blood. The transformation registered on his heat, pressure, and movement sensors." Paladin continues to fire his weapons, "but his sensorium was focused entirely on Eliasz' body."[8]

Erotic gunplay is, of course, no stranger to the classic western. In Zane Grey's *Riders of the Purple Sage*, the gunfighter Lassiter's long, heavy guns are the object of Jane Withersteen's fear and fascination. Late in the novel, Lassiter "unbuckled the heavy cartridge-belt, and laid it with the heavy, swinging gun-sheaths, in her lap." Without his guns, Lassiter "appeared shorn of strength, defenseless, a smaller man," and Jane, regretting her role ("Was she Delilah?") in that symbolic castration, "rose, and with blundering fingers buckled the belt round his waist where it belonged."[9] If the gun/penis analogy is not as direct as in *Autonomous*, there is lots of buckling and unbuckling here, and fingers "blundering" around unfamiliar parts, not to mention focused attention on laps and waists. As we noted about the John Wayne film *Red River* (1948) in *Weird Westerns*, we watch "two handsome young cowboys meet on a cattle drive and admire each other's guns: each man pulls his six-shooter from its holster and hands it over to the other to be weighed and fondled before they fire off together in a spontaneous bout of target practice, with each man shooting the other's weapons."[10] The scene with Eliasz and Paladin, if more explicitly rendered, nonetheless has a clear lineage to similar moments in the classic western.

Throughout much of the rest of the book, Paladin tries to make sense of this event, running searches on human sexuality in the background even as he remains on task in tracking down Jack. *Autonomous*'s bounty hunter story is an exploration of the nature and the bond of partnership, of the connections made by individuals working together to accomplish a violent task—a central thematic concern of the classic western as well. The human-robot pairing also suggests the common frontier narrative theme of interracial partnership, a feature of both classic frontier stories such as James Fenimore Cooper's white "man without a cross" Natty Bumppo and his "Mohican" companion Chingachgook and weird westerns such as the "final frontier" exploits of the human Captain Kirk and his half-Vulcan first officer Spock of *Star Trek*. The human-robot pairing relies on the foil of human intelligence and biological embodiment juxtaposed with artificial intelligence and mechanical embodiment as the science fiction version of individual humans negotiating difference and otherness.[11] What *Autonomous* brings to the surface and explores directly is the erotics of partnership, the imbrication of otherness, desire, and sexuality—elements as well (even if submerged, repressed, displaced) of the frontier narrative (as Leslie Fiedler in *Love and Death in the American Novel* long ago suggested).[12]

In her discussion of Joanna Russ's classic feminist science fiction novel *The Female Man*, Veronica Hollinger points out that the cyborg character Jael "works exactly to disrupt the naturalized relations among sexed bodies, sexual desires, and gendered behaviors which maintain heterosexuality's psychological and social hegemony."[13] "Technology," Susan S. Martins writes, "can interrupt the natural and the normalized."[14] When Jael has sex with her lover Davy ("the most beautiful man in the world"), who turns out to be an artificial construct rather than a human, she observes, "Alas! Those who were shocked at my making love that way to a man are now shocked at my making love to a machine; you can't win."[15] As Hollinger observes, "This particular sexual activity—the female cyborg fucking her automated/subhuman lover—falls outside the Butlerian arena of cultural intelligibility. It cannot be categorized as simply and straightforwardly heterosexual; but nor is it anything like homosexuality. Retrospectively, Jael's sexuality can most easily be located within the spacious non-category of queer. And what is most notable in Russ's construction of Jael is how technology—so often figured in science fiction as anathema to human/natural sexuality—is here what enhances and supports sexuality."[16]

Adding advanced technology to the western—queering the western by interrupting the naturalized and normalized genre expectations we might bring to a western story—opens up space for exploring classic western themes (e.g., encountering otherness and difference) in new ways. But what are we to make of *Autonomous*'s story of the developing bond between two bounty hunters? Surely, the bond between Natty Bumppo and Chingachgook could be described accurately as at least a homosocial one, while the slash fiction dedicated to imagining a romantic, homoerotic relationship between Kirk and Spock (commonly abbreviated K/S or Spirk) is so extensive, entire databases are dedicated to it, and scholar Henry Jenkins suggests their partnership may provide the earliest known work of slash fiction, dating to 1974.[17] But while the description of Eliasz becoming erect while stroking the phallic protrusion of Paladin's weapon suggests homosexuality, the ambiguity of AI gender makes such a reading incomplete at best. Paladin has neither sex nor gender, but the homophobic Eliasz perceives him as masculine: "Military bots, especially ones with armored bodies like Paladin's, were almost always called 'he.'"[18] Robots in this world have biological parts, including a human brain (which is used as an interface to aid in facial recognition).[19] Paladin attempts to track down the identity of the donor whose brain is encased in a protective container in his torso, eventually revealing to Eliasz, "She gave me this brain," information that helps Eliasz resolve his conflict: "Should I start calling you 'she'?"[20] "As a robot," Paladin "didn't care what pronoun people used," observing that "changing his pronoun would make absolutely no difference at all," but then "Paladin considered the implications of Eliasz' facial expression, which at the moment hovered between desire and fear. Of course: If Paladin were female, Eliasz would not be a faggot. And maybe then Eliasz could touch Paladin again, the way he had last night, giving and receiving pleasure in an undocumented form of emotional feedback loop."[21] Homophobia is an element of Eliasz's characterization. If Paladin is not homophobic, he picks up on and repeats his partner's language choices, and he recognizes that Eliasz's perceptions of gender and sexual identity are a barrier between them. After a moment's thought, Paladin responds, "Yes." From that point onward, Paladin is "she," and Eliasz and Paladin are coworkers, partners, and lovers, as well as highly trained, heavily armed killers.

Like a classic western, *Autonomous* is a story of violent frontier adventure, and it is also a story of transformation, rebirth, and renewal. However, it is not so much a story of regeneration through violence as regeneration in spite of violence. Paladin's identity change is not brought about by violent action, nor does that identity change alter her ability and capacity for violence. The bounty hunters do (or try to do) what they were hired for. The final showdown with the outlaw Jack does not go quite as planned, but Paladin (although severely damaged) and Eliasz survive. Together, they decide to set aside their guns and travel to a new frontier on a settlement on Mars. A human-bot relationship, Paladin observes, "wouldn't matter as much on Mars, where the labor shortage meant all were welcome, especially a bot who could work outside the atmosphere domes."[22] As part of this weird western's project of queering the western, we get an ending that suggests the classic genre's form while moving beyond it in radical ways. The bond of work that joins together cowboy partners in the western is here dissolved, and rather than moving on to a new job (a new town to tame, a new quarry to hunt, a new herd of cattle to drive) that allows them to remain together without changing the nature of their bond, the work relationship is set aside for romantic partnership. Rather than the lone cowboy hero who protects a community but is not part of it, they ride off into the sunset together, their new frontier not a place on the edge of civilization where they can escape from social belonging but one that offers new opportunities for community, a place where they can live as themselves. The frontier of Mars in *Autonomous* is a space of liberation that allows the free expression of their sexuality. In turn, sexuality ("giving and receiving pleasure in an undocumented form of emotional feedback loop") in *Autonomous* is liberatory, inspiring individual and social transformation.[23]

Rough Riders, Gay Cowboys, and Country Kink

Various forms of illicit, if not undocumented, pleasure have always been present in westerns, manifesting in sometimes sublimated, sometimes openly kinky ways. Whether it's a tight-lacing corseted saloon girl or the fetishization of the suffering male body, westerns are a deeply body-conscious and body-obsessed genre.[24] After all, westerns are no stranger to the concept of the "high body count" story, often while telling tales about the imposition, displacement, and expansion of bodies westward. Given its history, it's no surprise that the body-obsessed western has of course become an aesthetic touchstone for all manner of camp, kink, and titillation in a range of genres and formats.

The handsome cowboy clad in tight pants and Gay Pride–worthy leather chaps is a queer sex symbol that long predates *Brokeback Mountain*, or even the camera's worship of Robert Conrad's celebrated butt cheeks, shown off in the 1960s CBS series *The Wild Wild West* with specially tailored pants and short, tight bolero jackets. In her chapter on kink, camp, and queer masculinity, Sara Spurgeon points out that the barely hidden homoerotics of the western were already present in the earliest novels and films, from the male narrator's breathlessly detailed descriptions of the Virginian's muscled shoulders to a slew of Hollywood Golden Age westerns featuring tightly bonded pairs of men eating, sleeping, fighting, and whoring side by side, even as they can't take their eyes off each other.[25] Lee Clark Mitchell notes that long before Hollywood entered the field of play, many of the earliest historical descriptions of the cowboy focused not just on his supposed youthful, masculine virility but on his colorful costume, dwelling on high-heeled boots, large, fancy hats, and bright bandanas. When early Hollywood ropes itself to the western, Mitchell continues, the camera ensures our "eye is trapped and held up by fetish items associated with parts of the body, as our gaze is directed from . . . chests, legs, and various muscle groups to articles instead that either cover or exaggerate them . . . ornate buckles, gun belts worn low . . . chaps (with the groin area duly uncovered and framed), and tight-fitting . . . leather pants in the only genre that allows men to wear them."[26]

The queerness of this fetishistic gaze directed at the male body and its suspiciously high-heeled boots was already a cliché by 1923 when Harold Hersey wrote his hugely popular comic poem "The Lavender Cowboy."

Almost immediately set to music and first featured on film in the 1930 western *The Oklahoma Cyclone*, versions of "The Lavender Cowboy" were recorded by at least twenty known artists, including popular mainstream performers like Burl Ives, even though the suggestively homosexual lyrics (He was just a lavender cowboy, with only two hairs on his chest, and he rode on a filly called Daffy-Down Dilly, the prettiest horse in the West) meant the song was largely banned from radio play. Openly gay recording artist Tom Robinson included a cover of "The Lavender Cowboy" in 2000 on a Fan Club CD.[27]

The assumption of the cowboy's hypermasculine heterosexuality, in other words, has always been the flipside of his queerness—one version simultaneously supporting and undermining the other—and not just in Hollywood. In a deliberate bid to deny the press's characterization of himself as a queer-coded "Jane Dandy" or an American Oscar Wilde, Theodore Roosevelt deliberately reshaped his public image from swishy eastern sissy to manly, leather-clad cowboy. "Roosevelt's nickname 'Rough Rider,'" Christopher Le Coney and Zoe Trodd explain, "was enshrined into popular myth by the chroniclers of his exploits in the Spanish-American War, and the cowboy image that he had self-consciously cultivated became a well-entrenched icon—answering the fears of many Victorian Americans (including Roosevelt himself) who were witnessing the end of western expansion as the frontier region west of the Mississippi became increasingly domesticated and settled during the 1880s and 1890s." Despite the hilariously gay double entendre of his nickname, Roosevelt insisted his "vision of the cowboy was expressly in opposition to men possessing 'certain dreadful qualities of the moral pervert,' men 'who were not men.'"[28] As Roosevelt feared, the road from Rough Rider to Lavender Cowboy is a short one—indeed, they can be considered opposite sides of the same coin, united in part, as the nineteenth-century obsession with the cowboy's exaggerated, flamboyant costume suggests, via an aesthetic that fetishizes and celebrates the body and lends itself to the inherently sexy and subversive visual language of camp.

Weird western aesthetics play out as a potentially liberatory discourse in neo-burlesque and camp performances that seek to redirect attention to queer and feminist sexual expressions.[29] Given the parameters of burlesque (and its sister, neo-burlesque) and camp as rooted in the idea of fantasy and exaggeration, adding the western aesthetic to these performances inherently re-weirds the weird western. Musical superstar Beyoncé's fashion line Ivy Park released a Rodeo collection in 2021 that came with a full pictorial and video campaign rooted in kink, western, and fantasy cabaret. The video sizzle reel included denim tracksuits worn by Black ranchers, Beyoncé in a literal ring of fire wearing chaps with an extremely high-cut thong bodysuit (extra cheeky even by Bey's usual bodysuit standards), and pole dance carousel horses with a revolving cast of riders/dancers (a performance form originated by strippers) including Beyoncé herself as well as openly gay country singer Orville Peck. The clip, which runs just under two minutes, is a fascinating look at how traditional western visual tropes get weirded, in ways that are potentially liberating. Images of lariat roping get intercut with images of Beyoncé whipping her top braid like a rodeo showgirl—the traditional (read "realistic") scenes of western life and the classic western get replaced with a fantasy vision of the West that amps up the sex appeal. The entirety of the clip makes a powerful statement about the place of Black and queer people in the west—past, present, and future. Beyoncé's subsequent *Renaissance World Tour* in 2023 further amplified the visual work of the Ivy Park Rodeo collection with a futurist disco western aesthetic that added a healthy dose of ballroom culture. The show's finale sees Beyoncé airborne on a shiny chrome horse against a sea of concertgoers, many of whom followed the "dress code" and arrived with chrome and silver disco-esque cowboy hats.[30] In Beyoncé's western future disco renaissance, she overtly and unapologetically celebrates Black queer culture.[31]

Another relatively recent pop culture touchstone of weird western sex performance is contemporary burlesque queen Dita Von Teese's signature "Rhinestone Cowgirl" act, which she first created in 2006 and recently revived in 2023 for her current "Dita Las Vegas" burlesque residency on the famed Strip. Dita rides a pink velvet quilted mechanical bull with rhinestone bedecked horns while bumping, grinding, and ultimately stripping to "Hey Good Lookin'" (previously popularized by Hank Williams). The over-the-top aesthetic utilizes western kitsch as kink, exaggerating a major visual component of classic westerns in glam camp fashion. The nearly nine-minute routine opens with classic western film music while Dita stands in a power pose in front of her mechanical bull and swipes a bedazzled pistol across her face before putting it into her holster and stepping slowly forward like a cowboy approaching for a high-noon style shoot out. Each step forward with her hands on her holsters is drawn out for dramatic emphasis and exaggeration, and the fact that every facet of her sexy cowgirl costume, from cowboy hat to chaps to boots, is covered in sparkling silver rhinestones makes the entirety of the production a classic example of burlesque fantasy and camp—providing the voyeur with a presentation of sex and the western that could only exist on a theatrical stage.[32]

The fantasy and exaggerated western aesthetics in these more recent burlesque and burlesque-adjacent performances are part of a larger and longer history of western-inspired sex performance that teases the boundaries of seeming binaries such as past/future and voyeurism/agency. Sally Rand's "Nude Ranch" from the 1936 Fort Worth Exposition was part of the *Casa Mañana* spectacle directed by burlesque and Broadway producer Billy Rose. *Casa Mañana* or "The House of Tomorrow" included a wide range of programming from a "Pioneer Palace" and state-of-the-art theater design for his "Frontier Follies."[33] In addition to the big Broadway-styled showgirl chorus revues, the bill included several "peep show" style sideshows capitalizing on the controversial publicity that comes from topless entertainment.[34] The "most popular and controversial" feature of *Casa Mañana* was Rand's "Nude Ranch," spuriously billed as an "educational exhibit."[35] The titled placard above the entrance to this elaborate sideshow presents sex performance as a kind of revision on the traditional, with the "D" of "Dude" conspicuously crossed out and replaced with an "N." Not only does this revise a common western phrase, but it also removes the clearly masculine gendered connotations. Inside the attraction, a fully dressed Rand (famous for her nude fan dance act) played hostess to fifteen nude "cowgirls" wearing ten-gallon hats, glittery cowboy boots, holstered "six shooters," and green neck bandanas who demonstrated "healthful" activities such as archery and sitting atop a horse. The supposed educational element came from a narrator lecturing on the benefits of exercise and good diet.[36] The exploitative and voyeuristic aspects of the Nude Ranch curiously bring into conversation language of the "past" frontier and some of its aesthetic shorthand with the premise of a "future" (The House of Tomorrow) that is seemingly liberated from previous sexual restraints and conventions via sex performance.[37]

However, the notion that sexy western aesthetics in a weirded fantasy vision can be liberating is one that should be carefully considered. Kink as a concept plays into the notion of desires that are considered unusual or strange, which is why kink and countercultural impulses have sometimes been strange bedfellows. If, as Willie Nelson croons, "Cowboys Are Frequently, Secretly Fond of Each Other," but that fondness is only presented as a kind of fetish or kink, how does that then further reinforce, even if inadvertently so, narratives of queer and or feminist sexualities as deviant?[38]

Some of the essays in *Hell-Bent for Leather* take up the question of whether sex and sexuality can serve as a form of liberation in the weird western. "Human/alien sexual congress," Michael G. Cornelius observes in the introduction to *The Sex Is Out of This World: Essays on the Carnal Side of Science Fiction*, "has long been part of the science fiction tradition."[39] Alien, robot, cyborg, whatever science fictional form the Other may take, encounters with otherness in speculative works also provide a method of rethinking human sexuality. However, if speculative explorations of alien sexuality sometimes suggest the liberatory possibilities of newly discovered sexual practices and/or of sexual relationships beyond proscribed heterosexual procreative norms, science fiction tradition also reveals "a reflection and redaction to our own ethos in regard to representing acts of physical, sexual conjunction."[40] "Science-fictional representations of sex acts involving aliens," Alcena Madeline Davis Rogan observes, "are therefore bound to reinscribe the epistemological and ontological lineaments of the human sexual experience."[41] Thus, "the old cultural anxieties that relate to intimate interactions between the controlling subject and that which represents difference echo the racism, colonialism, and xenophobia of Earth's troubled social history (and present)."[42]

As Rob Latham writes in "Sextrapolition in New Wave Science Fiction," we see in the "New Wave" science fiction of the 1960s and 1970s a "new sense of sexual openness."[43] Ursula K. Le Guin wrote in a review of a 1971 novel that "freedom from censorship, and the resulting advent of sex to science fiction, are altogether good." However, she went on to wish that male writers would be more responsible with that freedom and would create women characters as more than "a pair of styrofoam boobies."[44] Latham observes, "The difficult balancing act LeGuin is negotiating here" involves "acknowledging the progress achieved in overcoming censorship while bemoaning the resulting excesses" of a discourse that reiterated sexual exploitation of women more so than it advanced gender equality in sexuality.[45] At the same time that a "ludic sense of liberated energies lies at the core of New Wave sextrapolation," the texts from this important era of science fiction history also reveal depictions of sex and sexuality that reinforce—rather than challenge—sexual hierarchies.[46]

Overview of Chapters

We find a parallel dynamic in the stories of weird western sex and sexuality that we examine in this collection. The western's celebration of frontier freedom is sometimes reimagined in liberatory science fictional and fantastic forms, as demonstrated by the discussion of *Autonomous* above. Jennessa Hester's "The Daddy with No Name: The Kinky Cowboy Aesthetics of *The Mandalorian*" explores the erotically liberatory potentials of the weird western as celebrated in fan fiction and art engaging the Star Wars world of Disney's popular series and imagined relationships between its bounty hunter hero and his target. Hester argues that the numerous examples of fan fiction surrounding these characters "carry with them an affirmative and reparative power, one which allows audiences to enhance the already rich sexual spaces" present in weird westerns. The speculative technologies of science fiction also make possible imagining new western spaces, as Katie Googe reveals in her discussion of a hyperreal virtual frontier in the form of the fictional California town of San Junipero, where queer desire and intimacy thrive. In her chapter, "Beyond the Virtual Frontier: New Possibilities of Sex and Desire in *Black Mirror*'s 'San Junipero,'" Googe contends that like the West itself, this futuristic California is "part 'simulation and part inhabited, dynamic community,'" where queerness combined with technology can overcome even death.

Sex and sexuality in weird westerns, however, as in science fiction and straightforward westerns, may also replicate exploitive discourses, as Micah Donohue observes in "Re-creations and Inescapable Repetitions: Sontag's 'Pornographic Imagination,' Bacigalupi's *The Water Knife*, and the Weird Western." Donohue argues that Bacigalupi's novel utilizes a pornographic gaze that both critiques and replicates the linked exploitations of the bodies of women and girls and of the body of nature. Calling the book "a pornographic and SF western that projects a history of water scarcity and wanton bloodshed in the US Southwest," Donohue reads Bacigalupi's vision of an ecologically devastated and sexually vicious near-future dystopia "as the inescapable repetition of an environmentally and economically disastrous past." Scott Pearce's analysis of director George Miller's 1979 vision of an apocalyptic Australia, *Mad Max*, also insists on recognizing the close ties between heteropatriarchy and a devastated natural world cast as a dystopic new frontier. In his chapter, "Lost Max: *Mad Max* and the Challenge to Masculine Dominance in 1970s Australia," Pearce argues that while "the narrative presents a vague crisis of resources, such as a lack of fuel, and the decline of social institutions capable of maintaining law and order, the inherent crisis within the film is one of a destabilized heterosexual masculine dominance" that becomes a critique of the patriarchal social system on which colonization and colonizing myths were founded.

Many writers in this collection demonstrate the ways sex and sexuality can be linked to a larger critique of the western and of the sexualized and racialized ideologies of western expansion and settler colonialism. Thus, as Miriam Brown Spiers argues in "'Touch Your Wound, Dear': *Eye Killers* and the Vampire of Manifest Destiny," sexual violence and sexual exploitation provide a potent metaphor for the violence of conquest and colonization. She analyzes Navajo/Laguna Pueblo author A. A. Carr's 1995 horror western, in which Native characters and their white ally must save a Navajo girl abducted by an ancient European vampire named Falke. Brown Spiers argues that the novel presents the vampiric character as "an unsubtle metaphor for Manifest Destiny" in which "indigenous knowledge offers an antidote to Falke's toxic masculinity, with its grounding in Euro-American patriarchy." Anne Mai Yee Jansen's "Qweirding the West: Re-forming the Nation in the Novels of C Pam Zhang and Emma Pérez" furthers the critique of settler colonial conquest and racialized and gendered exploitation, arguing that "the ways writers of color queer and/or weird the western as a genre reconceptualizes the US racial imaginary." Jansen contends in her analysis of queer novels by C Pam Zhang and Emma Pérez that these writers are "reanimating specters of colonialism on the frontier . . . through the portrayal of gender non-conforming protagonists and haunted landscapes." Jana Koehler's chapter, on the other hand, places Ishmael Reed's parody western *Yellow Back Radio Broke-Down* into conversation with the weird western short stories of Robert Howard, the white Texas author who also penned *Conan the Barbarian*. In "Ishmael Reed Takes on the Weird Western in *Yellow Back Radio Broke-Down*," Koehler explores the complicated intersections of race, class, and gender that exclude Black men from attaining power. "Howard's texts," she argues, "are fixated on the threat of Black women's sexuality by depicting stereotypes of hypersexuality associated with women of color," while Reed's text "interrogates the stereotypes of Black male hypersexuality in order to boost Black masculinity . . . often at the expense of women and those with non-normative sexualities."

Weird westerns frequently imagine the violence of contested frontiers as producing monstrous sexualities and violent new genders, often twisted by the poisonous effects of exploitative capitalism run amok in weird wild wests. Pointing to the history of the western as a genre that both critiques and promotes capitalist expansion and toxic, rugged masculinities, Elizabeth Abele analyzes two of the many films inspired by the classic 1953 western, *Shane*. In her chapter, "Coming Back to *Shane* to Redeem the Cyborg in *Soldier* and *Logan*," Abele argues that the genetically modified characters at the center of *Soldier* and *Logan* critique masculine conditioning that "restricts the full range of human connections, particularly for those called to 'serve.'" Joshua T. Anderson and Rebecca M. Lush's "Leatherface Families and Final Grandmas: The Reproductive Rites and Slaughterhouse Sexualities in the New 'Old West,'" analyzes the through lines of economic hardship, industrial violence, family legacies, and sexuality in *The Texas Chain Saw Massacre* (1974) and *X* (2022), where they argue that these postindustrial wests are haunted by a "final grandma," "a revision of Clover's famed 'final girl' that troubles the notion of final 'survivor' by raising questions about surviving whom or what." Leaning hard into the sexually subversive power of the monstrous, Meredith Harvey's chapter, "'What Makes You Worth $100,000?': Heists, the Commodification of Women, and Capitalism Condemned in *The Professionals* and *Army of the Dead*," uses the classic 1956 western *The Professionals* to point to the parallels between sex workers, gambling, and patriarchal marriage conventions in Zack Snyder's 2021 Las Vegas zombie apocalypse film, *Army of the Dead*. Harvey points out that in Snyder's opening sequence "the zombie showgirls are not framed as any more an aberration than the bachelorette, the patron, or the newlyweds in their consumptive desires." But while many viewers may note the homages to Romero's *Dawn of the*

Dead, Harvey claims, "*Army of the Dead* also possesses a less apparent predecessor, the western."

In westerns, the home is often imagined as the calm domestic antithesis of the saloon or gambling hall—even if the showgirls aren't zombies. But the home in westerns is frequently a site of contested and violent domesticities, a location where the western has traditionally engaged in its most ferocious policing of genders and sexualities, underscoring the often false promise the genre makes of freedom from social constraints in a landscape famous for imagining women as either schoolmarms or saloon girls, virginal ranchers' daughters in need of masculine protection from the threat of rape or hypersexualized and racialized cantina dancers who exist to serve the sexual appetites of men, whether they want to or not. For a genre that insists its version of domesticity is a defense of the traditional nuclear family, violent domesticities abound in both standard and weird westerns. Jeffrey Chisum's "The Woman in Room 327: Western Domesticity and Oedipal Conflict in *The Shining*" examines home as both a place and a concept "crucial to understanding *The Shining* and the peculiar way that the film sits astride both the western and horror genres," describing the western domesticity presented in the film as a source of haunting violence and oedipal conflicts. Violent domesticities and sexualities extend into weird western video games as well as fiction and film. The video game *Bioshock Infinite*, which imagines the flying city of Columbia in 1912 as a new American West, is also obsessed with fathers, daughters, and monstrous sexualities. Christina Fawcett and Marc A. Ouellette's "Transgression on the Frontier: The Ludicity of Incest in *Bioshock Infinite*" explores the ways the game's climactic reveal—that the bounty hunter main character is actually the father of the young woman he's been hired to kidnap—"deploys a complex relationship with time, history, American Imperialism, the language of manifest destiny and the segregationist and self-loathing of the American past." Sara Humphreys argues that the western and the gameworld western have always "been ideological partners in the production, performance, and control of sex and gender" by forcing the player to "replicate gestures, movements, clothing, body shape, and sex-positions that constitute the expected conventional sex and gender performances found in and popularized by the western." As do Fawcett and Ouellette, Humphreys also considers the psychosocial structure of fathers and daughters in her analysis of the video game *The Last of Us II*. However, she asserts in "Dead Fathers and Monstrous Daughters in *The Last of Us II*," the game also challenges how gender and sexuality are understood "by creating moral quandaries concerning the ethical choices made by the main characters in the first game."

The concluding essay of the volume emphasizes the weird western's exploration of the possibilities of liberation through the joyful embrace of a variety of sexual practices. Demonstrating the long history of celebrating queerness and kink in weird westerns, Sara Spurgeon's "'Do I Bring My Own Leash, or Do I Pick One Up at the Door?': Kink, Camp, and Queer Masculinity in CBS's *The Wild Wild West*" examines the campy fun of the 1960s western steampunk series, suggesting the show's regular use of BDSM play centered on its male lead "reveals not just the homoerotic heart beating beneath the cowboy's broad, manly chest, but exposes as well the profoundly kinky and genderqueer nature of the genre's laboriously constructed version of American manhood."

The selections in this anthology suggest the complexity of the weird western as a hybrid form. Weirding the western, as many of our contributors note, opens up a space for critiquing the classic western and its imbrication in discourses supporting colonialism, capitalism, racism, patriarchy, and sexual oppression. However, our contributors throughout come to different conclusions about how effectively the texts they examine accomplish that critique. Donohue's analysis of *The Water Knife*, Pearce's detailed study of *Mad Max*, and Harvey's reading of *Army of the Dead*, for example, find that even though the weirding of the western in these texts may have in some ways troubled the western's classic form, they ultimately have reified the oppressive structures they seem to have set out to critique. Other essays here, such as the chapters by Hester (on *The Mandalorian*) and Spurgeon (on *The Wild Wild West*) that begin and end the anthology, find in the texts they examine a capacity for weirding and queering (or qweirding, to once again evoke Jansen's coinage) the western in liberatory ways. Considered as a whole, the chapters in *Hell-Bent for Leather: Sex and Sexuality in the Weird Western* create a dialogue that goes back and forth between those two perspectives, unraveling the complex interplay between the western and the weird western—between sex and sexuality as a structure of oppression and sex and sexuality as a pathway toward liberation.

Notes

1. Zattoni et al., "The Impact of COVID-19 Pandemic on Pornography Habits."
2. Johnson, Lush, and Spurgeon, "Westworld(s)," 2. In our definition of weird westerns, we build on Paul Green's expansive definition of the term in *The Encyclopedia of Weird Westerns*, where he describes the weird west or a weird western as "a comparatively recent label of a genre that incorporates supernatural, fantasy and sci-fi elements in a Western frontier theme." Green, *Encyclopedia*, 5.
3. Johnson, Lush, and Spurgeon, "Westworld(s)," 6–7.
4. Meljac and Hunt, "Strange Country," 68.
5. Newitz, *Autonomous*, 244.
6. Forde, "Olivia Dunham," 74.
7. Newitz, *Autonomous*, 76.
8. Newitz, *Autonomous*, 77.
9. Grey, *Riders*, 226.
10. Johnson, Lush, and Spurgeon, "Westworld(s)," 7.
11. Such human-robot pairings can be seen in other speculative westerns such as the Tonto and Lone Ranger interlude in Stephen Graham Jones's *The Bird Is Gone*, which explores the tension of difference and otherness with its mechanical and twitchy Lone Ranger, who spouts canned dialogue tracks in contrast to the humanness of Tonto. Jones, *Bird Is Gone*, 132–33.
12. The episode "Long, Long Time" from *The Last of Us* (season 1, episode 3) highlights the romantic relationship of Bill and Frank, who find love and connection on the apocalyptic frontier. The episode brings into relief the traditional markers of hypermasculinity including guns, ammo, and violence in a setting that is essentially a "fort" on the new speculative frontier, with tender moments of domesticity and care where the frontier setting provides the space for these two men's sexual and romantic relationship to flourish out of closeted contexts.
13. Hollinger, "'Something Like a Fiction,'" 154.
14. As quoted in Hollinger, "'Something Like a Fiction,'" 152.
15. As quoted in Hollinger, "'Something Like a Fiction,'" 154.
16. Hollinger, "'Something Like a Fiction,'" 154.
17. Jenkins, "'Welcome to Bisexuality, Captain Kirk,'" 187.
18. Newitz, *Autonomous*, 184.
19. The human brain in a robot is a plot device central to Anne McCaffrey's *The Ship Who Sang*, where Helva, a human woman's brain that is implanted into a spaceship, experiences sexual desire for her male human pilots.
20. Newitz, *Autonomous*, 184–85.
21. Newitz, *Autonomous*, 185.
22. Newitz, *Autonomous*, 300.

23. Newitz, *Autonomous*, 185.
24. Tight-lacing is a practice of corsetry that is sometimes a feature in BDSM communities, tied to not only body modification but also sensory experience of the restraint and pressure afforded by an overly tightened corset.
25. For more on the homoerotics of the western, see Vito Russo's *The Celluloid Closet: Homosexuality in the Movies* (1987); Lee Clark Mitchell's *Westerns: Making the Man in Fiction and Film* (1996); Robert Lang's *Masculine Interests: Homoerotics in Hollywood Films* (2002); C. Le Coney and Z. Trodd's chapter "Sonnet Subtexts and Palatable Stories: Gay Cowboys and the Heterotopian Frontier of Modern-Classic Westerns," from Paul Varner's edited collection *Westerns: Paperback Novels and Movies from Hollywood* (2007); William Handley's edited collection *The Brokeback Book: From Story to Cultural Phenomenon* (2011); Barbara Mennel's *Queer Cinema: Schoolgirls, Vampires, and Gay Cowboys* (2012); and Hiram Pérez's *A Taste for Brown Bodies: Gay Modernity and Cosmopolitan Desire* (2015), among others.
26. Mitchell, *Westerns*, 165.
27. Queer Music Heritage, "Lavender Cowboy."
28. Le Coney and Trodd, "Sonnet Subtexts," 137.
29. As defined by scholar and burlesque performer Lynn Sally, neo-burlesque began as an underground performance movement in the 1990s that "references burlesque of the 1940s–1960s . . . while recontextualizing it with modern themes." Sally, *Neo-Burlesque*, 2.
30. During the last leg of her Renaissance World Tour, Beyoncé issued a "dress code" for Virgo season, which she announced on her social media and website with a chrome cowboy hat graphic. Attendees should wear their "most fabulous silver fashions to the shows 8.23–9.22! We'll surround ourselves in a shimmering human disco ball each night. Everybody mirroring each other's joy. Virgo season together in the house of chrome." Story posted to Beyoncé's official Instagram stories on August 23, 2023 (which only appears for twenty-four hours).
31. Beyoncé brings the union of western and disco futurist sexuality full circle in the ending chapter of her *Cowboy Carter* album, released in 2024. In the penultimate song "Sweet Honey Buckiin," lyrics such as "look at that horse" and "buckin' like a mechanical bull" seamlessly serve as western sexual double entendre and redefine the soundscape of country and western to include mechanical beats and dancefloor grinds.
32. Dita Von Teese, "Rhinestone Cowgirl," Dita Von Teese website, February 27, 2023, https://dita.net/burlesque/cowgirl/; The Vontourage (@vontourage), photo of Dita Von Teese with Vontourage dancers Alek Palinski and Elio Martinez

during Rhinestone Cowgirl, Instagram, August 2, 2017, https://www.instagram.com/p/BXTpqXhhzr2/?hl=en.
33. Jones, *Billy Rose*, 89.
34. Jones, *Billy Rose*, 89.
35. Jones, *Billy Rose*, 90.
36. Jones, *Billy Rose*, 92; Zemeckis, *Feuding Fan Dancers*, 173.
37. Notably, much of this past language aligns with Roosevelt's rhetoric surrounding his own transformation from East Coast frailty to virile western masculinity via the "west cure." Interestingly, extending this formula to the Nude Ranch girls overturns the traditional neurasthenia treatment for women of the "rest cure."
38. Originally written and recorded by Lubbock, Texas, musician Ned Sublett in 1981 and covered by Willie Nelson in 2006, the duet version in 2024 featured Nelson and Orville Peck. Tomás Meir, "Willie Nelson Thinks Queer Message in Orville Peck Video Is 'More Important Than Ever,'" *Rolling Stone*, April 5, 2024, https://www.rollingstone.com/music/music-country/orville-peck-willie-nelson-dropcowboys-are-frequently-secretly-fond-each-other-1234999336/.
39. Cornelius, "Sexing Science Fiction," 8.
40. Cornelius, "Sexing Science Fiction," ebook.
41. As quoted in Cornelius, "Sexing Science Fiction," ebook.
42. Cornelius, "Sexing Science Fiction," ebook.
43. Latham, "Sextrapolation," 66.
44. As quoted in Latham, "Sextrapolation," 66.
45. Latham, "Sextrapolation," 66.
46. Latham, "Sextrapolation," 70.

Bibliography

Beyoncé X Adidas: Ivy Park Rodeo. Directed by Daniel Sannwald, performances by Beyoncé, Orville Peck, Tobe Nwigwe, Monaleo, and Glynn Turman. Parkwood Entertainment, 2021.

Cooper, James Fenimore. *The Last of the Mohicans: A Narrative of 1757*. Philadelphia: Carey & Lea, 1826.

Cornelius, Michael G. "Sexing Science Fiction." Introduction to *The Sex Is Out of This World: Essays on the Carnal Side of Science Fiction*, edited by Sherry Ginn and Michael G. Cornelius. Jefferson NC: McFarland, 2012.

Forde, Teresa. "Olivia Dunham and the New Frontier in *Fringe*." In *Women's Space: Essays on Female Characters in the 21st Century Science Fiction Western*, edited by Melanie A. Marotta, 72–86. Jefferson NC: McFarland, 2019.

Green, Paul. *Encyclopedia of Weird Westerns: Supernatural and Science Fiction Elements in Novels, Pulps, Comics, Films, Television and Games*. Jefferson NC: McFarland, 2009.

Grey, Zane. *Riders of the Purple Sage*. New York: Harper and Brothers, 1912. Reprint, New York: Grosset & Dunlap, 1971.

Handley, William R., ed. *The Brokeback Book: From Story to Cultural Phenomenon*. Lincoln: University of Nebraska Press, 2011.

Hersey, Harold Brainerd. "The Lavender Cowboy." In *Singing Rawhide: A Book of Western Ballads*, 13–16. New York: George H. Doran, 1926.

Hoar, Paul, dir. *The Last of Us*. Season 1, episode 3, "Long, Long Time." Aired January 29, 2023, on HBO.

Hollinger, Veronica. "'Something Like a Fiction': Speculative Intersections of Sexuality and Technology." In *Queer Universes: Sexualities in Science Fiction*, edited by Wendy Gay Pearson, Veronica Hollinger, and Joan Gordon, 140–60. Liverpool, UK: Liverpool University Press, 2008.

Jenkins, Henry. "'Welcome to Bisexuality, Captain Kirk': Slash and the Fan-Writing Community." In *Textual Poachers: Television Fans and Participatory Culture*, 185–222. New York: Routledge, Chapman & Hall, 1992. Updated 20th anniversary ed., New York: Routledge, 2013. Page references are to the 1992 edition.

Johnson, Michael K., Rebecca M. Lush, and Sara L. Spurgeon. "Westworld(s): Race, Gender, Genre in the Weird Western." Introduction to *Weird Westerns: Race, Gender, Genre*, edited by Kerry Fine, Michael K. Johnson, Rebecca M. Lush, and Sara L. Spurgeon, 1–36. Lincoln: University of Nebraska Press, 2020.

Jones, Jan. *Billy Rose Presents Casa Mañana*. Fort Worth TX: TCU Press, 1999.

Jones, Stephen Graham. *The Bird Is Gone: A Manifesto*. Tallahassee FL: FC2, 2003.

Lang, Robert. *Masculine Interests: Homoerotics in Hollywood Films*. New York: Columbia University Press, 2002.

Latham, Rob. "Sextrapolation in New Wave Science Fiction." In *Queer Universes: Sexualities in Science Fiction*, edited by Wendy Gay Pearson, Veronica Hollinger, and Joan Gordon, 52–72. Liverpool, UK: Liverpool University Press, 2008.

Le Coney, Christopher, and Zoe Trodd. "Sonnet Subtexts and Palatable Stories: Gay Cowboys and the Heterotopian Frontier of Modern-Classic Westerns." In *Westerns: Paperback Novels and Movies from Hollywood*, edited by Paul Varner, 136–57. Cambridge, UK: Cambridge Scholars Publisher, 2007.

Meljac, Eric, and Alex Hunt. "Strange Country: Sexuality and the Feminine in Robert Coover's *Ghost Town*." In *Weird Westerns: Race, Gender, Genre*, edited by Kerry Fine, Michael K. Johnson, Rebecca M. Lush, and Sara L. Spurgeon, 67–91. Lincoln: University of Nebraska Press, 2020.

Mennel, Barbara. *Queer Cinema: Schoolgirls, Vampires, and Gay Cowboys*. New York: Columbia University Press, 2012.

Mitchell, Lee Clark. *Westerns: Making the Man in Fiction and Film*. Chicago: University of Chicago Press, 1996.

Newitz, Annalee. *Autonomous*. New York: Tor, 2017.

Pérez, Hiram. *A Taste for Brown Bodies: Gay Modernity and Cosmopolitan Desire.* New York: NYU Press, 2015.

Queer Music Heritage. "Lavender Cowboy: Charting a Song's History." March 2005. https://www.queermusicheritage.com/mar2005lavender.html.

Russo, Vito. *The Celluloid Closet: Homosexuality in the Movies.* New York: Harper Collins, 1987.

Sally, Lynn. *Neo-Burlesque: Striptease as Transformation.* New Brunswick: Routledge University Press, 2022.

Zattoni, F., M. Gül, M. Soligo, et al. "The Impact of COVID-19 Pandemic on Pornography Habits: A Global Analysis of Google Trends." *International Journal of Impotence Research* 33 (2021): 824–31. https://doi.org/10.1038/s41443-020-00380-w.

Zemeckis, Leslie. *Feuding Fan Dancers.* Berkeley: Counterpoint, 2018.

HELL-BENT FOR LEATHER

PART 1

The Daddy with No Name

The Kinky Cowboy Aesthetics of *The Mandalorian*

JENNESSA HESTER

Of the narrative elements most commonly associated with the weird western, none make quite as immediate or visceral an impact as that of aesthetic contrast. The subgenre's ability to take the well-worn myths of the American frontier and combine them with the ever-shifting shapes of sci-fi, horror, and fantasy persists as its most obvious and defining feature. It is also what makes the form so appealing; there is a reason Cynthia Miller introduces the concept of the weird western by noting how it intertwines "Steam men . . . Dinosaurs . . . Aliens . . . Vampires" and other strange sights with the familiarity of "traditional Western plots."[1] Indeed, it is the subgenre's reliance on surface spectacle that allows it to remain marketable and appealing to popular audiences while at the same time permitting its participation in the complex investigations of sex and gender so beautifully highlighted throughout this collection. What is perhaps most astonishing about these tales' willingness to cross space with cowboys, however, appears only once one sets aside this generic formalism and looks at the individual phenomenological relationships that readers and viewers, listeners and players form with these hybrid texts. Specifically, these personalized points of address carry with them an affirmative and reparative power, one that allows audiences to enhance the already rich sexual spaces created by frontier mash-ups through the addition of their own bodily proclivities and desires. Nowhere is this easier to see than in the recent Disney+ streaming sensation *The Mandalorian* (2019–present), a show whose text contains all the typical trappings of the subgenre, yet whose atypically overwhelming fan response provides unique insights into the profound sexual impact weird westerns can have on those who most fully embrace them.

Star Wars as a Weird Western

Before discussing *The Mandalorian* proper, it is important to examine the various narrative and cultural histories from which it will draw, starting with its parent series' connection to the western genre. The *Star Wars* franchise is no stranger to the mythic American frontier. When the first film made its way to cinemas in 1977, many reviewers highlighted its clear ties to classic cowboy movies. Roger Ebert, for instance, noted that the story's "heroes are from Westerns" and that their nostalgic influences play on "old thrills, fears, and exhilarations we thought we'd abandoned" as children.[2] Similarly, an anonymous *Time* magazine writer argued that the tale's narrative fabric seemed collated from "almost every western ever screened," with elements of fantasy, sci-fi, and swashbuckling thrown in for good measure.[3] Even more, both of these articles took time to emphasize the inherent strangeness of the enterprise, with the latter dedicating a whole section toward understanding why creator George Lucas embraced such a "weird idea" at all.[4] For many Americans alive at the series' inception, *Star Wars* came across partially or entirely as a play on the western genre, one that transformed the gunslinger flicks of old into something new and novel.

In the decades following its initial release, several people have examined the western influences embedded within *Star Wars*' narrative and aesthetic foundations. Andrew Gordon, for example, interrogated the story's direct ties to media like the Lone Ranger serials and the works of John Ford, formally outlining the methods by which such tales successfully transitioned from the "wide open spaces of the frontier" to space, that final frontier.[5] Meanwhile, Stephen Graham Jones (Blackfeet) explained how the movie subverted those classical tropes and provided the "Indian role models" he needed in the form of Leia (Carrie Fisher), "with her Hopi hairdo," and Han Solo (Harrison Ford), "that living embodiment of an Indian who is not going to wait to get his request to cross the reservation line approved."[6]

However, for as different as these and other interpretations of *Star Wars* might be, they tend to share at least one major element: a focus almost exclusively on the series' first film. When conceiving of the franchise as a western, weird or otherwise, critics tend to omit any discussion of its myriad permutations, from its prequels and sequels to its ancillary media and merchandise. Nowhere is this easier to see than in Paul Green's *Encyclopedia of Weird Westerns*, which only contains entries for the original film and a small handful of spin-offs related to *The Clone Wars* (2008–20) television show.[7] And to be clear, Green's text is notably more inclusive than others on this front; some similar encyclopedias, like Michael Pitts's *Western Movies*, do not provide references for even the debut picture.[8] This observation is by no means a slight against critics but rather a reflection of how *Star Wars*' public perception has shifted over time. Despite never abandoning its frontier aesthetics, those elements were nonetheless buried beneath other popular aspects of the franchise (such as lightsabers and the mystical Jedi order), or even absorbed and rendered invisible by the story's overwhelming international popularity (for example, Han Solo is now rarely compared to classical western rogues but has become the archetype to which modern rogues find themselves compared). In other words, *Star Wars* has remained a weird western franchise but has not provided a way for audiences to easily and consistently access the affectual material associated with the subgenre for an exceedingly long time.

Star Wars as Sexual Storytelling

Star Wars' relationship with sexuality follows a remarkably similar pattern. Upon the franchise's debut, as Roger Ebert was writing the glowing and cinephilia-centric review mentioned previously, Ed Franklin was preparing an equally glowing piece for influential leather magazine *Drummer*. Nestled neatly between two erotic photos—the first, a pornographic still of a gay couple engaging in anal sex; the second, an explicit advertisement of a man pleasuring himself with his "new sensational" male masturbator[9]—Franklin's article lays out the most important aspects of the cinematic sensation sweeping the nation:

> For boys (of all sexes) there is Carrie Fisher, Eddie and Debby's lovely, if low-busted, daughter, interestingly flawed by what appears to be a bungled nose job in the Nannette Fabray traditions. For the girls (ditto) there is either the gee-golly-gosh teenager portrayed by 25-year-old Mark Hamill or sexily cynical Harrison Ford's impersonation of a wholesome Burt Reynolds. . . .

Unfortunately, in this "long ago and far, far away galaxy," everyone is excessively overdressed (don't let that central figure on the ads fool you—no such male cleavage appears on the screen), even in the intimacy of their Solari-like desert habitations (courtesy of Tunisia). But this is a small price to pay for the fastest two hours in recent movie history.[10]

Though originating in an explicitly queer publication, Franklin's words speak to one of the initial major appeals *Star Wars* had for viewers of all orientations. In the tradition of adventure cinema, part of the story's spectacle was seeing attractive characters interact with each other, creating an environment of constant sexual tension that occasionally spilled over into more obvious exhibitions of embodied desire (see Leia's now infamous slave bikini, donned under duress by Carrie Fisher). Indeed, Fisher discussed the sexual side of her role in a 2008 memoir, noting, "I was even a kind of pin-up—a fantasy that geeky teenage boys across the globe jerked off to me [sic] with some frequency."[11]

Just like with its western genre influences, *Star Wars* has never severed its relationship with sexuality. However, desires that were once identifiable via mere surface reading have since grown harder to spot, obscured by increasingly complex and convoluted plotlines about mystic chastity and psychic connections and virginal conception. Some scholars have attempted to explain the exact nature of this shift, as with Roger Kaufman's argument that homoerotic archetypes persist in characters like Obi-Wan Kenobi (Ewan McGregor) and Jar Jar Binks (Ahmed Best), symptomatic readings of whom yield "resplendent symbolic imagery of fulfilled homosexual personhood."[12] With this said, though, the individuals most invested in sussing out the series' hidden lewd details are not scholars or critics but *Star Wars* fans themselves. This sometimes occurs on social media platforms and other digital spaces, where users pair off various characters—such as Anakin Skywalker (Hayden Christensen) and Obi-Wan, known as Obikin, or Rey Skywalker (Daisy Ridley) and Kylo Ren (Adam Driver), known as Reylo—and explore the romantic and sexual desires that were allegedly omitted from the films. It just as often plays out at sci-fi conventions and similar venues of nerdy congregation, where sexy *Star Wars* cosplay remains a common sight and Slave Leia outfits have become so popular as to be considered "lewdly passé."[13] And of course, the world of pornography is rife with galactic nudie films and pictures, a genre so popular that erotic website xHamster released tracking data for it in 2017.[14]

In each of these instances, *Star Wars*' most dedicated fans are approaching the films as "active participants," subsisting within a psycho-consumer cycle where they "appropriate corporate-generated imagery, and then embellish or transform it with personal artistic expressions . . . due to their personal identification with the texts."[15] These viewers recognize that the franchise they love is a sexual space, as it always has been, and use the aesthetics provided them to express and explore various aspects of their erotic identities. Moreover, those aesthetics are often amorphous or alien, relying as they do on design choices that obscure faces and similar bodily characteristics that typically constrain the worldbuilding of popular art. As a result, *Star Wars* places far fewer limitations on fans' sexual ideation, a design choice that has yielded a notably diverse range of erotic identification practices. To be sure, some devout viewers might feel content fawning over clearly human characters like Anakin or Rey, while others might lock into the semiobscuring but nonetheless racialized erotics of Queen Amidala (Natalie Portman) and her bright white face paint, the performed minstrelsy of Jar Jar Binks, or "the disembodied blackness of James Earl Jones as Darth Vader, the voice of intergalactic doom."[16] However, many other fans fall for individuals who possess odd traits like neon skin or animal appendages, a fact evidenced by the popularity of search terms like "Chewbacca Pussy" on xHamster.[17] Meanwhile, a sizable portion of active participants go even further and treat the series' aesthetics as a blank slate upon which to foist their own self-constructed personas, finding within its obfuscatory battle armor or definitionally elusive alien species a kind of empty psychological canvas upon which to paint their distinct forms of sexuality.

Because *Star Wars* no longer foregrounds elements of desire within the films themselves, this process of affectual identification and aesthetic appropriation is not readily accessible to all audiences. However, it is essential to note here that the materials necessary to foster this form of address are not solely invented by fans but are demonstrably present (in some form or another) within the franchise itself. The ideations outlined above do not stem from "wishful or willful misreadings" of George Lucas's spacefaring adventures; rather, they are the result of a "recognition and articulation of the complex range of [sexuality] that has been in popular cultural texts" like *Star Wars* since their earliest days.[18] Though each fan's expression of their sexuality by way of Jedi aesthetics will differ, they all pull from the same reservoir of erotic material, an aesthetic pool hidden away from the franchise's more casual viewers—much like its connections to the western genre.

Even more, *Star Wars*' unique erotic aspects are further heightened by those genre connections. Scholars have routinely highlighted American frontier narratives as examples of repressive storytelling. Taken broadly, this means that the gunslinging "hero almost never has sex, and when he does it's only implied, not shown, denial of sex being central to the kind of deprivation the Western finds essential."[19] When such tales discuss such feelings directly, it is often in the form of a vice, à la the saloon and its sex workers who might "entrap the hero in the very things the genre most wishes to avoid."[20] More narrowly, this repression takes on a range of forms depending on the particular aesthetic elements a narrative chooses to foreground. In some cases, as Christopher Le Coney and Zoe Trodd note, there exists a "latent homosexuality" within westerns that, while invisible, "evokes the closeted lives of many gay men."[21] This manifests most prominently in the homosocial relationships between cowboys and their same-gendered companions, a genuinely lustful partnership shielded by gestures toward damsels and heterosexual courtship. In other instances, as pointed out by Eric Meljac and Alex Hunt, the sexual dynamics take on more socially sadomasochistic functions, creating through bodies the genre's "metanarratives of male dominance, female submission, and the vanished and silenced native."[22] Such analyses, and several others like them, run through academia and paint a compelling portrait of westerns as agents of repression. And yet, for as constrictive as the genre might be on a formal and social level, such a fact has not impeded audiences from approaching and treating westerns as sexual products. This is most apparent in gay and leather subcultures, where frontier paraphernalia like "ropes, riggings, and so on" play a prominent role in queer performance and lustful encounters.[23] And yet, one need not retreat to a local dungeon to find evidence of cowboy-tinged sexual ideation, as it presents itself on the bare surface of the American historical record. The general perception of John Wayne, the most famous cowboy in Hollywood history, is that he was in no way a sex symbol. Despite being remarkably "handsome in his youth," the star "nonetheless became identified as a man of courage and action rather than a bedroom virtuoso."[24] Or at least, so the story goes. In reality, behind this chaste facade, the famed actor served as an outlet for his audience's desiring gaze. Most notably, women of the time "claimed to find a sensuality in the way he walked and the wiggle of his posterior."[25] Wayne even commented on this popular perception of himself, noting that he gets "hot when they say I wiggle my rear. . . . God knows, if I don't do anything else, I move well."[26] This view of the actor has not changed, as unambiguously evidenced by contemporary works such as the short story "Dear John Wayne" by Sherman Alexie (Spokane/Coeur d'Alene), which both queers Wayne and details an affair between him and a Spokane woman, where she observes, "His penis was huge! It was a movie star's penis, for sure";[27] as well as Lady Gaga's recent song titled after the actor, in which she exclaims, "I need a real wild man, I'm strung out on John Wayne!"[28] And of course, Wayne is by no means an exception to otherwise stolid rules, as comparable western stars like Clint Eastwood enjoyed a similar sexual status in their youth.

The Mandalorian as a Weird Western

At the connection point between these historical strands—*Star Wars* as a weird western, *Star Wars* as a deeply sexual media franchise, and the western as a genre of desire—lies the focus of this chapter, *The Mandalorian*. Created by Disney veteran Jon Favreau, the streaming show follows a galactic bounty hunter known as Mando (Pedro Pascal) as he attempts to take a young alien back home to his family. Though Mando has a real name, he does not readily share it with the world; in the same way, he hides his face behind a suit of religious armor, only revealing it in a small handful of scenes. Similarly, while the show eventually gave the bounty hunter's young companion an official name, most people simply refer to him as "Baby Yoda" due to his striking resemblance to the franchise's beloved sage. Throughout the series, this odd duo bond with each other as they make their way through increasingly dangerous scenarios in the outskirts of space.

When the pilot episode debuted on Disney+, fans were immediately struck by the show's clear western influences. Unlike the various *Star Wars* feature films released around the same time, which tended toward religious mysticism and high melodrama, this new project seemed to borrow heavily from the gunslinger stories of old: its self-contained narrative structure from classic rootin'-tootin' cowboy serials, its aesthetics from Hollywood's dirty and dangerous frontier as constructed in Monument Valley, its tone from the swagger-filled spaghetti westerns of Sergio Leone. These genre trappings were apparent to audiences from the episode's very first sequence, which borrows from a variety of western films and blends them together into a succinct show teaser.

For a specific comparison to illustrate this fact, look no further than Leone's *For a Few Dollars More* (1965). In addition to Mando lifting both his name and attitude directly from Clint Eastwood's Manco (or The Man with No Name), the protagonists' introductions in these two projects contain remarkable similarities. They each begin with medium-long shots of the heroes walking into small settlements. The streets seem abandoned, stripped of life, feelings emphasized by the inclement weather conditions beating down upon the mysterious central figures. And yet, Mand/co seems entirely nonplussed. After a few moments, they each make their way to the entrance of a saloon, the establishment's doorway creating a diegetic frame around them. They briefly observe the hectic activities occurring inside, then enter. Each gunslinger is searching for a bounty, which they find at a small table situated away from the bar. Fistfights break out, ones that force our characters to use the saloons' spatial features as weapons, and when the heroes eventually come out on top, they each respond with a similar threat. For Mando, "I can bring you in warm, or I can bring you in cold."[29] For Manco, "Alive or dead, it's your choice."[30] In both cases, the spatial positionality of the characters as being *on top* merges with their comparable expressions of aural control, thereby presenting them as dominant masculine figures in the tradition of the John Wayne eroticized cowboy. And of course, as our protagonists go about their business, they are each accompanied by brief, airy musical riffs played on woodwind instruments, either a flute from classic composer Ennio Morricone or a bass recorder from new talent Ludwig Göransson. The comparison between these two introductions is by no means perfect, and not only because the sequence in *For a Few Dollars More* is longer and, as a consequence, contains a few notable diversions. However, of importance here is simply that *The Mandalorian* utilizes enough frontier elements (structural, aesthetic, sonic, dialogic, and so on) that such similarities come easily to viewers with any level of familiarity with the genre. From its first moments, *The Mandalorian* is unmistakably a western.

And yet, at the same time, the series is still distinctly and without a doubt *Star Wars*. For all the ways in which the show's opening sequence mimics *For a Few Dollars More* and its contemporaries, the differences are stark and obvious. While Manco hunts down his bounty by asking a bar patron for directions, Mando utilizes a futuristic tracking device with sonic qualities resembling a submarine's sonar. While Manco dons his now-famous poncho and wide-brimmed hat, a six-shooter strapped to his hip, Mando glistens in his religious armor made from an imaginary steel called Beskar, a laser gun strapped to his hip (alongside a medley of other fantastic weapons concealed on his person). These contrasts between frontier mythos and galactic imaginings go on and on—human versus alien characters, wanted posters versus holographic bounty pucks, hanging lanterns versus electronic lights—and continue throughout the entirety of the series. Like the original 1977 film, *The Mandalorian* provides its viewers with a thoroughly weird blend of well-worn western tropes and those distinct sci-fi aesthetics for which *Star Wars* has become known. Though the show is often treated by fans as a new phase in the franchise's life, it represents nothing if not a return to form. It pulls the galaxy's frontier origins back into focus, providing a way for fans to easily and consistently access that affectual generic material.

The Mandalorian as Sexual Storytelling

When taken in isolation, *Star Wars*' return to the weird west undoubtedly warrants critical analysis and discussion, the rumblings of which are already audible within the pages of public periodicals. But when viewed in the context of a conversation about sexual ideation, the streaming show might seem to some degree interchangeable with its contemporaries. After all, on a purely textual level, *The Mandalorian* offers little with regard to bodily desire save for general innuendos and any information discernible from deeply symptomatic and psychoanalytic readings. Indeed, one could reasonably argue that a series like *Westworld* (2016–22) lends itself far better to sexual discourses since it utilizes such elements as an essential surface feature.

However, what *The Mandalorian* lacks in clear analytical fodder, it makes up for in a few important ways with regard to audience reception. First, the series enjoyed a level of popularity that exceeded the boundaries of the episodes themselves, reaching a level of cultural awareness in the form of memes, merchandise, and online chatter that few other weird westerns can compare to. As a consequence of this remarkable success, more fans became active participants of the show than is typical for media properties. This makes it easier to locate and evidence particular patterns within audience responses, and it also indicates that they are not social abnormalities propped up by a small coalition of dedicated but nonrepresentative viewers.

Second, as outlined earlier in this chapter, *Star Wars* fans already have distinct ways of appropriating its content for sexual uses, meaning any elements added or altered by the weird western subgenre will stand out. Even better, because *Star Wars* started off life within that subgenre, its reinvigoration of those elements now does not feel out of place to most audiences. For this reason, viewers are less likely to abhor the frontier influences as gimmicky or noncanonical, instead embracing their inclusion and (consciously or not) allowing their sexual ideations to weave back and forth seamlessly between *Star Wars* and the Wild West. Since weird westerns rely on aesthetic contrast to operate, *The Mandalorian* provides a unique opportunity to demonstrate what happens when the elements it combines interact with each other mutualistically as opposed to parasitically.

With these two qualifiers in mind, *The Mandalorian*'s initial reception becomes a vital point of focus. Upon the series' debut, it appeared as if the vestibules holding back viewers' desires did not simply open but crumbled under the sheer weight of lustful phenomenological pressure. Fans and critics alike immediately conceived of Mando as a sex symbol and they did not hesitate to let the world know it, leaving comments on social media platforms about how "horny" the gunslinger makes them and how they wish to "sit on his lap" or "get a bounty on [their] head so large that Pedro pascal [*sic*] will come and murder" them.[31] These feelings were so overwhelming, both in scope and intensity, that some critics actually started to question why the character left such an impression on them, as well as whether or not this impression was valid. Lizzie Logan, for example, noted that she was "a little surprised to find myself lusting after . . . the DILF," uncertainly supposing that it is "not *not* normal to be attracted to a character without a human face."[32] Josephine Rozenberg-Clarke was even more direct, asking in an article title if it is "Okay to Want to Fuck the Mandalorian" before detailing her own sexual receptive practices in relation to the show: "There's something delicious about never being able to see [Mando], even if logistically the mask and armour make any kind of intimacy difficult. No kissing, no touching, can he even release his bits from that armour? Is there a boner door? Does the codpiece detach? Folks, this is what I'm sitting here thinking about while I watch The Mandalorian with my long-time partner, while pretending to just be invested in the ~storyline~."[33] The repeated comments about Mando's concealed face, ones consistent with the general fan reaction to the show, are particularly revealing with regard to *Star Wars* and the weird western subgenre.

On the one hand, such statements clearly evoke the function of the franchise's alien aesthetics as a blank sexual canvas. Much of people's attraction to Mando stems from the fact that he is not a discernible and objectifiable body but a mirror that reflects the viewer's own lustful proclivities back at them. Unlike traditional movie characters, who mold themselves in particular ways to evoke specific types of arousal, the galactic gunslinger is sexy precisely because fans get to construct him as such. To borrow Logan's phrasing, "Like the Force, true hotness comes from within. Though we can always sense it, it remains invisible. . . . The imagination is where the hottest stuff usually happens," and Mando's amorphous design provides a "sexy, mysterious" figure upon which one can direct those lustful imaginings.[34] By way of the protagonist's concealed person, the show creates a phenomenological possibility space where any form of desire—straight or gay, vanilla or kinky, human or alien—becomes fair game, both a reasonable assumption to make about the character and one the story cannot contradict. The show is only able to accommodate this specific form of sexual ideation because of its ties to *Star Wars*, the weird half of this genre mash-up.

On the other hand, those statements also demonstrate the western's role in encouraging such active sexual participation from fans. When speaking of Mando's hidden face, lusty viewers typically qualify the observation with a description of their favorite character traits. In addition to his aforementioned mysteriousness, people often "thirst" after the gunslinger's deep and distinct voice, his tendency to avoid conversation unless absolutely necessary, his ability to defend vulnerable people (Baby Yoda and otherwise) from danger, his clear moral code, and most commonly of all, the particular albeit difficult to define "energy" he exudes through his actions and body language.[35] To fans of frontier narratives, these comments should feel immediately familiar, as they are all aspects of the archetypal Hollywood cowboy. These qualities are either formal conventions built into the stories themselves, à la Jane Tompkins's argument that westerns are "at heart antilanguage" that consistently emphasizes doing over speaking, or they are popular conventions carved into the public consciousness by noteworthy performances, as with the Man with No Name's deep voice evoked via Pedro Pascal's oral acting or the unique vibes of John Wayne's shaky rump as captured by his grandson Brendan Wayne, who served as one of Pascal's body doubles.[36] Indeed, while Mando leaves a lot of room for personalized sexual ideation, he nonetheless possesses a number of fixed aspects that are largely inseparable from common lewd descriptions of him.

At initial glance, this observation might seem like it thwarts the erotic elements brought to the series through its connection to *Star Wars*. However, it is important to remember that shows like *Westworld* have encouraged viewers to treat the frontier as a place of sexual exploration, providing them with the tools necessary to unlock the western's latent potential as an erogenous genre. As a result of this fairly new socio-narratological context, Mando's cowboy traits do not end up serving as fixed markers of a singular sexuality. Instead, they act as aesthetic signals indicating to fans that they can, and *should*, eroticize the show and the mythic space in which it tells its story. The weird west does not mandate the sexualization of cowboys, even though many will choose to do so; it reconfigures the frontier as a type of phenomenological address, an affectual medium through which the sexual material of the weirding genre (sci-fi, fantasy, horror, and so on) becomes accessible to even the most casual of audiences.

The Mandalorian as Reparative Storytelling

By making what was once exclusive to active participants available to all, this subgenre's unique form of address serves a distinctly reparative function. As Eve Sedgwick argues, modes of interpretation that make it "possible to find ways of attending to" hidden or fractured parts of the self provide individuals an opportunity to extract meaningful "sustenance from the objects of culture."[37] Given that the weird western subgenre engenders within its audience a sexually affirmative affective positionality, the natural result is that many of the people who engage with such stories will be able not only to enjoy their fantasies but also to construct a more genuine and expressible erotic identity (or heal one that society has deemed unacceptable).

For *The Mandalorian*, this sexually reparative function has manifested in a uniquely visible way within the ageplay community, specifically those who identify with the Daddy Dom/little girl and Daddy Dom/little boy lifestyle. Daddy/little is a form of kinky power exchange in which a masculine individual exerts control over a partner. Unlike purely sadomasochistic relationships, those who participate in this form of role play typically model their interactions around conceptions of parenting as opposed to slavery, with the Daddy Dom serving as a strict but nurturing caretaker to someone who has adopted a childlike or infantile persona. Importantly, Daddy/little couples are composed of consenting adults, and the fulfilling aspects of the relationship rely on that fact, especially for the submissive partner. This is because what adult children seek is the ability to *regress*, a process that professional ageplayer Penny Barber describes as "removing [one's] adult layer and exposing the vulnerable, childlike layer underneath that longs to learn and please a parental figure, to experience unrestrained emotions and simple joys."[38] Indeed, the pleasure of this form of power exchange necessitates the little having a grown-up self, one who can revel in the temporary freedom and release provided by regression. However, despite such relationships being entirely legal and, once again, occurring between consenting adults, Daddy/little couples nonetheless endure frequent accusations of "mental and moral failings," leading many to conceal or repress their kinky sexuality out of the unfounded belief that they have a social or psychological disorder.[39]

Thanks to *The Mandalorian*'s status as a weird western, these littles have found a way to watch the show reparatively and appropriate its aesthetics into their marginalized erotic identities, a phenomenological process that takes three steps. First, in approaching the galactic frontier as an inherently sexual space, these individuals have managed to take Mando's amorphous lewd form and project their own desires onto him. This has led to the reconfiguration of the gunslinger as a Daddy, with his moments of discipline (as when he lightly censures Baby Yoda for improprietous decisions, such as removing a silver cap from one of his ship's control levers) and nurture (as in the frequent scenes in which he gently holds or carries Baby Yoda) mimicking the qualities littles seek in their partners. This perception of the character has led many to refer to him as Daddy Mando, with some fans even producing merchandise featuring the moniker. For one illustrative example among many, see fetish shop CunningLinguistCo.'s Daddy Mando heart pin.[40]

After establishing the gunslinger's kinky status, littles then began refashioning his ward into an aesthetic surrogate for their marginalized selves. Just like with Mando and many of the franchise's other characters, Baby Yoda's bodily status is to some degree indeterminate. Though referred to and treated as a child by all other characters, he is canonically fifty years old, and the extent of his cognitive abilities is constantly brought into question. More importantly, the character does not read to most viewers (from this community or others) as a legitimate infant but as a regressed version of a much older character. As the unofficial fan name implies, Baby Yoda is appealing not because he resembles an actual youngling but because he seems like a "cute" or "chibi" version of the franchise's indisputably adult sage. In this way, he actually mimics a little's identity even more closely than Mando does a Dominant's. The weird western's reparative address reveals that Baby Yoda is first and foremost an infantilized version of a preexisting being, just like the submissive viewer, and provides the affective space necessary to connect with him on that level.

Finally, after determining their personal interpretations of the two characters, littles began using the refashioned aesthetic personas to express their sexual identities. This is easiest to see in the prevalence of Baby Yoda memes among Daddy/little communities, many of which feature references to both the emotional structure of such relationships and their sexual aspects. To highlight but a few of them:

> An image of Baby Yoda looking disappointed, his ears turned down and a frown pulled across his face, with user-generated text reading, "When he's not kinky and refuses to give you a spanky spank."[41]
> An extreme close-up shot of Baby Yoda beginning to cry, with user-generated text reading, "When daddy says 'no' Littles be like."[42]
> A shot of Baby Yoda holding a cup, a blank expression on his face. User-generated text reads, "Listening to my co-workers talk about

their vanilla sex lives knowing that if I start talking about my kinks I'll get turned into HR."[43]

An image of Baby Yoda reaching up toward the left side of the frame, his hand outstretched. User-generated text reads, "Me after I've been a brat all day but now I am ready for cuddles."[44] *Brat* refers to a particular type of Daddy/little role play in which the submissive intentionally disobeys their Dominant.

These memes have no clear sources, no clear authors, and show a significant amount of digital degradation. However, such facts all demonstrate just how popular such image macros are, passing through the devices of a large number of littles who see their own identities reflected in the scenarios depicted. Though seemingly innocuous, these social artifacts evidence the culmination of a major phenomenological journey—one that found its origins in *Star Wars* and classic frontier narratives, that gained life through the release of *The Mandalorian* and the popularization of the weird western subgenre, and that now serves as a source of sexual empowerment and reparativity for the erotically marginalized.

Conclusion

The most obvious consequence of this analysis is, of course, a reassessment of what *The Mandalorian* offers on a textual and receptive level. Given the examples provided above, it is reasonable to assume that fans' unique sexual ideations extend well beyond the show's central Daddy Dom Mando/infantilized Yoda relationship, even if such readings have not made their way into the public record. Reasonable starting places for such readings might include the Mandalorian signet ceremony, which in many ways resembles the practice of collaring within sadomasochistic communities; the show's emphasis on highly noticeable and spiritualized clothing, reminiscent of the care and respect shown to leather, rubber, lingerie, and other frequently sexualized garments; and the power dynamics of the show's Imperial officers, whose regimentation and uniformity may indicate further connections to dominant and submissive positionalities.

More notable for readers of this collection, though, are the potential implications of this chapter on weird westerns as a whole. What the distinctly kinky reception of *The Mandalorian* offers is another mode by which we might approach texts situated within the genre, an additive interpretive lens that can enhance and amplify existing criticism in novel ways. The people who engage with weird westerns, whether for personal or academic reasons, encompass a broad range of sexual identities. The various tales analyzed throughout this book help bring those desires out, providing the unique aesthetic lexicons by which audiences can tap into the erotic material that lay dormant within the world of the western, as well as within themselves. In doing so, these stories empower readers and viewers to go beyond passive sexual enjoyment and become *active participants* in the appropriation and integration of frontier sexuality into their own desiring identities. The weird western is a genre of incredible, individualizable erotic and reparative possibility; *The Mandalorian* asks us to embrace that fact fully and hunt for the offbeat perversions hiding just beneath the leather.

Notes

1. Miller, introduction to *Encyclopedia of Weird Westerns*, 4.
2. Ebert, review of *Star Wars*.
3. *Time*, "Star Wars."
4. *Time*, "Star Wars."
5. Gordon, "Star Wars," 318.
6. Jones, "The Truth about Yoda," 88–89.
7. Green, *Encyclopedia of Weird Westerns*, 231–33.
8. Pitts, *Western Movies*, 334.
9. Franklin, "Drummer Views the Flicks," 63.
10. Franklin, "Drummer Views the Flicks," 62.
11. Fisher, *Wishful Drinking*, 9.
12. Kaufman, "Homosexual Romance," 128.
13. Reagle, "Geek Policing," 2871.
14. xHamster, "Awakening 'The Force.'"
15. Shefrin, "*Lord of the Rings, Star Wars*," 273.
16. Nama, "R Is for Race," 159.
17. xHamster, "Awakening 'The Force.'"
18. Doty, *Perfectly Queer*, 16.
19. Tompkins, *West of Everything*, 84.
20. Tompkins, *West of Everything*, 86.
21. Le Coney and Trodd, "Sonnet Subtexts," 141.
22. Meljac and Hunt, "Strange Country," 68.
23. Meljac and Hunt, "Strange Country," 81.

24. Davis, *Duke*, 121.
25. Davis, *Duke*, 121.
26. Davis, *Duke*, 121.
27. Alexie, *Toughest Indian*, 343.
28. Lady Gaga, "John Wayne."
29. Filoni, "Chapter 1: The Mandalorian."
30. Leone, *For a Few Dollars More*.
31. Valdivia, "People Are Thirsting."
32. Logan, "Why Is the Mandalorian So Hot?"
33. Rozenberg-Clarke, "Is It Okay to Want to Fuck the Mandalorian."
34. Logan, "Why Is the Mandalorian So Hot?"
35. Valdivia, "People Are Thirsting."
36. Tompkins, *West of Everything*, 50.
37. Sedgwick, *Touching Feeling*, 150–51.
38. Barber, *Age Play*, 109.
39. Barber, *Age Play*, 8.
40. CunningLinguistCo., "SECONDS: Daddy Mando hard enamel pin (desert sunset version)—best dadalorian in the galaxy," *Etsy*, 2020, http://etsy.com/listing/975379884/seconds-daddy-mando-hard-enamel-pin (listing discontinued).
41. u/fxckinghydra, "when he's not kinky and refuses to give you a spanky spank," Reddit, December 9, 2019, https://www.reddit.com/r/me_irl/comments/e8jz5s/me_irl/.
42. u/sahinox, "When daddy says 'no' Littles be like," Reddit, January 4, 2020, https://www.reddit.com/r/PewdiepieSubmissions/comments/ejwhf6/oh_no/ (removed by moderators).
43. His Sluts Owner, "Listening to my co-workers talk about their vanilla sex lives knowing that if I start talking about my kinks I'll get turned into HR," Pinterest, 2019, https://www.pinterest.com/pin/89790586309468274/.
44. Unknown Facebook user, "Me after I've been a brat all day but now I am ready for cuddles," Facebook, 2019 (circulated through multiple discontinued Facebook groups).

Bibliography

Alexie, Sherman. *The Toughest Indian in the World: Stories*. New York: Open Road Integrated Media, 2001.

Barber, Penny. *The Age Play and Diaper Fetish Handbook*. San Francisco: Pennyroyal Press, 2011.

Davis, Ronald L. *Duke: The Life and Image of John Wayne*. Norman: University of Oklahoma Press, 2001.

Doty, Alexander. *Making Things Perfectly Queer*. Minneapolis: University of Minnesota Press, 1997.

Ebert, Roger. Review of *Star Wars*. RogerEbert.com, January 1, 1977. https://www.rogerebert.com/reviews/star-wars-1977.

Filoni, Dave, dir. *The Mandalorian*. Season 1, episode 1, "Chapter 1: The Mandalorian." Aired November 12, 2019, on Disney+.

Fisher, Carrie. *Wishful Drinking*. New York: Simon & Schuster, 2008.

Franklin, Ed. "Drummer Views the Flicks." *Drummer*, June 1977, 62–63.

Gordon, Andrew. "Star Wars: A Myth for Our Time." *Literature/Film Quarterly* 6, no. 4 (1978): 314–26.

Green, Paul. *Encyclopedia of Weird Westerns: Supernatural and Science Fiction Elements in Novels, Pulps, Comics, Films, Television and Games*. 2nd ed. Jefferson NC: McFarland, 2016.

Jones, Stephen Graham. "The Truth about Yoda." *Transmotion* 5, no. 2 (December 2019): 88–89.

Kaufman, Roger. "Homosexual Romance and Self-Realization in *Star Wars*." In *Sex, Politics, and Religion in Star Wars: An Anthology*, edited by Douglas Brode and Leah Deyneka, 101–15. Lanham MD: Scarecrow Press, 2012.

Lady Gaga. "John Wayne." Digital. Track 4 on *Joanne*. Interscope Records, 2016.

Le Coney, Christopher, and Zoe Trodd. "Sonnet Subtexts and Palatable Stories: Gay Cowboys and the Heterotopian Frontier of Modern-Classic Westerns." In *Westerns: Paperback Novels and Movies from Hollywood*, edited by Paul Varner, 136–55. Newcastle: Cambridge Scholars, 2008.

Leone, Sergio, dir. *For a Few Dollars More*. Produzioni Europee Associati, 1965.

Logan, Lizzie. "Why Is the Mandalorian So Hot?" *Vulture*, December 21, 2020. https://www.vulture.com/article/the-mandalorian-hotness-investigation.html.

Lucas, George, dir. *Star Wars*. Lucasfilm, 1977.

Meljac, Eric, and Alex Hunt. "Strange Country: Sexuality and the Feminine in Robert Coover's *Ghost Town*." In *Weird Westerns: Race, Gender, Genre*, edited by Kerry Fine, Michael K. Johnson, Rebecca M. Lush, and Sara L. Spurgeon, 67–91. Lincoln: University of Nebraska Press, 2020.

Miller, Cynthia J. Introduction to *Encyclopedia of Weird Westerns: Supernatural and Science Fiction Elements in Novels, Pulps, Comics, Films, Television and Games*, 2nd ed., edited by Paul Green, 4–13. Jefferson NC: McFarland, 2016.

Nama, Adilifu. "R Is for Race, Not Rocket: Black Representation in American Science Fiction Cinema." *Quarterly Review of Film and Video* 26, no. 2 (2009): 155–66.

Pitts, Michael R. *Western Movies: A Guide to 5,105 Feature Films*. 2nd ed. Jefferson NC: McFarland, 2013.

Reagle, Joseph. "Geek Policing: Fake Geek Girls and Contested Attention." *International Journal of Communication* 9 (2015): 2862–80.

Rozenberg-Clarke, Josephine. "Is It Okay to Want to Fuck the Mandalorian Even Though He Wears a Mask 24/7." *Pedestrian*, December 4, 2019. https://www.pedestrian.tv/entertainment/the-mandalorian-is-hot-there-i-said-it/.

Sedgwick, Eve Kosofsky. *Touching Feeling: Affect, Pedagogy, Performativity*. Durham NC: Duke University Press, 2003.

Shefrin, Elana. "*Lord of the Rings, Star Wars*, and Participatory Fandom: Mapping New Congruencies between the Internet and Media Entertainment Culture." *Critical Studies in Media Communication* 21, no. 3 (2004): 261–81.

Time. "Star Wars: The Year's Best Movie." May 30, 1977. https://time.com/4153583/star-wars-the-years-best-movie/.

Tompkins, Jane P. *West of Everything: The Inner Life of Westerns*. Oxford: Oxford University Press, 1993.

Valdivia, Pablo. "People Are Thirsting Over the Mandalorian Despite Never Seeing His Face." *BuzzFeed*, December 3, 2019. https://www.buzzfeed.com/pablovaldivia/mandalorian-pedro-pascal-hot.

xHamster. "Awakening 'The Force.'" December 14, 2017. https://xhamster.com/blog/posts/736643.

Beyond the Virtual Frontier

New Possibilities of Sex and Desire in *Black Mirror*'s "San Junipero"

KATIE GOOGE

2

The opening scene of the *Black Mirror* episode "San Junipero" doesn't look much like a western. The first shot of neon lights reflecting on the ocean fades into a brightly illuminated seaside town. The camera cuts and pans past a poster of the 1987 film *The Lost Boys* and the pink and purple neon entrance of a bar while Belinda Carlisle's "Heaven Is a Place on Earth" plays from a car radio. While this seems far from the vast landscapes and rugged gunslingers of a stereotypical western, "San Junipero" moves the western's defining nostalgia for the freedom of a limitless—but imaginary—frontier into the digital age. Using western themes, the episode presents a new hyperreal virtual frontier where queer desire and intimacy can thrive away from the stagnation and repression of "civilization."

Black Mirror, a science fiction anthology series created by British writer Charlie Brooker, is known for stories about the ways in which technology conditions and mediates human connections, frequently with a pessimistic and even horrific bent. The 2016 episode "San Junipero" explores these same themes but in the form of a love story. The episode takes place in what is presumably a near future, where the elderly and terminally ill can access a fully immersive virtual reality. There they experience life as young people in the simulated California beach town of San Junipero. The living are limited to five hours a week on Saturday nights, and based on that "trial run," they can decide to upload their brains after death and live forever in San Junipero, where a digital cloud replaces the heavenly clouds as the ideal afterlife. Visitors can choose a time period to visit or inhabit, and the viewer sees the 1980, 1996, and 2002 versions of San Junipero, though most of the episode takes place in a re-creation of 1987. Like the West itself, the town is part "simulation and part inhabited, dynamic community," where the dead and dying can live, change, grow, and even fall in love.[1]

The episode follows the relationship between Kelly (Gugu Mbatha-Raw) and Yorkie (Mackenzie Davis), a couple who meet in San Junipero. Kelly is a terminally ill "visitor" to the simulation who spends her weekly time in San Junipero partying, engaging in casual sex, and enjoying a brief period of youth. She is not planning to upload her brain after death out of respect for her husband and daughter, both of whom predeceased her and did not upload their brains. Yorkie is a shy woman who became paralyzed in a car crash nearly forty years ago while running away from her homophobic parents. She uses the simulation to experience the life she feels she missed while she was unresponsive in the hospital. She plans to marry one of her nurses so that the state will allow her to be euthanized and live in San Junipero full-time.

Kelly and Yorkie's romance is conducted almost entirely in the digital world of San Junipero, and very little of the episode is set outside the simulation. The physical world only becomes important—or visually present on-screen—when Yorkie (now played by Annabel Davis) allows Kelly (Denise Burse), who lives in Nevada, to come visit her in her hospital in California. There, Yorkie's nurse Greg (Raymond McAnally) tells Kelly and the viewers about Yorkie's paralysis and desire to die and live in San Junipero full-time. Kelly proposes to Yorkie in the simulation, allowing Yorkie to marry someone she's "connected with" instead of Greg. After the two marry, Kelly signs off on Yorkie's assisted suicide. On their "honeymoon" that Saturday night in San Junipero, Yorkie tries to convince Kelly to stay in the virtual reality with her after death, but Kelly is committed to following her husband. The two fight, and Kelly abruptly leaves the simulation. At the very end of the episode, Kelly opts for euthanasia, the credits roll, "Heaven Is a Place on Earth" plays once again, and Kelly joins Yorkie in San Junipero.

Off the Edge of the World

This episode approaches the concept of the western from a very specific position. Its use of a western location inevitably conjures certain associations that have become integral to the mythology of the American West. Since the late nineteenth century, the West has become "a wide-open region, wholly imagined, populated not by men but by legends, where thrilling adventures test the metal of Anglo-American resolve."[2] This West never existed, but the myth took root. It became a significant part of not just American culture but American national identity, and even spread its influence outside of the United States and to genres other than the western. As a result, the West has become "by the very nature of its mythic representations, a type of hyperreality, a simulation reproducing images conforming to some already defined, but possibly non-existent, sense of Westness."[3] "San Junipero," however, takes this idea of the West as reproduced images one step further by placing its California beach town in an actual virtual reality. San Junipero has no location on a map; instead, it is a futuristic invention where the characters can escape into a nostalgic 1980s.

The episode's play of past and future reflects the preexisting temporal bidirectionality of the western myth. For well over a century, the American West has represented both nostalgia and progress, both past and future. In 1893 Frederick Jackson Turner presented "The Significance of the Frontier in American History," which glorified a frontier experience that it simultaneously declared closed. By the beginning of the twentieth century, it was understood that the old, noble, free West was well and truly dead. However, Turner specifically mourns the West as having died as part of the nation's march of progress, thus tying the West to the future. Nathaniel Lewis identifies this contradiction as one between a West that "has been slipping away, eroding, and declining . . . a palimpsest of the Edenic past," and one that offers "a glimpse of the West as a perpetual future."[4] Because the West died to give new life to the United States, it exists in both the nostalgic past and the endlessly potential future.

The future orientation of the West has made it and the associated frontier experience one of the most popular metaphors of science fiction. David Mogen explains that science fiction narratives can "assimilate traditional myths into speculative visions" and "transport the 'sense of wonder' traditional stories still evoke to . . . our possible futures."[5] This transportation often uses the western landscape to create stories that complicate our understanding of authenticity, progress, and myth. Many of these science fictional westerns, such as the original *Star Trek* series or the later *Firefly*, draw on the American West and its associated mythology for both aesthetics and conflicts. Others "do not use explicit images of western landscapes or figures . . . to emphasize their cutting-edge millennial technology and not hark back to an antiquated rural, agrarian life-style," and yet "they invoke deep cultural myths about certain traits of an American 'national character'—rugged individualism, practical genius, contempt for artificial social conventions—that are inextricably linked with the American West."[6] "San Junipero" is among this latter type, using metaphors and themes of the West rather than the aesthetics that other science fictional texts have adopted.

While the episode is set in both a physical and a virtual West, "San Junipero" truly becomes a western in its treatment of the simulation as a new frontier. Beth Levy comments that the mythological excess and exuberance of the West gives the impression that "the American frontier [will] fall off the edge of the world," which is one of the basic premises of much western-influenced science fiction.[7] After the closure of the western frontier, popular culture began to imagine other similar spaces. Despite the long association between science fiction and the frontier, Robert Murray Davis argues that the difference between the western and science fiction is that the western is haunted by "the presence of history . . . while the SF hero [has] all history theoretically before him."[8] Both the western and the science fiction story are connected to the idea of the frontier, but each suggests a different relationship to temporality.

Different eras of science fiction imagine different frontiers as technology opens new possible futures. In the 1990s, cyberpunk authors were inspired by the "wild west" of the internet to create new cyberspace frontiers. As early as 2000, authors such as Helen McLure wrote about the connection between the electronic frontier and western mythology. She notes that "the electronic frontier encompasses many of the dualities and tensions of the American West. Like the western frontier, the e-frontier is vitally significant to American economic and strategic interests . . . yet the cyber frontier also appeals on a popular level to many romantic, nostalgic western myths about endless horizons, unlimited opportunity, and untrammeled freedom."[9] While technology itself changed significantly in the years between McLure's commentary and "San Junipero," the conception of the digital world as an untamed expansion of our lives has remained an important cultural myth.

"San Junipero" specifically chooses to portray virtual reality as the new frontier. This shift feels appropriate for a piece of media that aired more than forty years after the last person walked on the moon but the same year as the Oculus Rift, the first major commercially available virtual reality headset, went on the market. This change in technology shapes the ways in which cultural myths exist, allowing for a greater homogeneity across physical spaces that used to be more culturally distinct. Commentators from the United States and United Kingdom alike have adopted the myth of digital technology as a new frontier. In 2018 the British National Society for the Prevention of Cruelty to Children started a campaign that included the Twitter hashtag #WildWestWeb to encourage greater internet regulation.[10] This metaphor has different valences across different cultural contexts and uses, but the association of a new digital world with a frontier is a popular one.

This points to the power of the myth of the American West even outside the United States. The United Kingdom especially has a long history of adapting the western genre, since it was British emigrants who created the prototype of the western mythology. Richard Slotkin notes that aspects of the cultural myth of the West derive "from the utopian ideals of certain of the original colonists . . . which assert[ed] that this New World is to be liberated from the dead hand of the past."[11] This connection is likely the cause of the trend that Richard Cracroft notes in British westerns, "where, probably because of shared culture and language, British western authors showed more awareness than their European neighbors of current American western history."[12] Even in genre fiction, the American West is a recurring feature. The first of Arthur Conan Doyle's Sherlock Holmes novels, *A Study in Scarlet* (1887), features an extended description of Mormon life in Utah in the 1840s, while the iconic British science fiction television program *Doctor Who* featured a western in only its third series in 1966 with the serial "The Gunfighters" and then returned to the theme in 2012 with the episode "A Town Called Mercy." Much like the western, British genre fiction was codified in an imperialist context. At the time, "the British Empire was riding the crest of rampant nationalism and imperialism, and Britons, full of dreams, looked at the American West less through the eyes of seekers than through the eyes of exploiters."[13] Charlie Brooker's "San Junipero" continues in this tradition of both British westerns and British science fiction and does so deliberately. In an interview reflecting on the third series of the show, the first that was produced by the U.S.-based

Netflix, Brooker notes that the episode "was a deliberate raspberry-blow to people who said we'd gone all American now. So it was quite amusing to me to go, 'Right, okay, we'll set this one in California.'"[14] This suggests that Brooker is deliberately invoking California as the most American place possible from the British perspective of the United States.

California: The Final Frontier

The episode takes place both in the simulated West of San Junipero and in the real-world location in which the elderly Kelly and Yorkie live. The coexistence of these two Californias creates an additional relationship between the virtual frontier of San Junipero and the historical western frontier. It is as if the creators of the simulation considered Belinda Carlisle's claim that "we'll make heaven a place on earth," and decided that if heaven did exist on earth, it would be in California. Since "the West is, and always has been, many different spaces—real and imagined," the western landscape can be broad enough to accommodate a simulated reality of itself.[15] It is notable that despite seeing other time periods in San Junipero, the show never mentions or depicts any other possible locations for the afterlife. As far as the episode itself is concerned, heaven may be California in 1980 or 2002, but it is always California.

California's location on the ocean, at the edge of the old physical frontier, makes it especially resonant as a virtual frontier. Mogen sees California as imbued with the "qualities of the 'figurative frontier' . . . partly because of its geographical (and symbolic) location as the final 'West.'"[16] California thus represents the outermost possibilities of the West. California first gained national prominence due to the gold rush, and the association of California with great risk for great reward has only continued as the newer myths of Hollywood and Silicon Valley have grown. Lewis notes that California, "at once America's ultimate reality and ultimate fantasy, may be said to exist *beyond*: beyond the horizon, beyond the present, beyond representation. The West is the ever-distant site of national destiny, where dreams will someday be fulfilled."[17] In western mythology, impossible dreams of being rich, famous, and happy come true in California, so it is the perfect site for a virtual frontier beyond normal expectations.

Once the end of the frontier is reached, there must be a new goal, since "the West is always moving somewhere else."[18] In science fiction, it often moves to the future, and in the American imagination, California is the future. Silicon Valley is the biggest symbol of this, and its mythology involves creating technology that seemed impossible only a decade ago but now populates our everyday lives. As McLure notes, "Elements of the Old West survive in the gold rush mentality and lawlessness and crime that have accompanied the opening of the electronic frontier," and some of the people who flock to the frontier still dream of a better future.[19] This association creates an obvious link between California in the present and the company that offers a highly realistic virtual reality and brain uploading service in the episode. As the final frontier, the California myth involves surpassing what is attainable and reaching for an ever-moving future.

As the end of the continent, California can represent even the most extreme and uncrossable frontiers, including that between life and death. While Yorkie and Kelly are not dead for most of the episode, it is established early on that the virtual town's primary function is as an afterlife, since "eighty, eighty-five" percent of the population consists of "full-timers" who are already dead. There is a long history in both medicine and myth of humans trying to extend their lives indefinitely, but even with current technology, death remains inevitable. However, once the frontier line has been pushed as far as possible, what is left is California, just as the characters, having reached the ends of their lives, are left with only the choice between a simulated California town and—at least in Kelly's perspective—nothingness.

Virtual Sex and Real Queers

As part of California's beyondness, it has a long history of vibrant queer culture and rich queer life. This association began with the early cowboy narratives where the hero "is queer: he is odd; he doesn't fit in; he resists community; he eschews lasting ties with women but embraces rock solid bonds with same-sex partners; he practices same-sex desire."[20] While this queer cowboy narrative existed alongside a sometimes violent, homophobic culture, in the twentieth century, the link between the West and queerness has continued. San Francisco became mythologized into the gay haven in the United States. Across time, the West grants permission to break rules, including the unwritten rules of heterosexuality and domesticity.

In the present moment, California is known for its progressive, queer-friendly politics. Even within California, the most progressive and accepting places are the large coastal towns, and from the first shot, the episode visually emphasizes San Junipero's location on the ocean. San Junipero in particular is not a reflection of the physical location and complicated history of California but rather an idealized version of a new frontier. This California would be perfectly accepting of queerness, and an interracial queer relationship, because the virtual frontier is even more future-looking than the state that exists in our present reality.

The limitlessness of the simulation is specifically connected to both sex and sexuality. While the episode is frequently described—including by its creators—as a love story, the key to the episode's happy ending is not actually love but desire. Yorkie and Kelly certainly express a connection and an interest in each other, but that interest starts as purely sexual and never is referred to as love. Love is always reserved in the episode for relationships that exist outside of the simulation, while the motivation of the characters within San Junipero is desire. Even Kelly and Yorkie's marriage that exists outside the simulation is never explained in terms of love. That legal relationship is brought about by the restrictions of the outside world. At the beginning, Kelly and Yorkie's relationship is framed as exploration and excitement. As much as they both enjoy their first meeting, it's apparent that Kelly is not interested in anything more than a single sexual encounter, and Yorkie doesn't seem to know what she wants, as evidenced by her turning Kelly down the first time Kelly propositions her. When Yorkie confronts Kelly about avoiding her after their first sexual encounter, Kelly is quite clear about what she wants. She explains, "This means fun. Or it should, and this, this is not fun." Yorkie's response to Kelly doesn't even ask for love or affection. She just says, "Maybe you should feel bad. Or at least feel something."

Even at their marriage, Kelly offers to marry Yorkie not out of love or out of even potential love but because she's someone Yorkie is "connected to," which is interesting given that Kelly and Yorkie have met a total of three times and Yorkie has known her nurse Greg for three years. The connection then does not seem to be about love or a long-term relationship but instead desire. That is, after all, the kind of connection that Yorkie, as a paraplegic lesbian, can never have with Greg in the real world. The future beyond the frontier line is the place where the traditional domestic love story gives way to the unrulier forces of desire and allows them to have their own triumphs.

In this and throughout the episode, the freedom of San Junipero seems to specifically be linked to the free expression of sexuality and the exercise of sexual desire. The entire premise of the simulation is to provide the dead and dying opportunities that they can no longer have in the real world, and many of those opportunities are linked to sex. Producer Annabel Jones explains, "It's a cliché, but when you're old you're still mentally and emotionally alive to all experiences. It's just your body that's letting you down. And so to be free of that and go and fuck as much as they want, and drink as much as they want . . . why wouldn't these two mature women want to be doing this?"[21] The primary locations the episode shows in the simulation are all connected to sex. The characters meet at Tucker's bar, where Kelly and others find sexual partners. Most of the other scenes in the simulation take place in Kelly's house, which is the site of Kelly and Yorkie's sexual liaisons. The only other significant location is the Quagmire, which is even more obviously designed to facilitate sexual encounters. Even the timing of the visits to the simulation—Saturday from 7 p.m. to midnight—seems specifically designed to be a time when people will want to go out to bars and meet potential partners. While Yorkie's motivations for wanting to be in the simulation are somewhat more complicated, Kelly is immediately honest about using the simulation to have the sex she could not have while she was married. She has had sex with Wes before the beginning of the episode and is initially insistent that she doesn't want to sleep with anyone more than once, to the point of avoiding Yorkie when it seems like she will be too attached.

This is an interesting feature of a text that takes cues from both westerns and science fiction, two genres that are famously erotically charged without conventionally ever actually portraying sex or sexuality. Nicola Griffith notes in her essay about science fiction and bodies that "some characters in cyberpunk espouse the superiority of the non-corporeal world. People are 'wetware' or 'meat puppets,' merely the means by which information uploads and propagates itself. . . . The ultimate aim of the human mind, some characters seem to be saying, is to upload, to become one with the machine.... Along with the urge to upload comes a certain contempt for the associations of the flesh. Skin to skin sex is not as desirable as slipping into a body suit and data glove and jacking into a juicy bit of software."[22] "San Junipero" in many ways pays homage to this cyberpunk legacy. It does valorize the upload as the path to happiness, but essential to the upload is genuine sexual sensation. The simulation does not replace sex that people could be having in the physical world, but simulated sex replaces the sex that they can no longer have in the physical world. In this context, "sexuality symbolizes something real.... [It] is a placeholder for various forms of boundary transgression, including boundaries between selves, and between normative and deviant expressions and desires."[23] The freedom of the simulation is ultimately a freedom to participate in joyous, sensual sex, including sex that is taboo in the unsimulated world.

This limitless sexual freedom is somewhat complicated by the portrayal of the other location where characters go to have sex in the simulation: the Quagmire. The bar is introduced by Kelly, who explains upon first meeting Yorkie that she had met and hooked up with Wes at the Quagmire. Yorkie asks what that is, and Kelly responds, "If you don't already know what the Quagmire is, you probably don't wanna know." The mystery remains until after Yorkie and Kelly's first sexual encounter. When Yorkie cannot find Kelly again, both Yorkie and the viewers leave the pop songs and neon lights of Tucker's and first experience the simulation's alternative bar. The Quagmire is isolated outside of town, industrial, and the music is louder and harsher. The patrons are tattooed, dressed in leather, and sporting extreme body modifications. While the episode does not include explicit sexual acts in the club, the scene was clearly designed to demonstrate the extremes of kink that were possible in the simulated world. There is even a brief shot of one patron strangling another with what looks like plastic wrap. Producer Annabel Jones recalls shooting the interiors in a "dodgy club in North London. Naked butts, nipple tassels and pierced bits everywhere."[24] The entire scene evokes motorcycle and fetish culture and extreme BDSM.

While the episode is overwhelmingly positive about queer sexuality between Kelly and Yorkie, its portrayal of the Quagmire suggests both the simulation's limitlessness and the show's actual sexual limits. The very naming of the bar evokes something that should be avoided and is difficult to get out of, a direct contrast to the ethic of consent in actual BDSM communities. The episode portrays this setting from the perspective of the sheltered and sexually inexperienced Yorkie and thereby frames the Quagmire as a place of danger and boundary-crossing that goes too far. While the viewer knows that Kelly does frequent this bar, or at least has visited it before, the episode does not use her perspective to normalize it but rather uses Yorkie's perspective to exoticize it. The visible presence of extreme kink in this virtual frontier reflects an idea going back as far as Turner that on the frontier, people are more comfortable "breaking the bond of custom, offering new experiences, calling out new institutions and activities."[25]

However, the extreme practices, from strangulation to public sex to bare-knuckle boxing all seem to be pushed to this one location outside of the "normal" range of tastes that in-town locations like Tucker's cater to. Even beyond the frontier, BDSM and related practices are still pushed outside society and portrayed as shocking and perverse in contrast to the episode's celebration of casual queer—though presumably vanilla—sex in Kelly and Yorkie's relationship. This decoupling is especially interesting given that historically, "sadomasochists and other sexual 'deviants' are often thrown together into one large group of sexual outcasts."[26] The episode will reference Kelly's presence in the Quagmire but will never show it and will detach the relationship between Yorkie and Kelly from any association with the kinds of sex exhibited in the Quagmire.

However, the existence of this boundary-pushing sex is essential to the ethos of the San Junipero simulation. It may not be common or acceptable, but an afterlife based on letting people have the sex that they cannot physically have in their dying bodies necessarily must include a place to have sex that is considered extreme. As Lewis Call explains, "Fantasy is central to kink because it allows desire to expand beyond the boundaries imposed by biology," and San Junipero consistently offers that which is beyond biological and social boundaries.[27] The ultimate relegation of BDSM to outside the acceptable practices of even the limitless afterlife reflects what Weiss calls "understanding via pathologizing," wherein "SM is understandable only when it is the symptom of a deviant type of person with a sick, damaged core. . . . They allow the mainstream audience to flirt with danger and excitement, but ultimately reinforce boundaries between protected and privileged normal sexuality, and policed and pathological not normal sexuality."[28] Kelly embodies this practice when she acknowledges that she has used the Quagmire to find casual sexual partners in the past, but she ultimately holds herself apart from them. She refers to the patrons of the Quagmire, and to Wes, the partner she met there, as "lost fucks . . . trying to feel something, anything." While the motivations of the patrons of the Quagmire are never fully explored, Kelly seems to believe that they are only there trying to make up for the unvaried and too-safe experience of the simulation. In this same conversation, however, she distinguishes herself from them because she is not planning to stay in San Junipero forever but will ultimately die and leave the simulation. However, both her own actions and her own relationships point out the contradiction in her statement. Neither she nor Wes are already dead, and yet they, too, enjoy the boundary-pushing of the Quagmire. It cannot just be about people who have been in the simulation for too long and gotten bored. This contrast is the main function of the Quagmire within the episode, creating a complicated place in between the permissible and the acceptable sexual boundaries of the simulation.

The extreme sexuality of the Quagmire and even of Tucker's bar creates another contrast in the episode, this time between the simulation and the world outside. While the world of San Junipero is hypersexualized, the unsimulated world outside is completely sexless. Historically, science fiction has been known as the genre whose "writers and readers seem to prefer their characters to pop nutrition pills rather than delight in a gourmet meal, dwell 24/7 in sterile environments rather than wander through a wood, and jack into virtual sex rather than touch another human being."[29] The irony of "San Junipero" is that the descriptions of a sterile, sexless science fiction world seem to apply far more to the world outside the simulation than the messy, sensual world of San Junipero. All the sex in the episode happens in the virtual reality. Yorkie explicitly says that she has never had sex before meeting Kelly in San Junipero, and Kelly, who had a husband and a child and therefore did presumably have sex outside of the simulation, never mentions it. Instead, she talks about the emotional aspects of her relationship with her husband and the thwarted desire of crushes on women when she was with him. The only relationship that is physically present outside of the simulation is Yorkie and her nurse Greg, who plan to have an entirely sexless marriage.

Real (Disappointing) Wests

While "San Junipero" consistently encourages the viewer to identify the virtual reality with the "Wild West," the simulated town is not the only West in the episode. Most of the episode takes place in the utopian, idealized virtual reality where the characters dance, have sex, and fall in love. However, the women also live in a different West, one that includes the specific real locations of Carson City, Nevada, and Santa Rosa, California. The episode contrasts these two settings to show why the characters are so desperate to escape into the simulation.

Until they "pass over," that is, end their lives in the physical world, and move to the simulation full-time, Kelly and Yorkie are dependent on nurses and caretakers for all their basic needs. In the virtual world, this labor is pushed out of view. In order to maintain the illusion that the episode is really taking place in the 1980s, the characters actually go out of their way to avoid talking about the labor outside the simulation that makes their lives possible. Even when the nurses and caretakers are physically present, the camera remains focused on Yorkie and Kelly, with Kelly's caretaker literally fading into the background after she helps Kelly into Yorkie's hospital room. The only person in the physical world who gets any significant screentime or mention is Yorkie's nurse Greg, and very little is made of the practical aspects of his job. He is almost exclusively discussed in terms of his legal and emotional support of Yorkie, though presumably he is also responsible for her physical well-being. The simulation renders all of this labor invisible in order to create the perfect illusion of freedom and independence for its inhabitants.

The possibilities of the virtual frontier in "San Junipero" are first represented by the lack of physical limitations within the simulation. Everyone is eternally young, healthy, and able-bodied. While this is not true in westerns, and especially not in the historical frontier West, it connects to the mythology of the frontier as a place of youth and potential. In Santa Rosa, California, Yorkie is paralyzed, and Kelly uses oxygen and needs assistance to walk, but in the idealized San Junipero, both women walk, dance, run, and have sex without issue. As Allison Ross observes in her article on the episode, the narrative positions virtual reality as "a place of endless possibilities and endless permissibility."[30] Even the most common of physical disabilities seem to be gone in San Junipero. Yorkie explains that her glasses "don't do anything" anymore. Everything that paralyzed or plagued the characters in the real world no longer has an impact on their bodies.

Not only does the virtual reality "cure" the characters, it makes their unblemished young bodies invincible. The characters' invincibility is first revealed when Kelly punches a mirror, and her hand does not bleed. Even the mirror is repaired when she looks back up at it. The conventional western portrays the frontier as a place of superhuman feats and larger-than-life figures. "San Junipero" uses virtual reality to literalize this mythology with bare-knuckle fights that don't draw blood and people who walk away unharmed after being thrown through the windshield of a car. Kelly even asks Yorkie at one point if she has her "pain slider set to zero," suggesting that physical pain is optional in this virtual world. These new possibilities in San Junipero are part of the allure of the simulation, and they reinforce the limitlessness of the virtual world.

However, there are complications to this apparently utopian existence. The first is that while the characters' bodies no longer have wounds, they still carry the mental scars from their trauma. This is most apparent in Yorkie, who, after decades, still feels the effects of her car crash. She is visibly upset by a racing game in the arcade and shows nervousness around driving, especially when Kelly goes off-road. Though she seems to begin to heal through repeated safe exposure to cars in San Junipero, the simulation cannot immediately cure everything. Kelly's flawed interpretation of the patrons of the Quagmire also suggests that she believes that human problems like boredom persist in the simulation. Taken together, these moments suggest that dissatisfaction arises and preexisting mental health problems persist even within this seemingly perfect world.

The flaw in the utopia that has received the most critical attention, though, is in the way that the simulation's physical "perfection" erases disability and undermines the work of current disability activism. No one in the infinitely customizable world of San Junipero is visibly disabled or even visibly over thirty. In this way, the very perfectible, limitless physicality of the simulation can become a restriction. As Alison Kafer notes, so much of contemporary discourse around physicality suggests that it is "the very absence of disability that signals [a] better future. . . . A future with disability is a future no one wants."³¹ San Junipero represents both the past and the future, but in reshaping the past into a utopian future for queer desire, it eliminates the real disabilities and diversity of bodies that existed in the past and present. This is not unusual, since "the value of a future that includes disabled people goes unrecognized, while the value of a disability-free future is seen as self-evident."³² While some people would want to "cure" their physical limitations, in their review of the episode, Kayla Rosen objects to the seeming universality of that choice, claiming that they personally would spend their time in San Junipero "mourning the loss of crip community, crip wisdom, crip magic."³³

Despite the virtual world's flaws, the episode intends for the viewer to see San Junipero as a perfect, utopian afterlife that connects the virtual frontier to the imagined Edenic landscape of the frontier West. However, the role of technology changes in the move from physical space to technological space, as technology does not ruin the "perfect" world but creates it. Unlike the hard work and violence that "won" the West, life in San Junipero is seemingly free from labor, obligation, and even pain. All the work that goes into the lives of the inhabitants is rendered invisible, and they are only left with leisure and pleasure.

In the idealized San Junipero, everyone is young and healthy, an achievement of Disneyland's goal to create "a city without pathologies."³⁴ Outside the simulation, however, disability, age, and disease are part of life. "The American West has always been represented as 'new,' a place of immense promise and growth," but in "San Junipero," only the created world can provide that, while bodies and minds stagnate in the material California and Nevada.³⁵ Neither of the protagonists will survive for much longer in the physical world, but the new virtual West allows for "the belief in the possibility of regeneration."³⁶ Indeed, we are not supposed to wish for their survival outside the simulation. As Rosen notes, "Every sympathetic character wishes for [Yorkie's] death, and the audience is meant to as well."³⁷ When Kelly hears that Greg is planning to assist in Yorkie's suicide, she specifically tells him, "You're a good man." Later, Kelly becomes the character most skeptical of the utopia that San Junipero offers, but even she does not question that Yorkie is better off in the simulation than in the physical world. Both the ending of Kelly staying in San Junipero and the portrayal of Yorkie throughout the episode support this view. The liberation Yorkie feels in the simulation is portrayed through her joy and surprise at the smallest experiences. This is most notable, though, in the scenes where Yorkie sticks her feet out into the rain or in the sand, just sitting with the sensations that she has not felt in so long. However ableist the episode's biopolitics, the episode is clear that the two Wests represent a choice of either a perfect future in idealized bodies and "without pathologies" or a present that is limited in time and potential by the characters' age, illness, and disability.

It is the perfect implementation of the "west cure" rhetoric that defined the early days of western writing. By setting out for the frontier, a young man's ills would be cured by fresh air and labor, as the virtual reality cures the characters in "San Junipero." However, the cure is not permanent, and Kelly and Yorkie both continue to experience pain and disability when they return from the frontier, until, at least, they "pass over." It is also notable that the main beneficiaries of this VR cure are two women, since the west cure was the response to male malaise, while a "rest cure" of food, quiet, and isolation was instead recommended for women. An essential part of the cure in "San Junipero" is the physical freedom and the social access that the simulation gives the elderly and disabled. Yorkie especially seems to revel in the simulation's natural world, tying that to her own west cure. In contrast, both women are forced into a version of the rest cure in the real world, with their limited mobility and lives in medical facilities. This is ultimately portrayed as something to be escaped in the West of the simulation.

Just as the frontier West appealed to those who wanted to escape eastern law and society, San Junipero lacks the rules and restrictions that exist outside the simulation. As far back as Turner, there is the idea that "the frontier is productive of individualism. . . . It produces antipathy to control, and particularly to any direct control."[38] In the virtual world, the possibilities are limitless. Since nobody can be physically harmed, everything from safe driving laws to the laws of physics is redundant. The difference between the virtual reality and the physical reality creates "two simultaneous worlds . . . one utopic 'fantasy,' the other dystopic 'reality,' and the design of the episode allows for movement between these intersecting and fluid states of non-being and being."[39] As part of Kelly's role in initiating Yorkie into the simulated world, she even tells Yorkie on their first meeting, "Let's not limit ourselves," which seems to be something of a mission statement for San Junipero.

This is in direct contrast with the perpetual regulation of the California in which Yorkie physically resides. That world imposes "the five-hour weekly limit" on visits to San Junipero, which Kelly bitterly notes is in place because "they don't trust us with more." Even more strictly, the "state's got a triple-lock on euthanasia cases. You gotta have sign off from the doc, the patient, and a family member." This rule prevents Yorkie from ending her own life and moving permanently to San Junipero. Her religious parents refuse to authorize her euthanasia and instead leverage the power of the state to keep her alive against her will. By the episode's logic, the limitations of the unsimulated California highlight the superiority of the completely free virtual world.

The solution to the regulations surrounding Yorkie's euthanasia demonstrates the difference between the two worlds. Kelly breaks the rules to go to San Junipero, where she can speak directly with Yorkie. There, she proposes and the two kiss passionately. This marriage in physical reality to the object of Yorkie's queer desire from virtual reality is what allows Yorkie to escape the regulation enforced by her homophobic parents. Kelly can then sign off on Yorkie's euthanasia so she can live permanently in a world free from regulation and repression. As Ross notes, "The storyline's relationship to marriage signals and signifies its larger commentary on dystopia and utopia—marriage as an institution is manipulative and state-mandated to achieve ability and immortality, and marriage as an ideal is an affirmation of desire."[40] Within the simulation, the two women are connected by desire, while in the "real" West, their connection is about circumventing state control to allow them to move into the greater freedom of the virtual frontier. The connection between a lack of social regulation and the frontier is long-standing, even before the frontier was specifically western. Richard Slotkin observes that part of the New World/Old World dichotomy was about authority: "The most striking quality of life in the New World was the relative absence of social restraints on human behavior. . . . In Europe all men were under authority; in America all men dreamed they had the power to become authority."[41] The rhetoric around the simulation and the physical world echoes this relationship, where the simulation is completely unlimited, but the unsimulated world is perpetually restrained.

Not only do legal restrictions almost entirely vanish inside the simulation, but the unwritten, communally enforced social regulations also relax significantly. While the physical world contains homophobia as represented by Yorkie's parents, in San Junipero, Kelly assuages Yorkie's fears about "two girls, dancing" by saying, "Folks are way less uptight than they used to be, and . . . this is a party town, no-one's judging." Ross observes that, for Yorkie, in the physical reality "expression of her sexuality is linked to danger and to loss of mobility. In San Junipero, however . . . she is able to express her desires without consequences: her virtual body is no longer paralyzed."[42]

While Kelly's life has not been as restricted as Yorkie's, she too discusses limitations from outside the simulation. The biggest hurdle to her experiencing queer happiness in the afterlife, according to the show's logic, is her dead husband. Just as the traditional western sets eastern domesticity and western bachelorhood as opposites, "San Junipero" contrasts the restrictive love and marriage of the real world with the boundless queer desire of the simulation. As Packard puts it, "Without a wife or children, without domestic possessions, without social status of any kind, the cowboy is 'free' in the sense that he adheres to no law but his own," which neatly reflects the appeal of the San Junipero simulation.[43]

In this case, restrictive domesticity is most specifically represented by Kelly's husband, Richard. He is first mentioned when Yorkie asks how Kelly knew that she was attracted to women, and Kelly answers, "I always knew. I mean, I'd be attracted to other girls. . . . I never acted on any of it. Never did anything. I was in love with him." While Kelly repeatedly protests her love for her husband throughout the episode, it is always referenced in the context of a restriction. In this instance, her love for him and her respect for their marriage prevented her from acting on her queer desire. Later, Kelly explains to Yorkie that she will not be taking the permanent afterlife offered by the simulation because she and Richard had a daughter who died without the opportunity to go to San Junipero. Kelly expresses her grief, saying, "When they offered him this, to pass over, pass through, spend eternity in this fucking graveyard you're so fond of, he said 'How can I? When she missed out, how can I?' And so he went. And I wish I could believe he's with her now, that they're together, but I don't. I believe they're nowhere." This is the moment of greatest conflict between Kelly and Yorkie, where it seems like queer desire might not be enough to give this episode a happy ending. While the narrative does support the idea that Kelly genuinely loved her husband in that speech, it also posits that love as something that is preventing Kelly from taking her own version of a happy ending. In order to get to the final scene of Kelly and Yorkie driving off into the sunset together, Kelly has to leave behind the ideas of her husband and reject the monogamous heterosexual domesticity that he represents.

Like They Saw in Some Movie

The virtual world is created to cater specifically to the characters who are within the simulation, so it is a replica of the 1980s that is exact enough for the characters' minds to accept, but not so exact that it actually includes all the messy, real, and difficult parts of that era. Like many monuments to a western past, San Junipero "appeal[s] to the frontier," or in this case the 1980s, "as a tradition that ought to be recovered and preserved."[44] This fidelity is primarily for the characters but also works on the viewer. There is no indication in the first half of the episode that there is any world outside. All the technology and all the media is strictly eighties. It is the same kind of hyperreal simulation that Umberto Eco identifies with Disney World, where "once the 'total fake' is admitted, in order to be enjoyed it must seem totally real."[45] In this case the construct is the 1980s, and the realism is perhaps more important because the inhabitants of the simulation did presumably experience the 1980s and would know if a given song or film is anachronistic.

Once the viewer learns the truth, however, it is apparent that the simulation is a funhouse mirror version of the eighties, not the genuine article. The soundtrack consists of nothing but classic eighties hits; all the décor is pink and blue neon; the clothes are all exaggerated versions of eighties apparel. This stereotypical rendering of the eighties demonstrates the extent to which outside forces can "cajole [people] into voluntarily displacing, fragmenting, and disfiguring memory beyond recognition."[46] Even those who might know better accept and perpetuate this mythically "frozen, one-dimensional idealization of space."[47] The falseness of this simulation is highlighted when the characters visit other time periods, and the San Juniperos of 1980, 1996, and 2002 are as exactly stereotypical of those eras as the 1987 version is. In this, the simulation becomes something like a ghost town, where the real 1980s change "from a[n] unstable, marginal region of uncontainable mobility into a frozen, 'preserved' tradition. It simultaneously resurrects and dehistoricizes the ghost town with an infusion of 'history' repackaged as amusement."[48]

The Hollywood version of the eighties isn't even for the viewers but for the characters who want "a nostalgized vision of what Southern California was like 30 years ago—the freedom of cruising its streets and the kind of careless, libidinal adolescence that used to be possible" but that never existed in reality.[49] The people in the simulation don't want to re-create the totality of their youth. They want a 1980s where two women can get married and AIDS doesn't exist. The romantic version of the West—and of the 1980s—as it exists in the contemporary imagination is a creation of California. Our cultural memory of the decade is as much a nostalgic remembrance of youth as portrayed by John Hughes films as a time people still remember. The creators of "San Junipero" explicitly reference this mythologized 1980s rather than a real one, with the production designer noting that he wanted to visually reference classic eighties films like "*Pretty in Pink* and *Ferris Buller's Day Off*. Once again, the goal was to settle the audience into a place they know and give them a stereotype that they can enjoy." The director follows this comment by discussing how in these films "the mood was far more optimistic, almost to the point where you could classify it as a genre. The genre of eternal optimism!"[50]

Similarly, Hollywood sold John Wayne films about the limitless West where a man could be a man, and Disney turned the concept into the family-friendly Frontierland. Lewis believes that "because the real [West] has always seemed so vast and extraordinary (beyond representation), we can identify the production of the real at work from the beginning. . . . With reality so contested, the production of simulacra was probably inevitable."[51] And indeed, the world's top producers of simulations have more than mined the western landscape. Frontierland—and its logical, though fictional, successor *Westworld*—offers all the thrills and possibility of the West without the discrimination, toil, and peril. As Handley notes, "By virtue of its distance from reality, this 'authentic' Western image takes on a life of its own, preserved in a static realm beyond experience."[52] Any changes must come as updates, artificially imposed by the simulation's human creators.

"San Junipero" moves this static West into virtual reality, creating the 1980s as a film set, the way our John Hughes–tinted memories want them to be. As Ross observes, the episode's "utopia is marked by cinematic tropes and artifice, signaling its constructed nature. Built from the replaying of experiences, the afterlife offers nothing beyond a blending of stored bites and bytes, reconstituted to accommodate the inhabitants' desires. People dress as if they are characters in their own Hollywood films."[53] Late in the episode, Kelly criticizes Yorkie's decision to stay in San Junipero, asking her, "You wanna spend forever somewhere nothing matters?" objecting to the false glitz in language that echoes similar accusations against Hollywood.

The association with Hollywood is especially interesting, given that *Black Mirror*'s series three, which includes "San Junipero," was the first produced by the U.S.-based streaming company Netflix, rather than the British Channel 4. However, even Hollywood money could not buy an authentic United States. Producer Laurie Borg explains that for "San Junipero," "our biggest challenge was creating period America on a tight budget. . . . I knew we could not afford to film in the US, but also knew South Africa could deliver 'period' Americana streets and coastlines."[54] Of course, nothing is representative of Hollywood quite like inauthenticity, something that the show itself acknowledges when Kelly comments of the patrons of the bar, "People try so hard to look how they think they should look. Looks they probably saw in some movie." Even an episode of television feels the need to acknowledge the gap between film and reality. Indeed, like mainstream film, the simulation's selling points are a safe, constructed reality in which young, beautiful people live out fantasies that would not be possible in the real world.

This episode's relationship to Hollywood is complicated by its allusions to another weird urban California text: *The Lost Boys*, whose poster appears in one of the opening shots of the episode. The first shot of the lights of the town across the water seems to deliberately echo the opening of Joel Schumacher's 1987 vampire film, presenting a contrast between the wholesome suburban image of the John Hughes films that the designer specifically mentions referencing and this darker, more countercultural vision of the 1980s. "San Junipero" both appropriates and responds to Schumacher's film, portraying an immortal youth of partying as utopian rather than malevolent. It replaces the film's intense homoeroticism with an actual queer relationship and recenters the narrative around elderly women and their desires rather than young men. However, the more optimistic outlook of "San Junipero" also corresponds to an erasure and marginalization of the counterculture and alternate aesthetics portrayed in *The Lost Boys*. Where the film shows Santa Carla's boardwalk populated by young people in black leather with piercings and tattoos, the *Black Mirror* episode keeps the town and boardwalk a normative John Hughes–esque aesthetic and relegates that kind of "deviance" to the Quagmire. While both texts explore the relationship between age, gender, sexuality, and the allure of an immortal life on the California coast, the way in which "San Junipero" references *The Lost Boys* highlights the differences between the conclusions of the two texts.

Travels in Virtual Reality

Even before the viewer learns the truth about the town's existence in the cloud, San Junipero is not presented as an "authentic" California town in the 1980s. Unlike *The Lost Boys*' Santa Carla/Santa Cruz, it does not even seem to be based on a specific location in California. This virtual reality is a classic example of Baudrillard's hyperreal, where "simulation is no longer that of a territory, a referential being, or a substance. It is the generation by models of a real without origin or reality."[55] Kelly's comment that the inhabitants of San Junipero look like people out of a movie is necessary because of the decades of Hollywood conditioning media consumers to accept stylized inauthenticity as a marker of time period, not an actual plot device. It is the pinnacle of Eco's assertion that "there is a constant in the average American imagination and taste, for which the past must be preserved and celebrated in full-scale authentic copy; a philosophy of immortality as duplication."[56] Even when the viewer still thinks that San Junipero is set in the actual 1980s, the place is already marked by inauthenticity.

However, this simulated and mythologized experience that is displaced in both time and place is not fake but hyperreal. Much like the contemporary California tourist attractions Hsuan Hsu describes, San Junipero is "not [a] static representation . . . but [an] open-ended space . . . that both accommodate[s] and respond[s] to the experiences of individual visitors," and Kelly and Yorkie make this space their own.[57] Even as she is criticizing the rest of the people in the bar for their Hollywood impressions of the 1980s, Kelly compliments Yorkie's glasses, telling her, "I like these. They're authentically you." The viewer later learns that "authentic" Yorkie outside the simulation does not wear glasses or need them, since she is confined to a hospital bed and unable to move. The very afterlife premise of the episode resonates with Baudrillard's definition of hyperreality as a space where "they are already purged of their death, and better than when they were alive; more cheerful, more authentic, in the light of their model."[58] Ultimately, the glasses and the rest of the experience is not about authenticity but about re-creating a youth both Yorkie and Kelly were denied by heteronormativity and homophobia.

This hyperreal western text creates an interesting relationship between hyperreality, futurity, and nostalgia. Nostalgia is also an important and repeated term in the conception of "San Junipero." The entire idea began as "immersive nostalgia therapy," which allows those in the simulation to relive the best parts of their youth. However, because of the selective nature of nostalgia, it becomes a form of hyperreality since it is simulating a memory that never existed, not the real thing. As Eco notes, the philosophy of the hyperreal is "we are giving you the reproduction so you will no longer feel any need for the original," though he also notes that "for the reproduction to be desired, the original has to be idolized."[59] In the case of San Junipero, the desire is never to return to the actual 1980s but to return to the youth and freedom that the 1980s represent in the imaginations of the characters and, to some extent, the viewer.

However, in this hyperreal world, characters can experience deeper emotion and connections by opening themselves up to real experiences. Yorkie's response to Kelly's compliment about her glasses makes her vulnerable and opens up the possibility of authenticity in the simulation. She says, "I guess now they're kind of a comfort thing," opening a door for human connection that has no parallel in the physical world. Through their invulnerable, unrestricted, inauthentic proxy bodies in the simulation, Yorkie and Kelly genuinely connect to each other. This vulnerability aligns with Baudrillard's understanding of "simulation [that] threatens the difference between the 'true' and the 'false,' the 'real' and the 'imaginary.'"[60] "San Junipero" confirms that the West is a place of contradictions, "both romantic and modern, individualistic and communal, nostalgic and progressive."[61]

San Junipero is presented as more likely to foster open and authentic relationships than the physical world. The world contained inside the servers is both emotionally and physically real for those who are connected. Yorkie, especially, believes in the reality of the simulation. Late in the episode, she bangs on the hood of the car and tells Kelly, "Look at it! Jesus! Touch it! . . . It's real. This is real." Her reaction to San Junipero is similar to "imagery evoking [the] original encounter with the New World [which] creates a 'sense of wonder.'"[62] San Junipero is full of firsts in Yorkie's life that the narrative treats as real. She tells Kelly, "I've never been on a dance floor before," and after she and Kelly have sex, she admits that she has "never slept with a woman before. . . . Never with anyone." It is often observed that queer people who come out later in life frequently feel like they are experiencing the adolescence they were denied while in the closet. While Yorkie's story is more complicated, it has echoes of this real-world experience. Mackenzie Davis specifically links the realness of the situation to Yorkie's own authenticity, saying that "there's something beautiful about this woman choosing to be authentically herself in this moment of unlimited possibility. The thrill of her identity and her queerness is the event, the reason for all of this, not the opportunity to reinvent her exterior self and sell a coolness that would appeal to anyone else."[63] Yorkie's homophobia-linked paralysis prevented her from experiencing important firsts in the real world, but she is given a second youth in the virtual reality.

The restrictions of the real world, including Yorkie's physical limitations and the heteronormativity and mononormativity that prevented Kelly from exploring her attraction to women, fall away in San Junipero. There, both women are allowed to be openly queer and experience a meaningful relationship with each other. Even so, they are still hiding from the restrictions and judgments of the real world. Kelly admits, "No one knows about even half the shit I get up to," while Yorkie says, "Just the concept of me enjoying myself would blow [my parents'] minds." In this simulation there is both openness of sexuality and new sensation and experience. And the combination of science fiction and western themes help form a setting where Yorkie and Kelly can safely discover "profound and unprecedented emotional experience."[64]

All the significant moments of connection between Kelly and Yorkie take place in San Junipero. Not only do they meet and experience desire in the virtual reality, but Kelly demands to be allowed into San Junipero even against the rules so that she can propose to Yorkie on the beach in San Junipero rather than in the sterile hospital room. Their "honeymoon" also takes place in the simulation, and they both wear the wedding dresses that were not a feature of the actual wedding. Even less positive, but no less real, experiences take place within the simulated world. After their wedding, the two fight because Yorkie tries to convince Kelly to stay in San Junipero with her rather than dying without uploading in honor of her husband. Though the fight is painful, it represents a real challenge to their relationship, even a relationship based in a simulation.

Compared to San Junipero, the world outside seems inadequately conducive to human connection. Like "'civilization' in frontier fiction," it is "identified with stagnation, repression, and artifice."[65] Unlike the loud music, colorful neon, and crowded dance floors of the replicated 1980s, the images of the material world are often cold and sterile without much personality or specificity. The landscape is never in focus and the characters are all in pale colors against white hospital sets. The relationships in that world are less rich than those inside the simulation. Yorkie's parents no longer visit her in the hospital, and while Greg is kind and talks to her on the "combox," their relationship is one of convenience. The episode presents the world outside the virtual reality as holding only death and solitude for Yorkie and Kelly. The unsimulated world acts as the old world to San Junipero's frontier. It is a place where "people become . . . old . . . without ever having lived."[66] The simulated San Junipero meanwhile provides the same function as Disneyland, which "tells us that technology can give us more reality than nature can."[67]

Science fiction often functions in analogies, and the American West's mythological freedom and romanticized frontier experience has been a favorite in the genre for decades. "San Junipero," however, eschews the aesthetics of the western, and its pointed inauthenticity may seem at odds with the claim to genuine self-creation on the western frontier. Created by a British writer, filmed in South Africa, and featuring Canadian and British leads, its stand-in Southern California is no more representative of the actual physical location than the virtual reality San Junipero is of an existing place. However, "San Junipero," like "every story about the West[,] is a complicated swirl of truth and untruth, of events of the body and events of the mind, of interior experience and social exchange."⁶⁸ The show uses an imaginary, stereotypical, poorly remembered eighties in an idealized, theme park version of California. However, it is this very inauthenticity that allows it to realize its thematically western narrative of limitless happiness that is impossible in a "real" world upon which history has left a mark. The queer possibilities for the characters are perhaps the strongest marks of this, since the simulated science fiction world gives its queer protagonists full lives and happy endings in a way that the western genre still struggles to do. The long history of western fiction has shown that "the American West is more than a geography, it is a complex, unstable signifier," and it is the very instability of the concept of "the West" that allows *Black Mirror* to remove California to a simulation.⁶⁹ This virtual frontier is a place in which the inauthenticity of the West and the impossibility of representation open up possibilities of queer relationship and connection.

Notes

1. Campbell, *The Cultures of the New American West*, 154.
2. Packard, *Queer Cowboys*, 1.
3. Campbell, *The Cultures of the New American West*, 130.
4. Lewis, *Unsettling the Literary West*, 9.
5. Mogen, *Wilderness Visions*, 118.
6. McLure, "The Wild, Wild Web," 469.
7. Levy, *Frontier Figures*, 15.
8. Davis, "The Frontiers of Genre," 34.
9. McLure, "The Wild, Wild Web," 457–58.
10. NSPCC (@NSPCC), "In the average primary school class surveyed, one child has been shown an online nude/semi-nude image by an adult. We must act now to keep our children safe online and end the #WildWestWeb Find out more: http://bit.ly/2n0kku4," Twitter, August 29, 2018, https://twitter.com/nspcc/status/1035052014059876352.
11. Slotkin, *Regeneration Through Violence*, 3.
12. Cracroft, "World Westerns," 123.
13. Cracroft, "World Westerns," 123.
14. Brooker, Jones, and Arnopp, *Inside Black Mirror*.
15. Campbell, *The Cultures of the New American West*, 2.
16. Mogen, *Wilderness Visions*, 30.
17. Lewis, *Unsettling the Literary West*, 9 (emphasis in original).

18. Handley and Lewis, introduction to *True West*, 7.
19. McLure, "The Wild, Wild Web," 458.
20. Packard, *Queer Cowboys*, 3.
21. Brooker, Jones, and Arnopp, *Inside Black Mirror*.
22. Griffith, "Writing from the Body."
23. Weiss, "Mainstreaming Kink," 124.
24. Brooker, Jones, and Arnopp, *Inside Black Mirror*.
25. Turner, *The Frontier in American History*, 38.
26. Wilkinson, "Perverting Visual Pleasure," 185.
27. Call, *BDSM in American Science Fiction and Fantasy*, 10.
28. Weiss, "Mainstreaming Kink," 105.
29. Griffith, "Hard Takes Soft, Still," 392.
30. Ross, "Queer Futures in *Black Mirror*'s San Junipero."
31. Kafer, *Feminist, Queer, Crip*, 2.
32. Kafer, *Feminist, Queer, Crip*, 3.
33. Rosen, "*Black Mirror*'s 'San Junipero.'"
34. Campbell, *The Cultures of the New American West*, 136.
35. Campbell, *The Cultures of the New American West*, 1.
36. Mogen, *Wilderness Visions*, 32.
37. Rosen, "*Black Mirror*'s 'San Junipero.'"
38. Turner, *The Frontier in American History*, 30.
39. Ross, "Queer Futures in *Black Mirror*'s San Junipero."
40. Ross, "Queer Futures in *Black Mirror*'s San Junipero."
41. Slotkin, *Regeneration Through Violence*, 34.
42. Ross, "Queer Futures in *Black Mirror*'s San Junipero."
43. Packard, *Queer Cowboys*, 3.
44. Hsu, "Authentic Re-Creations," 308.
45. Eco, *Travels in Hyperreality*, 69.
46. Hsu, "Authentic Re-Creations," 316.
47. Campbell, *The Cultures of the New American West*, 10.
48. Hsu, "Authentic Re-Creations," 308–9.
49. Davis quoted in Campbell, *The Cultures of the New American West*, 141.
50. Brooker, Jones, and Arnopp, *Inside Black Mirror*.
51. Lewis, *Unsettling the Literary West*, 15.
52. Handley and Lewis, introduction to *True West*, 7.
53. Ross, "Queer Futures in *Black Mirror*'s San Junipero."
54. Brooker, Jones, and Arnopp, *Inside Black Mirror*.
55. Baudrillard, *Simulacra and Simulation*, 5.
56. Eco, *Travels in Hyperreality*, 17.

57. Hsu, "Authentic Re-Creations," 311.
58. Baudrillard, *Simulacra and Simulation*, 23.
59. Eco, *Travels in Hyperreality*, 35.
60. Baudrillard, *Simulacra and Simulation*, 8.
61. Levy, *Frontier Figures*, 16.
62. Mogen, *Wilderness Visions*, 33.
63. Brooker, Jones, and Arnopp, *Inside Black Mirror*.
64. Mogen, *Wilderness Visions*, 43.
65. Mogen, *Wilderness Visions*, 52.
66. Mogen, *Wilderness Visions*, 53.
67. Eco, *Travels in Hyperreality*, 71.
68. Limerick, *The Real West*, 16.
69. Campbell, *The Cultures of the New American West*, 2.

Bibliography

Baudrillard, Jean. *Simulacra and Simulation*. Translated by Sheila Glaser. Ann Arbor: University of Michigan Press, 1995.

Brooker, Charlie, Annabel Jones, and Jason Arnopp. *Inside Black Mirror*. New York: Crown Archetype, 2018.

Call, Lewis. BDSM *in American Science Fiction and Fantasy*. London: Palgrave Macmillan, 2013.

Campbell, Neil. *The Cultures of the New American West*. Edinburgh, UK: Edinburgh University Press, 2000.

Cracroft, Richard. "World Westerns: The European Writer and the American West." *Western American Literature* 20, no. 2 (Summer 1985): 111–32.

Davis, Robert Murray. "The Frontiers of Genre: Science-Fiction Westerns." *Science Fiction Studies* 12, no. 1 (March 1985): 33–41.

Eco, Umberto. *Travels in Hyperreality*. Translated by William Weaver. San Diego CA: Harcourt, 1986.

Griffith, Nicola. "Hard Takes Soft, Still." *Science Fiction Studies* 36, no. 3 (November 2009): 392–93.

———. "Writing From the Body." Nicola Griffith personal website. Posted May 23, 2015. https://nicolagriffith.com/2015/05/23/writing-from-the-body/.

Handley, William R., and Nathaniel Lewis. Introduction to *True West: Authenticity and the American West*, edited by William R. Handley and Nathaniel Lewis, 1–20. Lincoln: University of Nebraska Press, 2004.

Harris, Owen, dir. *Black Mirror*. Season 3, episode 4, "San Junipero." Aired October 21, 2016, on Netflix. https://www.netflix.com/watch/80104625.

Hsu, Hsuan L. "Authentic Re-Creations." In *True West: Authenticity and the American West*, edited by William R. Handley and Nathaniel Lewis. Lincoln: University of Nebraska Press, 2004.

Kafer, Alison. *Feminist, Queer, Crip*. Bloomington: Indiana University Press, 2013.

Levy, Beth E. *Frontier Figures: American Music and the Mythology of the West*. Berkeley: University of California Press, 2012.

Lewis, Nathaniel. *Unsettling the Literary West: Authenticity and Authorship*. Lincoln: University of Nebraska Press, 2008.

Limerick, Patricia Nelson. *The Real West*. Denver CO: Civic Center Cultural Complex, 1996.

McLure, H. "The Wild, Wild Web: The Mythic American West and the Electronic Frontier." *Western Historical Quarterly* 31, no. 4 (Winter 2000): 457–76.

Mogen, David. *Wilderness Visions: The Western Theme in Science Fiction Literature*. San Bernardino CA: Borgo Press, 1982.

Packard, Chris. *Queer Cowboys: And Other Erotic Male Friendships in Nineteenth-Century American Literature*. New York: Palgrave Macmillan, 2005.

Rosen, Kayla. "*Black Mirror*'s 'San Junipero' Is an Ableist Dystopia in Disguise." *Kayla Rosen Zines*, December 6, 2016. https://kaylarosenzines.com/2016/12/06/black-mirrors-san-junipero-is-an-ableist-dystopia-in-disguise/. Archived at Wayback Machine. Capture date February 23, 2019. http://web.archive.org/web/20190223021139/https://kaylarosenzines.com/2016/12/06/black-mirrors-san-junipero-is-an-ableist-dystopia-in-disguise/.

Ross, Allison. "Queer Futures in *Black Mirror*'s San Junipero." *Media Fields Journal*, no. 14 (2019). http://mediafieldsjournal.org/queer-futures/2019/7/1/queer-futures-in-black-mirrors-san-junipero.html.

Schumacher, Joel. *The Lost Boys*. Richard Donner Production, 1987.

Slotkin, Richard. *Regeneration Through Violence: The Mythology of the American Frontier, 1600–1860*. New York: HarperPerennial, 1996.

Turner, Frederick Jackson. *The Frontier in American History*. New York: Henry Holt, 1921.

Weiss, Margot D. "Mainstreaming Kink: The Politics of BDSM Representation in U.S. Popular Media." *Journal of Homosexuality* 50, no. 2–3 (2006): 103–32.

Wilkinson, Eleanor. "Perverting Visual Pleasure: Representing Sadomasochism." *Sexualities* 12, no. 2 (April 2009): 181–98.

PART 2

Re-creations and Inescapable Repetitions

3

Sontag's "Pornographic Imagination," Bacigalupi's *The Water Knife*, and the Weird Western

MICAH DONOHUE

Susan Sontag finds striking affinities between the western and science fiction (SF), and between SF and pornography. In "The Imagination of Disaster" (1965), Sontag links SF to the western, as both are recombinant genres, while in "The Pornographic Imagination" (1969), she binds pornography to SF, claiming that they "resemble each other in several interesting ways."[1] Both transform our understanding of the self and the world through the re-creation of established settings, tropes, characters, and symbols.[2] The reconstitutive shuffling of verbal and visual sources into new textual worlds and ways of being link these two imaginations and three genres. Pornography and science fiction, inscriptions of defamiliarization for Sontag, exemplify what Ursula K. Le Guin has argued speculative literature, in general, claims: "It doesn't have to be the way it is."[3] Paolo Bacigalupi communicates the opposite message as a dire warning in his novel *The Water Knife* (2015), a pornographic and SF western that projects a history of water scarcity and wanton bloodshed in the U.S. Southwest into a near-future dystopia. The future, in Bacigalupi's retelling, looms as the inescapable repetition of an environmentally and economically disastrous past.

Water Knife is a U.S.-Mexican borderlands SF novel that has repeatedly and insightfully been studied and critiqued as dystopian cli-fi about climate change and water depletion.[4] And indeed, much recommends an ecocritical approach to *Water Knife*. Not without reason does Shelley Streeby mention Bacigalupi's efforts to raise climate awareness through his fictions in the introduction to *Imagining the Future of Climate Change* (2018).[5] In her view *Water Knife* attempts, if with debatable success, something akin to Rob Nixon's appeal in *Slow Violence and the Environmentalism of the Poor* (2011) to "convert into image and narrative the disasters that are slow moving and long in the making" to promote climate activism.[6] But the novel can also be productively read as a weird western, as Michael K. Johnson, Rebecca M. Lush, and Sara L. Spurgeon define the genre in the introduction to *Weird Westerns: Race, Gender, Genre* (2020): "texts that utilize a hybrid genre format, blending canonical elements of the western with either science fiction, fantasy, horror, or some other component of speculative literature."[7] Bacigalupi blends western, noir, SF, cyberpunk, and borderlands tropes to render *Water Knife*'s seared landscapes and dust-choked characters. *Water Knife* also, I will argue, draws metaphorically and performatively—in its portrayal of sexual acts between characters—from a pornographic imaginary like the one Sontag describes. For Sontag, that imaginary, surveyed through readings of Georges Batailles's *Histoire de l'oeil* (1928), Pauline Réage's (Anne Desclos's) *Histoire d'O* (1954), and Jean de Berg's (Catherine Robbe-Grillet's) *L'Image* (1956), is a fantastic one where orgasmic release blurs into self-annihilation, and annihilation is, paradoxically, the liberation and realization of the self.[8] Bacigalupi, by contrast, offers no transcendence. His pornographic imagery figures into *Water Knife*'s allegory of an inescapable, dying world.

Metaphorically, the novel repeatedly references "collapse porn," Bacigalupi's troping of the related terms "disaster porn" and "ruin porn," which have been used to describe the widespread portrayal of environmental, political, and economic disasters in print and visual media.[9] In *Water Knife*, collapse porn simultaneously is the documentation of the borderlands' ongoing collapse into ecological and political ruin and an indictment of an audience insatiably consuming that ruin as specular pleasure. Lucy Monroe, a journalist and one of *Water Knife*'s three focalizing characters (along with Angel Velasquez, the eponymous "water knife," and Maria Villarosa, a Texan refugee), offers "the latest in collapse pornography" in the articles she routinely publishes on the doomed city of Phoenix, Arizona.[10] Performatively, the sex scenes in *Water Knife* visually approximate to so much material streaming in the cold but dazzling and lurid light of zeros and ones on hardcore internet tube sites. These scenes range from Maria's first sexual encounter, in which she loses her virginity in a male-female-female threesome, to a BDSM-coded encounter in which a recently tortured Lucy (the same self-described purveyor of collapse porn) is choked by her lover, Angel, and experiences "the slashes and bruises" of her life-threatening ordeal turn into an erogenous "map" of sexual pleasure. Bacigalupi explicitly connects Lucy's desire "to be annihilated"—a desire reminiscent of the fantasies discussed by Sontag in "The Pornographic Imagination"—to the crumbling cityscape around her.[11] The metaphoric and performative converge in Lucy's body in a lethal display of eroticized destruction.

Every aspect of Bacigalupi's novel, from accounts of intimate sex acts to descriptions of global commerce and Machiavellian politics, are fractal retellings of an all-encompassing doom. *Water Knife* weirds borderlands SF and the western not by "incorporating horror, supernatural, or fantasy elements and themes," Paul Green's recipe for the weird western that depends on an understanding of "weird" as having to do with "magical power" or "enchantment" of some kind.[12] A weird reading of *Water Knife* relies, rather, on an older meaning of the term as "fate" or "destiny."[13] Bacigalupi reconfigures western tropes and conventions—captivity narratives, prostitution, preoccupation with death, gratuitous violence, blunted language—into a work of borderlands SF that envisions an irreparably ruined future as the catastrophic conclusion to a worsening present and a traumatic past.

The narrative of *Water Knife* recapitulates nineteenth- and twentieth-century western and borderlands American history. The novel winks at Roman Polanski's *Chinatown* (1974), and it repeatedly references *Cadillac Desert* (1986), Marc Reisner's historical study of water (mis)use in the Southwest, as a "bible" for understanding the hellish plight of *Water Knife*'s near-future world.[14] If *Water Knife* refigures American history into a dystopian backdrop for its futuristic narrative, its sexual imagery is no less a recycling of past and present. Bacigalupi stages the graphic sex scenes in *Water Knife* from a definitively male, cisgender, and heteronormative perspective. Pornography can be subjectively emancipatory and politically transformative, but it can also be a disempowering repetition of social relations grounded in sexism, queer and transphobia, and other forms of oppression and violence.[15] Pornography shares this double—empowering, enervating—nature with SF and weird westerns.[16] The fusion of the pornographic with SF and western tropes is far more oppressive than liberating in *Water Knife*, but Bacigalupi does not do this naively or uncritically. Sex and sexuality are expressive features of the novel's larger portrayal and critique of what Bacigalupi calls a "broken future" in which no escape exists from an ecocidal history of technological progress and global capitalism.[17] The characters in *Water Knife* are inextricably bound to—and bound to participate in and document—the ongoing collapse of their world. *Water Knife* embodies this devastation through its socio-economically and physically violent sex scenes. The novel's fatal erotics symbolizes an ineluctable wreckage.

Maria, Sarah, and Ratan

Pornography has always played a part in the western, at least etymologically speaking. The *porn-* in pornography comes from the Greek *pornē* (πόρνη), or prostitute, and a *porneion* (πορνεῖον) was a brothel. How many prostitutes and brothels have appeared in western novels and films? As one example among many, Cormac McCarthy's *Cities of the Plain* (1998), the final novel in his *Border Trilogy*, begins in a "bloodred light"–lit Mexican brothel, replete with "whores in their shabby dishabille."[18] In *Water Knife*, "Texas bangbang girls," reduced to prostitution by the environmental laying waste of their home state, call out to prospective clients on the Phoenix streets. In fact Sarah, Maria Villarosa's friend and briefly her lover, plies that trade, and Maria, too, will moonlight in Sarah's company as a "bangbang girl" at a pivotal moment in the novel. But *Water Knife* is not a pornographic book in the sense of Bataille's *Histoire de l'oeil*, Réage's *Histoire d'O*, or Berg's *L'Image*—the novels that Sontag focuses on in "The Pornographic Imagination." That is to say, the "primary, exclusive, and overriding" fictional concern of *Water Knife* is not "the depiction of sexual 'intentions' and 'activities,'" as it is, for example, in *Histoire d'O*, where the Château de Roissy exerts such diegetic gravity that it pulls every character into its halls of torturous submission and sexual delirium.[19]

Water Knife is not a total erotic barrage à la Réage, Berg, or Bataille (or the Marquis de Sade, whose eighteenth-century *Justine* is an intertextual predecessor to all three). It rather incorporates the pornographic in a manner similar to how Sontag argues that the Icelandic Nobel laureate Halldór Laxness does in *Under the Glacier* (1968). He interweaves erotica, SF, philosophy, satire, allegory, and wisdom literature (among still other genres) into that virtuosic novel-as-tapestry.[20] Bacigalupi similarly twines genres in *Water Knife*, a braiding and hybridizing of forms that—as already noted by Johnson, Lush, and Spurgeon—is a hallmark of the weird western, just as it is a defining trait of SF according to Istvan Csicsery-Ronay Jr.[21] One of the threads that Bacigalupi works into *Water Knife* from the pornographic imaginary is the claim, tendentiously argued by Sontag, that "what pornography is really about, ultimately, isn't sex but death."[22] But for Sontag that aphorism is a paradox, a "spiritual paradox" that, in O's case for instance, is of "the full void," "the vacuity that is also a plenum," and of self-obliteration that is also absolute fulfillment.[23] In *Water Knife*, however, only the negative terms (death, void, vacuity, obliteration) will finally matter. Glimmers of the positive will be quickly and utterly extinguished by the shadows of a world so completely doomed by its history that no actions, even the most intimate expressions of human desire, escape corruption.

That corrupting violence will impact each of the focalizing characters in *Water Knife*. There is Angel Velasquez, the hatchet man who ruthlessly advances the Las Vegas–based water baron Catherine Case's hydrological designs on the region; Lucy Monroe, the Phoenix transplant and muckraking journalist; and Maria Villarosa, an orphaned teenage refugee in Arizona from the failed state of Texas—a not-so-subtle displacement and "structural appropriation" of Latin American migratory experiences—who hustles water to make ends meet.[24] Of the three storylines that Bacigalupi plaits into *Water Knife*'s narrative about the frantic search for a long-lost Pima (Akimel O'odham) deed to priceless senior water rights to the Colorado River, Maria's has by far the most pathos.[25] (Lucy, the Pulitzer Prize–winning collapse pornographer, is brutally tortured for information in the novel, but the impact of that scene is drastically lessened when, a short while later, it serves as morbid foreplay to her having sex with Angel, the slickly fatal water knife who seems dropped into the sand-crusted pages of *Water Knife* from the cyberpunk sprawl of early William Gibson.) This emotional intensity reaches its most fervent when, frantic for money to pay off debts to some local goons, Maria agrees to join her roommate, friend, and (unacknowledged) love Sarah for a night with one of her regulars.

Michael Ratan is an unscrupulous hydrologist who has acquired the Pima deed everyone is hell-bent to find. (He hides it in his well-worn copy of *Cadillac Desert*, which will ultimately come—folded invaluable paperwork and all—into Maria's possession.) Sarah knows none of this, but she has pinned her hopes on him for a ticket beyond the Arizona border, and she convinces Maria to tag along on a date because Ratan has cash that she and Maria desperately need. They go to a club; they do drugs; they dance; they make out; they leave in a chauffeured car, and Maria, body still singing with "bubble," feels her desire arc like electricity to Sarah. Ratan she tolerates as a phallic conduit for her wild passion. She wakes on Ratan's bed (Sarah and Ratan are there, still asleep), reeling from the drug's come down, struck by the knowledge that "she'd lost her virginity to a stranger." Uncertain how to process that fact, she reframes it, deciding that "she'd lost her real virginity to Sarah." Slipping quietly into Ratan's bathroom, she showers and washes her underwear in the sink. (He lives in one of the novel's sinfully luxurious arcologies, where enough wealth can purchase entry into an enclave of wet Edenic splendor.) Ratan interrupts her and has sex with her again, although she "hoped he wouldn't." "It was nothing," she thinks, "something she could pretend to like. She pretended Sarah was with her."[26] As Maria performs for Ratan, however, the modal verb transforms silently into an imperative. Her act *must* convince him of her feigned pleasure.

The first of the two sex scenes that *Water Knife* dwells on in graphic detail (the second, which I discuss below, involves Lucy and Angel) ends with Maria cast as Ratan's sexual performer, but that happens in such a way as to emphasize the general powerlessness and vulnerability of sex workers in zones of often racialized economic precarity. The scene is structured by its asymmetrical distribution of power—Maria and Sarah are, in a double sense, subjects of Ratan's lust—and its clearly related status as an economic transaction. They are with Ratan because "*he'll pay, he'll pay, he'll pay.*"[27] Bacigalupi, here, intentionally reproduces the worn western trope "of the female as commodity" that the SF western in the twenty-first century has vigorously challenged and, as Melanie A. Marotta claims, has in many cases moved beyond.[28] In an insightful study of Elizabeth Bear's SF western *Karen Memory* (2015), for example, Selena Middleton calls attention to how the women working in the novel's brothel—the Hôtel Mon Cherie—create a gynocentric community characterized by security and agency.[29] In the arcology in *Water Knife*, Maria and Sarah have neither. That everything is focalized through Maria's perceptions tragically underscores how little power she has in this moment, and in a world in which such moments regularly occur.

Maria's ménage à trois reproduces a reductive heteronormative pornography (literally, here, a writing of prostitution) in which lesbian sex is rendered ancillary to the satisfaction of the straight male gaze, a gaze that Bacigalupi repeatedly introduces without interrogating or overtly critiquing in *Water Knife*. Johnson, Lush, and Spurgeon write that weird westerns "reinforce" as well as "challenge" oppressive cultural norms.[30] Eric Meljac and Alex Hunt, in their reading of Robert Coover's *Ghost Town* (1998), "a postmodern parody of genre western tropes," provide an example of the latter, when they describe a "scene of bondage and sadomasochism" from Coover's novel in which "women are completely in control of the sexual situation."[31] Bacigalupi, by contrast, reintroduces a patriarchal sexual hierarchy that privileges male pleasure within an encompassing frame of heteronormativity that scaffolds a capitalist economic order in which sex workers are commodified as usable and disposable objects. The economic structure and phallocentrism of this scene, which is already a violation, generates only more violence. Shortly after Ratan accosts Maria in the bathroom, thugs burst into his apartment, demanding the deed they know he has.

Ratan struggles and they shoot him through the head. Maria tries to get Sarah to hide with her under the bed, but she is oblivious from the alcohol and drugs, muttering for Maria to leave her alone. Maria has just hidden herself when the man who shot Ratan comes into the bedroom, sees Sarah, and shoots her too. But it is not enough that Sarah is murdered in this fashion (or that Maria's just-awakened love for Sarah is brutally cut off), the novel also violently sexualizes her death, with one of the hitmen joking about posthumously raping her.[32] This conflation of sex and violent death is not unique but common in the novel. The character Jamie, for example, the one openly gay man in *Water Knife*, is tortured, raped, and killed in a horrific perversion of male-male sex.[33] Sex for Bacigalupi is about death, as pornography was for Sontag, but death in Bacigalupi's novel collapses the "spiritual paradox" that Sontag found in writers like Bataille, Réage, and Berg. In part this is because Bacigalupi's sexually explicit prose has none of what Sontag calls in another essay "the lyricism of erotic impulse."[34] His writing is straight to the point.

Bacigalupi's descriptions of sex are entirely without lyricism or poetry, and they read like they have come, in an inversion of the standard direction of adaptation, from adult film into literature. The following moment between Ratan with Maria is typical—both for its blunt sexual language and for its violence: "Maria felt Ratan's hands on her hips, felt his cock hard against her ass, felt him probing her sex with his fingers, pushing, pushing in, then pressing further. It hurt."[35] Echoing in Bacigalupi's writing is Jane Tompkins's claim that "the Western is at heart antilanguage," but in *Water Knife* the "antilanguage" of Bacigalupi's sex scenes becomes antilife. The antilanguage of *Water Knife* depicts a necrotic Southwest that represents an end to the futurity—however threatened, however bleak—that has always formed part of the western genre. For Tompkins, "the Western's attack on language is wholesale and unrelenting, as if language were somehow tainted in its very being."[36] In *Water Knife* it is being that is incorrigibly tainted by the horrific consequences of industrially caused and politically countenanced climate change. Bacigalupi uses sex, which always "hurts" in *Water Knife*, to symbolize not intimacy and connection but social ruin and natural collapse. Nowhere is that more evident than in Lucy's eroticized will-for-death (a longing that foreshadows her being shot and the uncertainty of her survival at the end of *Water Knife*). Her relationship with Angel metaphorically repeats the destruction that she documents as a journalist of collapse pornography.

Lucy and Angel

At almost the exact center of *Water Knife* (chapter 24 of 47), Bacigalupi underscores the genre affinities of the captivity narrative and the western.[37] Lucy is abducted, taken to an abandoned house on the outskirts of Phoenix, and bound securely to a chair. She has been kidnapped because some of Catherine Case's agents, acting on their own initiative, wrongly suspect that she has information about the Pima deed. From the outset, the scene is grotesquely sexualized. One of the torturers laughs about violating Jamie anally with a broom handle before killing him, and then he presses and "stroke[s]" his knife against Lucy's thighs and crotch before slicing off her t-shirt and remarking, "Nice tits." Once Lucy is stripped, she is whipped so badly with an electrical cord that her "body was crisscrossed with fire," "she was shaking with uncontrollable spasms of terror," and "her voice was hoarse from screaming." But the violence does not end there. The torturer returns to the knife he has put down and begins cutting Lucy. The novel reports that "she didn't stop [screaming] for a long time."[38] As she is being tortured, Lucy somehow has the mental wherewithal to appreciate the macabre irony that she is about to become a character in one of her own articles: "Just another body. Just another enticement for click-thru on some voyeuristic news site."[39] Except, of course, she is saved. In another recycling of old-fashioned westerns and pulp SF, the hero (Angel, in this case, who has been tracking Lucy for the same reason as her kidnappers) rushes in, gun blazing, to the rescue.

The scene above is remarkable for several reasons. First, it doubles and exaggerates the violent phallocentrism and heteronormative structuring of Maria's threesome with Ratan. Just as Ratan was at the center of that experience, Angel, ultimately, absurdly, will emerge as the true focus here. In the process of rescuing Lucy, he is shot. Despite the horrible torture that Lucy has endured, which the novel documents through her "ragged" and "animal-like" screams, she will perform field surgery on *his* bullet wound with a degree of efficiency that impresses Angel! He marvels over the fact that "most people would have been losing their shit right now, after going through what [Lucy had] gone through, but she'd just gotten up and gotten back in the game."[40] No one will accuse such language of lyricism, erotic or otherwise. Second, it begins to make explicit a connection between Lucy's embodied trauma and the collapse porn about Phoenix that has made her famous. Alexa Weik von Mossner discusses how Bacigalupi "uses the human body" to impact readers "on a visceral level" with the consequences of a worsening climate.[41] His visceral sexual imagery functions similarly. It connects violence against individuals to larger structures of inter- and impersonal violence that make the suffering Maria, Lucy, Jamie, and other characters undergo in *Water Knife* quotidian events. Finally, just as this scene can be read as the hyperbolic continuation of the violence that engulfs Maria, it also anticipates and will be explicitly invoked when Lucy (in another generic recycling that will come as no surprise whatsoever) is unable to resist Angel's "impossibly dark eyes" and goes to bed with him.

It starts, as often happens, with a humanizing story about a tragic past. Angel recounts the murder of his family by narcotraficantes when he was a boy living "down in Mexico." (Mexico exists in this novel only as a synonym for failed states, narco-politics, and cartel violence.) It turns out this dispassionate killer, who has left entire communities waterless to wither and be blown away by desert winds, has a heart-wrenching backstory, and it deeply moves Lucy. She cannot heal his emotional pain, but she can continue to minister to his physical wounds, which she does, and her ministrations lead directly to their having sex. It is worth noting, only because it again underscores the utterly phallocentric nature of Bacigalupi's writing about sex, that as she settles on top of him, she tries "to be gentle" so as "not to hurt *his wounds*."[42] In a troping of pornographic writing that goes back to Sade's *Justine* and can be seen in *Histoire d'O* and *L'Image*, the blatantly sexualized psychological and physical trauma that Lucy endured a day or so earlier while bound, whipped, and stabbed, in no way debilitates her sex drive. In fact, it fuels it.

Sontag, in her reading of a bondage-themed tradition of pornography that she traces back to the Marquis de Sade and Victorian authors like John Cleland, notes how the usually female protagonists of these narratives can endure extreme, crippling physical abuse and then miraculously recover in the span of hours—the pain having been nothing but an aperitif to stimulate the next course of masochistic sex.[43] Something of that tradition, and of its unbelievability, pertains to Lucy. She has been so badly hurt (her ragged screaming leaves no doubt about that), and scared so terribly, that only in an unreal pornographic setting such as Sontag describes would she respond to Angel as she does in *Water Knife*. Her "bruises," "whiplines," "cuts," "savaged breasts," "slashes," and "ravaged breasts" become sexually arousing marks of pain-as-pleasure, and Lucy, much as O or Anne in *L'Image* might, "revel[s] in the hurt" of Angel's hands and mouth on her tortured body.[44] By way of a comparison meant to further draw out this generic filiation of Lucy's, consider a somewhat similar episode that has a decidedly different outcome in Rebecca Roanhorse's *Trail of Lightning* (2018), a novel that is a work of southwestern cli-fi like *Water Knife*.

Although Shelley Streeby does not mention *Trail of Lightning* in *Imagining the Future of Climate Change* (the two books were published the same year), Roanhorse's novel has much to add to Streeby's project of exploring "how scholars, writers, artists, and organizers of color have used the term 'speculative fiction' and the 'speculative,' as well as others such as 'futures' and 'futurisms,' to describe the visionary work they are doing in imagining the future of climate change."⁴⁵ Like *Water Knife*, *Trail of Lightning* can be read as a weird western that amalgamates SF, horror, dystopia, cli-fi, and fantasy with Native American stories. The novel narrates the resurgence of the Navajo homeland, Dinétah, with all its magic and supernatural denizens, in the wake of cataclysmic flooding that destroys much of the United States and dissolves its colonial hold on tribal land and Indigenous peoples. In this, *Trail of Lightning* notably differs from *Water Knife*. The latter problematically rehearses the racist trope of "the vanishing Indian," figured most prominently in the novel by the Pima (Akimel O'odham), who are registered exclusively *by* their absence: only their name remains on the fought-for and bloodstained water deed. *Water Knife* evinces "a striking lack of specific and individuated American Indian characters," a troubling absence that Rebecca M. Lush has dissected in other weird western retellings of the American West.⁴⁶ *Trail of Lightning*, by contrast, depicts the empowered "survivance," to use Gerald Vizenor's term, of Native peoples continuing to assert their claim to political autonomy and self-representation.

Maggie Hoskins is a Diné monster hunter aided by the powerful and strikingly handsome medicine man Kai Arviso. Like Lucy and Angel, they eventually wind up in each other's arms, and (also somewhat like Lucy and Angel) this happens shortly after Maggie has been badly wounded in an erotically charged battle with her former mentor, Neizgháni. Moreover, Maggie has experienced traumatizing ordeal after ordeal in the novel, and the memories of what she has undergone are still very fresh. But where Lucy will find "pleasure" in Angel's tracing the lines of her wounds with his "lips and teeth and tongue," her "slashes and bruises" transforming into "a map of her survival" by the alchemy of his sensuous attention, Maggie, similarly attended to by Kai, will feel her "desire shu[t] off like a goddamn light switch."⁴⁷ The point here is not to debate which scene is more realistic (although there is appreciable irony in the fact that the magic-infused *Lightning* may contain more psychological realism than the hardboiled *Water Knife*). Nor is it to argue over the morality of sexual depictions in either book. As Helen Hester persuasively argues in *Beyond Explicit: Pornography and the Displacement of Sex* (2014), pornography is a capacious enough aesthetic mode to encompass liberating and socially transformative as well as reactionary, sexist, and racist content.⁴⁸ It is, rather, to underscore how Roanhorse and Bacigalupi knot sex and violence together for very different reasons in their novels.

The trauma of Maggie's recent and distant past interrupts the intimacy she longs for with Kai, but that interruption signals, both immediately and in the larger arc of Maggie's character through the novel, a need for healing that has not yet been completed. *Lightning*, whatever its dystopian shading, is a genuinely *post*apocalyptic novel that depicts with no small amount of hope a "sixth world" pushing fully into being through the detritus of capsized history. *Water Knife*, however, is, on its own terms, a truly *apocalyptic* novel. Reflecting on her surroundings earlier in the novel, Lucy thinks, without hyperbole, "This was true apocalypse. The world after all the rules had stopped existing."⁴⁹ Apocalypse, like porn, comes from a Greek word, *apokalypsis* (ἀποκάλυψις), which originally meant an uncovering, a revelation. *Lightning* reveals a world coming into existence (the "Big Water" that rushes across the continent presages birth, transformation, change); *Water Knife* shows one that has failed. The western has long dialogued with what Richard Slotkin, reimagining Frederick Jackson Turner, calls "the frontier myth as a theory of development."⁵⁰ That dialogue continues into the weird western, where the tone is generally more critical than celebratory, and the boundaries are conceptual as well as spatial. For Bacigalupi, *Water Knife* represents a terminal boundary, an ultimate apocalypse beyond which nothing exists. Sexual imagery cannot be separated from the novel's nihilistic portrayal of technological and economic destruction.

Fredric Jameson famously wrote in 1994 that "it seems to be easier for us today to imagine the thoroughgoing deterioration of the earth and of nature than the breakdown of late capitalism. Perhaps this is due to some weakness in our imagination."⁵¹ Those lines have been quoted, usually in slightly reworded form (and frequently without the second sentence), countless times. Jameson himself revised them, writing in a 2003 essay for *New Left Review* that "imagin[ing] capitalism" has *become* "imagining the end of the world."⁵² Bacigalupi imagines late capitalism in *Water Knife* as planetary deterioration that is simultaneously the accelerated demise of the innumerable individual lifeforms that are contained within and that constitute that world. This constellating of the global and the local, the specific and the general, and the individual and the communal finds its signal nexus point and allegorical personification in the character of Lucy. Her actions and words are microcosms of the larger narrative project of *Water Knife*: the telling of the climate-driven end of the world or, as Lucy puts it, "excavating" the bottomless pit of the "future as it yawned below them."[53] Bacigalupi plays on this doubling of Lucy as narrative character and symbolic register of impending doom as he describes her and Angel "fuck[ing] in the dark zone" of a condemned city inhabited by "people who faced the sawblade of collapse" without hope of escape.[54]

Lucy ceaselessly fantasizes about death with Angel. She pays rapt attention to his pistol, "the discarded tool of death" thrown to the floor as they hurriedly undressed; she imagines Angel as death, as her death ("He was death . . . taking her as death took all things"); and she aches "to lose herself entirely" and "be annihilated." To that end, she has Angel wrap his fingers around her throat and squeeze—"the crush of his fingers was overwhelming"—to the point of asphyxiation: "There was nothing of her now. She was gone. Her air was gone."[55] But Lucy's longed-for, breathless annihilation cannot be read as simply another instance of what Sontag describes as "the voluptuous yearning for the extinction of the self, for death itself" in the pornographic writers that she analyzes.[56] With O, with Anne and Claire in *L'Image*, that extinction is transcendent and dialectical. It is part of an almost Hegelian movement in which self-realization occurs through the ultimate *Aufheben* of self-demise. (Whether you accept the validity of that movement, however elegantly traced out by Réage and Berg, is another matter.) Lucy has no such realization, although she desperately seeks one. Rather than deepening Lucy's character, Bacigalupi intentionally flattens her, metaphorically equating her wounded body to a map. The whiplines, slashes, and bruises become cartographic representations—traced on an individual scale—of "all the horrors the world had to offer," horrors that Bacigalupi draws in much larger dimensions across the Phoenix cityscape and the devastated terrain of the U.S.-Mexican borderlands.[57] The writer of collapse porn is rewritten in *Water Knife* into the embodiment of her subject matter.

Lucy, "as she fuck[s]," identifies with the "mangled city," which is, in an allegorical sense, her own "ravaged" body writ large (just as it is, although this is less explicitly foregrounded in the narrative, Angel's scarred body, and Jamie's, and Maria's).[58] Helen Hester, near the end of *Beyond Explicit*, explores the ways in which the suffix "-porn" has moved in the popular idiom far beyond the obviously or gratuitously sexualized. She focuses on "warporn" and finds support in Sontag's *Regarding the Pain of Others* (2003) for her claim that "certain kinds of nonsexually explicit imagery are viewed as being particularly likely to trigger the itching, voyeuristic desire or lascivious curiosity typically associated with pornography."[59] In *Regarding*, Sontag returns to "one of the great theorists of the erotic," Bataille, to exemplify what Hester calls porn-like "voyeuristic desire" in *Beyond Explicit*.[60] Sontag dwells on Bataille's photo of a still-living but dismembered Chinese prisoner who undergoes the "death of a hundred cuts." This macabre image, for Bataille, represents "a mortification of the feelings and a liberation of tabooed erotic knowledge."[61] Violence for Bataille (and this is evident in his novel *Histoire de l'oeil*) represents "something more than just suffering." It is "a kind of transfiguration."[62] Bacigalupi disavows transfiguration. Like the western filmmakers that Lee Clark Mitchell analyzes in *Westerns* (1996), Bacigalupi crafts a world characterized by "violence as always brutal, never redemptive."[63] But unlike Sergio Leone or Sam Peckinpah, whose bloodshed nevertheless reinscribes, albeit ambivalently, a "commit[ment] to restoring the *status quo ante*," the violence in *Water Knife* translates history into a future of suffering, eroticized destruction, and death.[64]

In the collapse porn that Lucy writes, extreme violence is explicitly linked to "voyeuristic desire" and "lascivious curiosity"—as happens in the warporn that Hester investigates. Lucy, as we saw, envisions her own corpse as clickbait on a "voyeuristic news site" where hungry viewers salivate over the new day's fresh atrocities.[65] And as Sontag notes regarding Bataille, a bond forms between "mortification" and eroticism in *Water Knife*. Near the beginning of the novel, Lucy wonders if "she was just another collapse pornographer . . . eroticizing a city's death."[66] The remainder of *Water Knife* answers her question in the affirmative. Lucy does eroticize a city's violent death (as *Water Knife* generally eroticizes it), just as the brutal violence she suffers is eroticized in the novel. But the "transfiguration" that Bataille looks for in his atrocious photograph, or that O finds in dehumanization, never occurs. In the already ruined but still worsening world of *Water Knife*, sex and violence are inseparably fused. The erotic has become violent, and pain is invariably charged with fatal eroticism.

Weird Endings and *Water Knife*'s "Broken Future"

It is a small detail of debatable importance that Cormac McCarthy ends *Cities of the Plain* (1998) four years *after* the date of the novel's publication. Decades of Billy Parham's life are condensed into a short paragraph of rapid-fire sentences that culminates in "Days of the world. Years of the world. Till he was old." An old man (we find out a few pages later that he is seventy-eight years old), Billy is evicted from a hotel in El Paso, Texas, "in the spring of the second year of the new millennium," and makes his way to Arizona, where he meets an old Mexican man who may or may not be Death in what may or may not be a dream.[67] It is a *weird* ending, both fantastic (its allusions to Death, its playful rewriting of Jorge Luis Borges's "Borges and I," its dreams-in-dreams, its *mise-en-abyme* structure, its futuristic setting) and weird in a prophetic sense. It tells what will be: a drought-wracked, economically devastated Southwest where the blazing sun casts apocalyptic shadows. The epilogue of *Cities* reads almost like a prologue to McCarthy's *The Road* (2006)—or, intertextually, to Bacigalupi's *Water Knife*. The end of *Cities* alludes to an element of futurity that has always been a constitutive part of the western, and that Bacigalupi makes the central component of his weird western. There is a sense in which *Water Knife* is more western weird than weird western. According to the *Oxford English Dictionary*, a weird (used as a noun) was a seer—that is, "one pretending or supposed to have the power to foresee and to control future events." The future in *Water Knife* repeats and intensifies the violence of the past. Bacigalupi holds to McCarthy's borderlands dictum that "what has no past can have no future," and *Water Knife* mines the horrors of southwestern history for the materials to build a yet more horrible but equally inescapable future.[68]

McCarthy writes that every story "has its beginnings in a question."[69] *Water Knife* poses in harrowing terms what I see as a fundamental question of the weird western: what is the genre's relationship to the future, and is that future open or closed? For Ursula K. Le Guin, speculative fiction authors are "writers who can see alternatives to how we now live," and who are "visionaries of a larger reality."[70] O, at least in Sontag's reading of *Histoire d'O*, is such a visionary. The obvious null and sexual symbolism of her name does not preclude that "O" from being the weird image of an eye, less as an allusion to Bataille's *Histoire de l'oeil*, and much more as a way of emphasizing how O—with or without the Minerva's owl mask that she is forced to wear at the end of *Histoire*—sees herself and the world differently. Pornography can be such a reenvisioning. It is a poetics and ars combinatoria, as Sontag claims, of a vocabulary of sex acts that functions as a critique, an endorsement, or a utopian reimagining of human sexual and social life. Pornography, like SF and the weird western, veers between social transformation and stasis, between utopian hope and dystopian terror for tomorrow.

Bacigalupi depicts only terror. *Water Knife* winds to a nadir of hopelessness from which ascent is impossible. One of the first images in the novel of Phoenix "as a sinkhole . . . sucking everything down" provides a controlling metaphor for the vortical narrative of collapse in *Water Knife*. By the end of Bacigalupi's novel, that "gaping maw of disaster" is inescapable, and the final pages of *Water Knife* read like a coda to despair.[71] Lucy wants to return the Pima deed to Phoenix, giving the city water it desperately needs to survive—at least until the Colorado River dries up. Maria, however, sees things for what they are and not through "old eyes" blinded by dreams with no place in this "changed" world.[72] She shoots Lucy, recovers the deed, and gives the paperwork to Angel, who will use it to buy passage for each of them to Las Vegas and back into Catherine Case's good graces. *Water Knife* ends with Lucy terribly, perhaps fatally, wounded and Case, the "Queen of the Colorado," ruling unchecked over a dying, futureless Southwest. *Water Knife* concludes as it begins—with brokenness and bloodshed. Lucy is bleeding and Maria "wonder[s] if something was broken inside her."[73] It is a story that recapitulates the U.S.-Mexican borderlands' history of economically motivated violence and resource mismanagement. That history determines the mise-en-scène of what Bacigalupi calls a "broken future," and a broken future is all *Water Knife* displays for its readers.

Bacigalupi takes up but reverses Sontag's claim near the end of "The Pornographic Imagination" that "the traumatic failure of modern capitalist society [is] to provide authentic outlets for the perennial human flair for high-temperature visionary obsessions, to satisfy the appetite for exalted self-transcending modes of concentration and seriousness."[74] In the blisteringly hot temperatures of *Water Knife*'s near future, self-transcendence has become impossible. Sex, like everything else in *Water Knife*, symbolizes ruin and is a memento mori. That conflation constitutes the key critical contribution of *Water Knife*, which is admonitory, but it also defines its critical limit. Denuding its pages of hope at the same time that it oversaturates them with exploitation and violence, *Water Knife* tells a story (to quote one of Bacigalupi's tweets) of a "wretched, stupid, broken future."[75] In that ruined and banal tomorrow, the fast-approaching endpoint of global capitalism, true release is "the extinction of the self," not as the self-obliteration of orgasm in Sontag's pornographic imagination but as Angel's fist crushing Lucy's throat under the weight of what was and what Bacigalupi fears will be.[76]

Notes

1. Sontag, "Imagination of Disaster," 199; Sontag, "Pornographic Imagination," 321.
2. Sontag, "Pornographic Imagination," 329–30.
3. Le Guin, "It Doesn't Have to Be," 81.
4. Critics have variously praised and challenged *The Water Knife* for its portrayal of—and warning against—water shortages and climate change in the U.S. Southwest. See, for example, Farca, "There Will Be Blood"; Harris, "Expanding Climate Science"; Hsu and Yazell, "Post-Apocalyptic Geographies"; Pérez Ramos, "The Water Apocalypse"; Perrin, "Negotiating Water"; Schneider-Mayerson, "'Just as in the Book'"; Weik von Mossner, "Sensing the Heat"; and Yazell, "A Sociology of Failure."
5. Streeby, *Imagining the Future*, 18.
6. Nixon, *Slow Violence*, 3, 14–15. For critics who have questioned how successfully *Water Knife* promotes climate activism, see Schneider-Mayerson, "'Just as in the Book,'" 357; and Yazell, "A Sociology of Failure," 156–57.
7. Johnson, Lush, and Spurgeon, "Westworld(s)," 2.
8. Sontag, "Pornographic Imagination," 341–42.
9. Climate disaster porn is a widely used and hotly debated term, now lionized as a consciousness-raising, activism-promoting literary or journalistic form but also decried as an impediment to real environmental change and ultimately considered defeatist. For good discussions of the topic, see Atkin, "The Power and Peril"; Rastogi, *Postcolonial Disaster*; and Recuber, "Disaster Porn." For discussions of ruin porn, which is related but not identical to disaster porn, see Day, "Ruin Porn"; and Lyons, "Ruin Porn."
10. Bacigalupi, *Water Knife*, 27.

11. Bacigalupi, *Water Knife*, 212, 328, 331.
12. Green, *Encyclopedia*, 2.
13. See the entries for "weird" in *The Oxford English Dictionary*.
14. Bacigalupi, *Water Knife*, 219. See also Pérez Ramos, "The Water Apocalypse," 46.
15. Williams, "Proliferating Pornographies," 7–9; Hester, *Beyond Explicit*, 5, 9–10.
16. Sontag, "Imagination of Disaster," 212–13; Johnson, Lush, and Spurgeon, "Westworld(s)," 2.
17. In a 2015 interview with Amelia Urry about *Water Knife*, Bacigalupi discusses the "broken" and "accidental futures" depicted in his novels. Urry, "Can Fiction Make People Care."
18. McCarthy, *Cities*, 3.
19. Sontag, "Pornographic Imagination," 346.
20. Sontag, "Outlandish," 90.
21. Csicsery-Ronay, *The Seven Beauties*, 216–18.
22. Sontag, "Pornographic Imagination," 341.
23. Sontag, "Pornographic Imagination," 337.
24. Hsu and Yazell, "Post-Apocalyptic Geographies," 347.
25. The Akimel O'odham are a tribal nation located in present-day Arizona. Problematically, as I discuss in more detail below, their "presence" in Bacigalupi's novel is limited to their name on this deed and an aside in the novel that they sold their water rights to the city of Phoenix and "got a massive cash settlement" with which they bought "land up north." Bacigalupi, *Water Knife*, 282.
26. Bacigalupi, *Water Knife*, 212, 215.
27. Bacigalupi, *Water Knife*, 185 (my emphasis).
28. Marotta, "Where Are We Going," 13.
29. Middleton, "If He Can," 147–48.
30. Johnson, Lush, and Spurgeon, "Westworld(s)," 2.
31. Meljac and Hunt, "Strange Country," 67, 70.
32. Bacigalupi, *Water Knife*, 231.
33. Bacigalupi, *Water Knife*, 139.
34. Sontag, "Jack Smith's," 218.
35. Bacigalupi, *Water Knife*, 184.
36. Tompkins, *West of Everything*, 50, 52.
37. See Spurgeon, "Indianizing the Western," 155.
38. Bacigalupi, *Water Knife*, 257–60, 263.
39. Bacigalupi, *Water Knife*, 258.
40. Bacigalupi, *Water Knife*, 280.
41. Weik von Mossner, "Sensing the Heat," 174.
42. Bacigalupi, *Water Knife*, 326 (my emphasis).

43. Sontag, "Pornographic Imagination," 343.
44. Bacigalupi, *Water Knife*, 327–28.
45. Streeby, *Imagining the Future*, 26.
46. Lush, "Racial Metaphors," 255.
47. Bacigalupi, *Water Knife*, 328; Roanhorse, *Trail of Lightning*, 255.
48. Hester, *Beyond Explicit*, 3–10.
49. Bacigalupi, *Water Knife*, 137.
50. Slotkin, *Gunfighter Nation*, 16–21.
51. Jameson, *The Seeds*, xii.
52. Jameson, "Future City."
53. Bacigalupi, *Water Knife*, 29.
54. Bacigalupi, *Water Knife*, 330.
55. Bacigalupi, *Water Knife*, 329–31.
56. Sontag, "Pornographic Imagination," 339.
57. Bacigalupi, *Water Knife*, 329.
58. Bacigalupi, *Water Knife*, 329.
59. Hester, *Beyond Explicit*, 105.
60. Sontag, *Regarding the Pain of Others*, 98; Hester, *Beyond Explicit*, 106.
61. Sontag, *Regarding the Pain of Others*, 98.
62. Sontag, *Regarding the Pain of Others*, 99.
63. Mitchell, *Westerns*, 224.
64. Mitchell, *Westerns*, 254.
65. Bacigalupi, *Water Knife*, 258.
66. Bacigalupi, *Water Knife*, 29.
67. McCarthy, *Cities*, 264.
68. McCarthy, *Cities*, 281.
69. McCarthy, *Cities*, 277.
70. Le Guin, "Freedom," 113.
71. Bacigalupi, *Water Knife*, 29.
72. Bacigalupi, *Water Knife*, 448.
73. Bacigalupi, *Water Knife*, 448.
74. Sontag, "Pornographic Imagination," 350.
75. Paolo Bacigalupi (@paolobacigalupi), "The wretched, stupid, broken futures I write about are meant as warnings, not as user manuals, folks," Twitter, July 25, 2016, https://twitter.com/paolobacigalupi/status/757608362225831936.
76. Sontag, "Pornographic Imagination," 339.

Bibliography

Atkin, Emily. "The Power and Peril of 'Climate Disaster Porn.'" *New Republic*, July 10, 2017. https://newrepublic.com/article/143788/power-peril-climate-disaster-porn.

Bacigalupi, Paolo. *The Water Knife*. London: Orbit Books, 2015.
Bataille, Georges. *Histoire de l'oeil*. Originally published 1928. Paris: Pauvert, 1979.
Berg, Jean de. *L'Image*. Originally published 1956. Paris: Cercle du Livre Précieux, 1963.
Csicsery-Ronay, Istvan, Jr. *The Seven Beauties of Science Fiction*. Middletown: Wesleyan University Press, 2008.
Day, Iyko. "Ruin Porn and the Colonial Imaginary." *PMLA* 136, no. 1 (2021): 125–31.
Farca, Paula Anca. "There Will Be Blood: Water Futures in Paolo Bacigalupi's *The Water Knife* and Claire Vaye Watkins's *Gold Fame Citrus*." In *Make Waves: Water in Contemporary Literature and Film*, edited by Paula Anca Farca, 273–86. Reno: University of Nevada Press, 2019.
Fine, Kerry, Michael K. Johnson, Rebecca M. Lush, and Sara L. Spurgeon, eds. *Weird Westerns: Race, Gender, Genre*. Lincoln: University of Nebraska Press, 2020.
Green, Paul. *Encyclopedia of Weird Westerns: Supernatural and Science Fiction Elements in Novels, Pulps, Comics, Films, Television and Games*. Jefferson: McFarland, 2016.
Harris, Dylan M. "Expanding Climate Science: Using Science Fiction's Worldbuilding to Imagine a Climate Changed Southwestern U.S." *Literary Geographies* 6, no. 1 (2020): 59–76.
Hester, Helen. *Beyond Explicit: Pornography and the Displacement of Sex*. Albany: State University of New York Press, 2014.
Hsu, Hsuan L., and Bryan Yazell. "Post-Apocalyptic Geographies and Structural Appropriation." In *The Routledge Companion to Transnational American Studies*, edited by Nina Morgan, Alfred Hornung, and Takayuki Tatsumi, 347–56. New York: Routledge, 2019.
Jameson, Fredric. "Future City." *New Left Review* 21 (May–June 2003). https://newleftreview.org/issues/ii21/articles/fredric-jameson-future-city.
———. *The Seeds of Time*. New York: Columbia University Press, 1994.
Johnson, Michael K., Rebecca M. Lush, and Sara L. Spurgeon. "Westworld(s): Race, Gender, Genre in the Weird Western." Introduction to *Weird Westerns: Race, Gender, Genre*, edited by Kerry Fine, Michael K. Johnson, Rebecca M. Lush, and Sara L. Spurgeon, 1–36. Lincoln: University of Nebraska Press, 2020.
Le Guin, Ursula K. "Freedom." In *Words Are My Matter: Writings on Life and Books*, 113–14. Easthampton: Small Beer Press, 2016.
———. "It Doesn't Have to Be the Way It Is." In *No Time to Spare: Thinking about What Matters*, 80–84. Boston: Houghton Mifflin Harcourt, 2017.
Lush, Rebecca M. "Racial Metaphors and Vanishing *indians* in *Wynonna Earp*, *Buffy the Vampire Slayer*, and Emma Bull's *Territory*." In *Weird Westerns: Race, Gender, Genre*, edited by Kerry Fine, Michael K. Johnson, Rebecca M. Lush, and Sara L. Spurgeon, 255–88. Lincoln: University of Nebraska Press, 2020.

Lyons, Siobhan. "Ruin Porn, Capitalism, and the Anthropocene." Introduction to *Ruin Porn and the Obsession with Decay*, edited by Siobhan Lyons, 1–12. Cham: Palgrave Macmillan, 2018.

Marotta, Melanie A. "Where Are We Going and Whence Have We Come?" In *Women's Space: Essays on Female Characters in the 21st Century Science Fiction Western*, edited by Melanie Marotta, 1–24. Jefferson: McFarland, 2019.

———, ed. *Women's Space: Essays on Female Characters in the 21st Century Science Fiction Western*. Jefferson: McFarland, 2019.

McCarthy, Cormac. *Cities of the Plain*. Vol. 4 of *The Border Trilogy*. New York: Alfred A. Knopf, 2008.

Meljac, Eric, and Alex Hunt. "Strange Country: Sexuality and the Feminine in Robert Coover's *Ghost Town*." In *Weird Westerns: Race, Gender, Genre*, edited by Kerry Fine, Michael K. Johnson, Rebecca M. Lush, and Sara L. Spurgeon, 67–91. Lincoln: University of Nebraska Press, 2020.

Middleton, Selena. "If He Can Break It In, She Can Break It Out: The Public Impact of Domestic Machines in Elizabeth Bear's *Karen Memory*." In *Women's Space: Essays on Female Characters in the 21st Century Science Fiction Western*, edited by Melanie Marotta, 145–60. Jefferson: McFarland, 2019.

Mitchell, Lee Clark. *Westerns: Making the Man in Fiction and Film*. Chicago: University of Chicago Press, 1996.

Nixon, Rob. *Slow Violence and the Environmentalism of the Poor*. Cambridge: Harvard University Press, 2011.

Pérez Ramos, María Isabel. "The Water Apocalypse: Utopian Desert Venice Cities and Arcologies in Southwestern Dystopian Fiction." *Ecozon@* 7, no. 2 (2016): 44–64.

Perrin, Claire. "Negotiating Water in Times of Drought: An Ecocritical Study of Cli-fi Novels Paolo Bacigalupi's *The Water Knife* and Benjamin Percy's *Dead Lands*." In *Negotiating Waters: Seas, Oceans, and Passageways in the Colonial and Postcolonial Anglophone World*, edited by André Dodeman and Nancy Pedri, 165–80. Wilmington: Vernon Press, 2020.

Rastogi, Pallavi. *Postcolonial Disaster: Narrating Catastrophe in the Twenty-First Century*. Evanston: Northwestern University Press, 2020.

Réage, Pauline. *Histoire d'O*. Paris: J-J Pauvert, 1967.

Recuber, Timothy. "Disaster Porn!" *Contexts* 12, no. 2 (2013): 28–33.

Roanhorse, Rebecca. *Trail of Lightning*. New York: Saga Press, 2018.

Schneider-Mayerson, Matthew. "'Just as in the Book'? The Influence of Literature on Readers' Awareness of Climate Justice and Perception of Climate Migrants." *Isle* 27, no. 2 (2020): 337–64.

Slotkin, Richard. *Gunfighter Nation: The Myth of the Frontier in Twentieth-Century America*. Norman: University of Oklahoma Press, 1998.

Sontag, Susan. *Essays of the 1960s and 70s*. Edited by David Rieff. New York: Library of America, 2013.

———. "The Imagination of Disaster." In *Essays of the 1960s and 70s*, edited by David Rieff, 199–214. New York: Library of America, 2013.

———. "Jack Smith's *Flaming Creatures*." In *Essays of the 1960s and 70s*, edited by David Rieff, 215–19. New York: Library of America, 2013.

———. "Outlandish: on Halldór Laxness's *Under the Glacier*." In *At the Same Time: Essays and Speeches*, edited by Paolo Dilonardo and Anne Jump, 89–104. New York: Picador, 2007.

———. "The Pornographic Imagination." In *Essays of the 1960s and 70s*, edited by David Rieff, 320–52. New York: Library of America, 2013.

———. *Regarding the Pain of Others*. New York: Picador, 2003.

Spurgeon, Sara L. "Indianizing the Western: Semiotic Tricksterism in William Sanders's *Journey to Fusang*." In *Weird Westerns: Race, Gender, Genre*, edited by Kerry Fine, Michael K. Johnson, Rebecca M. Lush, and Sara L. Spurgeon, 150–73. Lincoln: University of Nebraska Press, 2020.

Streeby, Shelley. *Imagining the Future of Climate Change: World-Making through Science Fiction and Activism*. Oakland: University of California Press, 2018.

Tompkins, Jane. *West of Everything: The Inner Life of Westerns*. Oxford: Oxford University Press, 1992.

Urry, Amelia. "Can Fiction Make People Care about Climate? Paolo Bacigalupi Thinks So." *Grist*, July 9, 2015. grist.org/living/can-fiction-make-people-care-about-climate-paolo-bacigalupi-thinks-so.

Weik von Mossner, Alexa. "Sensing the Heat: Weather, Water, and Vulnerabilities in Paolo Bacigalupi's *The Water Knife*." *REAL* 33 (2017): 173–90.

Williams, Linda. "Proliferating Pornographies On/Scene: An Introduction." In *Porn Studies*, edited by Williams, 1–23. Durham: Duke University Press, 2004.

Yazell, Bryan. "A Sociology of Failure: Migration and Narrative Method in US Climate Fiction." *Configurations* 28, no. 2 (2020): 155–80.

Lost Max

4

Mad Max and the Challenge to
Masculine Dominance in 1970s Australia   SCOTT PEARCE

Mad Max (George Miller, 1979) is set in Australia "a few years from now," where society is seemingly on the edge of collapse. Law enforcement is losing sway as a ferocious motorcycle gang seizes control of the countryside, murdering, raping, burning, and looting as they go. Max Rockatansky (Mel Gibson), the film's protagonist, is part of the Main Force Patrol (MFP), a law enforcement department tasked with keeping the roads safe. The struggle to assert law and order and vanquish the villains, while also protecting family, is a well-worn narrative. Yet, Max fails to protect his family and, despite his killing of the ferocious motorcycle gang, the film ends with Max alone and lost, impotent and outcast.

Mad Max as a weird western is set on a somewhat recognizable frontier. There are tropes common to the western: civilization versus savagery, a socially minded white male savior protecting a helpless populace from antisocial villains, a need to defend vulnerable women, and a final showdown where the savior eliminates the villains. Conversely, *Mad Max* troubles these tropes by invalidating its white male savior and revealing his impotence and the fragility of his ideological founding. Further, the film is also concerned with the potential ramifications of a changing world. This concern is expressed primarily through its articulation of crisis. While the narrative presents a vague crisis of resources, such as a lack of fuel and the decline of social institutions capable of maintaining law and order, the fundamental crisis within the film is one of a destabilized heterosexual masculine dominance. Specifically, the film expresses an anxiety at how social and political change at the time of the film's production, particularly that wrought by the reformist federal government of Gough Whitlam, has critiqued and challenged the validity of a naturalized heterosexual masculine dominance. This, more broadly, is also a critique and challenge to the patriarchal social system on which colonization and colonizing myths were founded in Australia. The anxiety in the film as to the consequences such critique and challenge might begin is expressed in two distinct ways.

Firstly, it is expressed through the character of Goose (Steve Bisley), Max's friend and fellow MFP member. Goose is an ocker male, an Anglo-Australian male archetype. The term "ocker" was popularized on the Australian sketch comedy television show *The Mavis Brampton Show* (1964–68). It referred to a distinct version of the Australian masculinity: white, heterosexual, working class, egalitarian, usually easygoing, and often crude. However, variations predate this naming, although the characteristics remain mostly the same. Yet, despite his easygoing and jovial nature, his egalitarianism, and his determination to protect and serve his community, Goose is overcome by nefarious outsiders, a male biker gang of gay and/or bisexual Others. In this there is an expression of concern that the political and social changes immediately preceding the film have created a more welcoming political and social space for previously subjugated and derided sexualities, specifically the gay or bisexual man. More pressing is the concern that such a figure will cause disruption to hegemonic notions of sexual normativity, not only to ockers like Goose but to what they defend, the distinct gender boundaries that preserve the nuclear family. Further, a destabilizing or removal of the ocker male portends a challenge to the validity of Anglo-Australian national myths that are, likewise, premised on white heterosexual masculine dominance.

Secondly, this anxiety finds expression through Max, a more nuanced version of masculine domination than Goose. Max is married with a young son and demonstrates greater self-control than Goose. Max, however, is increasingly revealed as emblematic of the land he inhabits, its history of Anglo occupation, and the cowboy hero of classic westerns that are his forefathers, particularly those figures caught in the bind of a changing society, such as Tom Doniphon (John Wayne) in *The Man Who Shot Liberty Valance* (John Ford, 1962) and Jack Burns (Kirk Douglas) in *Lonely Are the Brave* (David Miller, 1962). While these westerns and others like them lament the closing of the frontier and the arrival of law-and-order bureaucracy, *Mad Max* laments the inability to close the frontier, a frontier in which heterosexual masculine dominance is incrementally losing power. Max, like Goose, is challenged by gay male Otherness and by the inescapable decline of the foundation myths that colonization has never been quite able to consolidate, and that are progressively revealed as flawed and unsustainable in a changing world, exemplified by the failure of Goose and Max to preserve their ailing society.

The "few years from now" consequences of crises in *Mad Max* are presented on a frontier that conflates disruptions to heteronormativity with disruption to social stability. This chapter first contextualizes *Mad Max* as a meeting of the western with a desire to preserve a distinct, but exclusive, Australian nationalist identity. It then examines the role of Goose and his position as a prominent form of heteronormative Australian sexuality, one that is deformed by gay male Otherness. It then focuses on Max as a western hero troubled by the binds of a colonial failure to conquer the land, as well as a personal failure to protect his family, which renders him ineffectual as a hero and as a heterosexual male.

Mad Max Is Weird

Defining *Mad Max*, in terms of genre, is a contested act. There are clearly recognizable character aesthetics with narrative tropes that tether the film to the western film genre but reposition it on a pre- or postapocalyptic frontier. The film is also distinctively Australian and was produced during a decade of incomparable upheaval and division. In naming *Mad Max* as a weird western, this chapter sees that the weird western is an adaptable and metamorphic genre that transcends, but also reflects, its point of origin, the western, as a uniquely American genre. Cynthia Miller and A. Bowdoin Van Riper, in *International Westerns*, see that "adapting the Western film to settings, audiences, and cinematic traditions beyond the United States enriches the genre with new geographic realities, new histories, and new collisions," and that these adaptations provide "new stories that could not be told anywhere else."[1] This is truer of the weird western than the western. The western typically strives to present an authentic view of the past, one that might not have actually occurred but could be reasonably believed to have occurred. Comparatively, the weird western incorporates aspects of the fantastic, which is not reasonably believed to have occurred or is set in an alternate context. The fantastic, however, is not separate from the real. For Rosemary Jackson, "Fantasy recombines and inverts the real, but it does not escape it: it exists in a parasitical and/or symbiotic relation to the real."[2] Fantasy then is the recognizable unreal, relocated. The ways in which this transpires in the weird western are multifaceted and contextual, but it allows for a refrontiering, a renarrativizing, and/or a reconquering of the past in ways that can highlight, challenge, or sidestep unaddressed historical and cultural trauma.

Mad Max is also an apocalyptic film. Whether, in terms of the setting, it exists before or after a world-changing disaster is not established, although it is certainly debated. John Hay asserts that "the post-nuclear disaster genre epitomized by the Mad Max series [is] highlighting Australia's ecological concerns and deep-seated distrust of nuclear energy."[3] However, such a position tethers *Mad Max* to its sequels and denies it individuation, but individuation is necessary to understand *Mad Max* and its relationship to national cinema in Australia, something that becomes increasingly irrelevant in its sequels. Constantine Verevis claims, "The near future of *Mad Max* is not post-apocalyptic, but rather depicts an increasingly lawless society in which conflict is staged on desolate country roads."[4] Likewise, Adrian Martin writes that the film "is not in fact post any apocalypse greater than a general breakdown of social order."[5] While Dan Hassler-Forest contends that "*Mad Max* established a genuinely nasty worldview, and a politics of absolute nihilism" and that in comparison to its sequels, it is "the odd one out—bereft as it is of utopian impulses beyond its fully apocalyptic politics."[6] What distinguishes *Mad Max* from its sequels is the context of production. It is this distinction that is paramount to understanding how the film engages with sex, sexuality, and gender in ways that challenge and endorse western tropes.

The national and international popularity of *Mad Max* led to *Mad Max 2* (1982) and two other sequels, *Mad Max Beyond Thunderdome* (1985) and *Mad Max: Fury Road* (2015).[7] *Mad Max*, as Delia Falconer points out, "was made entirely with private funds ($380 000)" for a national audience, filmed in six weeks, and edited on a loose schedule.[8] Its first sequel, targeted for national and international release, had, Adrian Martin points out, a "budget almost nine times larger than that of its predecessor."[9] It also "drops the horror references in favor of a more fulsome homage to the Western."[10] Theodore Sheckels identified the need for the *Mad Max* sequels to have international appeal as contributing to a shift in characterization. Max "becomes increasingly 'American' as his stories unfold. . . . He is a noble crusader for the lost children, not just a wanderer enacting revenge."[11] Indeed, the *Fury Road* entry was shot in Namibia and replaced Australian actor Mel Gibson as the titular character with British actor Tom Hardy. The *Mad Max* films, however, according to Stefan Zimmermann, all "use the Western genre's range of components, like the rural setting, the importance of landscape, and the immediacy of social commentary."[12] Likewise, they are all readily identified with variations in the postapocalyptic genre, but this becomes increasingly removed from their point of origin. The argument here is that unlike its sequels, *Mad Max* does not provide the same narrative closure, and its social commentary is more specific and potent. There is a hopelessness, an antisentimentality, as Hassler-Forest identified, that permeates through the film and that characterizes it as apocalyptic, not just in setting but in terms of commentary on the context in which it was produced.

In defining the term "apocalyptic," Teresa Heffernan returns to the root of the word, noting that "apocalypse, from the ancient Greek *apokalupsis*, is literally understood as a revelation or unveiling of the true order."[13] For nonsecular societies, apocalyptic narratives, as Elizabeth K. Rosen maintains, commonly provide a story "grounded in hope about the future," even if that future involved devastating disaster in the short term. In a modern secular context, however, apocalyptic narratives have "become instead a reflection of fears and disillusionment about the present."[14] It is this latter category that defines *Mad Max* as apocalyptic. *Mad Max* is a frightening premonition that argues that heteronormativity is under threat from the normalization of gay and bisexual identities in 1970s Australia. Gay males in *Mad Max* threaten the stability and social good of heterosexual masculine dominance. This threat comes because, according to the film, gay men menace traditional family structures and destabilize society.

The narrative framing of the film positions the viewer to see the film as an apocalyptic dystopia, with Max and his fellow law enforcement companions heroically struggling to maintain order. Such a framing reveals the dread within the film. Luana Barossi provides a salient reminder that "when dystopia is associated to characters who are part of a hegemonic group (to the narrative or as a social representation) and do not take into consideration the perspective of other groups, it carries the danger of collaborating to the maintenance of anachronistic prejudices."[15] The "scoot jockeys" and "nomad trash" that prowl the empty roads of *Mad Max* are motivated, seemingly, by their inherent savageness, their desire to rape and murder, and are juxtaposed to the civilizing endeavors of Max and Goose and other MFP representatives. In western parlance, the bikers are an incarnation of First Nations people who, in western films, for John A. Price, regularly "attacked the train or stagecoach" and were regularly presented "without historical accuracy or even sufficient fictional explanation. Indians were simply held as hostile to whites."[16] In the same way, *Mad Max* presents gay males as simply hostile to heterosexuality.

Context

Mad Max presents powerful white heterosexual males as necessary gatekeepers against what it envisions as social and cultural decline. And to safeguard such gatekeepers there must be a preservation of the patriarchal power structures that give them authority. In reading *Mad Max* as a weird western, the film pleads for a future that looks distinctly like the past, and it readily employs thematic concerns found in many westerns. Zimmermann points out that "westerns do not need to take place in the American West or have to be staged in the 19th century, as the specific elements and codes can be found in other types of films as well."[17] These codes, such as the conflict between right and wrong, good and evil, are often expressed through the role of the hero, who is most often a white male. Harry Schein identifies that "good men are the rightful owners from whom the bad men are trying to steal potency." The hero prevails because "he defends family and home—as an institution—draws his weapon quickly. He shoots seldom, but never misses."[18] Such codes are more overtly characteristic of classic or romantic westerns such as *High Noon* (Fred Zinnemann, 1952) and *Rio Bravo* (Howard Hawks, 1959), films that dominated the pre-1960s era but lost ground in the revisionist context of the 1970s where heroism, in films like *McCabe & Mrs. Miller* (Robert Altman, 1971), is less certain.

Mad Max uses the trope of the violent and confronting Other, a role regularly given to First Nations people, and consolidated in westerns such as *They Died with Their Boots On* (Raoul Walsh, 1941) and *Ambush* (Sam Wood, 1950). John Cawelti sees "the role of savage is more or less interchangeable between Indians or outlaws since both groups are associated with lawlessness, a love of violence, and rejection of the town's settled way of life."[19] Australian film could not turn to a canonical vision of First Nations people as a legitimate threat to the colonizing process, as the Australian colonizing myths had worked so determinedly to remove, minimize, and deny the existence of frontier conflict, real or fictional. And on the rare occasion when First Nations groups did appear in Australian films as opposing colonization, such as in *Bitter Springs* (Ralph Smart, 1950), the threat was minimal. Catherine Koerner reasons that in the "normative discourse of white settler Australians to be 'Australian' is invested in the denial of Indigenous sovereignty to protect their white settler Australian claims to sovereignty and national space" and that this then "reasserts white settler hegemonic power relations."[20] *Mad Max*, by positioning the gay male as a threat to dominant sexual norms and, more broadly, to the legitimacy of white nationalist identity, conflates two prominent social issues at the time of its production: sexual identity and national identity.

The arrival of *Mad Max* came after a decade of renewal in the Australian film industry. It also arrived at a time of seismic political, social, and cultural change in Australia. Serena Formica makes the point that "at the end of the 1960s, Australia did not yet have a national cinema, nor did it have a proper industry that could produce films aimed at both local and international audiences."[21] Renowned Australian film historian David Stratton agrees, noting that most films made in or about Australia from the 1940s through to the late 1960s were English or American productions, so that "Australian stories were being filtered through foreign eyes, and a strange variety of foreign actors were pretending to be Australians," such as "Ava Gardner, Fred Astaire, [and] Ernest Borgnine."[22] The emergence of a national cinema came through the founding of the Australian Film Development Corporation initiated by the Liberal-National government of Prime Minister John Gorton in 1970.[23] This body was tasked with funding Australian filmmakers to make films about Australia for Australians. However, it was the 1972 election of the Labor government under Gough Whitlam, which ended twenty-three consecutive years of Liberal-National rule, that is often credited with driving renewal in Australian film production.

Although short-lived, the Whitlam government of 1972–75 reshaped the political and social landscape of Australia through sweeping social transformations, particularly in education, healthcare, the arts, women's rights, and First Nations land rights.[24] A polarizing figure, Whitlam drew the ire of conservative opponents at home and pushed diplomatic relations with America to the breaking point. The Whitlam government and its aftermath served as the catalyst for dramatic change and unrest in many facets of Australian life. Chelsea Barnett makes the point that the "1970s continue to be remembered ... as a decade of upheaval and change. Indelibly linked to these lingering memories is former Labor prime minister Gough Whitlam."[25] Guugu Yimithirr activist Noel Pearson, speaking at Whitlam's 2014 funeral, stated, "Assessments of those three highly charged years and their aftermath divide between the nostalgia and fierce pride of the faithful, and the equally vociferous opinion that the Whitlam years represented the nadir of national government in Australia. Let me venture a perspective. The Whitlam government is the textbook case of reform trumping management."[26] The Whitlam government's 1972 Royal Commission on Human Relationships, the outcomes of which were overshadowed by the 1975 dismissal, were a catalyst for redefining an understanding of sexuality and gender in Australia.[27] Michelle Arrow, in "Making Family Violence Public in the Royal Commission on Human Relationships, 1974–1977," states that the Royal Commission "articulated and substantiated emerging feminist understandings of domestic violence. . . . It played a critical role in embedding feminist vocabularies and interpretations of such violence in public discourse." Further, it "interpreted domestic violence not as a personal pathology, but a product of dysfunctional, narrow gender roles and identities."[28] Arrow, in "'These Are Just a Few Examples of Our Daily Oppressions': Speaking and Listening to Homosexuality in Australia's Royal Commission on Human Relationships, 1974–1977," identifies another important aspect of the Royal Commission: "It facilitated and legitimated a kind of sexual citizenship for homosexuals, challenging the heteronormative model of citizenship, which had long dominated Australian political life."[29] And Steven Angelides believes the commission was "attempting to directly shape and alter public opinion and laws on the volatile issue of same-sex sexual practices."[30] By 1977 Australia had returned to conservative party rule, and the findings of the Royal Commission were not something the new government embraced, particularly as it challenged the prosocial character of the nuclear family. But also, for Arrow in "Making Family Violence Public," it "provided some of the most potent evidence of the failings of conventional family structures in contemporary Australian life."³¹ The findings also widened and endorsed the critique of heterosexual masculine dominance and its relationship to various forms of violence. And in doing this it likewise critiqued the impact of this dominance on the country's history of colonization.

Mad Max responds to this changing social and political context by presenting a dystopic vision of a future Australia where conventional heteronormative family structures are indeed failing. The failure, it articulates, comes not from any innate flaw but because of groups outside of the heteronormative tradition that prove themselves to be a violent threat to family and to broader society.

The Heterosexual Male and 1970s Australia

Heterosexuality and its prominent 1970s Australian male representatives are targeted and eradicated in *Mad Max* by Toecutter (Hugh Keays-Byrne) and his cronies. The 1970s Australian performance of hegemonic masculinity is represented in *Mad Max* predominantly through Goose. Goose is an ocker, the type found in popular early 1970s Australian films such as *The Adventures of Barry McKenzie* (Bruce Beresford, 1972); its sequel *Barry McKenzie Holds His Own* (Bruce Beresford, 1974), which included a brief appearance by then Prime Minister Gough Whitlam as himself; *Alvin Purple* (Tim Burstall, 1973); and *Don's Party* (Bruce Beresford, 1976). Theodore Sheckels defines the ocker as given to "drinking and generally rowdy behaviour," while Tom O'Regan sees the ocker as an "unabashed celebration of 'Australian,' particularly the vernacular, whether in speech, content, or action. . . . [It was] an inventive, usually male, anti-language for bodily functions, sex, drinking and women. Ocker implied a resolutely hedonistic outlook."³² The celebration of such a figure was deliberate and related to the push for Australian nationalism.

The ocker, and other incarnations of hegemonic masculinity in Australia, such as the Digger, differ from the American cowboy in a distinct way.³³ In westerns, the cowboy is often a celebrated or anointed individual. Will Wright, in what he calls the classical western plot, sees that "the distinction between the individual and society is clear and rigorous. . . . The hero is autonomous and unique."³⁴ More importantly, "the hero can take care of himself—he fears no one and needs no one—but society cannot take care of itself."³⁵ He can operate on the periphery of the law like Shane

(Alan Ladd) in *Shane* (George Stevens, 1953) or *as* the law like Rooster Cogburn (John Wayne) in *True Grit* (Henry Hathaway, 1969), but his individualism is clear. In Australia, the ocker is a communal figure connected to the Australian notion of mateship or camaraderie. Chelsea Barnett, in *Reel Men: Australian Masculinity in the Movies 1949–1962*, contends that "mateship was a key component of radical nationalist masculinity," as seen in the Australian historical drama *Sons of Matthew* (Charles Chauvel, 1949).[36] Contrariwise, Dennis Altman identifies that "racism was an essential element of the mateship myth."[37] Altman furthers the critique by stating that mateship as a "bonding has been turned into the basis of myths of both the national identity and social action," most clearly in the World War I drama *Gallipoli* (Peter Weir, 1981).[38] What connects the individualism of the American cowboy and the communalism of his Australian counterpart is that predominantly they are exclusive spaces, open only to white heterosexual men.

Michelle Arrow, in *Friday on Our Minds: Popular Culture in Australia since 1945*, claims, "The ocker was at the center of the film revival because governments wanted to cultivate a recognizably national genre that audiences would accept and recognize as Australian—as 'one of us.'"[39] Such a figure emerges, for Scott Murray, as a fixture of colonialist discourse, one that strived to assert a unique Australianness that was separate from the Britishness that dictated early Australian self-rule. Thus, the ocker becomes a reaction against colonial rule, colonial rule of Britishness over white Australia. Ocker figures were popular in Australia because "they dealt lovingly with aspects of the Australian character that the British-based values of the middle class viewed as contemptuous," particularly class hierarchies and formality.[40] Conversely, the ocker is for Neil Rattigan, "a white male, nearly always Anglo-Celtic (but not rigidly so), down-to-earth, unsophisticated, democratic, and unimpressed by authority."[41] Bruce Baer also identifies the exclusivity of the ocker and holds that "hostility and homophobia are the flipside of Australian homosociality" and mateship.[42] The ocker scorned what Arthur Phillips defined in 1950 as "The Cultural Cringe," that being a sense that in comparison to England, Europe, and America, Anglo-Australian culture was inferior. Phillips had declared, "We cannot shelter from invidious comparisons behind the barrier of separate language; we have no long-established or interestingly different cultural tradition to give security and distinction to its interpreters; and the centrifugal pull of the great cultural metropolises works against us."[43] The presumption was that any artist or intellectual must flee Australia to further themselves and avoid the uncultured masses. This played out through writers and academics such as Clive James, Brett Whiteley, and Germaine Greer, who were openly critical of Australia's perceived lack of refined cultural institutions and practices. The ocker films pushed back against "The Cringe." But as O'Regan identifies, "By the mid-1970s the public criticism levelled at ocker was intense."[44] The ocker male became, for many, an outdated, chauvinistic, tone-deaf trope. This was in part because the ocker, as Michelle Arrow states, "became a more reactive figure, a reassertion of 'traditional' masculinist national identity at a time when that identity was under challenge."[45] The Whitlam government reforms, despite their push to celebrate Australianness, drove the critique of the ocker. In *Mad Max* the ocker returns as the happy-go-lucky Goose, who succumbs to the divergent sexual identities in Toecutter's gang. Goose's appeal to the viewer is one that idealizes the past, that positions its loss as tragic and as having broader repercussions.

Goose is first introduced while sitting in a *Fat Nancy's Restaurant* cum petrol station recounting in cheerful and graphic detail, for an unwilling listener, a horrendous facial injury he saw at a crash scene. Goose is excited and enthusiastic in the telling of the story, but the listener is put off his meal and Goose eats it, as if that had been his plan all along. His participation in the opening sequence, as the MFP pursues an escaped criminal known as the Nightrider (Vincent Gil) in a wild car chase, is undone when Goose crashes his motorbike into a car and breaks his leg. Goose still maintains his sense of humor and relaxed nature. When the car owner exclaims, "Oh, my God! What's happening?" Goose, with a chuckle, responds, "I don't know, man. I just got here myself."[46] Goose, however, is not the only ocker character in the MFP.

MFP members Roop (Steve Millichamp) and Charlie (John Ley) are notified of the Nightrider chase as Roop watches, through his rifle scope, a young naked man and woman having sex. Such a framing sets the tone for the film as it is heterosexuality that is literally in the crosshairs, and the camera frames the scene through the scope. Roop and Charlie provide a comical determination to stay in the chase despite having multiple accidents and their car becoming increasingly battered. After Roop obliterates a caravan, Charlie's concern is not the occupants of the other vehicle but that he and Roop will find themselves in trouble, telling Roop, "He had his indicator on." As they drive on, Charlie declares, "People's lives are in peril!"[47] The purpose of these scenes is to establish the authority as easygoing, as ockers, not bound by rules-based procedure and okay with voyeurism for sexual gratification and the occasional destruction of private property. Here, also, is the connection between masculine identity, authority, and nationalism. These MFP officers are state representatives, agents of the status quo, characterized as much by their energy and enthusiasm for law and order as by their risk-taking and exuberance for sexual gratification, action, and adventure, even if it puts those they are supposedly protecting in danger.

Although the ocker was predominantly on the wane when *Mad Max* was released, he continued, and continues, to persist as a representative of Australian machismo. The national appeal of *The Paul Hogan Show* (1973–84), and then the international appeal of *Crocodile Dundee* (Peter Faiman, 1986) demonstrated the appeal and commercial viability of the ocker. Goose, like Max, also represents institutionalized authority. For Joane Nagel, "The culture and ideology of hegemonic masculinity go hand and hand with the culture and ideology of hegemonic nationalism."[48] Interestingly, *Mad Max* works to avoid any postcolonial critique of such figures by evoking *terra nullius*, in much the same way the British did before colonization. In doing so, in continually showing the land as open and uninhabited, and by showing only white faces in the film, *Mad Max* protects masculine and nationalist concerns about ownership of the past and entitlement to the future. Nagel asserts that when men go to war, as when Max and Goose and the MFP go to war against Toecutter's gang, they "are not only defending tradition but are defending a particular racial, gendered and sexual conception of self: a white, male, heterosexual notion of masculine identity."[49] The audience is positioned to sympathize with Goose and with Max and see them as a continuation of the settlement of an empty land, a land absent of the genocidal actions of historical colonization. They are likewise a continuation of characters established by prominent writers of the nineteenth-century Anglo-Australian experience, such as found in Henry Lawson's *Joe Wilson and His Mates* (1901).

Goose, Max, and the MFP are contrasted with Toecutter's biker gang, who are first seen as they arrive in a sparsely populated rural town. There are no gang markings on their clothes or other gang signs, but they all reverse their bikes in unison and rev their engines before disembarking to note their togetherness. Christopher Sharrett sees that "the outlaws are motorcyclists, referring to a long history in film genre of this group as the last rebel faction opposing middle-class complacency."[50] These bikers, comparatively, are not the unfairly maligned characters from *Easy Rider* (Dennis Hopper, 1969). When Toecutter removes his helmet, he reveals a stubble-covered face, part of an animal fur over his shoulder, and noticeable eyeshadow. The eyeshadow, a makeup typically associated with women, means Toecutter does not conform to an established notion of gender display, just as he will not conform to other established behavioral norms. Likewise, gang member Cundalini (Paul Johnstone), wearing pink heart-shaped sunglasses, and Mudguts (David Brack) immediately embrace and begin to dance a version of the tango. Doru Pop identifies the gang as infused with what the heteronormativity of the 1970s sees as "negative traits—homosexuality, sadist-masochism."[51] Rebecca Johinke raises the point that while the "bikies may have been cast as villains . . . their masculinity is never questioned. Their sexuality is disassociated from their gender and sex, and they are not weakened or effeminised by any comparisons with women."[52] The bikers do conform, for Will Wright, to the classic villain trope, for like the hero, "the villains are also strong and opposed to society. . . . Their strength makes them independent."[53] For the bikers to pose a legitimate threat to Max and Goose they must have a real and demonstrated capacity to potentially overcome them. Here the film seems, inadvertently, to promote the social constructivist position on gender and sexuality, akin to that found in Judith Butler's *Gender Trouble: Feminism and Subversion of Identity* (1990) and Pierre Bourdieu's *Masculine Domination* (1998). It also reveals that the distance between heterosexuality and homosexuality is not so vast. If Max and Goose embody a mateship, perhaps, so too do Toecutter and his cohort. It is this problematic subtext that troubles *Mad Max*.

Bourdieu attests that the differentiation between male and female, premised on a patriarchal social system and its institutions, is a "socially constructed difference" that inevitably "becomes the basis and apparently natural justification of the social vision which founds it."[54] Further, Bourdieu notes that "heterosexuality itself being socially constructed and socially constituted as the universal standard of any 'normal' sexual practice" comes to dominate.[55] The bikers in *Mad Max* are thus abnormal because of their sexuality. Kerstin Braun and Anthony Gray, writing about the Homosexual Advance Defense in Australian law, an informal interpretation of provocation, claim that "we see the caricature of the gay man as the evil, sex-crazed aggressor, seeking to attack the honour of the masculine, heterosexual man."[56] The Whitlam government passed a motion favoring decriminalization of homosexuality in 1973 but could not force states to legislate the change. At the time of *Mad Max*, homosexuality had been decriminalized in only South Australia (1975) and the Northern Territory (1976). Bourdieu states the heterosexual "family undoubtedly played the most important part in the reproduction of masculine domination and the masculine vision."[57] Just as the "Making Family Violence Public in the Royal Commission on Human Relationships, 1974–1977" identified problematic aspects of the nuclear family, so does Bourdieu identify the ways in which the nuclear family can function to subjugate those that cannot or will not engage in its replication.

Toecutter's gang is positioned not as outcast because they are gay or bisexual, but because their being gay or bisexual seemingly makes them dangerous, not only to heterosexual males but to broader society. Simon Watney claims that "the figure of the gay man interrupts yet also reinforces the social and psychic boundaries of desire, and the relations of gender which are inscribed within them"; they are "its necessary 'Other.' Without gays, straights are not 'straight.'"[58] That is, Goose and Max cannot be representatives of authority, both an authority over judicial process and an authority over appropriate gender behavior, without creating an Other in those that are not them.

In the rural town where Toecutter's gang passes time, Mudguts takes a drink from his milkshake and sprays it into the face of a young man from the town. Diabando (Howard Eynon) then attempts to kiss the young man who pushes his way free. Cundalini and Mudguts pursue the young man into a building while Diabando waits outside. The pursuit is slow and comical. Cundalini and Mudguts put on airs, mocking formality. The young man is wrestled from the building and dragged down the main street behind a motorbike. A young heterosexual couple, seemingly the same couple Roop spied on earlier in the film, having watched the proceedings from a distance, decide to flee in their Bel Air sedan. In their hasty retreat they narrowly miss running down Toecutter, who whistles and the gang, "whooping," immediately begins the pursuit. The Bel Air is run off the road and the gang manically assault the car, smashing windows and piercing panels. Falconer describes how the "young couple's car is 'raped' by bikie hordes before they are dragged through its shattered orifices and also raped."[59] The car and the heterosexual couple inside it are both markers of heteronormativity and reproduction. The car is a sedan, and it includes a backseat for future children, who mark not only the completed structure of the traditional family but its continuation through the next generation. The assault on the car is an assault on heteronormativity and its function as normalizing heterosexual sex. The fast-paced cuts of the scene, each barely a frame, as the car is shredded, torn, and smashed, demonstrate the frenzied and complete destruction of the vehicle as to render it irreparable. Hannah Graham and Rob White identify that in Australia, "cars act as symbols of masculinity," heterosexual masculinity.[60] The attack demonstrates the threat posed by the bikers and thus the need for Max to eventually eliminate them. Sharrett observes that although "Toecutter's gang sodomizes the young couple and destroys their auto . . . the destruction of the car is more prolonged than the abuse of the young people."[61] The attack is not specifically against the couple but is about what they represent to Toecutter's gang.

The aftermath of the incident is shown through Max and Goose's perspective as they arrive in their MFP car. The young man runs away from the scene, naked from the waist down, and clearly bleeding from the posterior. He is frightened, but apart from calling to him over the vehicle's PA system, no attempt is made to help him aside from a promise that Max makes to Goose to return later. Indeed, Goose insults the fleeing man, "Hey, fella, you're a turkey, you know that?"[62] Goose, on the other hand, comforts the girl who has been tied to the wrecked car and tenderly carries her to the MFP vehicle. There is the sense that the raped man has been emasculated and that his fleeing into the wilderness comes because he has lost some aspect of his identity that cannot be redeemed. Comparatively, the girl retains her femininity and can be saved by an untainted male.

Later, as gang member Bubba Zanetti (Geoff Parry) awaits the release of arrested gang member Johnny the Boy (Tim Burns) from MFP headquarters, a teenage boy inspects the wrecked Bel Air. He asks Bubba what happened to the car and then comments, "It looks like it was chewed up and spat out." To which Bubba responds, "Perhaps it's the result of anxiety."[63] Bubba's answer is striking and complex. The anxiety he mentions is a cornerstone of the film and the context in which the film was produced. Toecutter's gang destroyed the car and assaulted its occupants, in particular the young man, to claim dominance and power over him but also, for the film, to demonstrate the danger of the outsider, the gay male Other, that will attack and emasculate and deny space for continued heteronormative relations. Pop concludes that "the apocalypse Miller seems to make us afraid of is that of the transformation of 'standard' male identity."[64] Equally, Toecutter's gang establishes themselves as capable of violent, destructive sexual behavior, thus demonstrating the potential rise of a new hegemonic masculinity. This is, for Pop, "a negative projection of the possible effects of social revolutions against the existing order."[65] It argues for maintaining the status quo, and it also emphasizes the need to eliminate those who are not heterosexual. Their elimination, however, must come from a heterosexual male to stabilize heteronormativity and to demonstrate its comparative dominance.

Lost Max

Part of the weirding in *Mad Max* comes from modes of transportation. The horses of the western are replaced by cars and motorbikes. While this inevitably draws in elements of the road movie genre, it also, for Ffion Murphy, Rama Venkatasawmy, Catherine Simpson, and Tanja Visosevic, demonstrates the importance of the road and "its roots in the American frontier or Australian bush ethos."[66] The road, made or traveled, harks back to the Frederick Jackson Turner notions of "social evolution" and "the disintegration of savagery by the entrance of the trader, the pathfinder of civilization."[67] Turner's pathfinder can be seen to take forms other than the trader. The "disintegration of savagery" comes with the spread of the white male colonizer. Yet, *Mad Max* suggests that savagery takes many forms and there is therefore a need to restate what constitutes civilization, meaning pathfinders must periodically reemerge to perform recivilizing acts.

Murphy et al. further state that "American westerns and their Australian equivalent, the bushranger and drover films were arguably the forerunners to the contemporary road movie."[68] The distinction being, for Murphy et al., that American westerns or road films offered an escape of sorts across a border, normally into Mexico or beyond, such as in *Butch Cassidy and the Sundance Kid* (George Roy Hill, 1969), *The Wild Bunch* (Sam Peckinpah, 1969), or even *The Getaway* (Sam Peckinpah, 1972). Australia, an island continent, offers no such escape. Toecutter and his group cannot flee, and neither can Max. Conflict in such a context is inevitable.

Mad Max contains both narrative and character tropes that are common to both classic and revisionist westerns. In Toecutter and his gang, who rape and kill, there is the terror of savage Otherness and the fear of sexual perversion that Ethan Edwards (John Wayne) rages against in *The Searchers* (John Ford, 1956). In Max's elimination of Toecutter and his gang there is the desire for revenge because of violence committed against an intimate partner, as in *The Outlaw Josey Wales* (Clint Eastwood, 1976). The western demonstrates the need for conquest of the Other, for control, and for the elimination by whatever means, and it condones this by highlighting the danger of so-positioned antisocial groups. Peter Robson describes that in the western there is a "shift from random lawlessness and individual responses . . . [to] the emergence of official local law enforcement officers representing the community."[69] This transition marks the shift from the uncontrolled and volatile frontier to organization and civilization. For Robson, "this is the very essence of the Western genre."[70] It defines the objective of the colonizing process. *Mad Max* inverts this process through the decline of law enforcement and the pending loss of the civilization that colonization achieved.

Likewise, *Mad Max* inverts the function of space and landscape in the western. Stefanie Mueller, Christa Buschendorf, and Katja Sarkowsky argue that the "Western famously works with the binary of civilization versus wilderness embodied by the juxtaposition of two diametrically opposed types of space."[71] The objective is to civilize or control the wilderness because, as Mueller et al. state, the "natural environment is inimical to human beings."[72] The western genre provides, however erroneous and self-serving, a justification for historical colonization and its need to civilize. *Mad Max*, likewise, demonstrates the perils of the inimical environment, but it is a context in which that inimical environment thrives and prevails, rather than one in which it is consumed by civilization. In Australian cinema, Ross Gibson reasons that the "idea of the intractability of Australian nature has been an essential part of the national ethos."[73] The destabilization of masculine dominance in the *Mad Max* narrative brings to the fore these historical anxieties that linger in the Australian colonizing experience regarding the inability to conquer the land. Jane Jacobs and Ken Gelder contend there is "a modern Australian condition where what is 'ours' may also be 'theirs,' and vice versa: where difference and 'reconciliation' coexist uneasily. In an uncanny Australia, one's place is always already another's place and the issue of possession is never complete, never entirely settled."[74] Early Australian literature focused on white Australian indigenization. Mary O'Dowd believes that in this "silencing of Aboriginal presence we find evoked the 'Australian man:' white and taciturn. He is imagined into a harsh land where Indigenous people need scarcely be mentioned in the art and literature (and of course history) of the nation."[75] The importance of this absence is, as Aileen Moreton-Robinson states, "in the guise of the invisible human universal, whiteness secures hegemony through discourse by normalizing itself as the cultural space of the West."[76] Here is the power of absence, the power to shape narrative. This process continued with *Mad Max*, but emergent social change meant that the absence revealed more than it had previously been able to hide.

Max's actions, although persistent, are futile from the beginning because like his historical Anglo-Australian predecessors he cannot quite conquer or control the land, and ultimately he cannot maintain the facade that he has or that he will; despite this he still endeavors to save the ailing world around him. Max is distinguished from the other MFP members in the opening scenes of the Nightrider chase. As Roop, Charlie, and Goose all embrace the chase and eventually crash, these scenes are intercut with Max's slow preparation. The viewer does not see Max's face; rather, what is shown are his hands, his mirrored sunglasses, and his car. Max confronts the Nightrider head-on, literally driving at him. Max asserts his dominance, his prowess, his superior performance. It acts as a type of duel, a showdown, and Nightrider flinches. Moments later, Nightrider is consumed in a fireball and Max surveys the damage. For Johinke, this sequence positions Max "as a masculine hero, questing to defend the car-driving patriarchy from the threat of menacing gay scoot-jockeys."[77] Max, while not the ocker trope that Goose embodies, is a close relative, beholden to his car and exhibiting hoon qualities. "Hoon," like "ocker," describes a predominantly male disposition. Graham and White identify "hoon" as "a term commonly used in Australian culture to refer to young people, especially young men, who engage in what may be perceived as dangerous driving behaviour."[78] Hooning behavior is "a way of acting out what it is to be a man," through "risk-taking to feel adrenaline and the thrill of speed or danger while controlling a performance vehicle."[79] Given that Max drives directly at Nightrider, who has proclaimed himself "a fuel-injected suicide machine," the potential for his own death is clear, but so is his willingness to take risks others cannot, or will not, take to preserve authority.[80] The scene has resonance with John Wayne's Rooster Cogburn in *True Grit*. Max, on first appearances, is prepared, like Wyatt Earp (Henry Fonda) in *My Darling Clementine* (John Ford, 1946), to challenge those who threaten him and the community regardless of the personal cost. Although as the challenge becomes more personal, Max retreats from this position. Early in the film, he protects civilization, scant as it is. But his separateness from other members of the MFP is not highlighted. Max is not a loner, at least not at this point.

Max's position in the MFP, a group located in the derelict Halls of Justice, demonstrates a social conscience and a commitment to the ideals of state-sanctioned law enforcement. The condition of the Halls of Justice, as well as the arched sign at the opening with the letter U out of alignment and seemingly about to fall, clearly symbolizes the futility of the MFP's actions. These images foreshadow the film's ending when the U, as in Max, is removed from institutionalized justice. Still, Max maintains a commitment to justice, and while it is his own sense of right and wrong, it is also one fastened to those institutions he represents. In this he reflects not only the wealth of western figures but also established weird western figures, such as Rick Grimes (Andrew Lincoln) in *The Walking Dead*.

Max is married with a young child. He is the only character shown in the film with an intimate partner and child. This demonstration is important because as Bourdieu maintains, "in the least differentiated societies, women were treated as means of exchange enabling men to accumulate social and symbolic capital through marriages, which functioned as investments leading to the creation of more or less extensive and prestigious alliances."[81] Certainly, this has application in the world of *Mad Max*. Women seemingly exist in the film to be raped and attacked, but this occurs only to emasculate the men to whom they are identified as belonging. Michael Flood asserts that "heterosexual sex is a means to male bonding and masculine affirmation."[82] The loss of this position, because it is usurped by another man, particularly a gay man, negates such bonds and affirmations. In positioning women in this way, the trauma of sexual assault then belongs not to them but to their male partner. The capital that Max has, as Bourdieu identifies it, is that he protects patriarchal assumptions about gender and sexuality, and this gives him a righteousness in the film's narrative. His son, Sprog, a term that has its origins in the armed forces and refers to a recruit, is a tangible representation of Max's sexual potency, his ability to replicate and perpetuate his dominance.

In an evidently patriarchal world, there are no female police officers. For Johinke, MFP commander Fifi (Roger Ward), "with his shaved head, butch moustache and leather attire, is a decidedly camp character. Fifi's status is undermined by his unlikely name. . . . This diffuses his masculine credibility."[83] However, there is a long-established affinity for ironic nicknames in Australia. The NT News, reporting in 2020, identified that "a redhead will be Bluey, a short guy might get Lofty, and a bloke with a quiet disposition can only be Mad Dog."[84] The nickname Fifi could equally suggest a hypermasculine character. Nicknames are pervasive throughout the film, in the MFP, and in Toecutter's gang. Sarah Chevalier, in a study of Australian nicknames, found that "Australian men, whether on the playing fields, at the workplace, in the pub, etc. form close bonds, or ties of 'mateship.' To a certain extent this mateship manifests itself, and helps to perpetuate itself, via nicknaming."[85] Hence the MFP also includes Goose and Roop. Interestingly, the bikers also have nicknames: Nightrider, Toecutter, Mudguts. This naming suggests a connection between the normative and nonnormative versions of masculinity might be closer than Max or the MFP realizes, so that the masculine and sexual identities that separate them exist on a spectrum rather than a hierarchy, a spectrum that is now contracting. John Rickard believes that "the homoeroticism of mateship draws much of its power from the denial of homosexuality."[86] Such a denial is hard to maintain when it presents such a confronting challenge. There are, however, important distinctions between Max and Goose and other MFP members versus Toecutter and his group.

A clear difference is found in biological reproduction. Toecutter has a quasi-adopted son in Johnny the Boy. This distinguishes Toecutter from Max in that Toecutter is unable to reproduce an heir with a partner, so he fabricates one as a form of perpetuation. Toecutter and Johnny target Goose by sabotaging his motorbike. They then run the salvage truck that Goose is driving off the road. Goose, trapped upside down in a vehicle that is leaking fuel, cannot escape. Johnny is reluctant to do as Toecutter wants—to set the vehicle on fire. Toecutter tells Johnny, "This is a threshold moment, Johnny. Step through it." He then whispers, "The Bronze, they keep you from being proud."[87] Goose, like the couple in the Bel Air, had recently taken part in a heterosexual encounter. His authority, both as an enforcer of the status quo—law and order—and as an enforcer of sexual norms, is literally upended. For Johnny, the threshold that is crossed marks a rebirth, and his new form is one that replicates Toecutter.

When Max visits the badly burned Goose in the hospital, he is shocked at how Goose has been deformed. Indeed, Toecutter's gang strives to deform heteronormativity. Max, however, rather than seeking immediate revenge, clearly articulates his feelings about the situation to his wife, Jessie (Joanne Samuel). "He [Goose] was so full of living, you know? He ran a franchise on it. . . . And here I am tryin' to put sense to it when I know there isn't any."[88] That Max can so clearly express his emotional distress marks him as far more emotionally available than the western figures he follows, and it problematizes his connection to the western hero. Jane Tompkins emphasizes this point: "The Western equates power with 'not-language.' And not language it equates with being male."[89] It is hard to imagine John Wayne or Clint Eastwood expressing loss in such a way or expressing a fear of what might happen next. Max, though, when he attempts to resign from the MFP, tells Fifi, "I'm scared."[90] Again, Max demonstrates an emotionality, a vulnerability, uncommon in western figures. Johinke believes that "like many heroes from westerns or police dramas, Max prefers to spend most of his time in the masculine realm, with only occasional 'civilising' visits home."[91] That company is increasingly diminished, as if to suggest that the masculine realm is likewise diminished. The frontier, with Toecutter and his cronies, reveals itself as a space that has no allegiance to the type of masculine dominance Max represents. Max also contests Johinke's statement, as when pressed, he chooses family.

Max does not commit to duty over family, such as Will Kane (Gary Cooper) in *High Noon*, and Max is no Wyatt Earp (Burt Lancaster) *in Gunfight at the OK Corral* (John Sturges, 1957). Even weird westerns such as *The Walking Dead* have protagonists that put duty ahead of family. It is in this narrative turn that *Mad Max* again weirds Wright's classical western and the notion of the western hero. Wright states that "without the hero, society cannot survive." And for the hero, his "characteristics of strength, independence, and self-reliance are not truly social values." The conflict, for the hero, comes because "the social values of love, law, friendship, and family are not truly individual values, but without them the individual cannot be fulfilled" Thus, "there must be a negotiation between the two positions . . . and this negotiation centres on the threat of the villains."[92] It is this classical model that Fifi uses to try and persuade Max to stay with the MFP, arguing, "They say people don't believe in heroes anymore. . . . We're going to give them back their heroes." When Max describes this attitude as "crap," Fifi relents: "You got to admit, I sounded good there for a minute, huh?"[93] Fifi's appeal to Max's sense of public service and his reveal that his own promotion of such ideals is shallow rhetoric renders not only the MFP but the broader society impotent in terms of the capacity for performance of desired actions.

Max, however, has not abandoned his patriarchal duties, his desire for masculine dominance, as preservation of the family is still paramount. Max's behavior still adheres to Bourdieu's statement that "the dominant model of family structure and, by the same token, of legitimate sexuality" is "heterosexual and oriented towards reproduction."[94] Although Max has lost Goose, the potential is that he can be replaced through reproduction. Indeed, when Max and Jessie leave for a vacation of sorts, they travel along empty roads in their Holden HJ Sandman Panel-Van, a vehicle culturally associated with heterosexual sex. Rosemary Kerr notes, "Panel-vans . . . alternately known as 'shaggin' wagons'—such as the iconic Holden Sandman, had an elongated boot, ideal for carrying surfboards and gear, and they could also accommodate a mattress."[95] The rerelease of the vehicle in 2005 prompted the *Sunday Herald Sun* newspaper to state, "Panel vans are making a big comeback—and the trend may have parents of teenage daughters more than a little nervous."[96] Similarly, a 2015 reissue was met with the *Courier Mail* headline "Shaggin' Wagon's Second Coming."[97] The vehicle's storied history as a space for heterosexual sex in Australian films, such as in the iconic coming-of-age film *Puberty Blues* (Bruce Beresford, 1981), makes it an overt symbol of heterosexual sexual activity.

Conversely, Delia Falconer believes Max's response to Goose's death comes because of his uncertainty in himself and his capacity to conquer. This is historically informed by an inability of colonists to subdue the land, and "the film betrays an anxiety that a landscape without a definable 'centre' may offer no 'moral center' or set of values on which heroism may be based."[98] The reveal for Max, in the wake of Goose's death, is the futility in endeavoring to claim the hero position. Max, unlike Captain Sam Collingwood (George O'Brien) or Lieutenant Colonel Owen Thursday (Henry Fonda) in *Fort Apache* (John Ford, 1948), does not put honor before family. Nor does *Mad Max* include a Captain Kirby York (John Wayne), or even, like *The Man Who Shot Liberty Valance*, a Maxwell Scott (Carleton Young) to demand the perpetuation of a colonizing myth, a moral center that is demonstrably untrue. Fifi makes only patronizing comments toward such an end. Such myths in Australia were never consolidated, were never strong enough to hold their ground under challenge. Even the Clint Eastwood westerns, such as *The Outlaw Josey Wales* and *Pale Rider* (Clint Eastwood, 1985) through *Unforgiven* (Clint Eastwood, 1992), demonstrate the potency of the individual, his difference, and his capacity to right a perceived wrong and impose himself on the environment. Max might be the center of *Mad Max*, and the narrative structure of the film positions Max as the hero, but he understands the naivety of such notions.

The panel van that Max and Jessie travel in, much like the Bel Air earlier in the film, becomes a target for Toecutter's gang. When Jessie takes the panel van to the beach to buy her and Sprog an ice cream, she encounters Toecutter's gang. Gang member Starbuck (Nic Gazzana) comments, "Look what's turned up for Sunday dinner," to which Mudguts replies, "Main course and dessert!"[99] They see Jessie, and seemingly Sprog, as prey. Their intentions are consumption rather than exclusively sexual gratification, although their comments regarding Sprog position the gang and their sexual Otherness as without boundaries. It also provides evidence to further demonize gay and bisexual men, a sexuality the film already aligns with rape, murder, and social unrest, but now it adds child abuse to that mix. It also reinforces the perception that children could be, as Steven Angelides writes, recruited, which "referred to the danger of impressionable children being manipulated or seduced into the homosexual lifestyle."[100] Such fears are also an expression of the decline of heterosexual masculine dominance. Although Jessie escapes the gang, they track her and Max to a farmhouse. Jessie and an elderly companion, May (Sheila Florence), flee in the panel van, but in driving through the farm gate a piece of wood pierces the radiator, and the panel van, like heterosexual dominance, comes to a halt. May tells Jessie to run and stands next to the panel van, gun at the ready, as Jessie runs down the road. Jessie's decision to run down the middle of the road, considering the open fields around her, is an odd one. Her unwillingness to deviate, to carve her own path, leaves her vulnerable. In this context, adherence to the norms of a broken social system leaves one vulnerable to those who exploit its weaknesses. Max is unable to stop the gang, and they run Jessie and Sprog down.

Later, Max then uses the V8 Interceptor with MFP license plates and engages the siren as he pursues Toecutter and his gang. There are elements of a Wyatt Earp revenge ride, as in *Hour of the Gun* (John Sturges, 1967). The choice of sirens identifies Max's actions as police actions, a statement of institutionalized authority. Fifi had made this type of action a reasonable one earlier in the film, telling members of the MFP, "So long as the paperwork's clean, you boys can do what you like out there."[101] Most importantly, however, Max's wife is not dead, although his son is. In fact, as Max waits in the hospital following the gang's run down of Jessie and Sprog, the attending doctor says, "We got all her signs back last night," and instructs the nurse to "tell him [Max] she's going to be alright. Tell him not to worry."[102] Although Sprog has died, Max still has a wife, a wife he clearly loves. This is not to say her condition does not prompt in him murderous actions, but his motivation is not explicitly born of her loss. That Jessie remains alive suggests that hope remains in the sense that Max might be able to start over. This event motivates Max to focus his energies on eliminating the gang, although his motivation is more complex than it is often defined. For Sharrett the "vigilante-style revenge he takes on the murderers of his wife and child connects him to the figure of the lawman as the cynical, disaffected pragmatist known from *Dirty Harry* (1971)."[103] Hassler-Forest takes a similar perspective, that seeing "the gratuitous murder of his wife and infant child transforms Max from stoic cop to vindictive vigilante."[104] The argument here is that Max is no vigilante, his wife is not dead, and he bears little resemblance to Harry (Clint Eastwood) in *Dirty Harry* (Don Siegel, 1971) or any of its sequels. Harry is known for his one-liners after capturing criminals, such as "Go ahead, make my day," or "You've got to ask yourself one question: 'Do I feel lucky?' Well, do you, punk?"[105] As Max kills off various gang members, such as Bubba, Mudguts, Cundalini, and eventually Toecutter, he doesn't say a word. Indeed, in the final twelve and a half minutes of the film he says a total of thirty-four words. And these are instructions to Johnny the Boy as he leaves him in the same predicament that killed Goose. In this, Max becomes a man of action and not words, and again he embodies some aspects of his western forebears. Jane Tompkins says, "The Western is at heart antilanguage. Doing, not talking, is what it values."[106] Silence in westerns can be more revealing or powerful than words. The potent stare from Ethan Edwards (John Wayne) in the final scene of *The Searchers* is more confronting for the viewer than any words he could utter. Max, however, rather than being silent, is mute. His actions might have destroyed Toecutter and his group, but they are futile actions. The loss of Goose, combined with the futility of the MFP, along with his inability to save Sprog, has seemingly resigned Max to permanent loss. It is the loss of heterosexual dominance, of the nuclear family, of his own potency as a male, and an acceptance that there is no going back.

Conclusion

Mad Max closes with Max headed into the unknown, and his return to Jessie or the MFP is uncertain. However, Max must fail. He cannot, like Ethan Edwards, succeed in his endeavor and return to the wilderness. Ross Gibson believes that "stories of heroic failure were required by postcolonial society to help it make its peace, conditionally, with the continent it could not defeat."[107] Indeed, failure marks many of the Anglo myths in Australian history. From the much-loved "Waltzing Matilda," about an itinerant worker who drowns himself rather than be arrested, to the catastrophe of Australia's first participation in armed conflict following federation (1901) with the Gallipoli campaign of World War I in 1915, loss and defeat are revered.[108] Australia's most renowned outlaw, Ned Kelly, the subject of a dozen films and TV series, is celebrated for his stoic defeat and for his historically questioned final words as he stood on the gallows: "Such is life." In a 2011 study, "Ned Kelly Tattoos—Origins and Forensic Implications," Roger W. Byard found that, in Australia, "individuals with Ned Kelly tattoos . . . had an above average incidence of traumatic deaths compared to other forensic cases," and these were predominantly by suicide.[109]

Mad Max, with its clear character and narrative influences from the western, cannot escape its context, which not only weirds western notions of individualism and heroism but ultimately rejects them. Sheckels supposes that in Australian films, "one keeps waiting for the inevitable defeat, and, when it does not come, the film's vision is dismissed as sentimental or fantastic or too American."[110] Such failure is one that is also contextual to the disruptive period in which the film was made. For Sharrett this is "the sense of lost faith in collective myth, simultaneous with a cry for violence as expression of a far more profound feeling of distrust of a mythic past but also a resentment at being cut off from a period when belief in myth provided a sense of cohesion to civilization."[111] The future that Max drives toward is irredeemable and there is no real destination, no objective; the land becomes again defined by the concept of *terra nullius*. Only now it is one that invalidates the colonizer and the notion of heterosexual masculine domination. Yet this displacement is short-lived. Max will rise to become the hero, the savior, in the film's many sequels, just as many of the reforms of the Whitlam government were eroded in the decades that followed his time in office. What *Mad Max* reveals, even if temporarily, is the fragility of white male heterosexual identity in Australia, the insecurity and anxiety of maintaining normative performance, and the fear that inclusiveness will remove such figures from their privileged positions of authority.

Notes

1. Miller and Van Riper, *International Westerns*, xv.
2. Jackson, *Fantasy*, 12.
3. Hay, "The American Mad Max," 308.
4. Verevis, "Another Green World," 135.
5. Martin, *The Mad Max Movies*, 15.

6. Hassler-Forest, "Mad Max," 302, 305.
7. Released in the United States as *Road Warrior*.
8. Falconer, "'We Don't Need to Know the Way Home,'" 166.
9. Martin, *The Mad Max Movies*, 17.
10. Martin, *The Mad Max Movies*, 39.
11. Sheckels, "'New Wave' Cinema's Redefinition," 36.
12. Zimmermann, "'I Suppose It Has Come to This . . . ,'" 136.
13. Heffernan, *Post-Apocalyptic Culture*, 4.
14. Rosen, *Apocalyptic Transformation*, xiv.
15. Barossi, "Through Different Eyes," 2.
16. Price, "The Stereotyping of North American Indians," 159.
17. Zimmermann, "'I Suppose It Has Come to This . . . ,'" 136.
18. Schein, "The Olympian Cowboy," 330.
19. Cawelti, *The Six-Gun Mystique Sequel*, 35.
20. Koerner, "White Australian Identities," 99.
21. Formica, "When It All Started," 45.
22. Stratton, *The Last New Wave*, 4.
23. The Liberal-National Coalition is one of the two most prominent political groups in Australia. Politically, the Liberal-National Coalition is characterized by right to center-right policies. The other most prominent political party is the Labor Party, characterized by left to center-left policies.
24. Federal elections are held every three years. The Whitlam government, after winning power in 1972, forced a double dissolution election in 1974 after the opposition blocked supply in the Senate. The governor-general, the Crown's representative, dismissed the Whitlam government in 1975 when the opposition again blocked supply. In the election following the dismissal, Whitlam was resoundingly defeated.
25. Barnett, "Male Chauvinists and Ranting Libbers," 296.
26. Pearson, "Australia's Greatest White Elder," 17.
27. Michelle Arrow, in "'These Are Just a Few Examples of Our Daily Oppressions,'" 241, provides this succinct definition of a Royal Commission: "a large-scale public inquiry established by government but conducted by independent appointees, who investigate specific issues in order to inform policy or legal reform or to inquire into extraordinary incidents." The removal of the Whitlam government by the governor-general, John Kerr, who functioned as the Crown's representative, in collusion with the leader of the Liberal-National Coalition, Malcolm Fraser, and under advice from Chief Justice of the High Court Garfield Barwick, remains a divisive and contentious issue in Australian politics. Whitlam supporters commonly refer to the event as a constitutional coup d'état.

Opponents saw the dismissal as an example of the necessity of reserve powers to resolve a governmental crisis.
28. Arrow, "Making Family Violence Public," 82.
29. Arrow, "'These Are Just a Few Examples of Our Daily Oppressions,'" 235.
30. Angelides, "'The Continuing Homosexual Offensive,'" 175.
31. Arrow, "Making Family Violence Public," 93.
32. Sheckels, "'New Wave' Cinema's Redefinition," 32; O'Regan, "Cinema Oz," 76.
33. The term "Digger" was popularized during World War I by ANZAC (Australian and New Zealand Army Corps) soldiers. It became synonymous with egalitarianism and friendship.
34. Wright, *Sixguns & Society*, 138.
35. Wright, *Sixguns & Society*, 135.
36. Barnett, *Reel Men*, 32.
37. Altman, "The Myth of Mateship," 170.
38. Altman, "The Myth of Mateship," 172.
39. Arrow, *Friday on Our Minds*, 113.
40. Murray, "Australian Cinema in the 1970s and 1980s," 76.
41. Rattigan, *Images of Australia*, 16.
42. Baer, "Eyes Wide Shut," 222.
43. Phillips, "The Cultural Cringe," 299.
44. O'Regan, "Cinema Oz," 77.
45. Arrow, *Friday on Our Minds*, 115.
46. Miller, *Mad Max*.
47. Miller, *Mad Max*.
48. Nagel, "Masculinity and Nationalism," 249.
49. Nagel, "Masculinity and Nationalism," 258.
50. Sharrett, "The Hero as Pastiche," 82.
51. Pop, "*Mad Max*—Spare-Parts Heroes," 203.
52. Johinke, "Manifestations of Masculinities," 125.
53. Wright, *Sixguns & Society*, 139.
54. Bourdieu, *Masculine Domination*, 13.
55. Bourdieu, *Masculine Domination*, 84.
56. Braun and Gray, "Green and Lindsay," 110.
57. Bourdieu, *Masculine Domination*, 85.
58. Watney, *Policing Desire*, 26.
59. Falconer, "'We Don't Need to Know the Way Home,'" 166.
60. Graham and White, "Young People," 31.
61. Sharrett, "The Hero as Pastiche," 84.
62. Miller, *Mad Max*.
63. Miller, *Mad Max*.

64. Pop, "*Mad Max*—Spare-Parts Heroes," 203.
65. Pop, "*Mad Max*—Spare-Parts Heroes," 203.
66. Murphy, Venkatasawmy, Simpson, and Visosevic, "From Sand to Bitumen," 75.
67. Turner, "The Significance of the Frontier," 23–24.
68. "Bushranger" refers to outlaws. The first two decades of the twentieth century saw a robust Australian film industry, and early Australian films recounted tales of bushrangers, most famously Ned Kelly in *The Story of the Kelly Gang* (Charles Tait, 1906). Only fragments of the film remain from its original run time of sixty minutes. "Drover" refers to someone who herds sheep or cattle. Murphy, Venkatasawmy, Simpson, and Visosevic, "From Sand to Bitumen," 77.
69. Robson, "Developments in Revenge," 74.
70. Robson, "Developments in Revenge," 74.
71. Mueller, Buschendorf, and Sarkowsky, "Violence and Open Spaces," 13.
72. Mueller, Buschendorf, and Sarkowsky, "Violence and Open Spaces," 13.
73. Gibson, *South of the West*, 49.
74. Jacobs and Gelder, *Uncanny Australia*, 133.
75. O'Dowd, "Embodying the Australian Nation," 96.
76. Moreton-Robinson, "Whiteness, Epistemology and Indigenous Representation," 78.
77. Johinke, "Manifestations of Masculinities," 118.
78. Graham and White, "Young People," 29.
79. Graham and White, "Young People," 31.
80. Miller, *Mad Max*.
81. Bourdieu, *Masculine Domination*, 98.
82. Flood, "Men, Sex, and Homosociality," 349.
83. Johinke, "Manifestations of masculinities," 120.
84. NT News, "We Aussies Just Love a Bonza Nickname," Editorial section, World, August 29, 2020, p. 18, NewsBank: Access Australia 2021, https://infoweb.newsbank.com/apps/news/document-view?p=AUNB&docref=news/17D27DFBB26CFB38.
85. Chevalier, "Nicknames in Australia," 135.
86. Rickard, "Sentimental Blokes," 43.
87. "The Bronze" refers to law enforcement. It is seemingly specific to the film, although also clearly derived from the colloquial term "Copper," which refers to police officers. Miller, *Mad Max*.
88. Miller, *Mad Max*.
89. Tompkins, *West of Everything*, 55.
90. Miller, *Mad Max*.
91. Johinke, "Manifestations of Masculinities," 124.
92. Wright, *Sixguns & Society*, 148.

93. Miller, *Mad Max*.
94. Bourdieu, *Masculine Domination*, 89.
95. Kerr, *Roads, Tourism and Cultural History*, 110.
96. Matthew Schulz, "Sin Bins Hit the Road Again," *Sunday Herald Sun*, May 7, 2006, p. 27, NewsBank: Access Australia 2021, https://infoweb.newsbank.com/apps/news/documentview?p=AUNB&docref=news/11175380E868FC68.
97. Joshua Dowling, "Shaggin' Wagon's Second Coming," *Courier Mail*, March 27, 2015, p. 23. NewsBank: Access Australia 2021, https://infoweb.newsbank.com/apps/news/document-view?p=AUNB&docref=news/154511EE87CD15E8.
98. Falconer, "'We Don't Need to Know the Way Home,'" 166.
99. Miller, *Mad Max*.
100. Angelides, "'The Continuing Homosexual Offensive,'" 186.
101. Miller, *Mad Max*.
102. Miller, *Mad Max*.
103. Sharrett, "The Hero as Pastiche," 82.
104. Hassler-Forest, "Mad Max," 302.
105. Siegel, *Dirty Harry*.
106. Tompkins, *West of Everything*, 50.
107. Gibson, *South of the West*, 17.
108. "Waltzing Matilda" is a bush ballad by Banjo Patterson written in 1895. Brad West marks the song as "central to Australian national identity." But "the hero in the song is a vagabond swagman who steals a sheep and, when confronted by the authorities, commits suicide" (p. 127). Graham Seal goes further, positioning the song as the "unofficial national anthem of Australia and the international musical signifier for 'Australia' and 'Australians'" (p. 67).
109. Byard, "Ned Kelly Tattoos," 279.
110. Sheckels, "'New Wave' Cinema's Redefinition," 33.
111. Sharrett, "The Hero as Pastiche," 90.

Bibliography

Altman, Dennis. "The Myth of Mateship." *Meanjin*, no. 2 (1987): 163–72.

Altman, Robert, dir. *McCabe & Mrs. Miller*. Warner Bros., 1971.

Angelides, Steven. "'The Continuing Homosexual Offensive': Sex Education, Gay Rights and Homosexual Recruitment." In *Homophobia: An Australian History*, edited by Shirleene Robinson, 172–92. Alexandria NSW: Federation Press, 2008.

Arrow, Michelle. *Friday on Our Minds: Popular Culture in Australia since 1945*. Sydney NSW: UNSW Press, 2009.

———. "Making Family Violence Public in the Royal Commission on Human Relationships, 1974–1977." *Australian Feminist Studies*, no. 95 (2018): 81–96.

———. "'These Are Just a Few Examples of Our Daily Oppressions': Speaking and Listening to Homosexuality in Australia's Royal Commission on Human Relationships, 1974–1977." *Journal of the History of Sexuality*, no. 2 (2018): 234–63.
Baer, Bruce. "Eyes Wide Shut: Homosociality, Justice and Male Rape through an Australian Lens." In *Law, Lawyers and Justice: Through Australian Lenses*, edited by Karen Crawley and Kieran Tranter, 220–39. Melbourne VIC: Routledge, 2020.
Barnett, Chelsea. "Male Chauvinists and Ranting Libbers: Representations of Single Men in 1970s Australia." In *Everyday Revolutions Remaking Gender, Sexuality and Culture in 1970s Australia*, edited by Michelle Arrow and Angela Woollacott, 295–312. Canberra ACT: ANU Press, 2019.
———. *Reel Men: Australian Masculinity in the Movies 1949–1962*. Melbourne VIC: Melbourne University Publishing, 2019.
Barossi, Luana. "Through Different Eyes: Relative Dystopia in Post-Apocalyptic Topoi." In *Apocalyptic Projections: A Study of Past Predictions, Current Trends and Future Intimations as Related to Film and Literature*, edited by Annette M. Magid, 2–26. Newcastle upon Tyne, UK: Cambridge Scholars, 2015.
Beresford, Bruce, dir. *The Adventures of Barry McKenzie*. Longford Productions, 1972.
———, dir. *Barry McKenzie Holds His Own*. Reg Grundy Productions, 1974.
———, dir. *Don's Party*. Phillip Adams, 1976.
———, dir. *Puberty Blues*. Limelight Productions, 1981.
Bourdieu, Pierre. *Masculine Domination*. Cambridge, UK: Polity Press, 2007.
Braun, Kerstin, and Anthony Gray. "Green and Lindsay: Two Steps Forward—Five Steps Back Homosexual Advance Defence—*Quo Vadis?*" *University of Western Australia Law Review*, no. 1 (2016): 91–118.
Burstall, Tim, dir. *Alvin Purple*. Hexagon Productions, 1973.
Byard, Roger W. "Ned Kelly Tattoos—Origins and Forensic Implications." *Journal of Clinical Forensic and Legal Medicine*, no. 6 (2011): 276–79.
Cawelti, John. *The Six-Gun Mystique Sequel*. Bowling Green OH: Bowling Green State University Popular Press, 1999.
Chauvel, Charles, dir. *Sons of Matthew*. Greater Union Cinemas, 1949.
Chevalier, Sarah. "Nicknames in Australia." *Swiss Bulletin of Applied Linguistics*, no. 3 (2004): 125–37.
Darabont, Frank, creator. *The Walking Dead*. Idiot Box Productions / Circle of Confusion / Skybound Entertainment / Valhalla Entertainment, AMC Studios, 2010–22.
Eastwood, Clint, dir. *The Outlaw Josey Wales*. The Malpaso Company, 1976.
———, dir. *Pale Rider*. The Malpaso Company, 1985.
———, dir. *Unforgiven*. The Malpaso Company, 1992.
Faiman, Peter, dir. *Crocodile Dundee*. Rimfire Films, 1986.

Falconer, Delia. "'We Don't Need to Know the Way Home': The Disappearance of the Road in the Mad Max Trilogy." In *The Road Movie Book*, edited by Steven Cohan and Ina Rae Hark, 161–74. New York: Routledge, 1997.

Flood, Michael. "Men, Sex, and Homosociality: How Bonds Between Men Shape Their Sexual Relations with Women." *Men and Masculinities*, no. 3 (2008): 339–59.

Ford, John, dir. *Fort Apache*. Argosy Pictures, 1948.

———, dir. *The Man Who Shot Liberty Valance*. John Ford Productions, 1962.

———, dir. *My Darling Clementine*. 20th Century Fox, 1946.

———, dir. *The Searchers*. C. V. Whitney Pictures, 1956.

Formica, Serena. "When It All Started: Politics and Policies of the Australian Film Industry from the Revival to the International Breakthrough." *Studies in Australasian Cinema*, no. 1 (2011): 43–57.

Gibson, Ross. *South of the West: Postcolonialism and the Narrative Construction of Australia*. Bloomington: Indiana University Press, 1992.

Graham, Hannah, and Rob White. "Young People, Dangerous Driving and Car Culture." *Youth Studies Australia*, no. 3 (2007): 28–35.

Hassler-Forest, Dan. "*Mad Max*: Between Apocalypse and Utopia." *Science Fiction Film and Television*, no. 3 (2017): 301–6.

Hathaway, Henry, dir. *True Grit*. Paramount Pictures, 1969.

Hawks, Howard, dir. *Rio Bravo*. Armada Productions 1959.

Hay, John. "The American Mad Max: *The Road Warrior* versus *The Postman*." *Science Fiction Film and Television*, no. 3 (2017): 307–27.

Heffernan, Teresa. *Post-Apocalyptic Culture: Modernism, Postmodernism, and the Twentieth-Century Novel*. Toronto ON: University of Toronto Press, 2008.

Hill, George Roy, dir. *Butch Cassidy and the Sundance Kid*. Campanile Productions, 1969.

Hogan, Paul, John Cornell, and Bill Harding, creators. *The Paul Hogan Show*. 7 Network / Nine Network Australia, 1973–84.

Hopper, Dennis, dir. *Easy Rider*. Pando Company, 1969.

Jackson, Rosemary. *Fantasy: The Literature of Subversion*. London: Methuen, 1981.

Jacobs, Jane M., and Ken Gelder. *Uncanny Australia: Sacredness and Identity in a Postcolonial Nation*. Melbourne VIC: Melbourne University Press, 1994.

Johinke, Rebecca. "Manifestations of Masculinities: *Mad Max* and the Lure of the Forbidden Zone." *Journal of Australian Studies*, no. 67 (2001): 118–25.

Kerr, Rosemary. *Roads, Tourism and Cultural History*. Bristol, UK: Channel View Publications, 2018.

Koerner, Catherine. "White Australian Identities and Indigenous Land Rights." *Journal for the Study of Race, Nation and Culture*, no. 2 (2015): 87–101.

Martin, Adrian. *The Mad Max Movies*. Redfern NSW: Currency Press and Screen-Sound Australia, 2003.

Miller, Cynthia J., and A. Bowdoin Van Riper. *International Westerns: Re-locating the Frontier*. Lanham MD: Scarecrow Press, 2014.

Miller, David, dir. *Lonely Are the Brave*. Joel Productions, 1962.

Miller, George, dir. *Mad Max*. Village Roadshow, 1979.

———, dir. *Mad Max 2*. Kennedy Miller Entertainment, 1982.

———, dir. *Mad Max Beyond Thunderdome*. Kennedy Miller Entertainment, 1985.

———, dir. *Mad Max: Fury Road*. Village Roadshow Pictures, 2015.

Moreton-Robinson, Aileen. "Whiteness, Epistemology and Indigenous Representation." In *Whitening Race: Essays in Social and Cultural Criticism*, edited by Aileen Moreton-Robinson, 75–88. Acton ACT: Aboriginal Studies Press, 2004.

Mueller, Stefanie, Christa Buschendorf, and Katja Sarkowsky. *Violence and Open Spaces: The Subversion of Boundaries and the Transformation of the Western Genre*. Heidelberg, Germany: Universitatsverlag Winter, 2017.

Murphy, Ffion, Rama Venkatasawmy, Catherine Simpson, and Tanja Visosevic. "From Sand to Bitumen, from Bushrangers to 'Bogans': Mapping the Australian Road Movie." *Journal of Australian Studies*, no. 70 (2001): 73–84.

Murray, Scott. "Australian Cinema in the 1970s and 1980s." In *Australian Cinema*, edited by Scott Murray, 149–78. Crows Nest NSW: Allen & Unwin, 1994.

Nagel, Joane. "Masculinity and Nationalism: Gender and Sexuality in the Making of the Nations." *Ethnic and Racial Studies*, no. 2 (1998): 242–69.

O'Dowd, Mary. "Embodying the Australian Nation and Silencing History." *Arena Journal*, no. 37/38 (2012): 88–104.

O'Regan, Tom. "Cinema Oz: The Ocker Films." In *The Australian Screen*, edited by Albert Moran and Tom O'Regan, 75–98. North Sydney NSW: Penguin Books, 1989.

Pearson, Noel. "Australia's Greatest White Elder: Gough Whitlam." *Vital Speeches of the Day*, no. 1 (January 2015): 16–17.

Peckinpah, Sam, dir. *The Getaway*. First Artists, 1972.

———, dir. *The Wild Bunch*. Warner Bros.—Seven Arts, 1969.

Phillips, Arthur. "The Cultural Cringe." *Meanjin*, no. 4 (1950): 299–302.

Pop, Doru. "*Mad Max*—Spare-Parts Heroes, Recycled Narratives, Reused Visualities and Recuperated Histories." *Caietele Echinox: Utopia, Dystopia, Film*, no. 29 (2015): 185–206.

Price, John A. "The Stereotyping of North American Indians in Motion Pictures." *Ethnohistory*, no. 2 (Spring 1973): 153–71.

Rattigan, Neil. *Images of Australia: 100 Films of the New Australian Cinema*. University Park TX: Southern Methodist University Press, 1991.

Rickard, John. "Sentimental Blokes." *Meanjin*, no. 1 (2007): 38–46.

Robson, Peter W. G. "Developments in Revenge, Justice and Rape in the Cinema." *International Journal for the Semiotics of Law*, no. 1 (2021): 69–80.

Rosen, Elizabeth K. *Apocalyptic Transformation: Apocalypse and the Postmodern Imagination*. Blue Ridge Summit PA: Lexington Books, 2008.

Schein, Harry. "The Olympian Cowboy." Translated by Ida M. Alcock. *American Scholar*, no. 3 (1955): 309–20.

Seal, Graham. "Going for a Song: The Cultural Politics of 'Waltzing Matilda.'" *International Journal of the Book*, no. 2 (2013): 67–72.

Sharrett, Christopher. "The Hero as Pastiche." *Journal of Popular Film and Television*, no. 2 (1985): 80–91.

Sheckels, Theodore F. "'New Wave' Cinema's Redefinition of Australian Heroism." *Antipodes*, no. 1 (1998): 29–36.

Siegel, Don, dir. *Dirty Harry*. The Malpaso Company, 1971.

Smart, Ralph, dir. *Bitter Springs*. Ealing Studios, 1950.

Stevens, George, dir. *Shane*. Paramount Pictures, 1953.

Stratton, David. *The Last New Wave: The Australian Film Revival*. Melbourne VIC: Angus & Robertson, 1980.

Sturges, John, dir. *Gunfight at the OK Corral*. Paramount Pictures, 1957.

———, dir. *Hour of the Gun*. The Mirisch Corporation, 1967.

Tompkins, Jane. *West of Everything: The Inner Life of Westerns*. Oxford, UK: Oxford University Press, 1992.

Turner, Frederick Jackson. "The Significance of the Frontier in American History." In *Does the Frontier Experience Make America Exceptional?*, edited by Katherine E. Kurzman and Charisse Kiino, 17–43. Boston MA: Bedford/St. Martin's, 1999.

Verevis, Constantine. "Another Green World: The Mad Max Series." In *A Companion to Australian Cinema*, edited by Felicity Collins, Jane Landman, and Susan Bye, 133–48. New York: John Wiley & Sons, 2019.

Walsh, Raul, dir. *They Died with Their Boots On*. Warner Bros. Pictures, 1941.

Watney, Simon. *Policing Desire: Pornography, Aids, and the Media*. Minneapolis: University of Minnesota Press, 1997.

Weir, Peter, dir. *Gallipoli*. Associated R&R Films, 1981.

West, Brad. "Crime, Suicide, and the Anti-Hero: 'Waltzing Matilda' in Australia." *Journal of Popular Culture*, no. 3 (2001): 127–41.

Wood, Sam, dir. *Ambush*. Metro-Goldwyn-Mayer, 1950.

Wright, Will. *Sixguns & Society: A Structural Study of the Western*. Berkeley: University of California Press, 1977.

Zimmermann, Stefan. "'I Suppose It Has Come to This . . .': How a Western Shaped Australia's Identity." In *Crossing Frontiers: Intercultural Perspectives on the Western*, edited by Thomas Klein, Ivo Ritzer, and Peter W. Schulze, 134–48. Marburg, Germany: Schüren Verlag, 2012.

Zinnemann, Fred, dir. *High Noon*. Stanley Kramer Productions, 1952.

PART 3

"Touch Your Wound, Dear"   5

Eye Killers and the Vampire of
Manifest Destiny   MIRIAM BROWN SPIERS

In 1995, well before the current boom of genre fiction by Indigenous authors, Navajo and Laguna Pueblo writer and filmmaker A. A. Carr published *Eye Killers*, a vampire novel inspired by F. W. Murnau's classic 1922 film, *Nosferatu*. Carr, who is a "producer, director, and writer of screenplays," explains that *Eye Killers* "was almost like a film shot in . . . [*Nosferatu*'s] expressionist style, more dramatic, less melancholy, but somewhat like this."[1] The novel is quite a departure from the style of Carr's films, which include a documentary about his grandmother called *Laguna Woman* and "the Emmy award–winning *War Code: Navajo Code Talkers* (1996), which he produced with his mother, the filmmaker Lena Carr."[2] Carr notes, "The film comes first. *Eye Killers* came out of my love of film."[3] In the novel, an ancient European vampire named Falke kidnaps an Indigenous teenager, Melissa, to make her his bride. Melissa's Irish American English teacher and Keresan Pueblo and Navajo grandfather must join forces to defeat the monster and bring Melissa home.

As opposed to the more sympathetic, often romantic vampires common in pop culture of the 1990s and early 2000s—Angel and Spike on *Buffy the Vampire Slayer*, Louis and LeStat in *Interview with the Vampire*, or Edward in the *Twilight* series—Falke is pure evil, and his sexuality is inherently monstrous. He is an unsubtle metaphor for Manifest Destiny, quite literally preying upon a young Navajo and Keresan woman and forcing his vampiric way of life upon her. While *Eye Killers* obviously draws upon the tropes of the vampire narrative, Carr's novel also incorporates many elements of the western, from the invasion and conquest of the Southwest to the violent policing of "the imaginary lines between civilization and savagery" to the ultimate showdown between Good and Evil—in this case, two humans imbued with the power of the traditional Navajo beings Coyote and Changing Woman, who must combat an explicitly European vampire.[4] Because Carr "incorporates supernatural . . . elements in a Western frontier theme," *Eye Killers* can be situated clearly within the genre of the weird western.[5]

Rather than embrace western and vampire tropes, *Eye Killers* inverts them in order to recenter the narrative upon Indigenous characters and communities. As Carr himself explains, "I took that tradition—the vampire tradition—from where I was, and made it mine. I stretched it and made it work for my own purpose. And that was fun."[6] In so doing, Carr critiques some of the worst elements of Euro-American culture, making the masculine vigilante white man his villain, while establishing members of Madrecita's Navajo and Keresan Pueblo community as his novel's heroes. Carr's depiction of Navajo and Keresan cultures and Indigenous knowledge offers an antidote to Falke's toxic masculinity, with its grounding in Euro-American patriarchy. From this vantage, *Eye Killers* highlights many of the contemporary issues that affect southwestern Native communities and that are the direct result of the "intrusion on their lands and culture by an exterior, hostile outsider"—including struggles with addiction and the environmental and human destruction caused by open pit mining on or near reservations.[7] As Carr observes, there "are a lot of problems obviously—alcohol, drug abuse, gang-related behaviors, self-destructive behaviors, suicide. That has become a real crisis in our communities."[8]

Perhaps most striking is the parallel between Melissa's abduction and the troubling reality of Missing and Murdered Indigenous Women (MMIW) in both the United States and Canada. Although the MMIW movement gained national attention several years after *Eye Killers*' publication, the rate of violence against Indigenous communities has been a cause for concern for much longer. To give one example, in 1999 the U.S. Department of Justice published a report that concluded the "average annual number of violent victimizations . . . for American Indians . . . was more than twice the rate for the Nation"[9] for the years 1992–96. Demonstrating a keen awareness of this violence, Carr notes in a 2010 interview that "the statistics are only now being compiled and analyzed for the Native American population—you can see the extent of this crisis in real numbers."[10]

It may seem somewhat implausible or insensitive to place abduction-by-vampire within the theoretical framework of MMIW. But Melissa's experience, as well as the experience of the friends and family members who search for her, mirrors the very real stories of young women who disappear from Indigenous communities. Like Melissa, these women are often abducted by non-Native men and are frequently the victims of sexual assault—a lurking threat in *Eye Killers* regardless of Falke's claims that he loves Melissa and plans to marry her. And readers may struggle, initially, to understand Melissa's insistence that Falke "chose me to be his wife. And I've chosen to love him."[11] But *Eye Killers*' use of the vampire trope can help make familiar a real-world phenomenon that could seem counterintuitive: because vampires are capable of mesmerizing or hypnotizing their victims, it is unsurprising that Melissa claims to love Falke despite the fact that she is clearly his captive. In the same way, survivors of sexual abuse "may appear to be madly in love with their perpetrators. This is a survival technique—*if we're in love, this terrible thing couldn't have happened.*"[12]

As in the real world, the ongoing sexualization of Indigenous women and the devaluation of their lives translates American legal authorities' inability or unwillingness to find the missing women or prosecute their abductors. The police in *Eye Killers* not only fail to find Melissa but also warn her, in a clear instance of victim blaming, that she will be in trouble when she comes home. Again, this response is unsurprising when considered in its larger political context. As Muscogee (Creek) scholar Sarah Deer observes, "The crisis of rape in tribal communities is inextricably linked to the way in which the United States developed and sustained a legal system that has usurped the sovereign authority of tribal nations. This colonial legal system has failed Native women by supplanting women-centered societies with patriarchal, oppressive structures that condone and thrive on violence as a way to control and oppress members of marginalized communities. These oppressive structures are predicated on hundreds of policies, regulations, and philosophies that underpin American justice."[13] *Eye Killers* bears out this structure through a combination of the police's incompetence and their lack of concern for a young Indigenous woman's safety. Understanding that the American justice system will frame Melissa as a criminal rather than a victim, her community has no choice but to circumvent that system and rescue Melissa themselves.

By drawing on the tropes of the weird western, Carr calls attention to the ongoing crisis of violence against Indigenous women—what Deer refers to as "an enduring violence that spans generations."[14] In a 2010 interview Carr elaborates on this relationship between past and present violence:

> Our [the filmmakers'] different histories all had such an effect on our current lives, in modern life. . . . Our Native past in terms of our spirituality is always very much a part of our living present, it is always here, it is always around us, and it is always with us. And it is the same with the physical past, the things that happened to us—our conflicts, for us in the South West, with the Spanish invaders, the Conquistadors, and with the government, the white soldiers and all that. . . . But with the invading Europeans, we get a sense that we never really got over that, that original trauma, that original breakdown, people's deaths. . . . In the generations now, there is this inter-generational trauma. It is as if we have never really been able to get ourselves back to wholeness.[15]

Thus, by depicting Melissa's attacker as a vampire who personifies Manifest Destiny itself, *Eye Killers* traces contemporary crises in Native communities to their roots in colonialism.

Moreover, by inverting the typical dichotomy of a western, where the hero is a lone white man and the villains are "savages," *Eye Killers* also challenges non-Native readers to reimagine the familiar structure of the western from an Indigenous perspective. If, as Deer argues, the abduction and assault of Indigenous women is "a fundamental result of colonialism," then *Eye Killers* demonstrates Indigenous communities' ability to resist assimilation and protect Native women by drawing on traditional knowledge and building alliances—both among themselves and with those Euro-Americans who recognize their responsibility to work toward decolonization.[16]

In order to understand how *Eye Killers* achieves these goals, it is first useful to position the novel at the intersection of the western and the vampire story, itself already at the crossroads of gothic, horror, fantasy, and science fiction (or "SF"). Paul Meehan notes that the vampire novel became widely popular in the late nineteenth century, during which time "the Victorian dichotomy between logic and the irrational would produce a creature that partook of both science and the supernatural, a being with a foot in both worlds."[17] The genre's ability to challenge binaries points to both the malleability of the vampire narrative and the overall flexibility of generic distinctions—as demonstrated by Hans Robert Jauss's theory of the "horizons of expectation," which suggests that generic definitions necessarily transform over time. Or, as Vivian Sobchack argues, the definition of a genre "must accommodate the flux and change which is present in any living and popular art form."[18] Thus, while early critics may have insisted that vampires belonged squarely in the horror or gothic categories, that distinction has long been challenged by texts ranging from Richard Matheson's *I Am Legend* (1954) to Anne Rice's *Interview with the Vampire* (1976) to Stephenie Meyer's *Twilight* series (2005–8). These and many other writers blur the lines between horror, fantasy, and SF; judging by the popularity of their attempts, readers have expanded their horizons of expectation accordingly. Such generic fluidity suggests that vampires are particularly well-suited to the weird western, which also "incorporates supernatural, fantasy, and sci-fi elements."[19]

Ken Gelder suggests that the vampire "can be made to appeal to or generate fundamental urges located somehow 'beyond' culture (desire, anxiety, fear), while simultaneously, it can stand for a range of meanings and positions *in* culture. The simultaneity . . . explains why the vampire has lived so long."[20] Mary Hallab, drawing on Gelder's work, adds that "because of its unique bipolarity—both human and supernatural, alive and dead—the vampire leads us to a larger consideration of the nature of the individual and his search for significance in a vast and terrifying universe."[21] Such "bipolarity" (or "simultaneity") might help us see weird western vampires as another permutation in a long history of generic experimentation. In fact, adaptability is a characteristic the genre shares with the western itself, as Johnson, Lush, and Spurgeon argue: "The weird western literalizes [Neil] Campbell's metaphorical rendering of the western as an undead genre, haunting and haunted, and provides further evidence to support his argument that the western has survived by crossing generic boundaries and by borrowing from different traditions."[22]

But while *Eye Killers* is clearly and undeniably a vampire novel, its classification as a western is less immediately obvious. True, it is set in the desert Southwest: its protagonists travel back and forth between Albuquerque (where Melissa and her teacher Diana live) and the Pueblo community of Madrecita (where Melissa's grandfather Michael is a sheepherder).

However, the novel's thematic focus on the invasion and conquest of the West—both in the nineteenth century and in the 1990s, when the story takes place—marks *Eye Killers* more convincingly. As Johnson, Lush, and Spurgeon suggest, the western "utilizes the invasion and conquest of what we now call the American West in such a way that the region itself paradoxically 'functions as a symbol of freedom, and of the opportunity for conquest.'"[23]

Carr's depiction of Falke is a direct critique of that conquest. Although we never learn precisely where Falke is from, he remembers the Adriatic Sea and his own kingdom, "in the Semming Pass near Vienna," which places his origins in the heart of western Europe.[24] Other than these vague facts, we learn only that Falke is obsessed with a woman named Christiane, whom he considers his true love. Falke's first wife, Elizabeth, observes, "Falke's power was linked to [Christiane]. . . . What had she been? A sorceress? Saint? Something about that ancient, long-dead woman was the key to Falke's strength."[25] Carr later reveals that Christiane was a nun who loved Falke but rejected him because she was "betrothed to the Son of God."[26] His obsessive love of a woman associated with Christ through both name and calling leads Carter Meland (a White Earth Anishinaabe descendant) to argue that Falke is more a metaphor for Manifest Destiny than European identity or Christianity itself because, although Christiane is the catalyst for Falke's behavior, she does nothing to encourage it. Although the Europeans who believed in Manifest Destiny colonized the Americas in the name of Christ, their actions were based on an extreme interpretation of the tenets of Christianity.

Falke's problem, then, is not that he is devoted to Christiane (or to Christianity) but that he becomes unhealthily obsessed with her. He kidnaps and attempts to convert Melissa because he mistakes her for Christiane. Elizabeth observes that "death was not [Falke's] queen. . . . Christiane was. Passion weakened him; love did too. And it could have strengthened him so much."[27] And not only does Falke's love turn to obsession in both instances, but Meland points out that Falke is desperate to "resurrect the Christiane to whom he gave his heart . . . seeking to convert the young Native girl to his vision of what existence means, but killing her in the process."[28] By clinging to his beliefs and trying to force reality to conform to them, Falke's behavior mimics the European colonizers who forcibly converted Indigenous peoples to Christianity. Falke is similarly cruel and just as delusional, believing that his way is best, even if it means Indigenous peoples must be transformed against their will. The allegory highlights the ways that the philosophy of Manifest Destiny transformed Europeans and Euro-Americans into monsters.

Falke, like the West itself, "functions as a symbol of freedom, and of the opportunity for conquest."[29] He tries to persuade Melissa that becoming a vampire will free her from the confines of human life; in order to indoctrinate her more effectively, he kills Melissa's mother, Sarah, explaining that doing so was "a necessity to weed out faltering hearts."[30] Given that Falke's strategy, typical of many abusers, is to gain control over young women by isolating them, it is unsurprising that this was not Falke's first murder in the name of love—he did the same thing to Elizabeth's family. Indeed, Melissa's apparent isolation and dissatisfaction—she lives alone with Sarah, who struggles with addiction—may well be one of the reasons Falke targets her in the first place. Because her relationship with her mother is so fraught, Melissa clings readily to Falke and his promises.

However, Falke fails to abduct Melissa because he underestimates her close relationship with other members of her community. Diana is willing to put herself at serious risk on Melissa's behalf; Melissa's grandfather, Michael, leaves his sheep camp to join the fight; and other members of the Navajo and Keresan community at Madrecita offer their own help. Even though Melissa neither sees Michael often nor regularly observes Navajo or Keresan traditions, the community nonetheless accepts her and goes to great lengths to bring her home. By contrast, Falke's first wife, Elizabeth, was part of a frontier family traveling west in the late nineteenth century and therefore more easily isolated. Falke's murder of Elizabeth's nuclear family left her without any community or any reason to return to the living world; she comes, however grudgingly, to identify herself as Falke's wife. Like many victims of abuse, Elizabeth's isolation leads her to give up hope of escape.

In addition to the western's focus on freedom and conquest, Johnson, Lush, and Spurgeon argue that the genre is also "obsessed with the violence necessary to police the borders of white American masculinity as those borders grind against . . . imaginary lines between civilization and savagery."[31] Falke maintains these borders with physical violence, as when he attacks Diana, "gripp[ing] her face and toss[ing] her backward" and leaving bruises that cover "the lower right side of her face."[32] He does not kill Diana because he wants to warn her against searching for Melissa. Embracing the entitlement inherent to the concept of Manifest Destiny, Falke believes in his right to possess Melissa and to threaten or harm anyone who tries to stop him. Falke also reinforces imagined boundaries by casually dismissing Indigenous people as "savages," often using the term to address Michael. When Diana confronts Falke a second time, he invites her to "Stand before me, and we can discuss Melissa's future like civilized beings"—the implication being that discussion is something that Diana, a white woman, is capable of.[33] Furthermore, Falke's "civilized" discussion is a proposal to turn Diana into a vampire so she can serve as a "guardian" to Melissa.[34] The term invokes the paternalistic relationship both Europeans and the United States have historically assumed toward Indigenous peoples—and Falke further hopes that Diana's guardianship will "last for centuries, longer than I will exist, perhaps."[35] His plan, like Falke himself, emphasizes the outdated and inaccurate belief that Euro-Americans will likewise continue to guard Indigenous peoples in the future.

In this discussion of the savage/civilized binary, Carr draws on the model presented by James Fenimore Cooper: "Indians as noble savages . . . captive white women, tragic mixed-race women, and brave white male rescuers."[36] But here, Carr again inverts the expected tropes: the captive is Indigenous rather than white, while the villain, responsible for abducting Melissa and murdering countless others (primarily the young women he seduces before attacking), is the only white male character. Given Falke's age and the presence of Elizabeth and Hanna, both of whom he sired, he appears to have been preying on young women in the West for at least a century. It is therefore significant that Falke finally encounters resistance after abducting Melissa, an Indigenous girl. What sets Melissa apart is the strength of her community, as well as that community's belief in and understanding of supernatural forces. Only Falke treats the Indigenous characters as "savages"; *Eye Killers*, rather than focusing on a singular western hero, presents a diverse community of women and people of color unified in their resistance to gendered and racialized violence.

Having established that *Eye Killers* is grounded in western and vampire tropes, it is also vital to consider the novel's refocusing of both genres through a distinctly Indigenous lens. One of Carr's primary methods for conveying Indigenous values is the slow, careful formation of relationships between the novel's protagonists. Diana initiates this formation when she reaches out to Michael for help finding Melissa, but an equally important relationship is the one between three Navajo elders—Michael and two of his closest friends, Emily and William—and the Keresan community that adopted them. As Emily explains to Michael: "A long time ago, the old Navajos, passing through on their sad walk, left your great-grandmother with the Keresans. Your father understood the Keresan language. After he died, when your mother died too, the Keresans took care of you and raised you to be strong. You are family with them, *ba'ba'ah*. You and William and myself are Navajo, but we are Keresan, also."[37] The "sad walk" that Emily refers to is the Navajo Long Walk, the U.S. Army's forced removal of the Navajo from their homes in 1864. In that time of need, the Keresan community reached across cultural and political boundaries to offer assistance, much as Diana and Michael work together to help Melissa. In both cases, two distinct groups share knowledge, language, and traditions in order to strengthen one another against a more powerful mutual enemy. *Eye Killers* suggests that Michael and Emily's decision to share Navajo ceremonies with Diana is not so different from the Keresans' decision to share their language and home with Michael's father. Although Indigenous ceremonies are sacred and very rarely revealed to outsiders, Michael and Emily rely on Diana's participation in order to defeat Falke and bring Melissa home.

Emily's conclusion that she, Michael, and William are both Navajo and Keresan reinforces one of the novel's key themes: a person can be part of multiple communities and identify with more than one culture without sacrificing any of them. It is not necessary, as Falke believes, to be assimilated into a dominant monoculture in order to share that culture's benefits. Though Michael's Navajo relatives have lived with the Keresans for several generations, he still identifies as Navajo; because he grew up in a Keresan community, Michael also identifies as Keresan. The two identities are not mutually exclusive: belonging is based not solely on blood, language, and culture but also on an acceptance of the responsibilities inherent to building and maintaining relationships. Thus, although she is not Indigenous, there is also room for Irish American Diana to enter into relationship with both the Navajo and Keresan communities, so long as she is willing to accept the responsibilities they place upon her.

For Diana to help rescue Melissa, she needs to accept the guidance of the Navajo and Keresan elders, who are the only ones prepared to recognize and respond to the monster in their midst. The non-Native characters, such as the local police and the high school's administration, blame Melissa's strange behavior and disappearance on drugs.[38] Diana, too, is incredulous at first, worrying that not even Michael's own community will take him seriously. But the elders to whom Michael reaches out have heard stories like his before, and they know how to proceed. Upon hearing Michael's story Emily responds, "[This] reminds me of something from the old days, but I can't remember all of it. Talk to them in Madrecita, my grandson. They will tell you something."[39] Emily is able to recall old stories that may apply to this situation—and she emphasizes oral stories rather than written ones, highlighting traditional storytelling's importance for passing knowledge on in Indigenous communities.

Emily's suggestion that they go to Madrecita reinforces the communal nature of Indigenous knowledge. In order to get the whole story, Michael and Diana will have to visit several elders, each of whom can provide a piece of the whole. The knowledge belongs not to a single expert but to everyone who has learned the tales. The collective sharing of the stories is a means of retaining information about unusual events, as well as a way to keep the knowledge from being forgotten. After visiting several Keresan and Navajo community members, Diana becomes "irritated with the chain of people they were supposed to talk to. Pretty soon, the whole pueblo would think Michael and she were a couple of loons."[40] But each link in the chain is necessary, as both the story's nature and the process of gathering it bring Diana further into the community. Since she is so accustomed to acting independently, it is especially important that Diana go through the ritual of meeting and learning to rely on other community members. As she follows the community's path, Diana begins healing from her own trauma.

While the Navajo and Keresan elders are willing to accept assistance from non-Native allies like Diana, they retain the responsibility for sharing knowledge and teaching Diana the necessary ceremonies to defeat Falke. At several points, Diana wonders "if she had any right to be here," emphasizing her respect for the Navajo and their sacred knowledge along with her awareness that she is a cultural outsider.[41] She is only allowed to participate because Emily, a Navajo medicine woman, is her teacher, and she is only invited to learn because she is already behaving respectfully and demonstrating her genuine concern for Melissa. This alliance—between a young Irish American woman, a Navajo elder, the Keresan community, and Coyote himself—is what defeats Falke. It reinforces the importance of Indigenous knowledge as a powerful tool, to be used with care, while also suggesting that such knowledge can be shared across cultural boundaries.

Sharing and the act of alliance-building flow in two directions. Based on her knowledge of mainstream American literature and popular culture, Diana identifies Falke as a vampire and can explain the distinctly European monsters to Michael and Emily. When Diana first observes that Falke matches the description of a vampire, Michael "rolled the word on his tongue. 'Explain these things to me. Maybe they're not skinwalkers after all.'"[42] Emily later reiterates, "I have not heard of these vampires before," indicating her reliance on Diana for this knowledge.[43] Another elder, Doris, also points out that there are "several men and women who are beginning to learn their medicines and strengths, but they have not seen what you have seen. They have not touched these creatures, what you call vampires."[44] When Diana hesitates to step in because she is non-Native, Doris responds, "You've seen much more than what we've seen, Diana. You know of these vampires. You are not Pueblo or Navajo, but you've told a story that Emily recognizes."[45] This specifically Euro-American cultural knowledge, in its similarity to Navajo and Keresan knowledge, is equally necessary to defeat Falke.

Since they fight not a traditional Navajo foe but one who represents settler colonialism and Manifest Destiny, it is fitting that an American descended from European immigrants should join them. As Vine Deloria Jr. (Standing Rock Sioux) argues, "The vast majority of Indian tribal religions . . . have a sacred center at a particular place," meaning they are centered in space rather than time.[46] The monster's place of origin therefore plays a particular role in the ceremonies that can be used against him. As Michael explains, "The one named Falke is not from this country. . . . So, the medicine we are preparing might not destroy him. . . . If he is so different from the evil things running here, if he is a vampire, how are we going to hurt him?"[47] A cure developed by the people from one place may be inappropriate or ineffective against a monster from elsewhere. Diana's experiences with Falke and mainstream hegemonic culture, as well as her ethnically European ancestry, make her useful for fighting European monsters. But because her hegemonic tradition now insists that monsters do not exist, Diana needs to learn the faith and ceremonies of the Navajo elders before she can take part.

Part of her hesitation seems to stem from the knowledge that her own ancestors had a fraught relationship with Indigenous peoples. When Michael places his hand on hers to show sympathy, Diana, rather than acknowledge this human gesture, thinks, "Indians do have red skin. She supposed her great-grandfather Zachary might have told her something else; how Indians were called redskins because of the colored war paint the warriors used to decorate themselves."[48] Elsewhere, Diana refers to Zachary as "the old Indian-fighter," painting a fairly clear picture of Diana's family's past interactions with Indigenous peoples.[49] Her train of thought demonstrates the hold that Diana's past still has over her, keeping her preoccupied with her family history and accompanying guilt and thus unable to focus on the chance to build a new relationship with Michael. The reference to Zachary is also a reminder of the western roots of the novel itself, an oblique acknowledgment of the racist rhetoric used against Indigenous people during the nineteenth century and the profit Diana's ancestors made from their suffering. Instead of using this history to exclude Diana from Michael and Melissa's community, *Eye Killers* argues that Diana should in fact become more involved. Diana can only help Melissa and Michael and address her own fear of abandonment by acknowledging her responsibility to her community.

When Diana continues to resist, Doris tells her, "It's time to heal the wounds that the government soldiers caused us, time to heal the hurt, the weeping, and distrust that still lives between our people. Emily has seen this in ceremony, Diana. You must accept it now."[50] Her explanation reinforces the metaphorical and ceremonial nature of Diana's role: Native and non-Native peoples cannot heal their wounds independently of each other. Refusing to engage or ignoring a hand extended in friendship only perpetuates the cycles of hurt and distrust. Nonetheless, non-Native allies must behave respectfully and responsibly toward their Native hosts.[51] They should not participate simply out of a sense of guilt or obligation; taking part in healing ceremonies will benefit them, too.

And in Diana's case, the healing is physical as well as metaphorical. Doris explains, quite clearly, "It's not only Melissa that needs healing. It is you, too."[52] She directs Diana by telling her, "Touch your wound, dear," referring to Melissa's bite mark on Diana's hand.[53] The wound suggests that Diana has been infected literally by vampirism and metaphorically by Manifest Destiny, which may explain why she has such difficulty accepting the elders' advice. Although *Eye Killers* rarely mentions the wound, it does hint that its infection is spreading. When Diana's ex-husband, Roger, pays her a visit, "oddly, her teeth began to ache."[54] The implication is that Diana could be growing eye teeth, with which she might feed on Roger. She pushes him away and the moment passes, but it is enough to suggest that Diana, too, is in physical danger.

Doris, however, offers an alternate interpretation, pointing out that Diana "cared enough to risk [her] life for Melissa."[55] Because Diana has shown such commitment, she is already an ally to the Navajo and Keresan communities. In addition to the literal wound on Diana's hand, Doris also refers to non-Native peoples' need to heal from the traumas of colonialism. It does not matter that the non-Natives were both the aggressors and the "victors"; they, too, suffer from the damage done, which includes broken alliances and a resulting isolation. Just as Diana finds herself alone despite the people with whom she interacts on a daily basis, non-Native peoples languish from a lack of community and the absence of a relationship with their Native neighbors.

In his discussion of Cherokee author Daniel Wilson's science fiction novel *Robopocalypse*, Scott Andrews (Cherokee) suggests that so long as Native literary criticism focuses exclusively on nationalism, the discussion will exclude cosmopolitan narratives. He identifies *Robopocalypse* as an example of a cosmopolitan narrative because it relies on the popular SF trope of impending apocalypse, in which all Earth's citizens must band together, regardless of ethnicity or nationality, in order to overcome the larger threat to our planet. Although the entire world is not about to end in *Eye Killers*, Carr employs a similar trope, suggesting that Falke is a threat to all humanity and that the only way for people to prevail is by banding together. Diana's relationship with Navajo and Keresan elders reflects this theme, as does Emily and Michael's model of dual citizenship. But Carr delineates between an alliance and a cosmopolitan melting pot: although *Eye Killers*' Native characters cooperate with Euro-Americans, they retain control of which information they will share, what they need to learn from their allies, and how to incorporate different kinds of knowledge into the appropriate ceremonies.

And the solution plays out neatly in the way the novel's heroes defeat Falke. The Indigenous elders draw on traditional knowledge, but their decision to include Diana in the ceremony exemplifies the need for traditions to change over time. As Emily explains,

> I have learned to do this ceremony.... But I have not heard of these vampires before. So I must make good my memory and change some things of this chant for it to work against them. What my sister taught me is very old. Much of what the other Navajos do has changed.... And I have changed things to protect us both [Emily and Diana]. For with this chant you must be purified properly. This I have not done for we are in a hurry. But the Holy Ones will purify you after your work is completed.[56]

Emily's emphasis on change in her own chant and in the chants performed by other Navajos highlights the importance of adaptation. She faces dual unusual challenges: Emily is preparing a Euro-American woman to perform a Navajo ceremony while also creating a chant to fight an unfamiliar monster. Given the combination of circumstances, Emily adjusts the chant to suit her needs. Her willingness to adapt echoes Deloria's observation that, within Native communities, "it was not what people believed to be true that was important but what they experienced as true."[57] Indigenous communities, Deloria argues, are better prepared to recognize and respond to the reality of a situation than Euro-Americans, who cling to a belief structure even after it fails to apply to the real world. In this case, we might compare Emily's and Falke's approaches. Falke remains obsessed with Christiane, attempting to force Melissa into his way of being. Emily acknowledges that there is a "right" way to perform the ceremony, but when the situation makes it impossible, she simply adapts.

Michael's goodbye to Diana further confirms Emily's decision:

I'm not through with this Eye Killer. Long ago, the first chanter sang a powerful song of fire, which destroyed it; but didn't break apart its body. That first chanter didn't understand the vampire way. And didn't have a warrior helping him who understood the vampire's chant. . . . That's why Eye Killer came back. . . . Grew again. But Emily remembered that first chanter's song, and where it was born. She gave it to you, *shi'yazhi*. You have broken Falke. And you helped me understand him too. Helped all of us.[58]

According to his explanation, Emily must incorporate a non-Native person into the ceremony; without Diana's knowledge of vampires, Falke's defeat would only be temporary. It is only through this combination of Indigenous and Euro-American knowledge that the particularly European monster can be destroyed. If Falke is a metaphor for Manifest Destiny, then the alliance between Diana, Michael, and the Navajo and Keresan community at large offers a metaphorical solution to its problems.

Rather than framing issues like MMIW as a problem only for Indigenous communities, Euro-Americans must take responsibility for the role America's culture and its legal systems play in both creating the problem and failing to address it. However, alliances should explicitly not follow the precedent of non-Native "heroes" who imagined themselves as white saviors swooping in to rescue Indigenous communities. A helpful example might instead be Diana's relationship with the Navajo and Keresan community, in which allies defer to the decisions of Indigenous nations. As Deer argues, "We know that Native women have the knowledge and wisdom to reframe the way in which the dominant system responds to rape, and therefore our tribal nations need to turn to the wisdom of these women in an effort to end this human rights crisis."[59] While non-Native allies may offer assistance, they, like Diana, must listen to Indigenous peoples and respect their sovereignty.

Deer further argues, "While many tribal-sovereignty activists may reject engagement with the federal systems that created the problems they seek to address, I make the case for working with the federal government to reform a system that has been deeply damaged by the failure to include tribal perspectives."[60] In much the same way, the Navajo and Keresan community in *Eye Killers* agrees to work with non-Native allies so long as the work takes place on their own terms. Non-Native communities and individuals must radically reimagine their relationship with Indigenous peoples—an act that includes acknowledging their existence in community with and their responsibility to tribal nations. Carr's weird western offers a model for this kind of relationship building: *Eye Killers* decolonizes the genre and demonstrates the power of Indigenous knowledge to resist the violence inherent to settler colonialism.

Notes

1. Kilpatrick, *Celluloid Indians*; Arrivé, "Aaron Albert Carr."
2. Kilpatrick, *Celluloid Indians*.
3. Arrivé, "Aaron Albert Carr."
4. Johnson, Lush, and Spurgeon, "Westworld(s)," 4.
5. Paul Green, as quoted in Johnson, Lush, and Spurgeon, "Westworld(s)," 3.
6. Arrivé, "Aaron Albert Carr."
7. Deer, *The Beginning and End of Rape*, xiv.
8. Arrivé, "Aaron Albert Carr."
9. U.S. Department of Justice, *American Indians and Crime*.
10. Arrivé, "Aaron Albert Carr."
11. Carr, *Eye Killers*, 318.
12. Deer, *The Beginning and End of Rape*, xvii.
13. Deer, *The Beginning and End of Rape*, xiv.
14. Deer, *The Beginning and End of Rape*, xi.
15. Arrivé, "Aaron Albert Carr."
16. Deer, *The Beginning and End of Rape*, x.
17. Meehan, *The Vampire in Science Fiction*, 23.
18. Sobchack, *Screening Space*, 18.
19. Paul Green, as quoted in Johnson, Lush, and Spurgeon, "Westworld(s)," 3.
20. Gelder, *Reading the Vampire*, 141.
21. Hallab, *Vampire God*, 1.
22. Johnson, Lush, and Spurgeon, "Westworld(s)," 10.
23. Johnson, Lush, and Spurgeon, "Westworld(s)," 3, with quote from Tompkins, *West of Everything*, 4.
24. Carr, *Eye Killers*, 99.
25. Carr, *Eye Killers*, 128.
26. Carr, *Eye Killers*, 263.
27. Carr, *Eye Killers*, 321.
28. Meland, "The Trickster Is History," 250.
29. Tompkins, *West of Everything*, 4.

30. Carr, *Eye Killers*, 316.
31. Johnson, Lush, and Spurgeon, "Westworld(s)," 4.
32. Carr, *Eye Killers*, 186, 235.
33. Carr, *Eye Killers*, 316.
34. Carr, *Eye Killers*, 318.
35. Carr, *Eye Killers*, 318.
36. Johnson, Lush, and Spurgeon, "Westworld(s)," 4.
37. Carr, *Eye Killers*, 153.
38. Carr, *Eye Killers*, 24.
39. Carr, *Eye Killers*, 153.
40. Carr, *Eye Killers*, 200.
41. Carr, *Eye Killers*, 57.
42. Carr, *Eye Killers*, 221.
43. Carr, *Eye Killers*, 279.
44. Carr, *Eye Killers*, 271.
45. Carr, *Eye Killers*, 244–45.
46. Deloria, *God Is Red*, 66.
47. Carr, *Eye Killers*, 221.
48. Carr, *Eye Killers*, 191.
49. Carr, *Eye Killers*, 191.
50. Carr, *Eye Killers*, 245.
51. Weaver, Womack, and Warrior, *American Indian Literary Nationalism*, xxi.
52. Carr, *Eye Killers*, 245.
53. Carr, *Eye Killers*, 245.
54. Carr, *Eye Killers*, 235.
55. Carr, *Eye Killers*, 245.
56. Carr, *Eye Killers*, 279.
57. Deloria, *God Is Red*, 66.
58. Carr, *Eye Killers*, 340.
59. Deer, *The Beginning and End of Rape*, xxii.
60. Deer, *The Beginning and End of Rape*, xxi.

Bibliography

Andrews, Scott. "Ugido Wado, Mr. Roboto." Paper presented at the Native American Literature Symposium, Prior Lake, Minnesota, March 2013.

Arrivé, Mathilde. "Interview with Navajo-Laguna Novelist and Filmmaker Aaron Albert Carr." *Revue de recherche en civilisation américaine* 2 (July 3, 2010). https://journals.openedition.org/rrca/328.

Carr, A. A. *Eye Killers*. Norman: University of Oklahoma Press, 1995.

Deer, Sarah. *The Beginning and End of Rape: Confronting Sexual Violence in Native North America*. Minneapolis: University of Minnesota Press, 2015.

Deloria, Vine, Jr. *God Is Red: A Native View of Religion*. Golden CO: Fulcrum, 2003.

Gelder, Ken. *Reading the Vampire*. New York: Routledge, 1994.

Hallab, Mary Y. *Vampire God: The Allure of the Undead in Western Culture*. Albany NY: SUNY Press, 2009.

Jauss, Hans Robert. "Literary History as a Challenge to Theory." Translated by Elizabeth Benzinger. *New Literary History* 2, no. 1 (1970): 7–37.

Johnson, Michael K., Rebecca M. Lush, and Sara L. Spurgeon. "Westworld(s): Race, Gender, Genre in the Weird Western." Introduction to *Weird Westerns: Race, Gender, Genre*, edited by Kerry Fine, Michael K. Johnson, Rebecca M. Lush, and Sara L. Spurgeon, 1–36. Lincoln: University of Nebraska Press, 2020.

Kilpatrick, Jacquelyn. *Celluloid Indians*. Lincoln: University of Nebraska Press, 1999.

Meehan, Paul. *The Vampire in Science Fiction Film and Literature*. Jefferson NC: McFarland, 2014.

Meland, Carter. "The Trickster Is History: Tribal Tricksters and American Cultural History in Contemporary Native Writing." PhD dissertation, University of Minnesota, 2002.

Sobchack, Vivian. *Screening Space: The American Science Fiction Film*. New Brunswick NJ: Rutgers University Press, 1999.

Tompkins, Jane. *West of Everything: The Inner Life of Westerns*. Oxford: Oxford University Press, 1993.

U.S. Department of Justice. *American Indians and Crime*. Washington DC: Office of Justice Programs, February 1999.

Weaver, Jace, Craig S. Womack, and Robert Allen Warrior. *American Indian Literary Nationalism*. Albuquerque: University of New Mexico Press, 2006.

6

Qweirding the West

Re-forming the Nation in the Novels of C Pam Zhang and Emma Pérez

ANNE MAI YEE JANSEN

> Always the lookout spots the Indians first spread north to south, barring progress. The Sioux or some other Plains bunch in spectacular columns, ICBM missiles, feathers bristling in the meaningful sunset. The drum breaks. There will be no parlance.
>
> —Louise Erdrich, "Dear John Wayne"

The western, even as a literary genre, typically evokes flickering pictures of white cowboys in whiter hats and was historically considered the domain of white men. But that's changing due to the innovative work of contemporary writers of color working within the genre. This essay focuses on weird westerns by C Pam Zhang and Emma Pérez, whose writing stands alongside those of other authors of color—both past and present—who have pushed the boundaries of the western genre. Writers of color have been engaging with the western for a long time (think John Rollin Ridge's famous 1854 novel *The Life and Adventures of Joaquin Murieta* as just one example); more recently, texts like Ishmael Reed's 1969 *Yellow Back Radio Broke-Down* and James Welch's 1974 *Winter in the Blood* are just a couple of the works published in the wake of the civil rights movement that exemplify this body of work. C Pam Zhang is a contemporary addition to the succession of Asian American writers (such as Frank Chin and Ruthanne Lum McCunn, who both published in the genre in the 1980s) who have linked the western to Asian American histories. Similarly, Emma Pérez is part of the lineage of Chicanx writers who are building on the work of both Mexican and Chicanx writers before them—including names like Carmen Boullosa and Kali Fajardo-Anstine—who have situated the western in relation to the United States and Mexico's complicated past. More recently, the weird western has gained in popularity; one needs only to look at the speculative elements in recent releases like Victor LaValle's

Lone Women, Tom Lin's *The Thousand Crimes of Ming Tsu*, and Isabel Cañas's *Vampires of El Norte* to see how the texts swelling the genre's ranks are continuing the rich legacy of decolonial and critical work performed by earlier writers of color.

The continued popularity of the western has significant implications for the politics of race in the United States. More than that, the ways writers of color queer and/or weird the western as a genre reconceptualize the U.S. racial imaginary. If the western is considered a quintessentially American genre based on a "formula" that operates "as an alternative to myth," then changing the formula fundamentally alters notions of Americanness.[1] Additionally, this mythical component is, as John G. Cawelti contends, "mainly political, cultural, and socio-psychological."[2] The capacity of the western to hold "political rhetoric and symbolism" is central to its power as a genre.[3] If, as Cawelti argues, the western is a genre that operates on the level of myth, then its rhetorical and symbolic malleability is central to its continued function as national mythos. More specifically, the figure of the cowboy has lasting power where sociopolitical mythmaking is concerned. In this vein, Sue Brower points out that the western is based on a set of gender and racial stereotypes, contending that "the Western archetype of the cowboy still possesses power as a symbol of American courage, strength, capability, and masculinity."[4]

Despite any symbolic power the cowboy and other western myths may continue to wield, several scholars have theorized the ways the genre has changed in the past few decades. Theories point to concepts of a New West and the Postwestern as two significant shifts the western has undergone in the past half century. Christine Bold has noted that the activism of the 1960s was echoed in literature, in some cases in the form of westerns that parodied "a formula which they considered a major representative of illusory American traditions."[5] In the same vein, Krista Comer locates the start date of literature of the "New West" in 1968, articulating that it "highlighted the relations of the indigenous and colonized to the spaces that existed *prior* to their transformation into 'the West'" and positing that it demonstrated an investment in alternate histories and their implications for the contemporary moment.[6] Coming out of the New West, in the introduction to *Postwestern Cultures: Literature, Theory, Space*, Susan Kollin suggests that the postwest critically reassesses the theoretical, geographical, and political limits of "a narrowly conceived regionalism that restricts western cultures of the past and present to some predetermined entity with static borders and boundaries."[7]

So what happens when writers stage an intervention in a genre that has too often been steeped in racism, colonialism, and heteropatriarchy? In their introduction to *Weird Westerns: Race, Gender, Genre*, Michael Johnson, Rebecca Lush, and Sara Spurgeon write that over "a hundred years after the official close of the last frontier in the American West, and despite being ostensibly anchored to a particular geographic location and a fairly precise point in history, the genre continues to be reinvented and hybridized."[8] The act of hybridizing the western genre is a powerful act of reshaping its myths. This genre-bending has powerful repercussions for narratives of race, gender, and nation. In the case of the weird westerns at the heart of this study, writers of color are reanimating specters of colonialism on the frontier by simultaneously weirding and queering (or, qweirding) the western in order to challenge the genre's historically flat representations of gender and sexuality. Through the portrayal of gender-nonconforming protagonists and haunted landscapes, C Pam Zhang's and Emma Pérez's weird westerns challenge hegemonic narratives of westward expansion and citizenship. Building on the kind of empowered resistance that Mishuana Goeman (Tonawanda Seneca) refers to as "(re)mapping," these writers are re-forming the nation through their play with genre.[9] In this essay, "re-forming" signifies both the process of forming anew something that had previously been formed (reshaping) and the practice of reformation as a process of changing, altering, or improving (refining).

This ability to re-form the western and its attendant mythologies is central to my reading of Zhang's and Pérez's novels. Together, these books demonstrate the power of weird westerns to queer the settler colonial project; their focus on gender-bending cowboys and restless ghosts serves to destabilize propagandistic narratives of citizenship and nationhood. By calling into question who and what the nation remembers and forgets, *How Much of These Hills Is Gold* and *Forgetting the Alamo, or, Blood Memory* redeploy western genre conventions and, in so doing, perform a powerful national revisionism that shifts the discourse around race, gender, and sexuality in relation to the frontier (as both geographical and critical construct).

Re-forming Gender and Nation in *How Much of These Hills Is Gold*

The impulse of the western to be engaged as an American genre—as a literary form that enforces or inscribes nationalistic values—is integral to my exploration of C Pam Zhang's novel *How Much of These Hills Is Gold* (2020). As Neil Campbell points out in his discussion of the book, the characters' lives are situated "within the wider history of anti-Chinese racism in a West already guilty of multiple crimes . . . revealed through both personal and institutional cruelty and abuse."[10] Within this context, Zhang's book dismantles the tired fantasy of an empty frontier conquered by white settlers. Instead, the text merges genres (the western and speculative fiction, specifically the ghost story) to confront heteropatriarchal visions of the Wild West. Given Johnson, Lush, and Spurgeon's contention that writers of color who engage with the tropes of the western often "weird" those tropes "in powerful, defamiliarizing, and even decolonizing ways," the generic hybridity and weirding of the western that characterize *How Much of These Hills Is Gold*, especially as they operate to disrupt archetypal characters, undermine racist narratives of Asian immigrants.[11] By populating the hills with ghosts, cowboys, and gender-bending prospectors, Zhang graphically reimagines Chinese immigration and labor in the nineteenth-century U.S. American West. The characters of rough-voiced Ma and anger-filled Ba dismantle Orientalist fantasies of sexually available women and perpetually foreign men. When their children, Lucy and Sam, are orphaned, their experiences seeking civilization (proper and feminine Lucy) and adventure (male-passing Sam) function to unravel the fiber of the conventional western.

Ma is characterized by her dichotomies: the difference between her pretty face and her ruined hands, her gentle appearance and her rough voice. At one point, when Ma plays into the local schoolteacher's Orientalist fantasies about her in order to obtain an education for Lucy, "Lucy is reminded that what makes Ma most beautiful is the contradiction of her. Rough voice over smooth skin. Smile stretched over sadness."[12] These contradictions are the products of trauma—specifically, the traumas borne of her immigration. When she arrived in the United States, she was part of a group of two hundred Chinese immigrant laborers. Her plot to avenge the abusive treatment toward this immigrant group at the hands of their white employers resulted in their accidental death by fire. Her attempts to save them resulted in a permanent change to her voice, which is described as "husky" and "unexpected against Ma's smoothness."[13] Ba tells Lucy that "her throat never did heal proper" and that her voice "was something made."[14] In other words, her voice carries with it the audible mark of her trauma. Deborah Madsen's proposal that "we might reread the American frontier as a national trauma narrative and the violence of that frontier history as a lingering wound in the national psyche" has interesting implications for Ma's character; if we understand her voice to be permanently re-formed by her trauma as an immigrant, then every word she speaks is inflected with that trauma.[15] The "wrongness in Ma's speech" is not the offensive "wrongness" of the stereotypical Chinese-accented English of conventional westerns, but instead the product of the West's rejection of her.[16] Her voice is scarred by her inability, as a Chinese immigrant, to secure justice for others like herself just as her hands—"roughened by callus, flecked blue by coal"—are scarred by her labor.[17]

The ways Ma's immigrant experience have marked her body signify her incompatibility with the land upon which she had once hoped to settle. At one point, she begins eating mud and "earthworms, pebbles, ancient twigs, buried eggs and leaf mold, the scritch-scratch of beetle legs. A feast of the land's dank secrets."[18] When Ba learns she has been eating mud, he realizes she is pregnant. However, taking the earth and its "dank secrets" into her body makes Ma ill, rendering her ordinarily robust frame skeletal and frail. Put simply, her body rejects the land that she takes into it. Ironically, despite this rejection her pregnant body simultaneously represents the frontier. Shortly before Ma abandons the family, their home is raided by white settlers in search of gold. When the men threaten to harm Lucy and Sam, Ma rises up from her hiding place, her "huge belly like a piece of the hills come alive" and speaks to Ba in Chinese—an act for which one of the men slaps her in the face, splitting her lip open.[19] The comparison of her body to the hills alongside the violent retaliation against her words—spoken in that voice marked by trauma—underscores the discordance between her immigrant status and the U.S. nation state. As Lucy reflects, the "hills may run flush with gold but none of it will be theirs" because of the laws that strip all rights to wealth or property from immigrants.[20] The violence with which Ma's subjectivity is enforced can be understood in terms of Madsen's idea that violence in the western is "a symbolic economy" that "articulate[s] a set of colonial and/or postcolonial conflicts over the legitimate possession of land."[21] As "the hills come alive," Ma's body *is* the land, and the racialized violence attempting to silence her trauma-inflected use of a foreign language can be understood as a colonial attempt to mandate whiteness in/on that land.

In the face of this racialized and gendered violence, Ma's actions undermine colonial attempts at domination through a false facade of submission. Here, it is helpful to consider Annette Kolodny's critical concept of the "pastoral impulse" in the American national and literary imaginary, which she defines as desire to understand the landscape as feminine in a way that conceptualizes the frontier as a mother.[22] With this in mind, Ma's fecund body-as-land becomes especially dangerous to these agents of white colonial patriarchy so that their violence operates as an attempt to bring her back into alignment with the pastoral impulse at the heart of colonial endeavors in the western. Given that the men are present because they wish to steal the gold Ba has claimed from U.S. American soil, Ma's response to their actions is especially significant: after they hit her, Ma "draws a crumpled handkerchief from the pouch inside her dress and holds it to her bleeding lip. When she drops the soiled cloth, her lips are sealed, her right cheek squirrel-swollen from the blow. Ma says no more" for the duration of the robbery.[23] In actuality, Ma has removed the largest lump of gold from the pouch between her breasts and placed it inside her mouth. However, the men interpret her injury and attendant silence as the desired outcome and give her no more trouble. Outwardly, she has conformed to their racialized and gendered expectations. Moreover, by taking the gold into her mouth, she *becomes* the gold-filled hills—embodying Gold Mountain and facilitating the illusion of the pastoral impulse—concealing within her body the very gold she will use to secure herself passage back to her home country.

While Ma rejects the frontier by appearing to conform to Orientalist visions of Asian women, Ba initially seems to conform to a different gendered stereotype: the Chinese immigrant laborer who busts his body working in the coal mines. But as the novel unfolds, his ghost reveals bits and pieces of his story to Lucy that destabilize this perpetual foreigner trope. Ba's ghost tells Lucy: "Like you I never grew up among people who looked like me. . . . If I had a ba, then he was the sun that warmed me most days and beat me sweaty-sore on others; if I had a ma, then she was the grass that held me when I lay down and slept. I grew up in these hills and they raised me. . . . If I had a people, then I saw those people in the reflecting pools, where water was so clear it showed a world the exact double of this one."[24] By situating himself as the child of the sun, grass, and hills, Ba subverts the perpetual foreigner trope that has plagued Chinese Americans (and their depiction in westerns) for over a century, re-forming it into a narrative of naturalization in which Ba (and, through him, Lucy and Sam) is descended from the frontier itself. Brower states that the "terrain [in westerns], both geographical and cultural, has also suggested a border dividing not just territory but also people who have a 'right,' who 'belong,' and those who do not. . . . One way or another, elimination of marginalized characters becomes morally justified and expected in the course of the typical Western plot."[25] However, by writing Ba as a character borne of the land—the frontier—Zhang derails the justification of his elimination and situates him as a figure more natural to the landscape than the white men who exert their power over him. Ba's statement, "I grew up knowing I belonged to this land, Lucy girl. You and Sam do too, never mind how you look," reinforces this point and situates Lucy and Sam as part of the landscape, too.[26]

Fittingly, as Lucy and Sam carry Ba's body with them in their initial flight east, away from the settlement town where they lived as a family, Ba's body disintegrates. When Lucy realizes what's happening, she begins taking the fallen appendages—first a finger, then his penis—and burying them in the dirt as she and Sam continue to travel east in search of a final resting place for their father.[27] The disintegration of Ba's body and Lucy's integration of his parts into the earth function to return him to the land from which he comes. In addition to his body being slowly (dis)integrated into the land, Ba's voice becomes the wind. Before they bury him, Lucy listens to the wind: "A wind unlike the daytime wind, a wind like a voice, low and blustering through the grass."[28] This wind begins to speak to Lucy, calling her *Cowaaaaaaard* and slapping her face as Ba did in life. In this way, Zhang merges Ba's body and consciousness with the landscape, making him part of the terrain upon which the rest of this weird western takes place. Moreover, Ba's gradual dismemberment functions to distribute him not only within but also across the land so that he is re-formed as an omnipresent part of the natural world (the wind).

From these two parents, both of whom defy the stereotypical roles allotted for Asians in westerns, come Lucy and Sam, who also re-form the West. On the very first page of the novel, we're introduced to Sam, a youth characterized by a consistent use of canned dialogue—the hackneyed lingo of stereotypical westerns. "'Pow,' Sam says. . . . 'Too slow. You're dead.' Sam cocks fingers back on pudgy fists and blows on the muzzle of an imagined gun."[29] Like most gunslingers, Sam seldom speaks, preferring instead to resort to physical violence. In this vein, Colin Irvine argues that the conventions of the western "have not evolved in substantial ways" over the past hundred years, and therefore "what a cowboy would say and how he would speak is strikingly similar to what a different character cut from the same cloth would say in a story written today. In essence, the language of the western genre, unlike that connected with reality, is a language written in a way that resists evolution."[30] This anachronistic characteristic of the language comes out in Zhang's novel through Sam's speech patterns. The first word Sam utters in the novel is "Pow"—a word he speaks on a few significant occasions. Sam also repeatedly uses the word "pardner," which aligns this character with the fixed period of western genre fiction. However, because Sam is neither the novel's protagonist nor a heroic figure, Zhang is able to accomplish some of the generic evolution Irvine describes as a seeming impossibility within the genre. Irvine goes on to posit that novelization allows writers to "use the genre in order to de-valorize and debunk the myths at the heart of the Western" through the "use of always evolving, contemporaneous language."[31] This is precisely what Zhang accomplishes with the cowboy lingo that falls flat coming from Sam, whom we know to be a beautifully fluid and dynamic character. The use of canned language functions to accomplish the de-valorizing and debunking of the nationalistic myths embedded in conventional westerns.

Beyond Sam's verbal caricature of cowboy-speak, Sam's body problematizes the heteronormative masculinity that typically defines the western cowboy. In his book *Westerns: Making the Man in Fiction and Film*, Lee Clark Mitchell argues that "from the beginning the Western has fretted over the construction of masculinity."[32] Sam, who is a female-bodied, male-passing character, complicates the conventional cowboy. Not only does Sam shirk conventionally female gender roles, but he also sews first a carrot, then a rock—significantly, pieces of the natural world—into his pants to simulate a penis. In so doing, Sam uses the frontier landscape to literally re-form his body, bringing it into alignment with the archetypal cowboy. At the same time, his act of physical transformation disrupts that same archetype by merging it with Sam's Asian body, which is narrativized as an inherent Other in the story of U.S. America. Sam's particular construction of masculinity, then, creates a space for him to be the cowboy he always has been, even as his gendered re-formation is incompatible with conventional narratives of nation, race, and gender.

Not only does Sam re-form gender through the frontier, but he also embodies the gendered behaviors expected of the western male protagonist. In his book *Gunfighter Nation*, Richard Slotkin writes, "In the traditional Western, women incarnate the Christian moral principles essential to a civilized order. Those principles are set off against the 'male' propensity for violence—although the safety of female order will depend on the assistance of at least one violent male."[33] Interestingly, Sam's character is distinctly uncivilized. He fights, yells, kicks, and is constantly described in terms of his dirtiness. When he and Lucy reunite as adults, his presence first takes the form of a tiger stalking the land. However, Lucy realizes that he has been the "tiger" all along—that in this land there "was never even the possibility of tigers," except that Sam defies possibilities and, as the tiger, unsettles the white settlers with his preternatural threat of animal violence.[34] Because Sam works according to his own set of morals, his re-formed male-passing body encompasses both the male and the female so that the "safety of female order" is obtained through the assistance of his own violence. He works to protect both himself and Lucy, at one point violently retaliating against a man who aimed to force himself upon her. Sam links that incident with his own experiences as a child traveling with a "mountain man," alluding to the man raping him when he found out about Sam's biological sex and stating that there aren't any good men.[35]

Ironically, Lucy's use of her own body in ways that go against "Christian moral principles" at the end of the novel further complicates this western trope. On the eve of their departure from San Francisco, which they're fleeing because of a Robin Hood–esque stunt Sam pulled, the gold man's debt collectors catch up with them and Lucy strikes a deal to save Sam's life: she becomes a sex worker in order to pay off the debt Sam incurred when he stole from the gold man. Remembering her mother's words—*"Always know what part of you they want"*—Lucy re-forms herself: "It's easy. She dug a grave years ago; now she throws into it every Sam and every Lucy that came before. All her soft rotting parts. The parts she keeps are her weapons."[36] In effect, she emotionally dismembers her body, discarding the "soft rotting parts" of her previous selves and weaponizing her sexuality—the parts of her "they" want. By dismembering and re-forming herself in order to assure Sam's safety, she disrupts the "female order" and knowingly subjects herself to sexual violence in order to protect her male-passing sibling. Unlike the assault to which Sam was subjected as a young male-passing cowboy, Lucy's willing use of her female body is a strategic move. While she is not literally undead, her bodily re-formation allows her to bury the remains of her previous selves and reanimate a different version of herself from the same grave.

Lucy re-forms herself multiple times before she is able to shape herself into a part of the western storyscape. After her initial separation with Sam, she re-forms herself as a docile Asian woman who follows in her white "friend" Anna's shadow. This role is both demeaning and untenable if she wishes to retain any agency, as she becomes a sort of pet with the added sexual dangers presented by Anna's upcoming marriage to a white man who desires Lucy. When she parts company with Anna, Lucy rips off the white linen and lace dress that represents her attempted foray into the territory of virtuous (white) womanhood.[37] Shortly thereafter, she asks Sam to shear her hair, attempting to stave off the sense of "old ghosts rising" as descriptors of Lucy's resemblance to Ma and Sam's resemblance to Ba increase in frequency and intensity.[38] When the haircut is done, the siblings bury Lucy's hair—"that long, shining hair that Ma intended to pass on to both her daughters"—in a grave, tossing a piece of silver on top of it as an attempt to keep it from haunting them.[39] However, the silver cannot keep the racialized and gendered legacy of Lucy's hair from pursuing her. Regardless, in this manner, Lucy re-forms herself as Sam's gender-neutral traveling companion. With her haircut that is "not a man's cut, not a woman's," Lucy accompanies Sam to a brothel—the same one she will end up working in—upon their arrival in San Francisco.[40] As a business, this brothel is built around exoticizing sexual fantasies of women.

During Lucy's initial visit, she observes seven girls lined up against a wall, each girl standing "against a square of paint. They look like drawings of princesses in storybooks, gilt-framed."[41] Lucy describes them as being like "the stories in Ma's books, the drawn princesses," going on to explain, "They're blank. . . . They remind me of pages."[42] When she returns to the brothel to work off her debt, Lucy is re-formed into a character in the nation's story about her. It takes three months for her to grow her hair out in order to accomplish her re-formation into the story of the exotic Asian woman—the stereotype, the embodiment of everything the United States has written about people who look like her.

The gendered violence Lucy experiences in this work marks her in much the same way Ma's voice and hands are marked by her trauma. When she is a child, Ba breaks Lucy's nose after she talks back to him and it sets crooked.[43] Ba says it's *"proper that you should have something to rememory you for sassing."*[44] Shortly after she becomes a sex worker, another man hits her, and "her nose breaks in the same place it did many years back. It heals straight, erasing the last mark of her old self."[45] These two breakages, both of which alter Lucy's face, signify the imposition of patriarchal control by Ba and the undoing of it by the unnamed John. By "undoing" I mean that Lucy, by acting in ways that do not align with the stories she is expected to become, renders herself illegible within the scope of the western. This illegibility plays with Orientalist stereotypes of inscrutability, queering them in a manner that aligns with Vivian Huang's argument that claiming "inscrutability from an Asian diasporic positionality" is, essentially, an act of queering that "cannot be accessed from without" and thereby cuts off the white gaze.[46] The shift in Lucy's physical appearance, then, makes space for a related internal transformation. When Lucy looks in the mirror upon final payment of the debt, "The nose is strange to her, as the face is strange, thin and stilled. . . . Her body is immortal, or rather it's died so many deaths in so many men's stories that she fears no longer. She is a ghost, inhabiting this body."[47] As a ghost given form by the body she still inhabits, Lucy takes on a sort of literal ghostliness, a possession, a re-forming of face and self that allows her to remain on the frontier if she chooses to do so. Having worked off her debt using the gendered power Ma discussed with her as a young girl, the novel concludes with Lucy poised on the brink of speech with the narration reading, "She opens her mouth.

She wants" but cutting off midsentence.[48] The incomplete sentence leaves the reader beholden to Lucy, denying them access to her interior landscape. More than that, Lucy has re-formed herself so many times, ultimately becoming a living ghost, that she is poised to haunt the West in the same way Ba did. She contemplates how Ba wanted to claim the land and Sam refused, eventually settling on what it might mean to be claimed by the land.[49] The act of burying her hair in the land allows her to be claimed by it, to become part of the frontier. Since she outwardly re-formed herself in the image of the storybook Asian sex worker, she occupies an archetype available to bodies like hers in the western. However, as an inscrutable living ghost claimed by the land, she defies not only death but also the archetype allotted for Asian women in the West.

Re-forming Memory and Nation:
Forgetting the Alamo, or, Blood Memory

Just as Zhang's novel engages with "weird" elements to re-form a variety of western archetypes, Pérez's novel *Forgetting the Alamo, or, Blood Memory* (2009) supplants the straight, white, asexual male protagonist of the conventional western and replaces him with Micaela Campos, a male-passing Tejana lesbian cowgirl. With her father and siblings dead, her mother sexually assaulted and trapped within the heteropatriarchal social structure, and her cousin Jedidiah "Jed" Jones running with the wrong crowd in the aftermath of the Battle of San Jacinto, Micaela finds herself traversing the bloody landscape in search of vengeance. During her wanderings, she re-forms her body into that of a cowboy, cutting her hair and changing her attire in order to pass as male. Along the way she falls in love with Clara, a mixed-race Black and Indigenous woman. As Micaela pursues the men who raped her mother, her younger sister, and herself—a man named Rove and the evil Colonel, a fictionalized military figure—she is helped by the networks of women woven across borders and by the ghosts that haunt the landscape. By queering the genre in this manner, Pérez re-forms dominant narratives of race, sexuality, and nation, narrativizing a Chicana feminist perspective into being. In her critical work *The Decolonial Imaginary*, Pérez argues that the entire discipline of history is "infused with morality, with how the documents 'should' be interpreted and written, with ponderings over what is and what is not the definitive story."[50] In *Forgetting the Alamo*, Pérez undermines this kind of moralistic version of history embodied by dominant narratives of what it means to be an "American" by imagining another side of that history, thus filling in the gaps made so visible in the western: namely, those surrounding women, Chicanas, and national boundaries. As Rosa Linda Fregoso points out, the "disavowal of the Mexicanist presence in definitions of U.S. citizenship and identity has been one of the major mechanisms for the consolidation of colonialist rule in states like California, New Mexico, and Texas during the nineteenth century and for the maintenance of a dominant racial order throughout the twentieth century."[51] By working within the western, Pérez shifts the focus onto the gendered nature of violence in the context of the shifting U.S.-Mexico border in the mid-1800s—what Gloria Anzaldúa famously refers to as the "borderlands"—in a move that re-forms the disavowal of the Mexicanist presence during the formation of the United States.[52] Ultimately, Pérez's novel asks the reader to *forget* the Alamo and everything it stands for with regard to borders and disenfranchisement, mixing genre conventions (ghost stories, romance, and westerns) to interrogate national memory and heteropatriarchal colonialism.

Forgetting the Alamo uses hauntings to undermine colonial morality. One ghost who haunts Micaela is that of a man named Oscar—a man who stole her father's gun and kidnapped her, serving as one of her captors before she killed him to escape the Colonel. Despite having once appeared solely to torment Micaela by threatening sexual violence against Clara, Oscar visits Micaela on a different occasion to warn her that the Colonel is coming for her.[53] He says, "I guess I got to say I'm sorry so I will. I'm sorry. Thing is, son, I got to do me some good deeds or I'm stuck here."[54] The tension created by Oscar's role in Micaela's life when he was alive, his threatening presence in his first visit, and his attempts at making amends in his final visit bring together threads of disenfranchisement, gendered violence, and morality in the novel. In her book on cultural hauntings, Kathleen Brogan argues that ghosts in literatures by writers of color often signal "the need to identify and revise the cultural past," simultaneously providing "the vehicle for both a dangerous possession by and an imaginative liberation from the past."[55] Oscar's presence brings Micaela's past deeds into her present; interestingly, rather than forcing her to reckon with her own act of violence against him, Oscar expresses the need to apologize to her. In other words, his haunting is an act of penance (rather than vengeance) that he hopes will help counteract some of his own bad deeds. Rather than the "dangerous possession" Micaela initially fears from this specter, Oscar offers her a "liberation from the past" by allowing her to elude the Colonel once more while also signaling to her that her act of violence was morally justified. Adrianna Simone identifies Pérez's use of "the decolonial time lag, which dismantles the hierarchical, historical structure by not following a linear approach to history. The past, present, and future are no longer on a single, chronological line that moves from a beginning to an end."[56] I argue that the presence of Oscar's ghost further dismantles the historical structure by allowing living and dead characters to occupy the same space. In this way, Pérez critiques colonial morality. By destabilizing the border between life and death and offering words of remorse from a colonial agent, the novel's decolonial time lag dismantles normalized moral rhetoric around colonization—and all its implications for racialized, gendered, and queer subjects—and in so doing re-forms normalized historical narratives of nation in the borderlands surrounding the U.S.-Mexico border.

As part of this deconstructive work, the networks of women that undergird the narrative present a shadow-borderland that, while deprived of the overt forms of power maintained by cisgender male characters, constitute a matriarchal power system functioning in opposition to colonial heteropatriarchy. Pérez has discussed her intentional use of the term "lesbian" because it is "the self-identity for women who choose to be with other women—physically, psychically, and politically."[57] While Micaela is the novel's sole lesbian figure, characters such as Clara (Micaela's lover and mother to Jed's children), Miss Elsie (the owner of the local brothel), Ursula (Micaela's mother), and Miss Celestine (a clairvoyant who aids Micaela and Clara in New Orleans) work collaboratively to provide safe houses for one another, influence political decisions, and critique colonial practices of landownership. These women are positioned in prominent places within their communities, and they are depicted as *knowing* things (sure, Miss Celestine is a psychic, but Ursula also predicts her husband's death on the field of battle, right down to the white-handled knife in his chest). Alongside the portrayal of these uncanny ways of knowing, Theresa Delgadillo argues that Pérez's novel, by featuring resilient female characters who are leaders of their communities, illuminates "the tensions of colonial and independence movements," thereby centering Latin America and relegating U.S. America to the borderlands.[58] Arguably, the novel also relegates the male characters and their cruelty, violence, and greed to the metaphoric borderlands. Conversely, the communal network of women in Pérez's novel—characterized by various forms of love and resistance—is featured at the center of the frontier.[59] Case in point, Miss Elsie explicitly views her brothel as a kind of safe house for victimized women. She tells Ursula, "Alls I know is somebody's gotta give them poor girls a place to live cuz they been run out of their homes by some mean husbands or papas or brothers or uncles who raped them or beat them or expected them to be their dang selves. Well, let me tell you, here they got a home and I ain't never let a man raise a hand to them."[60] The intentionality with which Miss Elsie runs her business counteracts the misogynistic violence of the colonial culture that pervades the community. Her actions and those of other "knowing" women in strategic positions re-form the West by depicting a gynocentric shadow-borderland.

Despite this robust community of women, the novel unflinchingly portrays and critiques the heteropatriarchal colonial violences to which women of all ages, colors, and sexualities are subjected. Pérez's decision to center the novel on a Tejana lesbian in the "heteropatriarchal, Anglocentric genre of the Western" undercuts the ways women and people of color in conventional westerns tend to be evil, antagonistic, or rendered without voice, agency, or depth of character.[61] While essentially every woman and girl in the novel is the victim of sexual assault at some point in her appearance in the text, Pérez refuses a narrative of disempowerment. Instead, Adrianna Santos theorizes Pérez's novel as a "survival narrative"—a designation she defines as "a hybrid form of literature that emphasizes collective struggle and storytelling as radical acts of cultural survival that are key components of empowerment and healing and that challenge the cultural erasure of colonization."[62] The prevalence of sexual assault in *Forgetting the Alamo* functions, then, as a powerful counter to colonial narratives of U.S. nationhood, exposing the interwoven politics of heteronormative patriarchy, anti-Mexican racism, and nationalist anti-immigration sentiments during the period of time the United States began solidifying and policing its southern border in earnest.[63] By filtering the entire novel through Micaela's narration, Pérez re-forms the western, decentering U.S. America and white heteropatriarchal frontier narratives.

Inextricably linked to the multitudinous nature of sexual assault in the novel is the issue of colonization. To return to Kolodny's ideas on the pastoral impulse, figurations of the land as feminine shifted away from a land-as-nurturing-mother image to an implied "spectre of violation" haunting the nineteenth-century West.[64] Relatedly, Madsen contends that sexual violence toward women in westerns is "related to the idea of legitimacy and specifically of what constitutes a legitimate claim to property," explaining that westerns legitimize the colonial acquisition of Indigenous and Mexican lands by the United States so that "the issue of who should possess the land is intimately linked to who should possess the women."[65] What, then, are we to do with Micaela's female body that is subjected to sexual violence but that she subsequently re-forms as a male body that loves another female body? Micaela's attackers, disfigured white men who have obtained the deed to her family's land through dubious circumstances, can certainly be seen as metaphorically possessing the land they've stolen through the act of rape: just as they "possess" Micaela's body, so do they possess her land. However, when Micaela cuts her hair and dons her father's jacket, thereby re-forming her female body as male, she also undermines the legitimacy of their claim to her—and by extension, other Mexican women's—land by staking her own claim to maleness. Furthermore, her "possession" of another woman through a mutually consensual relationship underscores the legitimacy of American Indian and Mexican land rights while simultaneously discrediting the blatantly illegal and immoral actions of her attackers. In fact, near the end of the novel Micaela learns that her father deeded his lands to Jed (his nephew) rather than to her. Importantly, this deed was matrilineally inherited until it reached Micaela's father, having been given to him by his mother on her dying day only because she "had no daughters to whom she could will the land."[66] His decision to will the land to his nephew rather than his daughter signals the entrenchment of the colonial shift toward patriarchy. The subsequent acts of rape perpetrated against Ursula, Micaela, and Micaela's ten-year-old sister by white men can be understood as extensions of the illegitimate colonial claims to the land, in contrast to Micaela's legitimate claims to it through her Indigenous, Mexican, and Tejana heritage.

In addition to the decolonial implications Micaela's performance of gender has with regard to land rights, her re-formation into a male-passing cowboy also calls up the specters of gendered violence that continue to haunt the borderlands. It is highly significant that Micaela's re-formation from dutiful daughter to nameless revenge-seeker occurs on the battlefield in the aftermath of the Battle of San Jacinto. Upon seeing her father's ruined body after three days of searching, Micaela pulls the knife out of his heart, explaining that "something came over me, maybe ghosts or spirits because I didn't realize what I was doing nor did I remember having done it. It was as if a strong spirit forced my hand and I cut my cheek from eye to mouth in a crescent moon like my Tío Lorenzo's brand."[67] Here, the suggestion that "ghosts or spirits" guided her hand to mark her as her uncle had once marked himself signals the role of the dead (ghosts) in Micaela's transformation. The fact that Micaela indicates she was "wholly conscious" of subsequently using the same knife to cut off her long hair and removing her father's jacket from his dead body and putting it on herself highlights her own agency in this transformation. Through the act of replicating her uncle's scar on her own face, she marks herself as male. This scarification, while distinct from the other ways women's bodies are marked by gendered violence, operates similarly in the way both types of wounds "suggest the literal and figurative historical marking of the female body, straight or queer."[68] Interestingly, while this "marking" of Micaela's female body operates similarly to other types of gendered violence, the ghostly influence has important ramifications. Because Micaela is not solely responsible for the scarification, her re-formation as a cow*boy* is attributed to a larger community: the dead. Given the setting (a blood-soaked battlefield), the role of these "ghosts or spirits"—perhaps those recently killed by U.S. colonial forces or even the land itself—in guiding Micaela's hand to scarify her face is a qweirding one that grants her the freedom of mobility typically reserved for the western's wandering cowboy. This spectral scarification enables Micaela to perform her anticolonial resistance through the act of re-forming her body. Despite the fact that this act does, indeed, mark her body, it does so in a manner that affirms her inner sense of self. In that way, it re-forms the gendered violence of the conventional western by serving as the catalyst for Micaela's shift to a male-passing cowboy.

Similarly, the acts of cutting her hair and donning her father's jacket signal Micaela's re-formation to a masculine role. Halberstam argues, "Apart from the prostitute with a heart of gold . . . there are two main generic roles for women in the Western": the so-called tomboy, whose "character morphs quickly into a properly but not excessively feminine wife"; and the tough girl with a gun, who the western usually suggests "really needs a man."[69] Being a lesbian who takes a wife and conducts herself as the men around her do rather than becoming a wife who depends on a man, Micaela breaks out of both proscriptive roles offered by the conventional western. By passing as male, Micaela finds a way to invert the power structure of both U.S. and Mexican patriarchy and occupy a space outside of systems of power that privilege whiteness, maleness, and heterosexuality. As Cheryl Clarke argues, men "at all levels of privilege, of all classes and colors have the potential to act out legalistically, moralistically, and violently when they cannot colonize women, when they cannot circumscribe our sexual, productive, reproductive, creative prerogatives and energies" and that the figure of the lesbian is a decolonizing figure.[70] Micaela is a character who, through lesbian desire, gains access to legal, moral, and violent actions that are unattainable to her as a heterosexual woman. By refusing to be colonized by the men who populate the landscape of Pérez's novel, Micaela takes control of her own sexual and (re)productive energies.

As a matter of fact, Micaela doesn't simply take control of these energies; she actively displaces the men who would attempt to control her themselves. By embodying the position westerns conventionally allocate to white male protagonists, Micaela's character wrests certain political and social powers out of the hands of other male characters. For instance, Micaela's lover Clara uses Micaela's cousin Jed to get pregnant. Jed and Micaela share certain key characteristics: they are both long and lean, both have bad tempers, and both feel slighted by their respective fathers' lack of faith in them. Significantly, Jed dies almost immediately after he serves his purpose as unsuspecting sperm donor, and Micaela steps in to replace him as the father (as well as Clara's lover). As a father figure, Micaela explains the joy Clara's twin babies bring her when she greets them and sees "my eyes, Jedidiah's eyes, in their tiny faces."[71] Micaela's recognition of her own eyes in the twins' faces and her actions upon finding her father's body illustrate her complete re-formation from a young woman with no agency to a female father figure who protects the children who share her bloodline. In her reading of Halberstam's concept of "female masculinity," Karen Allison Fielder articulates how in "Chicana/o culture, female masculinity disrupts the entire power structure" and upends "an entire cultural symbolic order."[72] In this way, Micaela embodies a powerful form of culturally inflected female masculinity that lends her character the ability to work from within the weird western to write a gynocentric narrative of U.S. nation formation and give voice to women so often silenced by both history and genre.

Conclusions: Re-forming the West

The genre-bending characteristics of *How Much of These Hills Is Gold* and *Forgetting the Alamo* reanimate the western in order to critique and deconstruct nationalistic mythologies of race, gender, and belonging in the United States. The figure of the female-bodied, male-passing cowboy embodied by Sam and Micaela calls into question the so-called Code of the West as portrayed in westerns. The Code was a system that "marked the boundaries of right and wrong, civilized and wild, and good and evil, and it safeguarded the frontier from chaos and abandon."[73] By re-forming their bodies, Sam and Micaela alter the Code, blurring boundaries and flipping scripts so that rather than a moral Code lending logic to the landscape, the Code becomes a set of questions to be problematized. That Sam re-forms his body to align with his male identity while Micaela re-forms hers to grant her access to the male-dominated landscape underscores the multiple ways their passings call the Code into question. Who was right and who was wrong where immigration, colonial violence, and the western frontier were concerned? Who should be considered civilized, and who wild, in the Wild West? What kinds of violence constitute acts of good and what kinds of laws or actions constitute evil?

The agency attributed to women in Zhang's and Pérez's novels further re-forms the western. Lucy is no damsel in distress, and Miss Elsie is no hapless whore. Instead, these characters destabilize flat moralistic portrayals of white western femininity, offering fortitude and defiance to heteropatriarchal desires. Through these characters, the western brothel as a space of masculine sexual conquest is re-formed into a space of feminine resilience, exposing heteropatriarchal sexual violence to be both criminal and, on the frontier, colonial.

Qweirding the West is an act of dismantling. Dismembering. Killing off the "Old" of the Old West and Frankensteining together something else. Re-forming the frontier, the narrative, what's considered Wild in the West. It's a conjuring act, a simultaneous possession and dispossession, an exorcism.

Notes

1. Saunders, *The Western Genre*.
2. Cawelti, *Six-Gun Mystique Sequel*, 9.
3. Cawelti, *Six-Gun Mystique Sequel*, 7.
4. Brower, "'They'd Kill Us If They Knew,'" 47.
5. Bold, *Selling the Wild West*, xv.
6. Comer, "New West, Urban and Suburban Spaces, Postwest," 249–51 (emphasis in original).
7. Kollin, "Postwestern Studies," xi.
8. Johnson, Lush, and Spurgeon, "Westworld(s)," 1.
9. Goeman, *Mark My Words*, 4.
10. Campbell, *Worlding the Western*, 112.
11. Johnson, Lush, and Spurgeon, "Westworld(s)," 12.
12. Zhang, *How Much of These Hills*, 105.
13. Zhang, *How Much of These Hills*, 102.
14. Zhang, *How Much of These Hills*, 185.
15. Madsen, "Discourses of Frontier Violence," 186.
16. Zhang, *How Much of These Hills*, 101.
17. Zhang, *How Much of These Hills*, 89.
18. Zhang, *How Much of These Hills*, 81.
19. Zhang, *How Much of These Hills*, 149.
20. Zhang, *How Much of These Hills*, 151.
21. Madsen, "Discourses of Frontier Violence," 188.
22. Kolodny, *The Lay of the Land*, 8–9.
23. Zhang, *How Much of These Hills*, 150.
24. Zhang, *How Much of These Hills*, 163.
25. Brower, "'They'd Kill Us If They Knew,'" 50.
26. Zhang, *How Much of These Hills*, 164.
27. Zhang, *How Much of These Hills*, 24 and 30.
28. Zhang, *How Much of These Hills*, 44.
29. Zhang, *How Much of These Hills*, 3.
30. Irvine, "The Popular Western as Epic," 75–76.
31. Irvine, "The Popular Western as Epic," 80.

32. Mitchell, *Westerns*, 4.
33. Slotkin, *Gunfighter Nation*, 290–91.
34. Zhang, *How Much of These Hills*, 215. Neil Campbell considers the supernatural potential of Sam-as-tiger, contending that Zhang's tigers function "as reminders of an alien culture while disrupting the expected landscape of a western novel." Campbell, *Worlding the Western*, 108.
35. Zhang, *How Much of These Hills*, 238.
36. Zhang, *How Much of These Hills*, 266 (emphasis in original), 268.
37. Zhang, *How Much of These Hills*, 227.
38. Zhang, *How Much of These Hills*, 236.
39. Zhang, *How Much of These Hills*, 237.
40. Zhang, *How Much of These Hills*, 237.
41. Zhang, *How Much of These Hills*, 249.
42. Zhang, *How Much of These Hills*, 250, 254.
43. Zhang, *How Much of These Hills*, 4.
44. Zhang, *How Much of These Hills*, 4.
45. Zhang, *How Much of These Hills*, 268.
46. Huang, *Surface Relations*, 2.
47. Zhang, *How Much of These Hills*, 271.
48. Zhang, *How Much of These Hills*, 272.
49. Zhang, *How Much of These Hills*, 272.
50. Pérez, *Decolonial Imaginary*, xiv.
51. Fregoso, "Reproduction and Miscegenation," 324.
52. Anzaldúa, *Borderlands/La Frontera*.
53. Pérez, *Forgetting the Alamo*, 112.
54. Pérez, *Forgetting the Alamo*, 154.
55. Brogan, *Cultural Haunting*, 11, 29.
56. Simone, "Storytelling as Transformation," 33.
57. Pérez, "Queering the Borderlands," 125–26.
58. Delgadillo, "The Criticality of Latino/a Fiction," 609–10.
59. Santos, "Surviving the Alamo," 45.
60. Pérez, *Forgetting the Alamo*, 25.
61. Santos, "Surviving the Alamo," 40–41.
62. Santos, "Surviving the Alamo," 38.
63. Pérez, "Queering the Borderlands," 126.
64. Kolodny, *The Lay of the Land*, 73.
65. Madsen, "Discourses of Frontier Violence," 195.
66. Pérez, *Forgetting the Alamo*, 20.
67. Pérez, *Forgetting the Alamo*, 30.
68. Fielder, "Revising How the West Was Won," 40.

69. Halberstam, "Not so Lonesome Cowboys," 198–99.
70. Clarke, "Lesbianism," 128.
71. Pérez, *Forgetting the Alamo*, 206.
72. Fielder, "Revising How the West Was Won," 37.
73. Miller and Van Riper, introduction to *Undead in the West*, xiv.

Bibliography

Anzaldúa, Gloria. *Borderlands/La Frontera: The New Mestiza*. 3rd ed. San Francisco: Aunt Lute, 2007.

Bold, Christine. *Selling the Wild West: Popular Western Fiction, 1860–1960*. Bloomington: Indiana University Press, 1987.

Brogan, Kathleen. *Cultural Haunting: Ghosts and Ethnicity in Recent American Literature*. Charlottesville: University Press of Virginia, 1998.

Brower, Sue. "'They'd Kill Us If They Knew': Transgression and the Western." *Journal of Film and Video* 62, no. 4 (2010): 47–57.

Campbell, Neil. *Worlding the Western: Contemporary US Western Fiction and the Global Community*. Reno: University of Nevada Press, 2022.

Cawelti, John G. *The Six-Gun Mystique Sequel*. Bowling Green OH: Bowling Green State University Popular Press, 1999.

Clarke, Cheryl. "Lesbianism: An Act of Resistance." In *This Bridge Called My Back: Writings by Radical Women of Color*, 2nd ed., edited by Cherríe Moraga and Gloria Anzaldúa, 128–37. New York: Kitchen Table, Women of Color Press, 1983.

Comer, Krista. "New West, Urban and Suburban Spaces, Postwest." In *A Companion to the Literature and Culture of the American West*, edited by Nicolas S. Witschi, 245–60. West Sussex, UK: Wiley-Blackwell, 2011.

Delgadillo, Theresa. "The Criticality of Latino/a Fiction in the Twenty-First Century." *American Literary History* 23, no. 3 (2011): 600–624.

Fielder, Karen Allison. "Revising How the West Was Won in Emma Pérez's *Forgetting the Alamo, or, Blood Memory*." *Rocky Mountain Review* 66 (2012): 34–47.

Fregoso, Rosa Linda. "Reproduction and Miscegenation on the Borderlands: Mapping the Maternal Body of Tejanas." In *Chicana Feminisms: A Critical Reader*, edited by Gabriela F. Arredondo et al., 324–48. Durham NC: Duke University Press, 2003.

Goeman, Mishuana. *Mark My Words: Native Women Mapping Our Nations*. Minneapolis: University of Minnesota Press, 2013.

Halberstam, J. "Not So Lonesome Cowboys: The Queer Western." In *The Brokeback Book: From Story to Cultural Phenomenon*, edited by William R. Handley, 190–201. Lincoln: University of Nebraska Press, 2011.

Huang, Vivian L. *Surface Relations: Queer Forms of Asian American Inscrutability*. Durham NC: Duke University Press, 2022.

Irvine, Colin. "The Popular Western as Epic: A Bakhtinian Understanding of Time in the American West[ern]." *Journal of the West* 45, no. 1 (2006): 74–81.

Johnson, Michael K., Rebecca M. Lush, and Sara Spurgeon. "Westworld(s): Race, Gender, Genre in the Weird Western." Introduction to *Weird Westerns: Race, Gender, Genre*, edited by Kerry Fine, Michael K. Johnson, Rebecca M. Lush, and Sara L. Spurgeon, 1–36. Lincoln: University of Nebraska Press, 2020.

Kollin, Susan. "Postwestern Studies, Dead or Alive." Introduction to *Postwestern Cultures: Literature, Theory, Space*, ix–xix. Lincoln: University of Nebraska Press, 2007.

Kolodny, Annette. *The Lay of the Land: Metaphor as Experience and History in American Life and Letters*. Chapel Hill: University of North Carolina Press, 1975.

Madsen, Deborah L. "Discourses of Frontier Violence and the Trauma of National Emergence in Larry McMurtry's *Lonesome Dove* Quartet." *Canadian Review of American Studies* 39, no. 2 (2009): 185–204.

Miller, Cynthia J., and A. Bowdoin Van Riper. Introduction to *Undead in the West: Vampires, Zombies, Mummies, and Ghosts on the Cinematic Frontier*, edited by Cynthia J. Miller and Bowdoin Van Riper, xi–xxvi. Lanham MD: Scarecrow, 2012.

Mitchell, Lee Clark. *Westerns: Making the Man in Fiction and Film*. Chicago: University of Chicago Press, 1996.

Pérez, Emma. *The Decolonial Imaginary: Writing Chicanas into History*. Bloomington: Indiana University Press, 1999.

———. *Forgetting the Alamo, or, Blood Memory*. Austin: University of Texas Press, 2009.

———. "Queering the Borderlands: The Challenges of Excavating the Invisible and Unheard." *Frontiers: A Journal of Women Studies* 24, no. 2/3 (2003): 122–31.

Santos, Adrianna M. "Surviving the Alamo, Violence Vengeance, and Women's Solidarity in Emma Pérez's *Forgetting the Alamo, or, Blood Memory*." *Journal of Latina Critical Feminisms* 2, no. 1 (2019): 37–49.

Saunders, John. *The Western Genre: From Lordsburg to Big Whiskey*. New York: Columbia University Press, 2001.

Simone, Adrianna. "Storytelling as Transformation: Disrupting Cycles of Violence Through Feminist Sites of Remembrance, Love, and Forgiveness in Emma Pérez's *Forgetting the Alamo, or, Blood Memory*." *Ex-centric Narratives: Journal of Anglophone Literature, Culture and Media*, no. 3 (2019): 28–40.

Slotkin, Richard. *Gunfighter Nation: The Myth of the Frontier in Twentieth-Century America*. Norman: University of Oklahoma Press, 1998.

Zhang, C Pam. *How Much of These Hills Is Gold*. New York: Riverhead, 2020.

7

Ishmael Reed Takes on the Weird Western in *Yellow Back Radio Broke-Down*

JANA KOEHLER

Recent scholarship on Ishmael Reed's *Yellow Back Radio Broke-Down* views his use of the western genre as a trickster trope or neo-hoodoo charm, a parody that reveals the racist and Eurocentric dogma the western genre often embodies and inspires. Reed is a central figure in the Black Arts movement and African American fiction of the West, yet his use of supernatural and science fiction elements set him apart from the Black Arts movement, leading critics such as Paul Green to categorize *Yellow Back Radio Broke-Down* as a weird western.[1] For other critics, what sets the novel apart from traditional westerns is that Reed's protagonist, the Loop Garoo Kid, is a Black cowboy and hoodoo priest. For them, an African American in a western is weird enough to make it a generic anomaly. As Joshua Smith argues, "The racialized other has historically been the de facto horrific, incredulous, spiritual or muse-like figure in white-authored western fiction," supplying a weird element to fiction that would otherwise appear traditional.[2] However, Reed's novel also employs elements of the weird west even while he revises them in order to critique exclusionary western narratives that write out (and white out) the experiences of African Americans.

This discussion explores the complicated intersections of race, class, and gender that exclude Black men from attaining power and that open up the western frontier to new forms of racial expression. While other scholars have examined how Reed uses race in order to critique the western, few have explored how sexuality plays a part in this critique.[3] By putting *Yellow Back Radio Broke-Down* into conversation with Robert E. Howard's weird western "Black Canaan," this discussion reveals how these authors engage with issues of sexuality, race, and gender through alternative dimensions that call into question accepted narratives about the West. Comparing Howard's short story to *Yellow Back Radio* demonstrates how Reed responds to the racism in weird fiction. The hero of Howard's tale is a white cowboy named Kirby Buckner. He quells a rumored uprising of the Black citizens of Canaan on the Texas border, who are supposedly under the spell of the evil African conjure man, Saul Stark. To do so, Buckner must contend with a nameless Black woman, the "Bride of Damballah," whose sexuality challenges Buckner's identity as a white man. In Reed's novel, however, the Black conjure man and hero-cowboy are one and the same. Instead of bringing order, the Loop Garoo Kid's goal is to shake up the status quo; thus, Reed's novel and Howard's short story seem to differ in almost every way possible. In particular, Howard's text is fixated on the threat of Black women's sexuality by depicting stereotypes of hypersexuality associated with women of color. By contrast, Reed's text interrogates the stereotypes of Black male hypersexuality in order to boost Black masculinity and to emasculate white men. However, while Reed portrays Loop's sexuality as empowering, it is often at the expense of women and those with nonnormative sexualities, similar to Howard's work. Putting Reed and Howard into conversation thus evinces a much deeper critique of Reed's novel and its homosexual tropes of alterity and pathological difference.

Robert E. Howard, or "Two Gun Bob" as his friend H. P. Lovecraft nicknamed him, is often referred to as one of the first to infuse western fiction with weird elements.[4] Howard's most recognized fictional creation is Conan of Cimmeria, who later became known as Conan the Barbarian and helped launch the "sword and sorcery" fantasy genre, which "blends historical adventure fiction with Gothic or Lovecraftian horror."[5] But Howard was most interested in the western genre, which he focused on toward the end of his life, combining the western with weird fiction and in the process mixing two distinct genres to create a hybrid form that was considered monstrous in its own way, as the reception of his work in *Weird Tales* was branded "uneven."[6] Howard was proud of his Texan heritage and often wrote of the profound influences the stories he heard in childhood had on his writing. Significantly, many of these stories were told by "his family's cook and laundress, both formerly enslaved African American women, who told him stories of their youth, their time in slavery, and the ghost stories of the region."[7] These women were Mary Bohannon and Arabella Davis, and Howard called Davis "a black philosopher, if there was ever one."[8] Black women's voices served as Howard's inspirations and they signal a real racial history that haunts the West and the greater American imaginary.

However, Howard's stories reveal anxieties about the influence of Black women, specifically their sexuality, a notion that is best demonstrated in his short story "Black Canaan," published in the June 1936 issue of *Weird Tales*. The protagonist of this tale is Kirby Buckner, a white Texan landowner and cowboy who is also a de facto community leader due to his family's generational influence. He is from the town of Canaan, whose residents are described as "the sons and daughters of the white frontiersmen who first settled the country, and the sons and daughters of their slaves," alluding to the complex relationship between colonial westward expansion and the simultaneous expansion of chattel slavery into the western states.[9] Buckner returns to his hometown after hearing the warning, "Trouble on Tularoosa Creek!" from an elderly Black woman who mysteriously vanishes into a crowd after delivering her message.[10] Buckner understands this message to indicate "old hates seething again in the jungle-deeps of the swamplands," alluding to a violent slave rebellion that occurred in Canaan in 1845.[11] Since then, "the fear of a black uprising lurked for ever in the depths of that forgotten back-country; the very children absorbed it in their cradles."[12] Buckner discovers that a conjure man named Saul Stark, "a great big black devil that talks better English than I like to hear a nigger talk," has come to town, and his "aim [is] to kill all de white folks in Canaan."[13] Stark is accompanied by a beautiful mixed-race woman who attempts to waylay Buckner on his ride to Canaan. Her beauty bewitches Buckner, and she remarks, "I have made a charm you cannot resist!" rendering him powerless even to mention her to his white companions.[14] In another confrontation, Buckner is so paralyzed by her spell that he is unable to defend himself, leaving his white companion Braxton to shoot at her before she disappears. When Buckner finally arrives at Stark's hideout he sees a full ritual in progress, "The Dance of the Skull," whose climax, he believes, is his death at the hands of Stark. The nameless woman then appears and performs the dance, only to drop dead at its conclusion (Buckner explains to the reader that Braxton's bullet had struck her but that she used her magical skills to keep herself alive long enough to perform the ritual). The woman's death inspires instant chaos, dispersing the crowd of Black citizens and breaking the conjure spell. Stark attempts to stab Buckner but is ultimately defeated. Afterward Buckner discovers that Stark had been using his conjure skills to turn men into half-amphibious monsters, a horror so profound that Buckner is unable to share this secret knowledge with his white companions as the story concludes. Howard's story is indicative of a larger literary tradition of vilifying Black men as physically threatening and Black women as sexually dangerous. This is the tradition Reed counters through a weird reversal of sexual and racial prowess that has the conjure man ride off into the sunset victorious instead.

Yellow Back Radio Broke-Down focuses on the Loop Garoo Kid, a Black cowboy, hoodoo priest, and the eldest son of God, who was banished from heaven by a jealous Christ. Loop has since joined a circus troupe invited to the town of Yellow Back Radio. However, the troupe is ambushed by a group of cowboys sent by Drag Gibson, a rich, racist landowner who controls Yellow Back Radio through intimidation, trickery, and murder. Loop is the only one to make it out alive; he flees to the mountain caves that surround Yellow Back Radio, where he plots his revenge against Drag and the other town officials. Along the way, he encounters absurd characters, such as Bo Shmo and his neo–social realist gang; the "last Indian" of Yellow Back Radio named Chief Showcase; and Mustache Sal, a treacherous former love interest who bears the marks of being branded by Loop, who ultimately kills Drag, frees the town, and seems to return home to Heaven after Pope Innocent VIII comes to beg his forgiveness. By twisting and turning the typical cast of western characters, Reed weirds the West in a way that also critiques the conventions of gender and genre but conforms to dominant, heterosexual stereotypes of homosexuality and deviance.

Reed deliberately engages with the literary history of western fiction in *Yellow Back Radio Broke-Down* while simultaneously incorporating Black literature of the West. As Reed explains, "I based the book on old radio scripts in which the listener constructed the sets with his imagination; that's why 'radio'; also because it's an oral book, a talking book."[15] He continues, "Also 'radio' because there's more dialogue than scenery or description. 'Yellow Back' because that's what they used to call Old West books about cowboy heroes: they were 'yellow covered books and were usually lurid and sensational.' . . . *Yellow Back Radio Broke-Down* is the dismantling of a genre done in an oral way like *Radio*."[16] Contrary to early reviews that claimed that Reed must have been under the influence while writing this novel, Reed asserts, "I wasn't 'crazy' or 'on dope,' but extremely conscious of form when I wrote that book."[17] While Reed emphasizes the innovation that Black writers bring to the western genre, he simultaneously acknowledges his predecessors by invoking Nat Love, a Black cowboy who wrote about his participation in the West. Likewise, Loop offers an alternative way of thinking about the American West and speaks to the historical presence of Black cowboys. In this way, the "novel revises Turner's thesis by marking a glorious return of the marginalized races."[18] Stephen McVeigh notes that Reed uses the novel "in the first place to highlight African-Americans' traditional exclusion from this American narrative and subsequently works to dismantle it."[19] Reed's characters are familiar to an audience raised on westerns, even while these characters also embody marginalized conventions of Black writers. His novel may seem senseless, but that is part of his point: "So this is what we want: to sabotage history. They won't know whether we're serious or whether we are writing fiction."[20] By drawing on these overlapping histories of Black westerns and involvement in the West, Reed weirds the western to challenge the normalized American imperialist narrative.

Even more, Reed challenges the weird western as a subgenre that involves science fiction or fantastic elements in a genre that usually adheres to a version of realism. *Yellow Back Radio Broke-Down* embodies Reed's artistic philosophy, which he calls "Neo-HooDoo." As Robert Elliot Fox argues, this philosophy is "in many ways, a truly 'black' art," yet at the same time, "due to the undeniable mix of ingredients in the New World, it is also 'something else.'"[21] This mixture is no weakness, as Fox furthers notes, "Unlike those who argue for a black essentialism, Reed sees this hybridity as a virtue, rather than a defect or betrayal."[22] The term "hoodoo" refers to the Americanization of the voodoo religion that originated in Haiti, "a polygot faith which embraces syncretism and challenges the notion of bounded essences"; it also evokes the rock formation found in the West's most iconic settings.[23] These geological wonders include the Badlands of the northern Great Plains, the Four Corners region, and most spectacularly Bryce Canyon National Park and Arches National Park in Utah. In the first few pages of the novel, Reed establishes this parallel when introducing Zozo Labrique, a "charter member of the American Hoo-Doo Church."[24] Only a few pages later in a description of the location where a scout for the circus troupe was lynched, the narrator notes a nearby "hoodoo rock" on top of which "fat nasty buzzards were arriving."[25] This specific rock formation is characterized as "tall skinny spires of rock that protrude from the bottom of arid basins and 'broken' lands" and are "often described as having a 'totem pole-shaped body.'"[26] Through weathering, the softer rock is eroded, leaving the hard rock in precarious positions that appear to defy logic. Hoodoo formations seem poised to collapse at any moment, yet through a delicate balance retain their form. This image demonstrates the connection between the western genre and an African American western past, one that has been whittled away through white historical erasure, but this paradoxical balance is also an apt symbol for the novel itself. Reed walks a fine line between absurdist humor and critique, and he weirds the western space to connect two seemingly disparate traditions, revealing that geography was never fixed but always malleable.

As Ralph Ellison states, Black Americans have known all too well "the relationship between geography and freedom."[27] Todd Tietchen argues that "Reed's HooDoo West often loses all coherent boundaries, placing it in stark contrast to the mythic frontier, site of an unambiguous conversion mission which pitted forces of Christian light against forces of Satanic darkness."[28] Yet other critics argue that the landscape of the West, which is often defined as being open and empty, is actually dangerously "deceptive."[29] At one point in the text, Drag Gibson, stymied once again by the Loop Garoo Kid, exclaims, "HOW CAN HE BE IN TWO PLACES AT ONE TIME?"[30] This bewildered cry brings us to what Michael K. Johnson calls "the debate circling around whether we should regard the frontier as an actual and identifiable geographic region or whether we should examine the frontier experience as a process of change and transformation."[31] It also links back to Reed's idea of neo-hoodoo, specifically of "time sense," which is "akin to the 'time' one finds in the psychic world where past, present and future exist simultaneously."[32] In short, Reed explains, "voodoo says that the past is contemporary."[33] Drag's question could also be posed to the novel's setting: How can a place be two things at one time? This question can be complicated even further since Reed never provides a definitive time frame, as McVeigh observes: "The novel ranges from the eighteenth century to the present, combining historical events and cowboy myths with modern technology and cultural debris."[34]

Reed puts these differing time periods into conversation and bends the reader's perception of causality.

Reed's artistic philosophy becomes especially apparent in a comparative discussion of Howard's "Black Canaan." Although "Black Canaan" is by no means the only weird tale that contains questionable racial ideology, it illustrates the type of attitudes Reed was up against as he wrote his weird western, especially with regard to conjure, the history of slave rebellions, and white fears of Black sexuality. Although the fiction of both Howard and Reed refer to histories of racial violence, for vastly different reasons, they also betray anxieties over less overt forms of violence. For Howard, this violence is embodied in Black women's sexuality and civil influence coded as conjure magic. In "Black Canaan," Buckner is driven home by the threat of violence in the form of Canaan's Black citizens' unrest, but he soon encounters a more subversive, and paradoxically seductive, threat in the form of the Bride of Damballah. He narrates:

> A strange turmoil of conflicting emotions stirred in me. I had never before paid any attention to a black or brown woman. But this quadroon girl was different from any I had ever seen. Her features were regular as a white woman's, and her speech was not that of a common wench. Yet she was barbaric, in the open lure of her smile, in the gleam of her eyes, in the shameless posturing of her voluptuous body. Every gesture, every motion she made set her apart from the ordinary run of women; her beauty was untamed and lawless, meant to madden rather than to soothe, to make a man blind and dizzy, to rouse in him all the unreined passions that are his heritage from his ape ancestors.[35]

Buckner is anxious because he cannot racially categorize this nameless woman's features, which defy his racial (and racist) expectations, but also because of the sexual attraction he feels for her, a prospect that he had previously considered impossible. He is also struck by her potent use of language, which seems to be connected to her conjure abilities and, consequently, her sexuality. She puts a spell on Buckner so that he cannot speak of her to his white brethren; it is ultimately a fellow white man who deals her a mortal wound, leaving Buckner with a masculine identity wounded by his impotence.

Howard's hypersexualized depiction of the nameless Black woman draws on centuries of racist and sexist discourse concerning the sexuality of Black women and men, much of which was supported by scientific communities, who painted Black women and men as more primitive and promiscuous than their white counterparts. Susan Bordo explains that "'Scientific' representations of the black woman's body, like evolutionists' comparisons of the skull shapes of African males and orangutans, exaggerated (and often created) relations of similarity to animals, particular monkeys."[36] Black women thus faced a double bind: "By virtue of her sex, she represents the temptations of the flesh and the source of man's moral downfall. By virtue of her race, she is instinctual animal, undeserving of probate and undemanding of respect."[37] David Pilgrim identifies this as the Jezebel stereotype, which "was used during slavery as a rationalization for sexual relations between white men and black women, especially sexual unions involving slavers and slaves."[38] A Jezebel was a Black woman who had a primitive and limitless sexual appetite that could not be satisfied with Black men and "desired sexual relations with white men; therefore, white men did not have to rape black women." Such views have continued into the modern era, silencing Black women's voices when they report sexual assault or abuse. Erin Chapman explains, "Overwhelmingly represented as either hypersexual or inhumanly strong, black women are rarely understood as victims of sexual assault, since sex with black women either presumes or does not require their consent."[39] Howard's character is both sexually hypnotizing and inhumanly (or supernaturally) strong, a trait that is coded as conjure magic but that actually reveals white men's anxieties about their sexual desire for Black women. Indeed, the Black woman in Howard's story is not especially interested in having sex with Buckner; it is Buckner who sexually desires her. Yet Buckner places the blame on her, in particular her Black body, as dangerous rather than questioning his own desires.

The Bride of Damballah unsettles and calls into question the dominance of the typical white, heterosexual, male western hero. Buckner finds the woman dangerous because she has a command of both supernatural and sexual powers, which reveals his own inadequacy. This attraction forces Buckner to question his place in society by challenging his very humanity while also destabilizing his identity as a cowboy and as a man. The woman renders him impotent in a way that strikes at cowboy lore; Buckner exclaims that when he attempts to murder her, "I sat there like an image pointing a pistol I could not fire!"[40] This combination of sexuality and subordination in turn inverts the long history of sexual violence of white men against Black women, both during and after plantation slavery. The woman herself recalls this: "White men are fools, too. I am the daughter of a white man, who lived in the hut of a black king and mated with his daughters. I know the strength of white men, and their weakness."[41] This woman is the embodiment of the Black freedom that Buckner and the white community of Canaan cannot bear to consider. Although she also displays her knowledge of conjure magic through her spells, her real power resides in her ability to challenge Buckner's racial and gender assumptions.

In contrast, the Black women in *Yellow Back Radio* do not fare much better. There is Zozo, a hoodoo priestess, who is desexualized as an old woman with a face that was "black wrinkled and hard" and Black Diane, otherwise known as Erzuli, the Haitian African spirit similar to Christian conceptions of the Virgin Mary, who has been in a sexual relationship with Loop in the past but does not appear within the action of the text itself.[42] The novel's main Black woman (although she rarely appears in the action of the text itself) is Mighty Dike, a "bulldyker octoroon," who takes up with a white man named Royal Flush Gooseman, an "aging unscrupulous fur trapper."[43] She is also described as wearing "a wide belt . . . on her hips from which dangled chalky trophies from former lovers, penises which had been made into plaster of paris casts."[44] Her name seems to be more of an insult than an indication of her sexual orientation. Either way, Reed depicts Mighty Dike as a sexual deviant who has chosen a white man over a Black man, Loop. Unlike Mustache Sal, who usually accepts a sexual proposition when she is offered, Mighty Dike resents Loop's whip play, stating, "I'll have him subpoenaed and thrown in jail if I see him again."[45] Mighty Dike's characterization draws on the Jezebel stereotype in regard to her large sexual appetite and desire for white men, a desire that Reed finds pathological since he views the white men in the novel as emasculated and weak.

Reed's depictions of Black men may likewise appear to simply reify racist stereotypes, especially given that Loop's initial characterization is foregrounded by a description of his violent sexuality. Indeed, the novel introduces him as "a bullwhacker so unfeeling he left the print of winged mice on hides of crawling women."[46] But rather than reinforcing racial stereotypes of Black men, Reed demonstrates that this strand of violence in the novel is most in keeping with the white, heterosexual male western tradition since it is geared toward women. Loop is no exception to this pattern. One of Loop's sexual proclivities is to brand women, a troubling image since it again brings to mind the horrors of slavery. Loop brands Mustache Sal, a white woman (or perhaps man?) who seems to find sexual gratification in the pain, and Mighty Dike, who resents the violence and wants him punished for the "way he used to brand me and beat me leaving those welts in the shape of bats on my fine yellow frame."[47] Both of these women are described as being formally part of Loop's "stable" of women.[48] Although Reed is able to imagine a western hero who does not continue the tradition of needless killing, he nevertheless does not create a space where women are safe from this cruelty. In part, this violence against women seems to be an attempt to shore up Loop's sexuality and therefore his masculinity at the expense of Black women. As Patrick McGee writes, "Black men are able to claim membership in the public sphere of American democracy only by demonstrating a masculinity—and, by implication, a patriarchal relation to the other gender—that is equal to that of white men."[49] But this strategy in turn never succeeds but results in violence to "enforce white supremacy."[50] Black critics might call this violence against women "backward, embarrassing, and counter-productive."[51] Yet these actions can be traced back to the normalized version of the western where masculinity relies on dominance. McGee further notes how critics typically condemn a writer on moral, individual grounds but fail to take into consideration the writer's context.[52] As Reed explains, "the lurid scenes are in the book because that is what the form calls for. They're not in there to shock."[53] While almost all the other characters bite the dust, Loop lives, indicating that he does not inhabit a self-destructive identity but a new one that is, in fact, regenerated through violence. In this case, the Black cowboy is the hero, overturning the stereotypical death of minorities so that the lone white cowboy hero may live. Loop's success, however, is predicated on violence toward women and men with nonnormative sexualities, a fact that complicates Reed's valuable critique.

In order to contextualize these moments of violence, it is productive to view Loop through the lens of the western itself to see how he rejects and conforms to the conventional notions of a cowboy hero, much of which implicitly revolves around gender and sexuality. The Loop Garoo Kid goes by many names that merge into one, as other scholars have noted, and as Reed explains in the title of an earlier poem, "Loop Garoo Means Change Into."[54] With such a name, the reader knows to expect surprises. Although the western has normalized the cowboy figure as white, heterosexual, and violent, "the frontier represents as well a space where the masculine ideal can be interrogated."[55] McVeigh agrees, noting that Reed's text embodies "a reversal of the form's traditional narrative structure. In Reed's reconfiguring of the western, the outsiders are the heroes and traditional American society represents villainy."[56] Reed does so through his protagonist, particularly in regard to Loop's choice of weapons and when he chooses to wield them, both of which are deeply enmeshed in Loop's sexuality. While these narrative choices legitimize Black men and restore their experiences in the West, this empowerment comes at the expense of women and gay men.

One of the most striking aspects of Loop is that he carries a whip, an oddity for a western hero in a land where gunfights are the norm. Indeed, if men in a western do not possess or use a gun, they are typically seen as "not men at all."[57] The gun comes to stand in for the man's sexuality, and its absence denotes his weakness and femininity, as evidenced in "Black Canaan," when Buckner cannot pull the trigger to shoot the nameless Black woman. If a whip does appear in a western, it is usually a woman who wields it, a fact that effectively feminizes the weapon and those who use it.[58] Thus, Loop's choice of weapon weirds the figure of the hero-cowboy and at the same time parodies the western phallus. Reed plays on the latent homosexuality in western films when men admire each other's guns in a scene where a foreman laments, "Those kids said some nasty things about the six gun. . . . Said we ought to unzip our pants and draw it from there."[59] As Eric Meljac and Alex Hunt explain, "Western gear—ropes, rigging, and so on—is not unknown in the realm of sexual fetish."[60] The younger generation recognizes this homosexual theme in westerns, but such a thought is horrifying to the old-timers who prefer to view their male bonds as platonic. Finally, the whip, especially when brandished by Loop, harkens back to plantation slavery in the American South since slaveholders and overseers often used the whip to punish enslaved persons. In many ways, Loop is the specter of slavery come back to punish whites who benefited from this institution; he embodies America's ignominious past as well as its greatest fear: a Black man with power, the figure at the center of Howard's text in the form of conjure man Saul Stark. These details challenge the typical and the weird western, which rarely grant agency to minority characters.

Although Loop is described as hyperviolent, he does not display this violence in the narrative space of *Yellow Back Radio Broke-Down* (except against Mustache Sal). Johnson concludes that Reed challenges the "violent masculine ideals [that remain] central to articulations of the frontier myth."[61] For instance, when he confronts John Wesley Hardin, summoned from the dead by Drag Gibson, Loop does not kill him. The resurrection of Hardin is significant not only because he was a prolific murderer and famed gunslinger but also because his first murder was that of a former slave named "Maje," which began Hardin's life as an outlaw.[62] As Hardin rants about all the Black men he has killed, which by middle age "had become an obsession," "a white python fell from the chandelier and coiled itself around John Wesley Hardin, its ruby red tongue and eyes staring directly into the famous gunslinger's face."[63] The snake strangles Hardin, Drag Gibson's "last hope" until his "hair had turned completely white. His pupils were crosses."[64] This strangulation summons the history of racial violence and lynching, most often carried out using a noose. It also indicates Loop's hypersexuality: Loop literally overpowers Hardin with the symbol of his Black masculinity, which is a weird combination of his (male) gender and (female) sexuality. The white snake is an especially important figure as it represents Damballah, the loa Loop uses in his hoodoo rites, who is "the world itself, a serpent made round like the ouroboros of Gnosticism."[65] If the western is about man's struggle to contain savagery and nature, then Loop's reclamation of nature and the power it offers is a forceful contestation. In short, Loop simultaneously reclaims the symbol of racial violence (noose) and female sexual deviance (whip) in order to remake his Black masculinity. For the majority of the text, Loop does not confront his enemies directly but conquers them through conjure and their own paranoia alone in his mountainside cave. In other words, he chooses to "liberate through the force of imagination rather than firepower," a clear rejection of western masculine ideals and a technique Reed seems to employ in his own text.[66]

Another liminal figure who disrupts the western, even as a stock character, is Chief Showcase, a Native American man who is hypersexualized to demonstrate his kinship with Loop and their shared superiority over the white men in the novel. In an early critique of *Yellow Back Radio*, Madge Ambler compares Chief Showcase to Booker T. Washington, who was willing "to play one of the enemy against the other" and who "represents the particular people in the minority groups who live off the fat of the ruling class only to infiltrate and destroy them from within."[67] Chief Showcase not only rescues Loop but also demonstrates for him the power of duplicity, that the best way to attack the enemy is indirectly. "I'm trying the same thing on him he [the white man] put us through," Showcase explains. "Foment mischief among his tribes and they will destroy each other."[68] Part of this mischief involves pursuing the women of Yellow Back Radio. Like the Loop Garoo Kid, Chief Showcase is also depicted as hypersexual in an effort to establish his superior masculinity. When Drag sends his men to capture Loop after the cowboy disrupts Drag's wedding to Mustache Sal—who Robert Davis argues is a "very thinly disguised Mary Magdalene"—Showcase volunteers to stay with the women, "his arms outstretched [above them] and a slight grin on his face."[69] This action situates him in direct contrast to Drag, who cannot stand to have them present: "All of you women clear outta here you're bringing me down."[70] After Mustache Sal has an affair with Showcase, she thinks, "Something else, this Indian. . . . They ought to change his name to Chief Feelgood."[71] Showcase is also feminized through his love of fine things, such as French champagne, "imported hookahs, [French avant-garde fashion designer] Pierre Cardin originals, moccasins decorated with rhinestones, aqua-blue headdress, [and] world-wide aeroplane credit."[72] As he tells Loop, "We Crows are called the Beau Brummels of the Indians," a reference to an English dandy who lived a life of fashionable decadence.[73] Just as his helicopter "stirred up the sand so that Loop couldn't make out its dimensions," Chief Showcase's identity is equally perplexing.[74]

The male partnership that briefly forms between Loop and Showcase has roots in the twentieth-century western, which both hints at and simultaneously eschews homosexuality between cowboys. The name "The Loop Garoo Kid" echoes the western tradition of two male cowboys who, after some initial differences, become an inseparable pair. Although the archetypal image of the cowboy depicts him as a loner, in the space of westerns it is more often that while "the male hero may begin and end his quest alone . . . he often has male company along the way."⁷⁵ Showcase initially may seem to be the updated version of Tonto to Loop's Lone Ranger but acts more like a Sundance Kid to Loop's Butch Cassidy. Although they share similar agendas, rather than follow Loop as Tonto would, Showcase has his own plans. The two are immediate friends, with Showcase noting that "Indians and black people have been roaming the plains of America together for hundreds of years. . . . Dick Gregory represented our Washington tribes in their treaty fights" and "the Seminole fought invasion after invasion against the Fiend to protect black fugitive slaves."⁷⁶ Together they represent "a positive image of multiethnic unity."⁷⁷ However, the relationship between the two men comes perilously close to threatening their heterosexuality. The only contact Loop and Showcase can have after their initial meeting is through their shared sexual relationships with Mustache Sal. In this way, Mustache Sal is both a nontypical and a stereotypical character whose gender and sexuality is left in question. Accordingly, like the stereotypical homophobic cowboy, the only alternative is for Reed's heroes to use women for sex and to eschew intimacy.

Similarly, Buckner is paired throughout the main action of the story with Jim Braxton, his friend who dies while protecting Buckner. But unlike Loop and Showcase, Braxton is not Buckner's equal. Buckner is heir of landed gentry and thus holds implicit authority over his fellow white citizens, who look to him to avert the potential rebellion. Buckner describes Jim as "a tall, lanky man on an equally gaunt horse."⁷⁸ Braxton first appears just after Buckner's first encounter with the nameless Black woman. Buckner does not initially recognize Braxton, pointing a gun at his chest and almost firing before recognizing his friend. Later, in a daze brought on by the sight of the nameless Black woman, he strikes at Jim with his gun barrel, an insult to which Jim never even responds. Jim goes along with whatever Buckner orders except to turn back and save himself: "Go on, then; I'm with you, come heaven or hell," a fairly romantic statement of his loyalty, which proves fatal moments later when he is attacked by a river monster.⁷⁹ Braxton's value is not in his personality or skills but rather in his whiteness. When he first appears, Buckner sighs and thinks, "The sight of another white man had somewhat steadied my nerves."⁸⁰ The end of Howard's story fits genre conventions by having Buckner returned to his loner status: his friend is dead, and he has no wife to return home to. In a typical western, the story cannot end with the hero in the arms of a woman. Such an action would be read as a submission to domesticity, which lessens the cowboy's appeal that is based on male freedom and individualism. Instead, "loneliness is almost always resolved for the cowboy in the western by another cowboy and not by a woman."[81] However, Buckner's solitary existence is not a voluntary one. Instead, it is a forced exile brought about by his traumatic experience with the nameless Black woman. Like the typical cowboy, Buckner is usually a stoic man of few words, but because of the woman's curse his silence is compulsory. Even though he physically overcomes Stark, Buckner is psychologically damaged by his encounter. His failed masculinity undermines the authority granted to him by his race and class, leaving him isolated from his white community.

The white men in Reed's novel are likewise depicted as failed examples of masculinity, an apt reversal of racist white texts such as Howard's that deny humanity to Black and Indigenous characters. However, one troubling aspect of this ridicule that is often ignored by critics is Reed's treatment of homosexuality, which is depicted as pathological and deviant. Drag Gibson's character is the most disconcerting. He is coded as queer through his actions, such as when he "removed a tube from his pocket and applied it to his lips" and later "wiped smudges of mascara that showed above his batting lashes."[82] His name is significant because, as he conveniently explains, "Drag is not only nickname for the horseman who rides to the rear of the herd catching the dust, bringing up the stragglers and sick among the cattle but my name is also shorthand for something scaly, slimy and huge with dirt."[83] What he does not mention is that "drag" is also an obvious reference to the act of cross-dressing. Drag's homosexuality is paired with his failure to perform as a cowboy, the icon of the American West. Through a binary view of gender, that emasculation renders Drag a woman, a role he performs through dress and use of makeup. The gay or sexually deviant male characters featured in Reed's novel function as caricatures of the U.S. government, and their homosexuality is meant to highlight the degradation of the nation.[84] At the same time, these characters acknowledge the western as a site of queer desire, one that can be used to critique America's imperialist reliance on dominant masculinity. Yet this critique is never fulfilled since the narrative does not venture beyond this comedic intent.

One of these humorous events occurs as Reed shows that sexuality is intertwined with politics, coupling Drag's drag performance and pathological sexuality with his capitalist imperialist motives, disturbingly demonstrated in the scene in which he French kisses his beloved green mustang. Although this scene may seem inconsequential and mainly employed for the sake of humor, the horse is a figure one should pay close attention to in westerns, as Jane Tompkins argues. Since horses are ubiquitous in this genre, they are often overlooked; however, precisely "because of this strange invisibility they are the place where everything in the genre is hidden."[85] As Reed explains, "In a Western, the macho male hero always prefers his horse to women."[86] Drag Gibson is not meant to be a character at all but the personification of abstract ideas of capitalism. "That is an old tradition in Afro-American culture where abstract forces are referred to as though they are real or as if they were people."[87] The novel tells us that Drag's horse "served as a symbol for his streams of fish, his herds, his fruit so large they weighed down the mountains, black gold and diamonds which lay in untapped fields, and his barnyard overflowing with robust and erotic fowl."[88] The horse clearly embodies Drag's ownership of nature, which he exploits for his own gains, both sexually and materially. Drag's treatment of his horse is reminiscent of the way slaveholders sexually abused their slaves, an evil that was justified through the denial of a slave's humanity and their label as property, rendering them sexually available objects to be exploited at the owner's whim. Indeed, as Tompkins states, "The horse, like a colonized subject, makes a man a master."[89] The kiss displays Drag's complete dominance, which is essential to the stereotypical cowboy's identity. Reed weirds the figure of the horse, so essential to westerns, to signal the abuse of both African Americans and Native Americans through the figure of the corrupt gay cowboy. While his dominance and ruthless attitude make Drag hateful in the eyes of the audience, it is his supposedly degenerate sexuality that drives the nail home for Reed.

Tietchen argues that Reed's text erases and censures homosexuality like contemporary westerns in an attempted critique of Euro-American masculinity and mastery.[90] While this is partly true, not recognizing Reed's queer critique also erases the novel's more intricate critique of race and colonialism. Scholars have largely ignored Reed's queer critique, which prefigures scholarship on the gay cowboy but also casts homosexuality as a sign of degeneracy, corruption, and weakness. By portraying these white authority figures as queer and incompetent, the Loop Garoo Kid and Chief Showcase become virile and dominant characters who have overpowered the perverted and pathetic institutions of the U.S. government. At the same time, Reed acknowledges the queer bond between cowboys and makes them shockingly apparent. Likewise, Howard demonstrates the powerful influence Black women have in their communities, but rather than lauding this trait, he vilifies it as being a threat to the white male dominance espoused in the traditional western. In order to avoid a misidentification of Reed as a queer writer (or Howard as a feminist), it is better to view his novel from the perspective of the weird west. Such a weird reading is key since it allows for an examination of how race operates in Reed's novel, but it also makes space for considerations that are often obscured within westerns, mainly gender, sexuality, and queerness. As Tietchen writes, this "is one of the most important functions of the trickster: the trickster attempts to reveal the multiple dimensions essentialist models hope to deny."[91] Following Tietchen's definition, Reed is the ultimate trickster, but he is by no means the first—or the last. As Reed himself prophesizes in the text, "I wouldn't be surprised if bad medicine steals the patents and calls them his own. Honkie. Devil."[92] Reed highlights the racist assumptions that belie weird westerns like Howard's by wielding an African American and queer critique of the western and larger national narrative it often supports. However, in his attempt to legitimize Black men's experiences in the West, he ends up reifying the homophobic and sexist aspects that the majority of weird western fiction rarely questions and often supports.

Notes

1. Green, *Encyclopedia of Weird Westerns*.
2. Smith, "*Uncle Tom's Cabin* Showdown," 315.
3. See Davis, "Scattering the Myths"; Jaupaj, "'What If I Write Circuses'"; Johnson, *Black Masculinity*; Tietchen, "Cowboy Tricksters"; Schmitz, "Neo-HooDoo"; and Weixlmann, "African American Deconstruction."
4. Indick, "The Western Fiction of Robert E. Howard," 99; Shanks and Finn, "Vaqueros and Vampires in the Pulps," 3.
5. Unlike traditional fantasy fiction that preceded Howard, in sword and sorcery fiction "the supernatural element is often portrayed as unnatural—intruding into the story world and threatening the existing paradigm rather than being a

natural, inherent part of the world." Everett and Shanks, *The Unique Legacy of Weird Tales*, xv.
6. Shanks and Finn, "Vaqueros and Vampires," 10.
7. Shanks and Finn, "Vaqueros and Vampires," 19.
8. Howard quoted in Louinet, "Pigeons from . . . Bagwell," 4.
9. See "Black Canaan" in Howard, *Horror Stories*, 379.
10. Howard, *Horror Stories*, 379.
11. Howard, *Horror Stories*, 379.
12. Howard, *Horror Stories*, 384.
13. Howard, *Horror Stories*, 385.
14. Howard, *Horror Stories*, 395.
15. Reed, *Conversations*, 63.
16. Reed, *Conversations*, 63.
17. Reed, *Conversations*, 64.
18. Jaupaj, "'What If I Write Circuses,'" 45.
19. McVeigh, *The American Western*, 149.
20. Reed, *Conversations*, 37.
21. Fox, "Ishmael Reed," 345.
22. Fox, "Ishmael Reed," 345.
23. Tietchen, "Cowboy Tricksters," 332.
24. Reed, *Yellow Back Radio Broke-Down*, 10.
25. Reed, *Yellow Back Radio Broke-Down*, 14.
26. National Park Service, "Hoodoos."
27. Ellison, *Going to the Territory*, 131.
28. Tietchen, "Cowboy Tricksters," 339.
29. Folsom, *The American Western Novel*, 31.
30. Reed, *Yellow Back Radio Broke-Down*, 83.
31. Johnson, *Black Masculinity*, 10.
32. Reed, *Conversations*, 63–64.
33. Reed, *Conversations*, 139.
34. McVeigh, *The American Western*, 150.
35. Howard, "Black Canaan," 381.
36. Bordo, *Unbearable Weight*, 9.
37. Bordo, *Unbearable Weight*, 11.
38. Pilgrim, "The Jezebel Stereotype."
39. Chapman, "Rape Fantasies," 144.
40. Howard, "Black Canaan," 381.
41. Howard, "Black Canaan," 382.
42. Reed, *Yellow Back Radio Broke-Down*, 12; Davis, "Scattering the Myths," 413.
43. Reed, *Yellow Back Radio Broke-Down*, 92.

44. Reed, *Yellow Back Radio Broke-Down*, 93.
45. In typical westerns, Jack Halberstam explains, "a woman with a gun," and thus, power, "is either mad, bad, or a big old dyke." This formula holds true for *Yellow Back Radio Broke-Down*, whose female characters are not rendered as complexly as their male counterparts. Halberstam, "Not So Lonesome," 192; Reed, *Yellow Back Radio Broke-Down*, 93.
46. Reed, *Yellow Back Radio Broke-Down*, 9.
47. Reed, *Yellow Back Radio Broke-Down*, 93.
48. Reed, *Yellow Back Radio Broke-Down*, 11.
49. McGee, *Ishmael Reed and the Ends of Race*, 69.
50. McGee, *Ishmael Reed and the Ends of Race*, 69.
51. Martin, *Ishmael Reed*, 77.
52. Although there are key exceptions to this trend, the western, especially in Hollywood films, is not exactly a feminist utopia. As Jack Halberstam notes, women are typically ignored in favor of the seemingly less complicated male bond, which heightens the cowboys' displayed masculinity and maintains their status as nonconformists. Halberstam, "Not So Lonesome," 191.
53. Reed, *Conversations*, 63.
54. Reed, *Conjure*.
55. Johnson, *Black Masculinity*, 10.
56. McVeigh, *The American Western*, 151.
57. Halberstam, "Not So Lonesome," 191.
58. Halberstam, "Not So Lonesome," 192.
59. Reed, *Yellow Back Radio Broke-Down*, 51.
60. Meljac and Hunt, "Strange Country," 81.
61. Johnson, *Black Masculinity*, 10.
62. Parsons and Brown, *A Lawless Breed*, 16.
63. Reed, *Yellow Back Radio Broke-Down*, 116.
64. Reed, *Yellow Back Radio Broke-Down*, 117.
65. Tann, *Haitian Vodou*, 99. Another challenge Reed gives to white men's dominance is that white women, namely Mustache Sal, freely prefer the sexual company of Loop and Showcase over white men in the novel. Reed uses Sal's extraordinary sexual appetite to again shore up his characters' masculinities. In doing so, her sexual choices overturn the lie Black women such as Ida B. Wells exposed that often justified the lynching of Black men in the American South at the turn of the century.
66. Davis, "Scattering the Myths," 416.
67. Ambler, "Ishmael Reed," 127–28.
68. Reed, *Yellow Back Radio Broke-Down*, 40.
69. Davis, "Scattering the Myths," 412; Reed, *Yellow Back Radio Broke-Down*, 81.

70. Reed, *Yellow Back Radio Broke-Down*, 81.
71. Reed, *Yellow Back Radio Broke-Down*, 111.
72. Reed, *Yellow Back Radio Broke-Down*, 57.
73. Reed, *Yellow Back Radio Broke-Down*, 42.
74. Reed, *Yellow Back Radio Broke-Down*, 37.
75. Halberstam, "Not So Lonesome," 194.
76. Reed, *Yellow Back Radio Broke-Down*, 42.
77. Weixlmann, "African American Deconstruction," 59.
78. Howard, "Black Canaan," 395.
79. Howard, "Black Canaan," 402.
80. Howard, "Black Canaan," 396.
81. Halberstam "Not So Lonesome," 191.
82. Reed, *Yellow Back Radio Broke-Down*, 19, 22.
83. Reed, *Yellow Back Radio Broke-Down*, 47.
84. It is worthwhile to compare Drag Gibson to Percival Everett's George Armstrong Custer, who also dresses in "ladies unmistakables" in Everett's novel *God's Country*. Custer's depiction demonstrates the tension between homoeroticism and homophobia that exists within the western genre; after overcoming his surprise at the sight of Custer in women's underwear and makeup, the white narrator, Marder, notes that the colonel "didn't look half bad." However, this detail also serves as a humorous episode, resulting in Custer's further emasculation on the basis of his supposedly deviant sexuality. Everett, *God's Country*, 182.
85. Tompkins, *West of Everything*, 105.
86. Reed, *Conversations*, 181.
87. Reed, *Conversations*, 181.
88. Reed, *Yellow Back Radio Broke-Down*, 19.
89. Tompkins, *West of Everything*, 116.
90. Tietchen, "Cowboy Tricksters," 338–39.
91. Tietchen, "Cowboy Tricksters," 337.
92. Reed, *Conversations*, 39.

Bibliography

Abraham, Linus K. "The Black Woman as Marker of Hypersexuality in Western Mythology: A Contemporary Manifestation in the Film The Scarlet Letter." *Journal of Communication Inquiry* 26, no. 2 (2002): 193–214. https://doi.org/10.1177/0196859902026002005.

Ambler, Madge. "Ishmael Reed: Whose Radio Broke Down?" *Negro American Literature Forum* 6, no. 4 (1972): 125–31. https://doi.org/10.2307/3041201.

Bordo, Susan. *Unbearable Weight: Feminism, Western Culture, and the Body*. Berkeley: University of California Press, 1993.

Chapman, Erin D. "Rape Fantasies and Other Assaults: Black Women's Sexuality and Racial Redemption on Film." In *Black Female Sexualities*, edited by Trimiko Melancon, and Joanne M. Braxton, 141–58. Rutgers University Press, 2015.

Davis, Robert M. "Scattering the Myths: Ishmael Reed." *Arizona Quarterly* 39, no. 4 (Winter 1983): 406–20.

Ellison, Ralph. *Going to the Territory*. New York: Random House, 1986.

Everett, Justin, and Jeffrey H. Shanks, eds. *The Unique Legacy of Weird Tales: The Evolution of Modern Fantasy and Horror*. Lanham MD: Rowman & Littlefield, 2015.

Everett, Percival. *God's Country*. Boston: Faber & Faber, 1994. Reprint, Boston: Beacon, 2003.

Folsom, James K. *The American Western Novel*. New Haven: College and University Press, 1966.

Fox, Robert Elliot. "Ishmael Reed." In *The Oxford Companion to African American Literature*, edited by William Leake Andrews et al., 344–47. New York: Oxford University Press, 1997.

Halberstam, Jack. "Not So Lonesome Cowboys: The Queer Western." In *The Brokeback Book: From Story to Cultural Phenomenon*, edited by William R. Handley, 190–204. Lincoln: University of Nebraska Press, 2011.

Howard, Robert E. *The Horror Stories of Robert E. Howard*. New Canadian Library, 2015.

Indick, Ben P. "The Western Fiction of Robert E. Howard." In *The Dark Barbarian: The Writings of Robert E. Howard, a Critical Anthology*, edited by Don Herron, 99–116. Westport CT: Greenwood, 1984.

Jaupaj, Artur. "'What If I Write Circuses': Revisiting Novel Writing and Neo-Hoodoo Aesthetics in Ishmael Reed's *Yellow Back Radio Broke-Down*." *Journal of Black Studies* 45, no. 1 (2014): 37–58.

Johnson, Michael K. *Black Masculinity and the Frontier Myth in American Literature*. Norman: University of Oklahoma Press, 2002.

Johnson, Michael K., Rebecca M. Lush, and Sara L. Spurgeon. "Westworld(s): Race, Gender, Genre in the Weird Western." Introduction to *Weird Westerns: Race, Gender, Genre*, edited by Kerry Fine, Michael K. Johnson, Rebecca M. Lush, and Sara L. Spurgeon, 1–36. Lincoln: University of Nebraska Press, 2020.

Louinet, Patrice. "Pigeons from . . . Bagwell." *Dwelling in Dark Valley* (e-zine, Robert E. Howard Electronic Amateur Press Association) 1, no. 4 (2002). http://www.robert-e-howard.org/Louinet/dwelling4a.htm.

Martin, Reginald. *Ishmael Reed and the New Black Aesthetic Critics*. London: Macmillan, 1988.

McGee, Patrick. *Ishmael Reed and the Ends of Race*. New York: St. Martin's Press, 1997.

McVeigh, Stephen. *The American Western*. Edinburgh, UK: Edinburgh University Press, 2007.

Meljac, Eric, and Alex Hunt. "Strange Country: Sexuality and the Feminine in Robert Coover's *Ghost Town*." In *Weird Westerns: Race, Gender, Genre*, edited by Kerry Fine, Michael K. Johnson, Rebecca M. Lush, and Sara L. Spurgeon, 67–91. Lincoln: University of Nebraska Press, 2020.

National Park Service. "Hoodoos." National Park Service, U.S. Department of the Interior, November 8, 2014.

Packard, Chris. *Queer Cowboys: And Other Erotic Male Friendships in Nineteenth-Century American Literature*. New York: Palgrave Macmillan, 2005.

Parsons, Chuck, and Norman Wayne Brown. *A Lawless Breed: John Wesley Hardin, Texas Reconstruction, and Violence in the Wild West*. Denton: University of North Texas Press, 2013.

Pilgrim, David. "The Jezebel Stereotype." Jim Crow Museum, Ferris State University, 2012. https://www.ferris.edu/htmls/news/jimcrow/jezebel/index.htm.

Reed, Ishmael. *Conjure: Selected Poems, 1963–1970*. Amherst: University of Massachusetts Press, 1972.

———. *Conversations with Ishmael Reed*. Edited by Bruce Dick and Amritjit Singh. Jackson: University Press of Mississippi, 1995.

———. *Yellow Back Radio Broke-Down*. Normal IL: Dalkey Archive Press, 2000.

Schmitz, Neil. "Neo-HooDoo: The Experimental Fiction of Ishmael Reed." *Twentieth Century Literature* 20, no. 2 (1974): 126–40.

Shanks, Jeffrey, and Mark Finn. "Vaqueros and Vampires in the Pulps: Robert E. Howard and the Dawn of the Undead West." In *Undead in the West II: They Just Keep Coming*, edited by Cynthia J. Miller and A. Bowdoin Van Riper, 3–25. Lanham MD: Scarecrow, 2013.

Smith, Joshua D. "Uncle Tom's Cabin Showdown: Stowe, Tarantino, and the Minstrelsy of the Weird West." In *Weird Westerns: Race, Gender, Genre*, edited by Kerry Fine, Michael K. Johnson, Rebecca M. Lush, and Sara L. Spurgeon, 67–91. Lincoln: University of Nebraska Press, 2020.

Tann, Mambo Chita. *Haitian Vodou: An Introduction to Haiti's Indigenous Spiritual Tradition*. Woodbury MN: Llewellyn, 2012.

Tietchen, Todd F. "Cowboy Tricksters and Devilish Wangols: Ishmael Reed's HooDoo West." *Western American Literature* 36, no. 4 (2003): 325–42.

Tompkins, Jane P. *West of Everything: The Inner Life of Westerns*. Cary NC: Oxford University Press, 1993.

Weixlmann, Joe. "African American Deconstruction of the Novel in the Work of Ishmael Reed and Clarence Major." *Melus* 17, no. 4 (1991): 57–79.

PART 4

Coming Back to *Shane* to Redeem the Cyborg in *Soldier* and *Logan*

8

ELIZABETH ABELE

Shane (George Stevens, 1953) belongs to a group of post–World War II westerns that address the dehumanizing required for a man to be a "hero." In the decades since, *Shane* has continued to resonate in the popular imagination, not only for Shane's single-handed rescue of the Starrett family and their community but for his subsequent exile. As one example, *Shane*'s influence on director Clint Eastwood is clear from *High Plains Drifter* (1973), where the arrival and departure of the Drifter who saves the community mirror the opening and closing of *Shane*. In addition, his 1985 *Pale Rider* is an uncredited adaptation that transposes the conflict from big rancher/small farmers to big miner/prospectors. *Shane* also has influence beyond the western, particularly in films that are part of late twentieth-century questioning of ideal masculinity. For instance, in the action thriller *The Negotiator* (1988) Samuel L. Jackson's character names *Shane* as his favorite western—a choice that Kevin Spacey's character questions because the hero dies at the end. The debate over whether Shane dies at the end becomes a key question in *The Negotiator*—why do American men valorize tales that ask martyrdom (or at best exile) of their heroes?

Two films revisiting the landscape of *Shane* specifically explore the limitations and potential tragedy of the cyborg hero: the science fiction *Soldier* (Paul W. S. Anderson, 1998) and the superhero *Logan* (James Mangold, 2017). These films represent a significant revision and deepening of the classic western. In *Soldier*, Todd 3465 (Kurt Russell) belongs to a race of soldiers trained and molded from birth. Unfortunately, he and his kind have been replaced by a new breed of soldiers whose DNA is combined before conception, moving one more step from human to a manufactured man. *Logan* is the final chapter for the X-Man known as Wolverine (Hugh Jackman). Though a naturally born mutant like other X-Men, his violent potential was enhanced by the military, infusing his skeleton with a rare

177

metal. His identity as a soldier as well as his augmented body make him a perpetual outsider, even among mutants. *Logan* presents the most personal mission of the mutant previously known as Wolverine.

As *Shane* indirectly addressed the violent history of World War II veterans and Cold War operatives, *Soldier* and *Logan* reflect more contemporary concerns about the masculine conditioning restricting the full range of human connections, particularly for those called to "serve." Shane (Alan Ladd) arrives without warning at the Starrett farm, which may look to be the quiet homestead of Joe Starrett (Van Heflin), but actually the farm is at the crossroads of an ongoing war between an entrenched, all-male cattle enterprise and a new community of homesteading families. Shane longs for relationships with the Starretts that had been out of reach for a man with his history: friend, lover, father, neighbor. However, Todd was raised to not even be aware of the possibility of these relationships, only of his place within his squad as he was sent to wars, across planets. In his almost two hundred years, Logan has found himself in quasi-military bands or alone, since his attempts at intimate connections generally lead to death. Todd and Logan's training and violent past, even if in service to society, creates an obstacle to their being ever fully human, parallel to the obstacle that presents Shane from remaining on the Starrett farm.

In her 1985 "A Cyborg Manifesto: Science, Technology, and Social-Feminism in the Late Twentieth Century," Donna Haraway defines the cyborg as a hybrid of machine and organism, existing as a figure constructed within social reality as well as in fiction, with modern war "a cyborg orgy."[1] She further notes the cyborg's value for revealing societal contradictions fruitful for feminism, socialism, and materialistic analysis. Instead of seeing the cyborg as a super-being, Haraway presents him as less than a man.[2] Beginning in the 1990s, feminist cultural critics regularly documented the constraints that patriarchy and ideology had placed on men, constraints that had tightened with the growth of industry and technology.[3]

Appearing just before Haraway's essay, the film *Blade Runner* (Ridley Scott, 1982), cowritten by *Soldier*'s screenwriter David Webb Peoples, portrays cyborgs manufactured by Tyrell Corporation—Replicants—who are desperately fighting for their humanity and their lives. This film dramatizes many of the issues within Haraway's essay: society has no appreciation for the Replicants' service, commissioning blade runners to assassinate them. Peoples wrote *Soldier* as a sidequel to *Blade Runner*, with the Replicants and the Adam Project Soldiers as parallel projects created by the same military-industrial complex. The Transigen Corporation in *Logan* replicates the work of Tyrell Corporation in their mission to create cyborg-soldiers that deliberately reduce the human element.

This essay will place *Soldier* and *Logan* as films building on *Shane*'s longing for human connection. These two films likewise connect to other late twentieth-century science fiction films featuring cyborgs who attempt to reclaim their human desires. As Haraway describes, "But basically, machines were not self-moving, self-designing, autonomous. They could not achieve man's dream, only mock it."[4] Despite the enhanced abilities of these men in service, these cyborg heroes seek the autonomy to dream of a life worth living. *Soldier* and *Logan* combine the landscapes of the western *Shane* and the sci-fi cyborg film, placed firmly within the context of a reexamination of the sacrifices required of "ideal" men. As *Soldier* expands the dystopia of *Blade Runner*, *Logan* disrupts the assumptions of the X-Men multiverse. While *Soldier* intentionally promotes a better model of masculinity for both those in service and their served community, *Logan* allows its weary protagonist a rest, making way for a fresh start for the next generation. These films engage in the ongoing conversation about contemporary American masculinity, including the threat of military-industrial manipulation.

The American Isolate Killer

The central question of *Shane* is the community's ambivalent relationship to the killer: though the community cannot survive without his expertise, his presence disturbs their foundation. Critics have noted Alan Ladd's conflicting qualities: "[His] calm slender ferocity make[s] it clear that he was the first American actor to show the killer as a cold angel."[5] Not coincidentally, this description connects to D. H. Lawrence's overview of American literature: "The essential American soul is hard, isolate, stoic, and a killer. It has never yet melted." This split between the heroic killer and the hearth is not unique to the western but is foundational to the American literary tradition. In *Love and Death in the American Novel*, Leslie Fiedler details this sharp divide in the American tradition between the lone heroic man and the family man—a divide that does not occur in the British literary tradition. Among his examples is James Fenimore Cooper's Natty Bumppo, who through five novels never kissed a woman.

Natty's sexuality and humanity is particularly relevant as the progenitor of the western hero, a man who is one with the landscape, with no permanent home or community. Fiedler describes Natty's particular sexuality: "The virility of Natty is heroic not genital and cannot survive in marriage anymore than in the hearth." However, "the forest breeds an equally tender passion between males."[6] In this construction of ideal American manhood, marriage is an emasculation: homosocial companionship within a wild landscape is the only appropriate love for a true man.

The American heroic path has commonly required the absence (or repression) of heterosexual desire—a desire that is removed by training, in service of the patriarchy and nation-building. In *Between Men*, Eve Kosofsky Sedgwick confirms that patriarchy depends on the solidarity of men and the exclusion of women, occurring on the continuum of male homosocial and homosexual bonds. This fine line between homosocial and sublimated homosexuality remains a question in these all-male units that deliberately exclude or undermine any heterosexual ties that could interfere with their mission.

Further connecting Natty Bumppo to this discussion of cyborg heroes is that among his nicknames is not only "Hawkeye" but, just as importantly, "La Longue Carabine." Though Natty is an eighteenth-century character, he is likewise a cyborg, a man known for his enhanced parts—his trained eye and his rifle—that make him deadly. Though Shane may rise out of the landscape on his horse, his entry into the narrative is defined by the gun on his hip. As Joey is pretending to hunt a deer, Shane appears in his view. Joey asks if he knows how to shoot before he asks Shane his name or any other personal detail. Though the western represents a less technological period, gunfighters like Shane function as cyborgs, with their identities inseparable from their revolvers. And like contemporary cyborgs, their perfection is merely a caricature of masculinity, without the complexity allowed to husbands, fathers, sons, or lovers.

When Ryker and his men arrive to threaten Starrett, the visibility of Shane's gun and his confident lean are enough for them to retreat; all he has to say is, "I am a friend of Starrett." Without firing a shot, he is marked as a gunfighter. However, his training is not without costs. Shane lives at constant attention. In the opening scenes, he jumps twice at the sound of metal behind him, preparing to draw on Joey and a calf. As a gunfighter, his life is always in peril. At the same time, friends and foes expect him to fight, even if he'd prefer to be a farmhand. Even Joey prefers to see Shane wearing a gun, feeling that it is a part of who he is—"It goes with him"—while not caring whether his father chooses to wear a gun.

Yet instead of his fusion with his gun making a gunfighter like Bumppo or Shane more than a man, it actually points to what he lacks, in regard to both his sexuality and fertility. Amanda Fernbach describes the irony of the cyborgs "who exhibit an array of technoparts in order to define a new technomasculinity. Like the fantasy of the fetishized woman, the fantasy of the technoman also disavows lack, although male rather than female lack is disavowed by these technoprosthetic fetishes."[7] Joey represents the son that Shane cannot produce.

Soldier's Todd has a technomasculinity that goes beyond a gun, with his mind constrained and body augmented. To prepare for the film, Kurt Russell trained three to four hours per day for eighteen months.[8] Russell's temporarily enhanced body was needed to emulate Todd's artificial training from birth. Despite Todd's hypermasculinity, as demonstrated by his body and operation as a killing machine, his body is "masking male lack with phallic prosthetics."[9] Todd and the other *Soldier*'s bodies are displayed and objectified in their excess, but their ability to kill masks their sexual and emotional impotence. Not coincidentally, *Shane* was more recently integrated into *Logan*, another film with a cyborg protagonist. This film marks the obsolescence of the X-Men, specifically Logan/Wolverine, the mutant whose memory and humanity were erased by the military when they augmented his claws; his phallic prosthetics are for killing only. The daughter that Logan protects was fertilized and incubated in a laboratory—asexual reproduction. Their impotence is essential to keeping them on mission, disentangled from women or children.

The implied castration of these protagonists may be easy to overlook since it is functional and not literal. Since the castration of American heroes is gradual and invisible, it evokes neither outrage nor pity for these men who are expected to serve—who appear content to live and die alone and unloved. As Haraway explains, "[The cyborgs] were not man, an author to himself, but only a caricature of that masculinist reproductive dream."[10] Though these alterations may not be visible, that does not make them any less traumatic—as demonstrated by Shane and other reluctant cyborg heroes.

Shane as the Beloved American Killing Machine

These sci-fi westerns deliberately built their new myths on *Shane* (1953), an American touchstone that reverberates as much as little Joey's call: "Shane—come back, Shane!" But what has repeatedly drawn people to *Shane* is the mutual longing in the call—that Shane wants more than anything to come back. Despite Shane being this ideal man that everyone immediately admires, he at the same time epitomizes the limits of the American hero, who is destined for exile without reward. *Shane*'s significance is documented by its appearance on numerous American Film Institute top one hundred lists, including its position as number three on AFI's top ten westerns, just behind *The Searchers* (1956) and *High Noon* (1952).[11]

Though Shane is immediately recognized as a fighter, Joe Starrett invites Shane to stay and work on the farm, allowing Shane to put up his gun and his buckskin, buying new clothes for his role working for Starrett. Starrett provides a different heroic model, worthy of Shane's service. He is a beloved father and husband, as well as the leader of this community. Starrett's commitment and passion consistently inspire his neighbors to hold on to their homesteads, standing up against the cattleman Ryker and his men. Joe and Shane quickly bond, recognizing the values that they share—courage, conviction, loyalty, and tenderness—but their different pasts dictate the divergent roles that they must play in facing Ryker.

However, instead of the film directly celebrating the bond between Shane and Starrett, it is Shane's attraction to Marian (Jean Arthur) that is constantly assumed—by Ryker, Starrett, and Marian herself. However, Shane never confirms it. When Marian asks if he is facing Ryker for her, he responds yes—but quickly adds that he is doing it for Starrett and Joey as well. Despite the heteronormative assumptions, Shane's most consistent connection is to Joey and his father. This connects to Sedgwick's observing in literature of the "use of women as . . . cementing the bonds of men with men."[12] Shane admires Starrett and sees his life as something worth having—with Marian part of that. Likewise, instead of Starrett being jealous of Shane, the fact that Shane could replace him as Marian's husband emboldens him to face Ryker.

Shane and Starrett's connection is profound and mutual. Jesse Gerlach Ulmer describes Joe Starrett's link to Shane when he invites him to supper: "There is something rather mystical about this scene, as if there exists a kind of supernatural bond between Shane and Joe. Nevertheless, their communication is expressed, and interpersonal alignment is established, through nonverbal means."[13] Starrett consistently sees Shane as a man and his friend, not just a gunfighter.

Second only to his bond with Starrett is Shane's bond with Joey. Joey's eyes watch Shane from the beginning; it is through his eyes that Shane performs. The dream of a son may have a stronger pull for Shane than that of a woman. He compliments the bashful boy for watching him: "I like a man who keeps his eye on things." To avoid disappointing Joey, Shane does not walk away from Ryker's men when they confront him the second time. However, Shane is cautious in teaching Joey to shoot. Though it is certain to cement the boy's regard for him, Shane wants more for the boy than his lonely path.

Echoing Fiedler, Susan Faludi observes that a wanderer like Natty or Shane is seen as "an emblem of virility." Yet "his heaps of dead pelts are the equivalent of the tycoon's consolidated fortunes, his killer instincts compensating for his service to the community."[14] Shane cannot point to pelts; the number of dead men on his conscience is his burden, his "brand." Daniel Worden describes the "obsolete cowpuncher or gunfighter who lives in no particular place and has no particular home"; Ryker and his men are as obsolete as Shane.[15] Significantly, Ryker's men seem to have little interest in women (no brothels or saloon girls around). Yet the cowpunchers at least enjoy each other's company, while the hired gun Jack Wilson (Jack Palance) keeps himself apart from even that fellowship. Jack Wilson is the epitome of the glittering, stone-cold killer who takes pleasure in cruelty—perhaps the man Shane was.

Shane also resembles Wilson in his use of language. In her work on westerns, Jane Tompkins notes, "For the really strong man, language is a snare. It blunts his purpose and diminishes his strength." She points to Shane as a prime example of the minimalist language that western heroes speak, "a desperate shorthand, comic, really, in its attempt to communicate without using words."[16] Ulmer confirms that this renunciation of language in Hollywood characters like Shane and the Virginian is "exploitative of self and others."[17] This paucity of language even extends to his name. Jack Wilson is allowed two names, as are Ryker's men. Only Shane has been linguistically reduced to one syllable, with no Christian name. His name and language reflect Shane's emotional constraints.

Soldier: Turning Men into Killing Machines

Soldier and *Logan* combine the classic narrative of *Shane* with the questions raised by late twentieth-century cyborg films: the more overt genetic source for *Soldier* is *Blade Runner*. *Blade Runner* was the most critically acclaimed 1980s cyborg film, with screenwriter Peoples placing *Soldier* within the same universe. Roy Batty (Rutger Hauer) and Todd were crafted by their common military-industrial complex quite differently—while Todd was molded after biological birth, the Replicants were fully designed and manufactured by Tyrell Industries. The Replicants and Soldiers are both replaceable commodities; as Harraway foresees, they are "bodies as commodities in its capitalist dystopia."[18] As commodities, their life or death is of little concern to their "owners"—who, as Batty notes, control them through fear.

Action films with protagonists who are cyborgs—men created or altered through technology—continued as a significant strain throughout the 1990s in films like *RoboCop* (Paul Verhoeven, 1987), *Total Recall* (Paul Verhoeven, 1990), *Face/Off* (John Woo, 1997), and *Gattaca* (Andrew Niccol, 1999).[19] Significantly, instead of these films problematizing the cyborg—the manufactured identity—these male protagonists ultimately find that embracing their hybrid selves is more satisfying than "natural" masculinity. Not coincidentally, Logan/Wolverine first appeared at this time in *X-Men* (Bryan Singer, 2000). Working within the context of a diverse team regularly challenged his hyper (white) masculinity, challenging him, like the 1990s cyborg heroes, to reclaim his humanity.

While the dynamics of *Shane* and cyborg narratives come together in *Soldier*, the film presents more optimistic resolution than the western, offering hope for contemporary men. While the first twenty minutes of *Soldier* document the deliberately dehumanizing/desexualizing process from Todd's birth to his disposal, the larger portion of the film evokes the western setting and mythology, allowing an opportunity for redemption *within* the community.

Soldier opens with infants crying in a sterile hospital nursery, where Todd is designated as "1A" and wheeled away. There is no *in loco parentis* offering this child comfort, only armed guards who deliver the infant to the Adam Project. This opening demonstrates Haraway's description of cyborgs as "the illegitimate offspring of militarism and patriarchal capitalism, not to mention state socialism."[20] The Adam Project hubristically creates a new breed of men, without the companionship of Eves. Their training goal is for Todd to perform "as a machine," removing any human reaction that could impede him from seeing everything and everyone as an object to be eliminated.[21]

Part of this conditioning is through directives spoken by a female voice on a loop: "Soldiers do not speak unless first spoken to by a superior officer. A Soldier shows no weakness; mercy is weakness and weakness is death. A Soldier likes to follow orders. A Soldier likes to kill. A Soldier needs no friends or family: war is his friend; the Forces are his family." This training deliberately stripped Todd and other Soldiers of anything that made them other than killing machines: their speech, their emotions, their connections, and their sexuality. At the end of the training, Todd and his squad are shown in a series of global and interplanetary conflicts. This is summed up with Todd 3465's record, with his confirmed and unconfirmed kills tallied for each mission. His life is his kills (his pelts).

The emotional desolation required of Soldiers is illustrated in the scene "Year 40: Between Wars." Traditional war films celebrate the homosocial fun of platoons between engagements. The Ryker men likewise enjoyed each other's company with cards or rowdy behavior. However, these Soldiers sit at attention on their cots, with no banter or shared activity, merely awaiting their next order. Despite the training tape's promise that "the Forces are your family," the squad offers no camaraderie or comfort.

As with the obsolescence of the gunfighter and cowpuncher, the Adam Project Soldiers also face obsolescence, with a "new batch" that is not only younger but "practically manufactured" through DNA profiles and recombination. These new Soldiers were created before birth: "The most promising monsters in cyborg worlds are embodied in non-oedipal narratives with a different logic of repression."[22] To prove the superiority of the new Soldiers, despite their lack of experience, their best Caine 607 (Jason Scott Lee) competes with Todd 3465. Finally, Caine is charged to take out Todd and two other Soldiers, killing two and besting Todd. However, Todd removes Caine's eye first—so though Caine escapes being discarded like Todd, he is humiliated and demoted for being less than perfect. Colonel Mekum (Jason Isaacs) yells, "You moron. Do you know how much it cost to breed you, to feed you, to train you? What good is this man now!" The Old Ones and the new Soldiers are equally commodities, only of value in perfect condition. As with the Replicants, there is no reward for their service and sacrifice.

As in a western, the focus shifts to a frontier community caught in the crossfire of these power brokers. As Shane emerged from the landscape, Todd rises from the trash heap: Arcadia 234 Waste Disposal Planet. He drags himself through the barren wilderness of this planet, stumbling through a graveyard to the communal settlement, established after their ship crashed. As *Shane*'s homesteaders could not get the attention of the U.S. marshal, these settlers have been ignored by the ships passing above. Yet the Arcadians demonstrate the ingenuity, the grit, and the democracy consistent with the best impulses of the western. Despite their crash landing and their planet's use as a dump site, there remains an optimism—they aspire to the name Arcadia, creating a place of innocence and simple pleasure. The Arcadians demonstrate frontier ingenuity, creatively repurposing the items dumped as they tend their gardens and raise their children.

It is significant that Shane's attempt at redemption ends with his exit through the cemetery—while Todd crosses a graveyard to find Arcadia and a new life, no longer a Soldier. Lee Clark Mitchell notes the centrality of cemeteries in the western, cementing the link between the landscape and death, with "the process of bodies being returned to their source."[23] If, as Mitchell posits, the western is about the process of making men, *Soldier* documents both the making and unmaking of Todd as a Soldier—as well as his rebirth as a man and human: "The process of beating occurs so that we can see men recover, regaining their strength and resources in the process of once again making themselves into men."[24]

Overall, Todd is unprepared for being part of a community, let alone a family. Mace (Sean Pertwee) and Sandra (Connie Nielsen) agree to take in the wounded Soldier. Todd is disturbed by the sound of them horseplaying and laughing with their son Nathan (Jared Thorne): "The cyborg does not dream of community on the model of the organic family. . . . The cyborg would not recognize the Garden of Eden."[25] Unlike Shane, Todd is more connected to Sandra than Mace. As Todd recuperates, his body is on display for her. Mitchell describes the common scenes of convalescence in the western as "watching [the male body] recover under a woman's gaze."[26] Not only does she see his well-developed physique, she also notes the words tattooed on his body. Mace reads the markings for Sandra, explaining that they are the names of military campaigns—another sign that his body is not his own. Yet when Todd looks at Sandra, it is not an objectifying gaze at her body but a look of puzzlement for her different way of being. Likewise, Sandra looks to Todd with more compassion than desire.

Overall, and unlike Marian, Sandra tries to understand Todd without judgment. She asks what he is thinking, what he is feeling:

TODD: Fear. Fear and discipline.
SANDRA: Even now?
TODD: Always.
SANDRA: Oh, my God.

When she hugs him, he remains stiff. Not only is he unable to feel sexual feelings for her, but he cannot accept her comfort—fear and discipline keep him separate. But he recognizes the family as a unit that he is now bound to serve.

The landscape of Arcadia differs significantly from the open ranges of the western. Instead of beautiful vistas, the planet has violent windstorms and lethal snakes. Their richest resources are not fields but dumps. This physical barrenness shifts the focus of the film from the impersonal to the "landscape" of the community itself. The lyrics of the song "The Night Ride Across the Caucasus" may describe a forest landscape, but it plays over a montage of Todd watching Sandra with her family. Todd's unexplored landscape is their intimacy and her kindness—as his gaze is learning to *subjectify*, to see human beings.

While women may be tangential to Ryker or to Shane, women are central to Todd's conditioning as well as his reprogramming. Though no women are visible within the Adam Project, the voice on the tape is female—the closest thing Todd knows as a mother. Though Mace is an advocate for Todd, it is Sandra who nurses him back to health and introduces him to the household chores. However, Todd's emotional development has been stunted, presexual. It is unclear whether he really understands the difference between genders, as he only refers to Sandra as "sir," a superior.

Likewise, he does not recognize the other men on Arcadia as like himself—as non-Soldiers, it does not occur to him to bond with them any more than with the female citizens. As he may be incapable of sexual desire for Sandra, he is equally incapable of a homosocial bond with Mace or the other Arcadian men, despite their extended arms. Todd may work alongside them but not truly with them.

However, like Shane, Todd is touched by the overtures of the boy, Nathan. Nathan gives Todd his puzzle, a prized possession that has nothing to do with Todd's fighting ability. Yet Todd does not want to make Nathan a Soldier—he only wants to keep him safe. Nathan is mute because he was stung by the poisonous snake that is common on Arcadia.[27] When Nathan sees a snake, Todd silently instructs Nathan to pick up a boot and crush it. When the boy hesitates and the snake springs, Todd catches it and throws it down—giving Nathan a second try at the snake. Mace intervenes, killing the snake with a hoe, yelling at Todd for endangering his son. Mace does not see the care in Todd's action, an act of love that is an important step for Todd. Unlike Shane, Todd does not train Nathan to be like him, just to be safe.

Several incidents lead Mace and the community to distrust Todd's ability to be a part of the community. As the community votes to exile Todd, Mace confesses his own doubts to Sandra, expressing his fear not just of Todd's strength but also of his apparent lack of emotion. Their leader echoes Haraway: "Because of your training, we do not believe that you can function in a community of families, of children, where the ability to fight is not the sole point of existence." Todd previously admitted to an Arcadian that he had been replaced "by a better Soldier." But it is being exiled from the community that leads Todd to shed his first adult tears. Though Todd's adjustment to community and caring is too slow and subtle to be obvious, this is a major step for him.

However, Todd's ability to fight has value when Colonel Mekum chooses Arcadia 234 to train his new Soldiers, since they are still "Between Wars."

He asserts that any civilians they may encounter are by definition "hostiles" since they are not there legally. (Ryker likewise ignored homesteading claims that interfered with his plans.) When Nathan saves his sleeping parents by killing a snake with a boot, Mace realizes that they voted wrong—that Todd can contribute to their lives. As he goes to bring Todd back, Mace is the first "hostile" killed. His dying words are for the safety of Sandra and Nathan, an order that Todd can follow.

Todd demonstrates that his connection to a community has actually made him a better fighter. In addition, Todd has combat experience, as well as specific understanding of the squad's methods. Even with Mace dead, his relationship with Sandra becomes no more sexually charged, more a heterosocial partnership. Sandra takes responsibility for managing the civilians while he systematically eliminates the new Soldiers. The last Soldier standing is Caine. What may give Todd the edge this time is that he is fighting for his community, not just out of fear. Todd's comrades, the Old Ones, are also on this mission as unarmed stewards. When they see the victorious Todd, they salute and follow him to take over the ship, grateful to be given an order again. Todd's victory is tied to both his homosocial and his community relationships.

Mekum's warship now becomes the Arcadians' ark to the Trinity Moons—their destination before the crash. Todd's reunion is not with Sandra but with Nathan, who signals for Todd to pick him up. As the retired Soldiers watch this intimacy with surprise, Todd holds Nathan as he monitors the ship's progress to their new frontier. As they ride together "into the sunset," to a worthy landscape, the Arcadians can hope for a better future. However, unlike *Shane*'s exclusion of alternate masculinities, the Arcadians' new settlement will include Todd and the Adam Project veterans. Rather than an exile or a martyr, Todd is now a member of the community and perhaps a father. While Shane told Joey that there was no coming back from the killing, these Soldiers are offered hope that they can recover their humanity and ability to connect in their new home.

Logan: Finding an Ending to Create a Future

The landscape and tone of *Logan* are markedly different from the previous films of the X-Men universe. Instead of the verdant northeast of Xavier's School for Gifted Children or the Canadian wilderness (Wolverine's preferred retreat), this is the dry, brown west of New Mexico and Mexico in the near future of 2029—a landscape reminiscent of an indie western. While *Logan* is structured less overtly like *Shane* than *Soldier*, the referents serve as a foundation for the finale of Charles Xavier (Patrick Stewart) and Logan (the last of the X-Men). Geoff Klock and Mitch Montgomery argue that this narrative "evolves by aggressively making space for itself, by being critical of the tradition that it participates in and thus justifies its own existence."[28] Instead of enjoying the rewards of their years of service, Charles and Logan are obsolete and in exile—a status that critiques both the western and superhero traditions.

Logan was to be the end of the character Logan/Wolverine, who appeared on-screen as an ensemble member in *X-Men* films and the protagonist in two previous films: *X-Men Origins: Wolverine* (Gavin Hood, 2009) and *The Wolverine* (James Mangold, 2013). Details on Logan have varied across these films, which Mangold addresses directly, giving him the space to craft this narrative. While strangers may call him "Wolverine," it is no longer a name he answers to, as he disavows any allusion to his past exploits: "Maybe a quarter of it happened, and not like this."

Logan shares key qualities with Shane, Todd, and other cyborg heroes. Like Shane, he has one ambiguous name.[29] He has no history before joining the X-Men, having lost his memory at the time of his enhancement. As in *Soldier* and *RoboCop*, his body was claimed as government property, leaving him little agency in its augmentation or deployment. Like Todd, he identifies as a soldier, long after his years of service have ended, with his dog tags regularly featured.[30] As often as Logan gives them away or discards them, they always come back: he fingers his dog tags early in *Logan*. His unconsummated love for the married Jean Grey (Famke Janssen) resembles Shane's dance with Marian, with his emotional recovery tied more to his mentorship of younger mutants.

While other mutants dealt with psychological pain from their mutation, Logan is the only one whose mutation causes him physical pain. In the first *X-Men* film, Rogue (Anna Paquin) asks him if the extension of his claws (through his skin) causes him pain; he replies, "Every time." While the focus is on Logan's incredible capacity to heal, this diminishes his even greater capacity for pain—his healing merely sets him up to be injured again. Prometheus similarly healed every time the eagles ate his liver, yet

Prometheus's cycle of healing and injury is recognized as torture. As Todd lives with constant fear, Logan's lot is pain.[31] Perhaps the ambiguity of Shane's death is that even if he literally survives, he will have no life. While Shane at least has the potential release of death, Logan cannot even count on that—Mangold includes Logan's suicide ideation in *The Wolverine* and *Logan* as his only way out. In both instances, duty prevents Logan's exit.

Unlike Shane and Todd, Wolverine finds little comfort in homosocial partnerships. For more than a century, he fought side by side with his brother Victor (Sabretooth), but he found Victor's more bestial nature repulsive. Once he joined the X-Men, he partnered with women or younger recruits more often than male X-Men—in between long stretches on his own. Though Logan demonstrates a capacity for sexual and emotional connections, he chooses a celibate and isolated life because he has too often witnessed the deaths of people that he tried to get close to.

Logan's filial relationship with Charles Xavier most separates him from these other weary fighters; his commitment to Charles drives Logan's choices in this chapter. Though Mangold references *Shane* at several points in this film, Klock and Montgomery note the film also connects to *Julius Caesar* and *The Aeneid*, in particular Aeneas transporting his father and child from a destroyed past "to find a new home, to find a new future."[32] Significantly Logan is approached in a cemetery to take on the mission of transporting a girl, Laura (Dafne Keen). Charles reads telepathically that not only is Laura a mutant, but she is also Logan's daughter. With the long absence of newly born mutants, Charles sees Laura's arrival as their awaited blessing.

Todd's conditioning in a controlled environment is echoed in *Logan* by the birth and childhood of Laura. However, as with Caine's cohort, her conception occurred in vitro, with DNA stolen from Logan. Yet the upbringing of Laura and the X-23 children did not even have the trappings of the Adam Project's military school, as the X-23 were confined to a laboratory where their "development" was monitored, never seeing the sun. Though the scientists blamed the children for their failure to become soldiers, the video that Logan watches reveals their inadequate training: only the nurses provided any human interaction and guidance (and that against orders). Smuggled out by a nurse, Laura is being tracked by Transigen to recover their "property." But with adamantine hand and feet claws, and no moral compass, Laura is even more lethal than her father—particularly now that Logan is suffering from the long-term effects of adamantine poisoning, a manifestation of the toxicity of his hypermasculinity.

Though Laura is more cyborg than her father, *Logan* presents an even more extreme example of the manufactured soldier. After their disappointment with X-23, Transigen moved to X-24: a complete clone of Wolverine, engineered to have all the rage but none of his humanity. As in 1980s cyborg films, *Logan* presents "a deep-set anxiety with the corporatization of this creation and the cancerous nature of the capitalist corporations."[33] In addition, Laura and X-24 both represent a theft from Logan, reinforcing the lack of control he has over his body.

As the movie opens with a general western setting, Transigen and their mercenaries add the conflict of corrupt capitalists like Ryker. Their initial showdown is followed by a western trek by Logan, Charles, and Laura—though technically moving east through Las Vegas to North Dakota. Supposedly, North Dakota is the site of Eden for the escaped mutant children, a mission that Charles insists that Logan fulfill. *Shane* is directly introduced as they stop at a hotel in Vegas. Charles watches *Shane* with Laura, explaining its significance to her. She watches not only the violence of Wilson and Shane but the gathering of the community surrounded by a mountain vista as they mourn their neighbor. She later listens intently to Shane's final words to Joey.

The next echoing of *Shane* comes when the trio is invited to the Munson farm. As they sit around the family table, Charles remarks to Logan, "This is what a family looks like. A home, people who love each other. A safe place." Despite his years at the Xavier School, Charles implies that Logan has never experienced this. After this meal that mirrors Marian's hospitality, Logan joins Will Munson (Eriq LaSalle) in restoring their water supply. When Munson is challenged by workers from the surrounding Canewood Beverage cornfields, Logan comes to his aid (as Shane supported Ryker). Unfortunately, breaking the *Shane* parallel is the arrival of Logan's double, X-24, who meets Canewood's reinforcements, killing not only them but also the Munson family and Charles. Logan's past not only prevents him from being a part of a family (even for one night) but bars him from being their protector; because of Logan, the Munson home was no longer "a safe place."

Yet despite their heavy losses, their trek to North Dakota is not in vain: Laura is reunited with her X-23 friends. From the beginning, the stakes of this film differ from other X-Men narratives, as Logan strives to protect "characters, not the fates of universes."[34] Yet Laura is not the innocent that Joey was, since Laura has killed like Logan:

> LOGAN: You're gonna have to learn to live with it.
> LAURA: They were bad people.
> LOGAN: All the same.

Unlike Joey or Nathan, Logan does not have to teach Laura to protect herself, just how to move away from the violence. Logan's final battle with Transigen and X-24 is to ensure the resettlement of the mutant children—a heterogenous community, male and female, of different abilities and races. Their showdown parallels both the one between Shane and the soulless Wilson, and the one between Todd and the upgraded model, Caine. Logan again demonstrates the advantage in fighting for someone and for a future. However, making this battle distinct is that Logan does not fight alone but collaboratively with Laura—as the other children dispatch the remaining Transigen operatives. Before the children leave to cross the Canadian border, Logan advises Laura, "Don't be what they made you"—referring both to Transigen's manufacture and her training to kill.

At the end of the film, Laura eulogizes Logan with Shane's final speech to Joey. But when she recites, "There's no living with a killing. There's no going back from one. Right or wrong, it's a brand. A brand that sticks," she is acknowledging that the X-23 likewise carry the brand. However, they can choose to go forward, going to a valley without violence and a different future—the same hope as the Adam Project veterans. For Logan, his pain is finally at an end, and he is mourned. Logan connects with Shane as he fully recognizes the limits and costs of his hypermasculinity, making it clear this is not a path to emulate.

Conclusion

Shane was released during a period of U.S. prosperity and peace, with returning World War II and Korean soldiers expected to return to their communities, forgetting their violent history. Joey unproblematically admires Shane's status as a gunfighter, mourning his exile—an exile that

Marian and Joe Starrett accept so that there will be "no more guns in the valley." However, the events of the 1960s shifted American awareness of the cost of serving one's country—in particular, as a soldier.

Todd and Logan's military service went beyond normal enlistment: Todd was "drafted" at birth; Logan served more than one hundred years and had his body modified by the military. Even after Logan left military service, he was recruited to the quasi-military X-Men as Wolverine. Though *Soldier*'s Todd is programmed with the same emotional and sexual constraints imposed on Shane (and other western heroes), he ultimately rejects them for the benefit of his community and himself. Since Logan serves without Todd's imposed restraints, he must live with the constant pain of separating himself from intimate relationships—in parallel to the constant pain of extending his claws and being shot. Yet he can assure the release of his daughter from a life of violent service.

Throughout American literature and popular culture, narratives valorize heroic protagonists as essential to the flourishing of communities and their children. Yet their service does not earn them a place at these hearths. Instead, their well-trained bodies present a barrier to emotional wholeness. Peter Lehman connected these fictional heroes to late twentieth-century men: "Men under patriarchy are not just empowered by their penis-phallus; they are also profoundly alienated from their own bodies, which are lost beneath its monstrosity."[35] In *Soldier*, Todd slowly awakens to life beyond fear and orders, leaving behind the programming that enslaved him. Logan battles with X-24 and Transigen to assure that the X-23 children—including his daughter—will not be lost beneath their lab-created monstrosity. *Soldier* and *Logan* do not offer an easy recovery for technomen, but these films provide hope of a new Arcadia or a new Eden—as a western should.

Notes

1. Haraway, "A Cyborg Manifesto," 6.
2. Haraway, "A Cyborg Manifesto," 11.
3. *Running Scared* (1992) by Peter Lehman; *Hard Bodies: Hollywood Masculinity in the American Era* (1993) by Susan Jeffords; *Manhood in America: A Cultural History* (1996) by Michael Kimmel; *Stiffed: The Betrayal of the American Man* (1999) by Susan Faludi.

4. Haraway, "A Cyborg Manifesto," 11.
5. "Alan Ladd," TCM, www.tcm.com/tcmdb/person/1122096%7c8828/Alan-Ladd/#overview.
6. Fiedler, *Love and Death*, 211.
7. Fernbach, "The Fetishization of Masculinity," 235.
8. "Soldier: Trivia," IMDB, https://www.imdb.com/title/tt0120157/trivia/?ref_=tt_trv_trv.
9. Fernbach, "The Fetishization of Masculinity," 236.
10. Haraway, "A Cyborg Manifesto," 11.
11. "AFI's 10 Top 10: The 10 Greatest Movies in 10 Categories," American Film Institute, https://www.afi.com/afis-10-top-10/.
12. Sedgwick, *Between Men*, 26.
13. Ulmer, "Shane and the Language of Men," 82.
14. Faludi, *Stiffed*, 11.
15. Worden, *Masculine Style*, 143. On the other hand, Starrett and his homesteaders won't live to see their eventual obsolescence in the West.
16. Tompkins, *West of Everything*, 51.
17. Ulmer, "Shane and the Language of Men," 73.
18. Haraway, "A Cyborg Manifesto," 75.
19. I looked at these films in depth in "Assuming a True Identity." In listing related films, I included *Soldier*. *RoboCop* particularly connects to *Soldier* as it features a cyborg who not only was the protagonist but who also evokes western tropes. The essay concluded by noting, "Through technological fantasies, certain Hollywood films present an allegory of contemporary society's artificial man—that may ironically be escaped through technology" (p. 454).
20. Haraway, "A Cyborg Manifesto," 9.
21. The Black Widow Ops program has many elements in common with the Adam Project in both the selection of participants and the elements of their training.
22. Haraway, "A Cyborg Manifesto," 8.
23. Mitchell, *Westerns*, 173.
24. Mitchell, *Westerns*, 174.
25. Haraway, "A Cyborg Manifesto," 9.
26. Mitchell, *Westerns*, 159.
27. Nonspeaking children often function in films as a trope to highlight privileged men who feel unable to speak. Director Guillermo del Toro has frequently used this construction. *Logan*'s Laura also appears mute for the majority of the film.
28. Klock and Montgomery, "Evolve or Die," 223.
29. "Jimmy" is only used by his half brother Victor (Liev Schreiber) in *X-Men Origins: Wolverine*.

30. At the end of *The Wolverine*, Logan declines to stay with Mariko (Tao Okamoto), explaining, "I am a soldier, and I've been away too long."
31. Not coincidentally, the official trailer was scored with Johnny Cash's cover of "Hurt": "I hurt myself today / To see if I still feel."
32. Klock and Montgomery, "Evolve or Die," 229.
33. Geck, "Corpus Christi," 69. Transigen takes on a more global "cancerous" position in their manufacture of corn syrup, which is likely responsible for the lack of mutant births.
34. Klock and Montgomery, "Evolve or Die," 229.
35. Lehman, *Running Scared*, 36.

Bibliography

Abele, Elizabeth. "Assuming a True Identity: Re/Deconstructing Hollywood Heroes." *Journal of American & Popular Cultures* 25, no. 3–4 (2003): 447–54.

Anderson, Paul W. S., dir. *Soldier*. Warner, 1998.

Faludi, Susan. *Stiffed: The Betrayal of the American Man*. New York: Harper Collins, 1999.

Fernbach, Amanda. "The Fetishization of Masculinity in Science Fiction: The Cyborg and the Console Cowboy." *Science Fiction Studies* 27, no. 2 (2000): 234–55. http://www.jstor.org/stable/4240878.

Fiedler, Leslie A. *Love and Death in the American Novel*. Rev. ed. New York: Stein and Day, 1966.

Geck, John A. "Corpus Christi, Corpus Cyborgenesis, and the Body Politic: The Passion Play of *RoboCop*." *Journal of Religion and Popular Culture* 32, no. 1 (2020): 65–80. https://doi.org/10.3138/jrpc.2017-0053.

Haraway, Donna J. "A Cyborg Manifesto: Science, Technology, and Social-Feminism in the Late Twentieth Century." In *Manifestly Haraway*, 3–90. Minneapolis: University of Minnesota Press, 2016.

Hood, Gavin, dir. *X-Men Origins: Wolverine*. 20th Century Fox, 2009.

Klock, Geoff, and Mitch Montgomery. "Evolve or Die: *Logan*, Repetition and the Excesses of Tradition." In *Superheroes and Excess: A Philosophical Adventure*, edited by Jamie Brassett and Richard Reynolds, 220–51. New York: Routledge, 2021.

Lehman, Peter. *Running Scared*. Princeton: Princeton University Press, 1992.

Mangold, James, dir. *Logan*. 20th Century Fox, 2017.

———, dir. *The Wolverine*. 20th Century Fox, 2013.

Mitchell, Lee Clark. *Westerns: Making the Man in Fiction and Film*. Chicago: University of Chicago Press, 1998.

Scott, Ridley, dir. *Blade Runner*. Warner, 1982.

Sedgwick, Eve Kosofsky. *Between Men: English Literature and Male Homosocial Desire.* New York: Columbia University Press, 1985.

Singer, Bryan, dir. *X-Men.* 20th Century Fox, 2000.

Stevens, George, dir. *Shane.* Paramount, 1953.

Tompkins, Jane. *West of Everything: The Inner Life of Westerns.* New York: Oxford University Press, 1992.

Ulmer, Jesse Gerlach. "Shane and the Language of Men." *Acadia* 53, no. 1 (2018): 72–88. http://www.degruyter.com/document/doi/10.1515/arcadia-2018-0005/html.

Verhoeven, Paul, dir. *RoboCop.* Orion, 1987.

Worden, Daniel. *Masculine Style: The American West and Literary Modernism.* New York: Palgrave Macmillan, 2011.

Leatherface Families and Final Grandmas

The Reproductive Rites and Slaughterhouse Sexualities in the New "Old West"

JOSHUA T. ANDERSON
AND REBECCA M. LUSH

The 2021 "Texas Heartbeat Act," also known as Senate Bill 8, put Texas once again at the center of the debate over sexual and reproductive rights. The bill, which at the time of this writing is still in effect, not only restricts a patient's access to an abortion after a heartbeat is detected, which can be as soon as six weeks, but also grants ordinary citizens the power to enforce the law by filing a civil lawsuit against any patient, physician, or pro-choice activist who helps to terminate a pregnancy.[1] If this sounds like a familiar story, it's because Texas is the site of the original *Roe v. Wade* (1973), the embattled Supreme Court ruling that protected reproductive rights in the United States until the Dobbs decision reversed course in June 2022. Texas is also the place that produced *The Texas Chain Saw Massacre* (1974), the movie that gave birth to the slasher genre in the back of an army green van, and the franchise that teaches us everything we need to know about the confused sex politics (and the violence it engenders) of Texas.[2]

The Texas Chain Saw Massacre sutures together concerns about economic hardship, industrial violence, family legacies, land claims, and ultimately forms of reproduction to highlight the bloody and tenuous conditions of the West and its bodies. Likewise, Ti West's *X* (2022), a film that pays overt homage to Hooper's *The Texas Chain Saw Massacre* and other iconic slasher prototypes, uses its 1979 Texas setting to retread some of the topics covered by its predecessor but with renewed attention to sex and reproduction via its focus on sex workers.[3] Key to both films is what we term the inclusion of the "final grandma," a revision of Clover's famed "final girl" that troubles the notion of final "survivor" by raising questions about surviving whom or what. Both *The Texas Chain Saw Massacre* and *X* depict a Texas that's the fabled place of exes and XXXs, where capitalist frameworks fuel consuming fantasies of the flesh, both cannibal and carnal.

Carol Clover defines the "final girl" in her landmark book *Men, Women, and Chain Saws* (1992) as "the one who did not die: the survivor."[4] The concept has become canon in horror scholarship and even horror films. Final girls in their traditional guise are depicted as young and sexually inexperienced, but nearly five decades of slasher films have seen these previous final "girls" live out their screen lives in franchise series to reach their new status as mothers or mother figures and grandmothers who continue to fight the same revenant-like slashers that simply will not stay dead. Recent examples include *Halloween*'s Laurie Strode (Jamie Lee Curtis) and *Scream*'s Sidney Prescott (Neve Campbell), who both returned to the big screen during the pandemic, with *Halloween Kills* (2021) and *Scream* (2022) both giving new meaning to self-aware horror and the politics of mask wearing.[5] Middle-aged Sidney and AARP-qualified Laurie having to continue the same fights that marked their late teen years has more than a little in common with the popular meme of an older white woman holding a sign saying, "I can't believe I still have to protest this fucking shit" in relation to abortion rights.[6]

The Texas Chain Saw Massacre and *X* convey stories of 1970s Texas in an iconographic western setting filled with cattle, armadillos, and farmsteads. They give us a weirded vision of that West through the horror genre's grotesque and macabre sensibilities that amplify the nearly supernatural power of violence that marks the bloodshed and body count of the films. Just as much of U.S. law hews to precedent, so much so that "originalist" is a specific positionality for some jurists, so too is the horror genre obsessed with precedents and an obsessive return to origins. *Texas Chain Saw Massacre* is a story about violent origins, whether it is the desire of the Hardesty children to visit their grandparents' homestead or its bizarre replaying of the national mythological origins such as Thanksgiving. *X*, as a film released in 2022 but set in 1979, can be seen as a horror film that situates its inspiration point (*Chain Saw*) as a new kind of origin that gets revisited and reinterpreted, relived, and reproduced. We argue that sex and sexuality function as the catalyst for these weird western blood-soaked stories that queer the notion of family and create the conditions necessary for the "final grandma."

The Texas Chain Saw Massacre and *X* are slasher-westerns that have more to teach us about the rituals of generational and gender violence in the extractive and exploitative economies of the rural West, where homemaking is tied to (and sometimes dried out and sutured to) the unmaking and "unmanning" of the western myths of rugged individualism and self-reliance. Final girls of times past continue to haunt the weird west as the "final grandma," a figure who shares a complicated legacy with the "final girl." Clover defines her "final girl" as "the one who encounters the mutilated bodies of her friends and perceives the full extent of the preceding horror and of her own peril. . . . If her friends knew they were about to die only seconds before the event, the Final Girl lives with the knowledge for long minutes and hours. She alone looks death in the face, but she alone also finds the strength either to stay the killer long enough to be rescued (ending A) or to kill him herself (ending B)."[7] Whereas the final girl is typically young, white, sexually inexperienced, and from the suburbs of the middle class, the final grandma is comparatively old, a survivor of (sexualized) trauma, and living alone, sometimes off the grid, with or without an alias, often with years of survival training under her belt. If the final girl faces death for long minutes and hours, the final grandma does so for years and decades, often returning for the sequels to continue the bad marriage between the slasher and the survivor.

The "final grandmas" we see in *Texas Chain Saw* and *X*, however, further trouble the canonical notion of the final girl who has simply aged out, as they invite us to consider generational trauma and the violence and burden of memory. The "final grandmas" of these films occupy a liminal space in a new "Old West" that hews to traditional, heteronormative values at the cost of all the characters. The "final grandmas" also are unstable referents in these films. They collapse new versus old and engage in a kind of monstrous reproduction, raising existential questions about the purpose of survival, whether protagonist, antagonist, monster, or human. In the original *Chain Saw* the role of the "final grandma" is performed by Leatherface, who through his series of masked personalities reproduces family lore and family roles. In *X* the final grandma figure, Pearl, an elderly woman whose voracious sex drive and desire to be seen as beautiful (and in her words "special") serves as a double to the young "final girl" Maxine, a stripper and sex worker in adult films who similarly has an insatiable need to be adored. The movie casts Mia Goth to play both of these roles to highlight the interchangeable nature of final girl and final grandma, doppelgängers whose (s)kinship highlights that cyclical reproduction. The final grandma of *X* (who gets her own dedicated origin story in the prequel film *Pearl*) is notably defined by sexual experience and desires, as is her final girl counterpart, Maxine. Notably both Leatherface and Pearl as "final grandmas" have strong links to the monstrous; thus they defy the more straightforward acceptance of the final girl as hero in horror.

In sum, the "final grandma" invites viewers to consider questions of survival, memory, and reproduction. As older women figures, "final grandmas" are viewed as disposable, outmoded, and barren, reminding viewers of the horror of aging and inevitable death. They also point out that the present and future generations cannot move forward if they have not reckoned with a past that continues to haunt and undergird the current society. The structures that the final grandmas have debatably "survived" have not been resolved or seen notable progress, hence why their younger counterparts are fated to repeat the same cycle of violence even when we think there's a chance of improvement that inevitably becomes a red herring.

Chain Saw and *X* unfold in the context of 1970s America, a decade marked by political and cultural upheaval, where foundational myths, including the notion of the American dream, became increasingly harder to see as viable. Films from the period reflect this state of "incoherence," as Berliner has argued, leaving 1970s American cinema dismantling the slick narrative coherence of the studio era, eschewing clean-cut formulas and characters in favor of art-house inspired character ambiguity.[8] In particular, Berliner sees 1970s film narratives as perverse in the sense of "turned around" as they "derail straightforward narration" and closure.[9] In this perverse narrative context, final girls become final grandmas who will survive to die another day. Horror films in particular force viewers to confront uncomfortable truths, and *Chain Saw* and *X* are not shy in presenting their critiques of American consumerist and industrialized culture. Poole, in his study of horror films and their ties to American empire, asserts that "horror is the lingua franca. Horror defined the American century" and that horror films such as *Chain Saw* are a "punch in the gut" that ultimately ask, "Who will survive America?"[10] The "final grandma" haunts Poole's rhetorical question in our reading of these films. If, as Poole asserts, American horror films "critique the American dream by showing us the mounds of corpses it's built on," *Chain Saw* and *X* remind us that these corpses are also part of an American consumption that we cannot escape.[11]

Both films participate in the "reproductive rites," or the stories and ceremonies that ritualize, ordain, and justify the settler's rights to inheritance and occupation of stolen ground, and "slaughterhouse sexualities," or the way sexual orientations align around the violence of the slaughterhouse, producing (s)kinships bound in leather that turn the tools of the skin trade into the weapons of sexualized domestic violence. The *Chain Saw* formula of Hooper's film and West's homage to it resemble and reassemble the confused reproductive rights of the frontier. Not to be confused with the leather families that formed in the BDSM community in response to the HIV/AIDS epidemic and that modeled complex forms of relational and sexual consent, the Sawyer's Leather(face) Family turns the domestic sphere into a stay-at-home slaughterhouse with literal forms of objectification, turning their victims into food and furniture, *skin* into a verb, *hide* into a noun, and taxidermy into performance art.[12] Once described as "the *Gone with the Wind* of meat movies,"[13] the film shows us how the sausage is made, or how the violence of the slaughterhouse economy produces violent domestic sexual orientations in the West. Likewise, *X* shows that the root cellar of the farmstead is really a nonconsensual sex dungeon where human victims and cattle become interchangeable. The settler farmstead is seen as the seat of unending carnal desires, despite the seeming regulation (i.e., suppression) from the televangelist-religious zealots whose voices roar in the background. Put simply, slaughterhouse sexualities reveal how sex in the West is closely aligned with the violence of capitalist consumption: we are what (or who) we eat or fuck in the West, where exploitation is an aphrodisiac.

Tobe Hooper's southern-fried slasher classic is the *Godey's Lady's Book* (1830–78) for the generation raised on images of the Vietnam War in the failing industrial economy of the 1970s, which would give rise to the myth of "trickle-down economics" of the 1980s.[14] The horrors of late capitalism abound in the film and create the context for production, consumption, and mass production in its slaughterhouse sensibilities. As Hooper once asserted, it's a film whose message is "this is America."[15] *The Texas Chain*

Saw Massacre follows five youthful wanderers—original final girl Sally Hardesty (Marilyn Burns), her brother Franklin (Paul A. Partain), and their friends Pam (Terri McMinn), Jerry (Allen Danziger), and Kirk (William Vail)—who travel the blighted burial grounds of Texas that were once home to their settler grandparents, as Sally tells a group of locals at a recently desecrated cemetery "my granddaddy's buried here."[16]

Arriving in a 1972 Ford Club Wagon van, Sally and her friends are introduced to a new breed of intergenerational horror through the out-of-work cannibal taxidermists the Sawyer family (a.k.a. the Hewitt family), including The Cook (Jim Siedow), The Hitchhiker (Ed Neal), and Leatherface (Gunnar Hansen)—the "first family" of the weird west. The Sawyer's faux-Indigenous, neo-Native performances of (s)kinship rely on a combination of settler fantasies of the frontier and the unsettling realities of economic and ecological violence that are central to settler homemaking practices in the industrialized West. The Sawyers are the weird west's best representatives of what Mark Rifkin describes as "an ensemble of imperatives that includes family formation, homemaking, private property holding, and the allocation of citizenship" that form "a series of potential 'detachable parts' fused to each other through discourses of sexuality."[17] In addition to making family out of the "detachable parts" of the frontier, the (s)kinship practices of the original slasher family are bound up with European gothic monsters, specifically Dracula, Frankenstein's monster, and Dr. Jekyll and Mr. Hyde. As J. Halberstam argued in *Skin Shows: Gothic Horror and the Technology of Monsters* (1995), the relationship between the 1974 original and Hooper's much campier, more playful sequel, *The Texas Chainsaw Massacre 2* (1986), is "not unlike the relation of *Frankenstein* to *Dracula* in terms of the various strategies and methods of generating horror."[18] Like Frankenstein's monster, the Sawyers are made up of ill-fitting parts—Leatherface, in particular, is a monstrous body who hides (or Hydes) under layers of sutured skin that map a history of domestic violence, or the violence within the home(land). And in an early scene, soon after the Hardestys and their friends pick up The Hitchhiker and learn that he has brothers, Franklin jokes: "I think we just picked up Dracula. . . . A whole family of Draculas."

The Sawyers inherit from both sides of the frontier's fantasies of romance and asexual reproduction: the (vampiric) European burden of selective memory and the settler's re-membered American self, both of which are repeatedly coupled and reproduced with the "Indian" at the frontier. As Frederick Jackson Turner declared in "The Significance of the Frontier in American History" (1893): "This perennial rebirth, this fluidity of American life, this expansion westward with its new opportunities, its continuous touch with the simplicity of primitive society, furnish the forces dominating American character."[19] The impact of the setting and themes first explored in *Texas Chain Saw Massacre* still resonate in more recent cinema, whether it's Fern (Frances McDormand) in *Nomadland* (2020), who might well be a descendant of the Sawyers and the Hardestys. Like the Sawyers, she is laid off from her job at the sheetrock plant and picks up gig work in the online shipping industry, which is still a slaughterhouse. She bears passing resemblance to Sally Hardesty, at least in the way we might imagine Sally would look if, after escaping the Sawyer house, she found another van, stayed off the grid, and roamed the West in her gas-guzzling mobile home. While *Nomadland* has earned the distinction of "serious drama," the sort that garners the big Hollywood awards and recognition while meditating on many of the cultural issues that underpin *Texas Chain Saw Massacre*, Ti West's *X* (2022) wears its homage closer to its skin in terms of genre and in the recentering of the sexual politics inherent in its predecessor.

Made for less than $140,000 and distributed by the Colombo crime family—who had recently cashed in on the porn classic *Deep Throat* (1972)—the original *Chain Saw* would go on to become one of the highest-grossing movies in Texas history, itself becoming a capitalist "franchise" that led the way for the Lone Star State to become the "Third Coast" in the film industry, behind Hollywood's West Coast and New York City's East Coast.[20] Written by Hooper and Kim Hinkel and starring a cast of unknown actors—most of whom were students at the University of Texas at Austin—the film tells the story of two western "families," the aptly named Sawyer family, who "saw and sew" their victims after they lose their manual labor jobs at the industrialized slaughterhouse, and the Hardesty Family (and friends), who travel by van to visit the old Franklin house, a dilapidated family estate that neither Sally nor her brother Franklin, who uses a wheelchair, seems eager to inherit.

Sally's remarkable transformation narrative from road tripper to original final girl begins in a newly liberated West, fresh off the passage of 1973's landmark Supreme Court decision in *Roe v. Wade*, in which Jane Roe filed a civil suit challenging the constitutionality of Texas's abortion law. However, after a fateful encounter with The Hitchhiker near an industrial slaughterhouse, Sally will be chased, captured, tortured, and baptized in the blood of her friends before narrowly escaping back onto the blistering Texas highway, herself a desperate hitchhiker. Sally's story arc, which begins during the hopeful sexual revolution of second-wave feminism, ends with all the ground-shaking force of an American jeremiad, with tough lessons about how to survive in a cannibalistic, kill-or-be-killed economy in which both the domesticity of the home and the mobility of the road are unnavigable traps.

This is not a West filled with wise settler ancestors; instead, Hooper's West is an unsettling burial ground haunted by destructive land policies and doctrines of death and dominance, including the still-fresh memories of chattel slavery and Indigenous genocide. In the opening frames, a radio DJ announces that "graverobbing in Texas is this hour's top news story" while infrared solar flares burn behind the title credits. The DJ tells us that authorities have discovered a "grisly work of art: the remains of a badly decomposed body wired to a large monument." Backlit with the Texas sunrise and framed by a skyline dotted with headstones, the grisly monument fills the screen: a monstrous, scarecrow-like figure holds a human skull, hinting at *Hamlet*'s Yorick or a weird western Statue of Liberty. The DJ continues his matter-of-fact report: a Texaco oil refinery has exploded on the Texas-Louisiana border; a cholera outbreak in San Francisco; strange suicide attempts in Houston; unidentified and mutilated corpses in Gary, Indiana; a deadly building collapse in Atlanta; an eighteen-month-old baby chained in the attic in Dallas. The DJ's voice fades out as the screen cuts to a dead armadillo—colloquially called the "Texas speed bump"—broiling on the highway. The earliest visual shots we get in the film's opening of the grisly monuments and desecrated body parts reassembled into grotesque altars we later learn are framed via the camera lens of The Hitchhiker, the film forcing us to see from the perspective of a Sawyer family member at its commencement, thus making the viewer complicit throughout.

This is how we enter the film: oil fires and outbreaks, suicide attempts and sociopathic violence, a sun burning too hot, and the inescapable stink of the dead blooming all around. As legendary horror film critic Joe Bob

Briggs declares in "They Came, They Sawed" (2004; published under his real name, John Bloom): "Before a single actor has appeared, before anything has happened at all, the film is pregnant with menace."[21] Before the van full of traveling youths picks up The Hitchhiker, the film furthers the foreboding atmosphere and impending cannibalism via Pam's astrology guide side chatter. She ominously notes that Saturn is in retrograde and is a "particularly bad influence now"; this level of detail is especially prescient since the Roman god Saturn, also known as Cronus in the Greek tradition, eats his own children, a grisly story that Goya's *Saturn Devouring His Son* visualizes as particularly monstrous.

X follows a ragtag group of sex workers and aspiring filmmakers in 1979 Texas who are all seeking their version of the American dream, whether it's to be famous, to make an avant-garde/artistic adult film, or to simply make money in the new market for home video entertainment. The group of strippers, sex workers, filmmakers, and budding entrepreneurs leave behind the city life of Houston, characterized by industrial views and a seedy Bayou Burlesque strip joint, to film their movie, "The Farmer's Daughters," at an off-grid Texas farm in an obviously economically depressed region. In their pursuit to "make a good dirty movie" they find that the locals, similar to *Chain Saw*'s Sawyer family, have an insatiable desire to consume that comes with its own bloodlust. The film's mise-en-scène has obvious crossover with *Chain Saw*, from the roadkill to the eerily uncanny dilapidated screen-doored farm homes that frame its foreboding shots of dark interiors and creepy altars of "folk art" (for the Sawyers their taxidermy creations, and in *X* Pearl's maquillaged doll art collection).

The Hardesty's van in *Chain Saw* is a fitting vehicle for our return to frontier conditions. Much like the frontier, vans have long been associated with domesticity and sex crimes—the vehicle of choice for soccer moms and sex traffickers—which explains why vans appear so frequently in slasher movies, because slashers are always inspecting the American home for weaknesses, the American family for signs of trauma and evidence of abuse. The shape of the van has changed considerably since its ancestors crossed the continent in those westward *Little House on the Prairie*–styled wagons. Likewise, *X* utilizes the 1970s van for its own frontier return, this time a more corporatized version boldly emblazoned with "Plowing Services" and steer-head logo on the side, a sexual double entendre that links Texas ranching and cattle-culture with the sex work of "plowing" and thrusting (and writhing and grinding) that are the hallmarks of the "good dirty movie" the characters seek to make, a film that features numerous scenes of "plowing" around an idyllic and nostalgic Texas farm of yesteryear.

In the absence of stable slaughterhouse work, the Sawyers turn to the feminized trades of home economics: The Cook sells cannibal barbecue at his gas-less gas station; The Hitchhiker sculpts rigor mortis art out of decomposing bodies and takes "family vacation" photos with the strangers who pick him up; Leatherface is the un-butch butcher whose rotation of masks makes him a cross between Little Red Riding Hood and the Big Bad Wolf's infamous grandma drag. Leatherface's ties to grisly fairytales are twofold via his position as a kind of "final grandma." Lanza describes the film as a "modern version of Hansel and Gretel," a fairy tale where the grandma figure turns out to be a cannibalistic witch, while the grandma drag of Red Riding Hood also evokes connotations of monstrous pregnancy.[22] In older variants of the tale the victims of the wolf's consumption slash their way out of his "pregnant" stomach and rebirth themselves in gruesome fairy tale blood. As Amy Kaplan writes in "Manifest Domesticity" (1998): "The border between the domestic and foreign, however, also deconstructs when we think of domesticity not as a static condition but as the process of domestication, which entails conquering and taming the wild, the natural, and the alien."[23] Leatherface is the weird western's best example of the ways in which domesticity is not a static condition. He has gone by many names: he is Bubba Sawyer in Hooper's campy 1986 sequel, Thomas Brown Hewitt in the 2003 remake of the 1974 original, and Jedidiah Sawyer in *Texas Chainsaw 3D* (2013). His skin masks, like the iconic cavalry Stetsons worn by Clint Eastwood's "Man with No Name," are constant but unstable identifying marks that have become collector's items in the refashioned West. His original "Killing Mask" is now owned by a collector in Illinois, his "Pretty Woman" mask is owned by The Hitchhiker actor Ed Neal, and his "Old Lady" mask was recently purchased by an unknown collector at Sotheby's Auction.[24] On the digital frontier, Leatherface, known simply as "The Cannibal" in the video game *Dead by Daylight* (2016), will no longer wear the face of Claudette Morel, a Black woman, because it retreads the minstrelsy of blackface, and as many gamers reported, it was often used to harass and target Black players.[25] As a slasher killer, Leatherface stands alone in his methods that re-create the racialized, sexualized, and gendered body in his own image. His he/him pronouns are as ill-fitting as his many masks, which are as suspicious and unconvincing as the "real" in real estate. Leatherface's constant refashioning of gender identity and sexual orientations extends to the way that he and his brothers rearrange and reconstruct the horror family tree.

If Sally Hardesty is the original final girl, as some have argued, Leatherface might be the original final grandma, in the way he resembles the folkloric wolf-in-grandma's-clothes and "adopts" fresh new faces to join his elusively queer family and their collection of victims who move beyond and between the taxonomies of gender and sexual identities.[26] As Carol Clover writes, "the appointed ancestor of the slasher film is Hitchcock's *Psycho* (1960)," because, she elaborates, it contains most of the seeds for the slasher formula: "The killer is a product of a sick family, but still recognizably human; the victim is a beautiful, sexually active woman; the location is not-home, at a Terrible Place; the weapon is something other than a gun; the attack is registered from the victim's point of view and comes with shocking suddenness."[27] However, it is Leatherface and his brothers that give us the means of production for reproducing monstrous families in and beyond the West. He is descended from the infamous cannibal taxidermist Ed Gein and a serial murderer in Houston, and his descendants are almost too many to name, including masked killers Michael Myers and Jason Voorhees, the rotation of self-aware Ghostface killers in the *Scream* franchise, Patrick Bateman in *American Psycho* (2000), Buffalo Bill in *The Silence of the Lambs* (1991), the chainsaw-armed Ash in Sam Raimi's *Evil Dead II* (1987), and Captain Spaulding and the "Firefly family" in Rob Zombie's *House of 1000 Corpses* (2003) and *The Devil's Rejects* (2005).[28]

Leatherface's West is not the Wild West of grass-fed beef and organic, free-range turkeys. Although filled with iconic establishing shots of the desolate, sun-scorched Texas prairie, the film takes place mostly indoors: the enclosed spaces of the slaughterhouse, the Victorian farmhouse, the "We Slaughter Barbecue" gas station, and the 1972 Ford Club Wagon. These indoor spaces are not elder-friendly, even though it appears everything inside and around the house has grown old.[29] The exterior of the home could double as a multigeneration art installation devoted to the failures of industrial economics: a generator buzzes in the absence of pollinating insects, a junkyard is filled with old VW Beetles, there's a human tooth on the front porch, and through the screen door, there's the bleached skull of a taxidermied buck. To move through the house is to be inside the ruins of the Cult of Domesticity and the realities of rural poverty, disability, and disillusionment: doors are draped with blackout curtains, and cracks of light reveal rooms hoarded with folk art made from bones, feathers, turtle shells, and the jaws of large mammals. Chickens are stuffed inside birdcages made for parakeets. Animal skins hang from the wall in the foyer. Pam hangs from a meat hook in the kitchen, where Leatherface butchers Kirk with a chainsaw. Leatherface will later "put on his face," changing from the Killing Mask to the Old Lady mask, which he wears while doting on his brothers during a weird western Thanksgiving celebration.

Similarly, *X* also explores the tension between the expansiveness of the landscape and the claustrophobia and decay of the ruins of the Cult of Domesticity. The interior of the main farmstead where Pearl resides is dark and faded and dank. By contrast the young people making their sex film reside in a "boarding house" on the farm's grounds that was originally used for soldiers during the Civil War. The boarding house, while also a relic of the past, is in nowhere near the same state of apparent disrepair as the main house, partially due to the film showing it to be a setting of much more vivacious activity. Boarding houses are spaces temporarily occupied, and their transitory nature suggests movement. The scenes set within the boarding house in *X* are mostly sex scenes shot for the main characters' porno film that highlight a sense of action and vitality. In a particularly key scene set in the boarding house, a sunlight-filled sex scene draws out the older Pearl from her gothic farm home to voyeuristically watch like a veritable peeping tom from outside the bedroom window. By contrast, Pearl's home is a mausoleum where she even fails to find sexual connection with her husband. If the cult of "true womanhood" upholds the doctrine of separate spheres for men and women, *X* shows just how separate and isolating this works in practice for a sex-starved Pearl. When Pearl does convince her equally aged husband to engage in sexual activity with her, it happens in the boarding house, not the family home proper (with a frightened Maxine hiding under the bed while the two older characters creak above her). The sterility of the main house is a feature that the prequel film *Pearl* also touches on, where we see a teenaged

Pearl (Mia Goth) sexually frustrated within her family's house because she feels she has been abandoned by her husband, who is abroad fighting in World War I. She even fails in her attempt to have her lover, a local cinema projectionist, have sex with her in her family's home, marking the home as an ongoing site of unwanted chastity and suffocating Victorian aesthetics (garish wallpaper and more abounds).

Of all of America's frontier (re)creation stories, the Thanksgiving myth is the one stuffed deepest inside *The Texas Chain Saw Massacre*. During one of the longest horror chase scenes in film history, which begins when Franklin is gutted by Leatherface in the woods, Sally is chased for six unhinged and uninterrupted minutes of screen time until she is finally brought to the table for the weird western's Thanksgiving meal. In the now infamous dinner table scene, which allegedly took over twenty-four hours to shoot with real meat rotting in the sweltering Texas heat, the cinematography turns to canted angles, emphasizing the slant horror of Sally's captivity. The Sawyer family does not merely "play Indian," to use Philip J. Deloria's term, but instead they play out the fantasy transformation story at the heart of Turner's "Frontier Thesis," in which the American frontier is part striptease, part drag show, as it "strips off the garments of civilization [of the European] and arrays him in the hunting shirt and the moccasin. . . . Before long he has gone to planting Indian corn and plowing with a sharp stick; he shouts the war cry and takes the scalp in orthodox Indian fashion."[30] Roughly the same story is on the menu during American Thanksgiving, the country's traditional feast of misremembrance.

The dinner scene reminds us that underneath the mask of America's Thanksgiving traditions is the carnage of The Brother's War. Although we trace the story of Thanksgiving back to the 1621 harvest meal between the Mayflower pilgrims and the Wampanoag, it was not a national holiday until it was enacted by President Abraham Lincoln in 1863 during the midst of the Civil War. Crediting Sarah Josepha Hale's decades-long efforts to promote the holiday in *Godey's Lady's Book*, Kaplan elaborates: "The power of Thanksgiving Day stemmed from its center in the domestic sphere; Hale imagined millions of families seated around the holiday table at the same time, thereby unifying the vast and shifting space of the national domain through simultaneity in time."[31] Recognizing the instability of our national origin stories might be particularly unsettling for Texans, who have long prided themselves on a culture of hypermasculinity despite having a feminized origin story, wherein during the "debates about the annexation of Texas and later Mexico, both sides represented the new territories as women to be married to the United States; Sam Houston, for example, wrote of Texas as presenting itself 'to the United States as a bride adorned for her espousals.'"[32] This imagery of a bride in her wedding garments is reflected in both the "Pretty Woman" mask that Leatherface wears to the dinner table and the way Sally is tied to a bone chair in a ceremony that reconstructs and recombines "virgin sacrifice" and the "fattened calf" wedding rituals. The horrifying and strangely comic scene accentuates the film's pitch-black humor, such as its depiction of Grandpa Sawyer, who looks like an identical twin to the cadaverous folk art in the first scene and who has been billed by his grandsons as the best cow killer in the West. The old man sucks blood from Sally's finger, which seems to confirm the family's vampiric (if not outright vampire) traits that were foreshadowed by Franklin soon after they picked up The Hitchhiker.

Far from Transylvania, the Sawyers make home in an always transitioning, yet deeply transphobic West. Although there is a long (and mostly long-forgotten) history of trans cowboys in the Wild West, the genre that tells its story has come to be synonymous with the straightening forces that police the boundaries of gender and sexuality.[33] The western's narrative drive toward settlement is never convincing in terms of gender and sexuality because, it turns out, even its most traditional heroes are often far from straight. The Lone Ranger, Clint Eastwood's "Man with No Name," John Wayne's "The Ringo Kid," and Gary Cooper's Will Kane all resist the drive toward heteronormative coupling, marriage, and domestication, while simultaneously representing a spectrum of "real men," despite the instability and slippages in what counts as proof of their straightness or manliness. The Lone Ranger spends most of his time on the trail with his Indigenous male companion Tonto. Eastwood's unnamed killer in *High Plains Drifter* (1973) is a sex criminal who is more shape (like Michael Myers) than person. The Duke's Ringo "Kid" clings to a nickname that suggests sexual inexperience, while Will Kane, whose name recalls both the Bible's first brother-on-brother murder and the last will and testament, has almost all of the qualities of a final girl in *High Noon* (1952) as he awaits a fateful confrontation with the Frank Miller gang, who, like the Sawyers, represents an outlaw western family who does not seem to be born of heterosexual coupling but forged in a process Richard Slotkin called "regeneration through violence."[34]

In the Sawyers' version of the West's regeneration through violence, Grandpa Sawyer is propped up by his grandsons in a ritual ceremony to prove that he's still the best killer around. The Cook (later named Drayton Sawyer in the sequel) attempts to soothe Sally's fears by recounting Grandpa's prowess on the killing floor: "You just hush. It won't hurt none. Grandpa's the best killer there ever was. Why he never took more than one lick they say. Did sixty in 5 minutes once. They say he could've done more if the hook-and-pull gang could've gotten the beeves outta the way faster. Now don't you cry none. Old Grandpa's the best. It won't hurt a bit." Sally is forced to bend over a bucket, awaiting the killing blow from Grandpa, but at his advanced age it is clear that he shares the vampire's tragic condition of outliving his own lifetime while relying more and more on "young blood" to survive. Far removed from his "prime beef" days, he can't even hold the sledgehammer, let alone swing it, making him one of the best representations of western fantasies of manliness collapsing under the realities of the rural body after a lifetime of exploitative labor. Grandpa is both the prop memorializing the fantasies of the West and the body that proves those fantasies false. Similarly, the "grandpa" figure in *X*, Pearl's husband, Howard (Stephen Ure), embodies a similar fear of manliness collapsing under the realities of the rural body as Howard fears sexual activity will kill him due to his weak heart. While the Sawyer grandpa collapses with the weight of slaughter, Howard fears collapsing from "plowing," to borrow the film's explicit comparison between sex work and ranch/farm work. And like any good slasher film where, as *Scream*'s Randy (Jamie Kennedy) tells us, "Sex equals death," Howard ends up dying after his big sex scene with Pearl. Because the Sawyers are more concerned with proving Grandpa's prowess than with killing Sally, she's able to escape for a footrace in what still might be the most frantic ending in horror history.

In the final chase scene, Sally escapes down a long dirt road with The Hitchhiker in close pursuit. When he catches her, he does not kill her. Instead, he repeatedly slashes his razor across her back with the glee and fervor of an orchestra conductor leading a symphony of chainsaws and generators. When she makes it to the highway, she narrowly dodges an empty cattle truck that barrels into The Hitchhiker. The truck driver, who appears to be the first BIPOC character in the movie, does not get any speaking lines. Instead, the unnamed truck driver has the words "Black Maria" stenciled on the side of his truck, a detail pregnant with possibilities. Is this Black Maria part of a fleet of cattle trucks with the Niña and the Pinta sent to "rediscover" the West? The name is also one that was colloquially used to refer to police wagons, which raises the question, Is Sally still imprisoned by the slaughterhouse sexualities that she only momentarily escaped? The truck bed setting portrays Sally as a good for transport, potentially making this vehicle just the latest iteration of the slaughterhouse and its violent kinks for sexual and industrial reproduction.

Left to wander the dangerous Texas highway bathed in blood and cackling in the back of a stranger's pickup truck, Sally Hardesty does not wait around for such answers. Her story is a blood relative to deeply American genres: the captivity narrative, the jeremiad, the slasher, and the western. Through this strange family tree, she is related to the Puritan final girl Mary Rowlandson and *Nomadland*'s final grandma Fern, and several other neo-western wanderers and homeless homesteaders who survive by the skin of (or in) their teeth. In its dismembering of America's Thanksgiving Day narrative, *The Texas Chain Saw Massacre* and its original final girl might help us to remember another American tradition: the presidential pardon of the Thanksgiving turkey. The practice of turkey pardoning, Michael Branch tells us, is tied to America's mythic origin story that skillfully serves up a settler fantasy of national unity while severing the remembrance of the Mystic River Massacre, as he concludes his essay "Freebirds" (2011): "We forgive the birds, and in so doing, we hope desperately that they might forgive us."[35]

Sally's story might also be one of forgiveness, but for whom? And for what? Perhaps it is the settler's long-practiced form of self-forgiveness that requires another kind of sacrifice. As Halberstam observes, "In its generic affinities to the western, the horror film does have a way of coding monstrosity in ethnic terms as white trash, rednecks, or redskins."[36] Halberstam's arguments regarding the gender and genre trouble produced in *The Texas Chainsaw Massacre* franchise, particularly Hooper's campy sequel, builds upon the groundwork laid by Clover, who posits that "if 'redneck' once denoted a real and particular group, it has achieved the status of a kind of universal blame figure, the 'someone else' held responsible for all manner of American social ills. The great success of the redneck in that capacity suggests that anxieties no longer expressible in ethnic or racial terms have become projected onto a safe target."[37] The forgiveness or pardon granted to Sally is part of the grammar of American innocence, which is crucially not a language of responsibility but of blame, guilt, and shame. The confrontation between Sally and the Sawyers plays out over and over again in slasher films, retesting the intersectional lines that cordon off the victim's body from the killer's body from the survivor's body from the bystander's body, all of which can change positions and orientations in a moment's notice. Slashers are loosely tied to the detective genre in that the original films in the series are almost always a whodunnit plot, where we anxiously await the reveal to see whom we can blame under the mask. The slasher film teaches us to be content with blame because we learn that no one in Haddonfield, or Camp Crystal Lake, or Elm Street, or Texas is responsible.

In the frantic final scene of *Chain Saw*, Leatherface falls and cuts his own leg with his chainsaw, making the violence of the film circular and never-ending. Missing the chance to chew up Sally, he stands and chaînés on his "wounded knee," a not-so-subtle reminder of his inheritance from the massacres of Indigenous peoples and the chainsaw's masked history directly linked to sexual reproduction.[38] As he wildly swings his chainsaw, sunrise bursting on the horizon like a Texas grapefruit, Leatherface reminds us that this is not an ending but a beginning expressed as a celebratory dance of continued turning steps evocative of the continuity of horror franchises that resist resolution and conclusion. It is a new ritual about how the American and the American family are *unmade* by the instruments and economics once used to "settle" the frontier. Like Teddy Roosevelt, Frederic Remington, Owen Wister, Charlotte Perkins Gilman, and other famous neurasthenia patients diagnosed by S. Weir Mitchell in the late nineteenth century, the Sawyers represent the anxieties of men being feminized or "final girled" *and* of women being trapped in domestic rooms with curdled yellow wallpaper. Once an affliction so common among the elite classes that Michael Vincent Miller titled the *New York Times* headline "Anybody Who Was Anybody Was Neurasthenic" (1991), neurasthenia seems to have run its course through the laid-off slaughterhouse workers, but we cannot know for certain because they do not have health insurance.[39] Inside the growl of Leatherface's chainsaw is a panicked rage, the angry barking search for another way through the forest, another way to survive. It is the sound of the western frontier being made over, the unifying national narratives transitioning from celebratory stories of nation- and homemaking into the horror stories of late-stage capitalism, legacies of land theft, and the threats of a dying but still deadly fossil fuel industry that revolve around the strange erotics of ecofascism and the end times.[40]

West's *X* engages in its own version of the capitalist slaughterhouse sexualities of *Chain Saw*. The film's title is a pun on the "X factor" or that unnamable "it" factor that both attracts and influences others, the X in XXX adult entertainment, and also "ex" meaning former. Sex, influence, and the desire to escape past conditions fuel the characters' capitalist drive of making it big economically in a kinky American dream where the home video market of "perverts" fills the economic and personal void felt by the main characters. The characters seem mostly doomed to repeat or confront what they've been trying to escape, whether it's Jackson (Scott Mescudi, a.k.a. Kid Cudi), the Black Vietnam vet who tries to reinvent himself as a porn actor but ultimately finds himself the victim of gun violence, or Bobby-Lynne (Brittany Snow), the stripper and sex worker whose American Dream is to get a paid-for house with her own pool where she can spend her day "tan[ning] these titties" but meets her end via an alligator attack that closely resembles the mural that decorates the Bayou Burlesque strip joint she works at while trying to make it "big."

For the main characters of *X* sex is a drive, work, art, human need, and also what creates an unexpected sense of family, united in their fears of death and decay. Whereas the Sawyers of *Chain Saw* queered the notion of family with their (drag) performance of traditional domestic roles, in *X* sex and sexuality creates an "it's all disco" philosophy, to quote character Bobby-Lynne, that brings together people of all genders and races before they get "too old to fuck." The haunting specter within the farmstead is old age, a condition that suggests a diminished X factor and loss of libido and thus loss of economic means.

Fears of aging take on an additional dimension not only in terms of the human life cycle but also in the fears and damage of aging values and outmoded social systems. Maxine explains to Lorraine (Jenna Ortega), the "church mouse" audio assistant of their film team who also decides she wants to act in their porn movie, "Letting outdated traditions control how you live your life will get you nowhere." Yet despite Maxine's rallying cry of resisting outdated traditions and insistence that she "will not accept a life [she] doesn't deserve," she is driven by the tradition of the American Dream and a "need to be famous" that privileges the currency of youth and beauty. Her talking points and mantras are just recast and recontextualized versions of what her televangelist preacher father (Simon Prast) spouts to the masses as he condemns sex and sexuality. Maxine finds herself in the precarious position of wanting to have her cake and eat it, too.

Maxine and Pearl function as doppelgängers that show the final girl and the final grandma to be two sides of the same coin. The main porno scene that R.J. (Owen Campbell) shoots in the cattle barn between Maxine and Jackson shows the overt slippage and boundary blurring of final girl and final grandma. When Pearl invites Maxine in for lemonade she comments to the younger woman, "Such a special face." The camera shots of the two women sharing lemonade visually mirror the intercut images of the porno scene of Bobby-Lynne and Jackson, infusing an uneasy sexualized tension between Maxine and Pearl. The lemonade scene is coded as illicit not only because of the sex scenes that interrupt it but because of Pearl secreting Maxine out of the house so her husband doesn't see her and saying, "It'll be our secret." The interchangeable nature of Maxine and Pearl, however, becomes more pronounced as Maxine films her sex scene with Jackson in the barn and a horny Pearl peers voyeuristically into the barn window. The film alternates between the widescreen and realistic color scale of the "present" of the film with R.J.'s camera perspective marked by shortened frame dimensions and the desaturated and hazy color scheme that is iconic to 1970s film technology. R.J.'s camera feed consistently shows Maxine engaged in sex, but the "real" view of the widescreen lens sometimes shows Pearl in Maxine's position. Final girl and final grandma are sometimes one and the same, but not necessarily united in whom or what they are fighting, due in part to their inability to acknowledge the social dynamics they are complicit in perpetrating.

The horror of *X* is Pearl's monstrous sexual desire that society deems inappropriate and revolting. R.J. tells her he doesn't "want to see it" when

Pearl attempts to bare her body to him. Her body is monstrous due to its age, and an "it" as opposed to part of her. When R.J. rejects Pearl, she kills him in classic slasher fashion, penetrating his body multiple times with her knife as Blue Oyster Cult blares "Don't Fear the Reaper." Pearl concludes her first kill scene with her own little ballet-inspired slasher victory dance like *Chain Saw*'s Leatherface, performing a stiff adagio that recalls her previous days as a dancer in her youth (a vocation that also doubles with Maxine's work as a dancer at the Bayou Burlesque).

While working out the difference between emotional connection via sexuality and sexuality as performance, Lorraine states, "The camera changes things," and the camera of *X* changes things by playing with genre and self-referentiality. Maxine does make it to the end of *X* as its unlikely final girl snorting cocaine and ironically muttering about "divine intervention." Her American Dream goals at the outset are presented as seedy and exploitative in their leveraging of sex work, and she's not portrayed as an idealized traditional final girl à la Sidney Prescott. Maxine's X factor may mean she draws people to her, but it doesn't necessarily valorize or idealize her for it. She's not the slasher feminist superhero fighting outdated traditions and slaying the patriarchy, but she is ultimately at war with herself and the limited roles and opportunities available to her as a woman in 1970s Texas, where sex work only appears to be the antithesis of the religious zealots she has perhaps unsuccessfully left behind.

The film engages in metacommentary to draw attention to the ongoing horror and genealogy of violence that continues to this day. The movie pays homage to a canonical horror work, while being a movie about characters making a movie, and the genre twists and turns that go from indie art-house porn to what the local sheriff says at the end when collecting evidence, including R.J.'s film reels, that it's "by the looks of everythin', I'd say one goddamn fucked up horror picture."

In a slant way, Hooper's and West's "frontier thesis" allows us to see the rot underneath our unconvincing stories about the capitalist American Dream that become like Leatherface's many masks and Pearl's makeup: covers for the violence that is both below and on the surface. Like the traditions of the western, slashers and final girls claim to have long memories, but they don't necessarily make good ancestors. Sometimes the slasher's killing spree is passed down from mother to son: Pamela and Jason Voorhees in *Friday the 13th* (1980), or Norma and Norman Bates in *Psycho* (1960). Sometimes, it appears motivated by incestuous and misogynistic impulses, such as Michael Myers in the *Halloween* franchise, or by revenge to atone for the sins of the fathers and mothers in a community, such as *Candyman* (1992), whose main character does to the Cabrini-Green projects of Chicago what Freddy Krueger does to the Elm Street suburbs of generic white America, and both turn the American Dream into a nightmare by reminding us of how the American family inherits a history of vigilante violence.

Hooper's and West's films explore the same territory but in a different America: the rural West. And as we say in real estate, it's all about location, location, location. "If you read enough of the reviews," Joe Bob Briggs once wrote, "you start to think that the scariest word in the title was neither 'Chainsaw' nor 'Massacre' but 'Texas.'"[41] Joe Bob was joking when he wrote this in 2004, but it certainly seems like the State of Texas wants to adopt the kill-or-be-killed politics of *The Texas Chain Saw Massacre*, which we might be better off treating as deadly serious. The film franchise sometimes referred to as the "grandaddy of slasher splatter horror" does not give us easy answers, and it is a veritable meat grinder for American political thought. It skewers liberal sensibilities by showing us how unsexy politeness politics is in a white-knuckle world. It reminds us that progressive fantasies of a community of workers are still far removed from the realities of the American Dream in rural America, where capital still rules the economics of fossil fuels, monoculture farming, and the industrial slaughterhouse.

Although things seem bleak from this vantage point, the slasher genre might now be producing something that the western so often fails to do: a lineage of women and queer survivors who return to adopt and protect new generations. In "Dear Final Girls" (2017), Stephen Graham Jones pens a letter written in the persona of Laurie Strode, Nancy Thompson (of *A Nightmare on Elm Street*), and Sidney Prescott with advice for the next generation of final girls after they survive their nights of terror: "Now you can walk out, into those end credits. But don't expect applause. You've graduated, see? It was that kind of ceremony. You're no longer the timid bookworm you were, once upon a lifetime. You've faced things most in your community have never even dreamed of. You've faced things that would have killed them in the opening scene. The girl you used to be, she's dead. You stand taller, now. At least for the moment."[42] The slasher has always shared the frontier's power for transformation narratives that almost always include transformations in gender and sexual identification, orientation, and performance. Their origin stories often explore generational conflict and the way it particularly leaves women and queer people vulnerable inside the American home, family, and middle-class communities, all of which harbor misogynist and homophobic violence.

At the same time, films such as *Chain Saw* and *X* dramatize the gender and generational trouble that is passed down through survivors at the intersections of the postsettler, postwestern, and post-horror. An unexpected reference to the *Texas Chainsaw Massacre* appears in superstar Britney Spears's memoir, an apparent non sequitur that is all the more poignant when one considers the thesis of her memoir may be her survival of her own trauma and hypersexualization while navigating layers of generational trauma, themes that have more than just a little in common with the trauma of final girls and grandmas.[43] The "post" of postcolonialism, postwestern, and post-horror implicitly questions whether we can ever be "post" anything but rather more aware of conventions and structures that we cannot seem to fully repudiate. *Texas Chain Saw* and *X* present visions of the West and Texas that constantly remind us that returns to origins and the past cannot be escaped. The more recent term "post-horror," which refers to stylized, recent horror works that attempt a contrived "elevated" or "artistic" aesthetic to focus on the horrors of vulnerability, ultimately raises the implicit rhetorical question of whether we can ever survive the horrors of our everyday lives.[44] *Texas Chain Saw* and *X* seem to suggest the unavoidable return, rendering the American western a horror and an enigma. As Cowan notes, "No matter how many explanations we offer, enigmas always leave us with more questions than answers."[45]

As the slasher genre ages, so too do its many final girls, and like Jones's letter, we are beginning to see a shift in the genre that returns to the postfrontier conditions of the suburbs or the slaughterhouse and sutures the waves model of feminism to the "waves" model of Turner's "Frontier Thesis." What remains might be more of the same—just a mutation of the same settler storytelling with its partial, blurry memory and romantic rewrites of a blood-soaked history, a mutation where apparent opposites, like Maxine and Pearl, actually mirror one another. However, it could also be a shift away from narratives of blame—since we have long pinned it all on the slasher killer(s)—and toward narratives of responsibility and recognized complicity. The survivors return and become (partially) knowledgeable ancestors with methods for surviving the harsh rules that keep being rebirthed and reproduced.

Put simply, this *is* your grandma's West. The place once settled by the Cult of Domesticity has been unsettled by the ritualized slashing of health care benefits, workers' protections, and reproductive rights. In this West, we bear witness to the grandmothers, the former final girls, who carry a vexed legacy both as survivors of generational violence and too often as coconspirators in some of the West's original sins of land theft and genocide. The final grandma is a self-reliant scream queen from the past five decades who continues to reappear on-screen, reminding us again and again that the frontier conditions of the free market can only be survived once you learn how to wield the genre's violent tools of instruction, which almost always double as domestic or industrial homemaking accessories: butcher knives, machetes, chainsaws. She is not merely the "one who does not die: the survivor." She is the one who *remembers*. And perhaps given the genre's capacity for violence and suture, she is also the one who *re-members* the parts that have been redacted, the parts that have been severed, and the parts still to be played in the new "Old" West.

Notes

1. Filipovic, "Is the Texas Abortion Law Backfiring on the People Who Pushed It Through?"
2. Which film is the "first" slasher is a topic of debate and argument within film scholarship. Many see *The Texas Chain Saw Massacre* as establishing the framework of the slasher film in a way that Hitchcock's *Psycho* does not. Others see John Carpenter's *Halloween* (1978) as the first "proper" slasher film, whose formula would become codified in the 1980s. Further others contend that *Friday the 13th* (1980) is the first. Additionally, the *Chainsaw* franchise has some spelling inconsistencies. The first film is *The Texas Chain Saw Massacre*, but Hooper's sequel and subsequent films render the key phrase as a compound word—*The Texas Chainsaw Massacre 2*. Only the first and original film uses two separated words. Some works mistakenly use the compound "chainsaw" when referring to the original film.

3. *X* includes a visual reference to *Psycho* with one victim's VW Beetle being drowned in the farm's pond, in addition to metacommentary via the dialogue where the characters, amateur filmmakers of adult entertainment (i.e., porn), discuss the virtues of Hitchcock's classic film. *Psycho* is often seen as the ultimate proto-slasher film. *Jaws* (1975) is sometimes seen as a forerunner to the slasher form as well, which *X* also references with a bloody alligator attack scene.
4. Clover, *Men, Women, and Chain Saws*, 35.
5. Similarly, the *Chainsaw* franchise relaunched on Netflix in February 2022, but it is not a proper "requel" (reboot + sequel) like the *Scream* and *Halloween* properties because the actors Marilyn Burns, Gunnar Hansen, and their director, Tobe Hooper, all died between 2014 and 2017. Kahane, "Politicizing the Mask."
6. "Politics/Government: I Can't Believe I Still Have to Protest This F—— S—," Know Your Meme, https://knowyourmeme.com/photos/1177200-politics-government.
7. Clover, *Men, Women, and Chain Saws*, 35.
8. Berliner, *Hollywood Incoherent*, 9.
9. Berliner, *Hollywood Incoherent*, 9, 11.
10. Poole, *Dark Carnivals*, 4, 17.
11. Poole, *Dark Carnivals*, 26.
12. Ryan, "American Master/Slave Story."
13. Wood, "11 Things You Didn't Know About *The Texas Chain Saw Massacre*."
14. This is the phrase that sometime western actor turned U.S. president Ronald Reagan used to encourage Americans to euphemistically embrace the "free market."
15. Poole, *Dark Carnivals*, 28.
16. Clover notes that Sally's final girl status results from her being saved by a passing truck driver; thus it is passive in comparison to Laurie Strode's more assertive defense and attack style in *Halloween*. See Clover, *Men, Women, and Chain Saws*, 36.
17. Rifkin, *When Did Indians Become Straight?*, 37.
18. Halberstam, *Skin Shows*, 140. Focused specifically on the sequel's lanky, genderqueer "final girl" Vanita "Stretch" Brock (Caroline Williams), Halberstam builds on the groundwork laid by Carol Clover to argue that Stretch, as a final girl, "represents not boyishness or girlishness but monstrous gender, a gender that splatters, rips at the seams, and that is sutured together again as something much messier than male or female." Halberstam, *Skin Shows*, 143.
19. Turner, "The Significance of the Frontier."
20. Ti West's inclusion of sex workers in *X* seems to acknowledge the porn roots that inform the production background of the original *Chain Saw*. Konda, "How *Deep Throat* Gave Us *The Texas Chain Saw Massacre*."

21. Bloom, "They Came, They Sawed."
22. Lanza, *The Texas Chain Saw Massacre*, 23.
23. Kaplan, "Manifest Domesticity," 682.
24. "Leatherface 'Kitchen/Old Lady' Mask from 'The Texas Chainsaw Massacre,'" Heritage Auctions, March 18, 2005, https://movieposters.ha.com/itm/movie-posters/horror/leatherface-kitchen-old-lady-mask-from-the-texas-chainsaw-massacre-bryanston-1974-/a/613-29411.s.
25. Campbell, "*Dead by Daylight* Removes Certain Cosmetics."
26. *Psycho* always looms large when thinking of slasher prototypes, even for the final grandma, as Norman Bates playacts as Mrs. Bates, his mother. In his drag costume he looks like a stereotypical granny.
27. Clover, *Men, Women, and Chain Saws*, 23–24. Some of the most iconic slasher films pay homage to Hitchcock's *Psycho*. For example, John Carpenter and Debra Hill cast Janet Leigh's daughter Jamie Lee Curtis to play the final girl in *Halloween* (1978). In Steve Miner's *Halloween H20: Twenty Years Later* (1998), Janet Leigh would make a cameo appearance alongside her daughter, who had reprised the role of Laurie Strode in the late 1990s, this time leaving fictional Haddonfield, Illinois, for fictional Summer Glen, California, where Curtis played a "final mother" living under an alias and employed as the head of a posh private school. Dr. Samuel Loomis, the iconic psychiatrist who obsessively hunts down his white-masked former patient Michael Myers with an Ahab-like ferocity and singularity of purpose in the *Halloween* franchise, was named after Marion Crane's boyfriend Sam Loomis (John Gavin) in Hitchcock's *Psycho*. In 1996 the Loomis name returned to haunt the slasher genre with Billy Loomis—one of two psycho killers in Wes Craven's postmodern, intertextual slasher film *Scream* (1996)—whose first name, "Billy," was inspired by Bob Clark's Canadian slasher *Black Christmas* (1974).
28. As writer Kim Henkel explained in the 2005 *Texas Monthly* essay "They Came, They Sawed" by John Bloom (a.k.a. Joe Bob Briggs): "I definitely studied Gein, . . . but I also studied a murder case in Houston at the time, a serial murderer you probably remember named Elmer Wayne Henley. He was a young man who recruited victims for an older homosexual man. I saw some news reports where Elmer Wayne was identifying bodies and their locations, and he was this skinny little ol' seventeen-year-old, and he kind of puffed out his chest and said, 'I did these crimes, and I'm gonna stand up and take it like a man.' Well that struck me as interesting, that he had this conventional morality at that point. He wanted it known that, now that he was caught, he would do the right thing. So this kind of moral schizophrenia is something I tried to build into the characters." Bloom, "They Came, They Sawed."

29. The Sawyer house recalls the description of Dracula's castle in Bram Stoker's classic *Dracula* (1897): "I myself am of an old family, and to live in a new house would kill me. A house cannot be made habitable in a day; and, after all, how few days go to make up a century. I rejoice also that there is a chapel of old times. We Transylvanian nobles love not to think that our bones may be amongst the common dead." Stoker, *Dracula*, 28.
30. Turner, "The Significance of the Frontier."
31. Kaplan, "Manifest Domesticity," 592.
32. Kaplan, "Manifest Domesticity," 585.
33. Imbler, "The Forgotten Trans History of the Wild West."
34. Slotkin, *Regeneration Through Violence*.
35. Branch, "Freebirds."
36. Halberstam, *Skin Shows*, 142.
37. Clover, *Men, Women, and Chain Saws*, 135.
38. A chaîné is a turning step from ballet whose name translates as "chain," thus providing a visual pun on the "chain" in "chainsaw." Pregnancy, it turns out, is relevant to the history of the chainsaw and to the monstrous methods of "reproduction" in the *Chainsaw* franchise. The first chainsaw was built in 1780 to cut through a woman's pelvic bone during troublesome childbirth. The procedure, known as a "symphysiotomy," involved a hand-cranked saw, which looked something like a steampunk dagger, slowly cutting open the birth canal without anesthesia.
39. Miller, "Anybody Who Was Anybody Was Neurasthenic."
40. Brown, "Lumbersexuality and Its Discontents."
41. Bloom, "They Came, They Sawed."
42. Jones, "Dear Final Girls."
43. Spears states she stayed up late watching *The Texas Chainsaw Massacre* before she decided to go to A Little White Chapel in Las Vegas for her first—and infamously covered—marriage, a milestone marked by her parents' swift intervention to annul the union. Even in this appearance *Chainsaw* is tied to issues of sex and sexuality, and how it is thwarted by family expectations and tradition. Spears, *The Woman in Me*, 106. Presumably Spears references the 2003 version of the film based on the spelling of the title.
44. Church, *Post-Horror*, 3, 11–12.
45. Cowan, *The Forbidden Body*, 18.

Bibliography

Berliner, Todd. *Hollywood Incoherent: Narration in Seventies Cinema*. Austin: University of Texas Press, 2010.

"Billionaire Space Cowboys Could Become Heroes by Focusing on Climate Crisis." *The Guardian*, July 25, 2021. https://www.theguardian.com/business/2021/jul/25/billionaire-space-cowboys-could-become-heroes-by-focusing-on-the-climate-crisis.

Bloom, John (a.k.a. Joe Bob Briggs). "They Came, They Sawed." *Texas Monthly*, November 2004. https://www.texasmonthly.com/arts-entertainment/they-came-they-sawed/.

Branch, Michael P. "Freebirds." *Orion Magazine*, November 16, 2011. https://orionmagazine.org/article/freebirds/.

Brown, Willa. "Lumbersexuality and Its Discontents." *The Atlantic*, December 10, 2014. https://www.theatlantic.com/national/archive/2014/12/lumbersexuality-and-its-discontents/383563/.

Campbell, Kyle. "*Dead by Daylight* Removes Certain Cosmetics Following Harassment Reports." *USA Today*, January 4, 2022. https://ftw.usatoday.com/2022/01/dead-by-daylight-cosmetics-harassment.

Church, David. *Post-Horror: Art, Genre, and Cultural Elevation*. Edinburgh, UK: Edinburgh University Press, 2021.

Clover, Carol. *Men, Women, and Chain Saws: Gender in the Modern Horror Film*. Princeton NJ: Princeton University Press, 1992.

Cowan, Douglas E. *The Forbidden Body: Sex, Horror, and the Religious Imagination*. New York: New York University Press, 2022.

Filipovic, Jill. "Is the Texas Abortion Law Backfiring on the People Who Pushed It Through?" *The Atlantic*, October 1, 2021. https://www.theatlantic.com/ideas/archive/2021/10/texas-abortion-law-even-more-absurd-practice/620265/.

Fine, Kerry, Michael K. Johnson, Rebecca M. Lush, and Sara L. Spurgeon. *Weird Westerns: Race, Gender, Genre*. Lincoln: University of Nebraska Press, 2020.

Foer, Jonathan Safran. *Eating Animals*. New York: Little, Brown, 2009.

Halberstam, J. *Skin Shows: Gothic Horror and the Technology of Monsters*. Durham NC: Duke University Press, 1995.

Imbler, Sabrina. "The Forgotten Trans History of the Wild West." *Atlas Obscura*, June 21, 2019. https://www.atlasobscura.com/articles/trans-history-wild-west.

Jones, Stephen Graham. "Dear Final Girls." *Juked*, October 31, 2017. http://www.juked.com/2017/10/stephen-graham-jones-dear-final-girls.asp.

Kahane, Leo H. "Politicizing the Mask: Political, Economic and Demographic Factors Affecting Mask Wearing Behavior in the USA." *Eastern Economic Journal*, January 5, 2021. https://www.ncbi.nlm.nih.gov/pmc/articles/pmc7783295/.

Kaplan, Amy. "Manifest Domesticity." *American Literature* 70, no. 3 (September 1998): 581–606.

Konda, Kelly. "How *Deep Throat* Gave Us *The Texas Chain Saw Massacre*." *We Minored in Film*, November 26, 2015. https://weminoredinfilm.com/2015/11/26/how-deep-throat-gave-us-the-texas-chainsaw-massacre/.

Lanza, Joseph. *The Texas Chain Saw Massacre: The Film that Terrified a Rattled Nation*. New York: Skyhorse, 2019.

Marulli, Larissa. "Chainsaws Were Originally Invented for Helping with Childbirth, Not for Cutting Wood." *Business Insider*, June 25, 2018. https://www.businessinsider.com/chainsaws-were-originally-invented-for-helping-childbirth-not-cutting-wood-2018-6.

Miller, Michael Vincent. "Anybody Who Was Anybody Was Neurasthenic." *New York Times*, July 7, 1991. https://www.nytimes.com/1991/07/07/books/anybody-who-was-anybody-was-neurasthenic.html.

Poole, W. Scott. *Dark Carnivals: Modern Horror and the Origins of American Empire*. Berkeley CA: Counterpoint, 2022.

Rifkin, Mark. *When Did Indians Become Straight?: Kinship, the History of Sexuality, and Native Sovereignty*. Oxford, UK: Oxford University Press, 2011.

Ryan, Jed. "American Master/Slave Story: Leather Titleholder Partners Speak about Family, Pride, PReP, and More." *Huffpost*, December 6, 2017. https://www.huffpost.com/entry/american-masterslave-stor_b_10056986.

Slotkin, Richard. *Regeneration Through Violence: The Mythology of the American Frontier, 1600–1860*. Norman: University of Oklahoma Press, 1973. Reprint, Norman: University of Oklahoma Press, 2000.

Spears, Britney. *The Woman in Me*. New York: Gallery Books/Simon & Schuster, 2023.

Stoker, Bram. *Dracula: A Norton Critical Edition*. Westminster, UK: Archibald Constable, 1897. Reprint, New York: W. W. Norton, 1997.

Stracqualursi, Veronica. "Majority of Americans Support Roe v. Wade Being Upheld, New Polls Show." *CNN Politics*, November 16, 2021. https://www.cnn.com/2021/11/16/politics/americans-abortion-roe-v-wade-poll/index.html.

Turner, Frederick Jackson. "The Significance of the Frontier in American History." American Historical Society, 1893–94. Accessed February 2, 2022. https://www.historians.org/about-aha-and-membership/aha-history-and-archives/historical-archives/the-significance-of-the-frontier-in-american-history-(1893).

Wood, Jennifer. "11 Things You Didn't Know about *The Texas Chain Saw Massacre*." *Esquire*, October 18, 2021. https://www.esquire.com/entertainment/movies/a23810/texas-chainsaw-things-you-didnt-know/.

"What Makes You Worth $100,000?" 10

Heists, the Commodification of Women,
and Capitalism Condemned in
The Professionals and *Army of the Dead*   MEREDITH HARVEY

Army of the Dead (2021) opens with a smooth military operation involving a zombie transfer, which is serendipitously disrupted by a car crash. Intercut with the scenes of the military transfer, the audience sees the cause of the accident: on their drive home from Vegas, a newly wed bride performs oral sex on her husband as a gift for "making an honest woman of her." In his distraction, her husband allows his car to swerve into the military convoy, resulting in an accident that brings about the zombie apocalypse, and in a subtle way it points to the evolution from oral sex, a consumptive alternative to sexual procreation, to oral consumption, the zombies' asexual but equally oral mode of reproduction. To further foreground the import of sex in the film, in our first view into this Vegas apocalypse, as "Viva Las Vegas" plays on, the zombies appear in the form of showgirls, who ravenously consume a male patron in a hot tub, a clear inversion of the patron's orgiastic fantasy. The scene then cuts to a man sitting at a slot machine, on oxygen, winning his jackpot, only to be consumed by the bachelorette zombies (and their zombie male strippers), for he was too consumed with his winnings to notice the apocalypse surrounding him. Such juxtaposition points to the parallels between sex workers, gambling, patriarchal marriage conventions, and zombies in that all in this scene are shown to be driven by a capitalistic need to consume, nowhere more so than in Vegas. Feminist scholar Nicola Smith critiques the ways capitalist societies "need and allow sex work to be constructed as an aberration in order to naturalize the appropriation of unpaid sexual labor that takes place primarily, if not exclusively, via the institution of marriage."[1] Yet in Zack Snyder's opening sequence, the zombie showgirls are not framed as any more an aberration than the bachelorette, the patron, or the newlyweds in their consumptive desires.

As the virus spreads, the film cuts intersperse images of people fighting zombies, and also posing with pictures of lost family members. One particular woman, listed in the credits only as "Soccer Mom" stands out as a superior fighter, whose aesthetic evolves from Soccer Mom to warrior as the song progresses. The sequence ends as Soccer Mom attempts to sacrifice herself for her child, whom she finds huddled underneath tables at a seedy lounge club. When the zombies grab Soccer Mom just feet from her freedom outside the war zone, the child refuses to leave her mother; instead the two clutch one another as the zombies consume them as a single unit. The heroes look upon the gory scene in tears, as the final brick in the shipping container wall is stacked atop Soccer Mom and the sequence concludes. The camera angle widens, and we see the wall surrounding Vegas, as well as the surrounding desert, and hordes of zombies teeming within. For those familiar with George A. Romero's *Dawn of the Dead* (1978), the omniscient wide shot seems reminiscent of the opening shot of the mall, an apocalyptic world in which the living dead occupy the familiar space of the living, but beyond its clear antecedent of Romero's zombie films, Snyder's *Army of the Dead* also possesses a less apparent predecessor, the western.

Paul A. Cantor argues, "Zombie tales and other apocalyptic scenarios turn out to be a way of imaginatively reopening the frontier in twenty-first-century popular culture. . . . All these apocalyptic shows are re-creations of that most basic of American genres, the Western."[2] Given the lineage that traces the zombie horror flick to the western, it is not surprising that in *Army of the Dead*, we see conventions of the zombie films but also the western, as demonstrated through both the setting of the film in the Las Vegas desert and its adherence to other western tropes. Operating within *Army of the Dead* such hybridity of genres situates the film into what Michael K. Johnson, Rebecca M. Lush, and Sara L. Spurgeon define as the weird western: "texts that utilize a hybrid genre format, blending canonical elements of the western with science fiction, fantasy, horror, or some other component of speculative literature."[3] The weird western not only situates itself within the canonical elements of the western but does so with intent that the audience will recognize "its acts of borrowing and its audacious generic joinings, inviting [them] to recognize genre conventions as conventions and actively participate in their interrogation."[4] This definition reminds viewers not just of the weird western's ability to adhere to conventions but how it places those conventions in the audience's path and begs for interrogation.

One avenue for such an interrogation presents itself in comparisons between western films and those films focusing on a more contemporary zombie apocalypse. Among the many western films that share heritage with this zombie film, one film that closely mirrors *Army of the Dead* within its generic formula is Richard Brooks's classic western, *The Professionals* (1966). In this chapter, I intend to show how the classic western *The Professionals* and the weird zombie western *Army of the Dead* utilize the conventions of their respective genres as well as those of their shared subgenre of the heist to disrupt the binary of savagery and civilization, and in doing so critique the treatment of women at the hands of powerful elite in late-stage capitalism. Based on Daryl Lee's generic reading of the heist and feminist scholars' examination of the relationship between capitalism and women's sexuality, I will look at how the two films adhere to and subvert generic conventions involving the commodification of women as sexual objects, and how the latter film includes accountability into its mode of critique.

Cowboys, Zombies, and Heists in the American West

While the zombie-infested Vegas strip does not embody the open frontier and premodern space of the western, key signposts throughout the film point to western heritage of *Army of the Dead* in ways that invite interrogation, including the desert landscape surrounding Vegas and the postmodern implications of the fallen Vegas. Furthermore, Snyder himself reflects on the generic connections in an interview in *Esquire* when he speaks of the conceptualization of the film's protagonist, a veteran of the zombie wars: "In my mind it's always a story of veterans. I just personally find the story of the old gunfighter that put their guns on for one last fight to be more interesting that the rookie gunfighter who goes into battle and isn't sure what's going to happen."[5] Such language situates the film as a weird western, with his usage of the word "gunfighter," but it also clearly situates the film's conventional characters within the long tradition of other veterans of lost causes, as hired guns with a mission.[6] In this case, we see the veterans of the zombie wars, those same heroes from the opening sequence, on a mission to liberate two women from zombie captivity, and more importantly to steal $200 million from a casino vault and escape with the money before the federal government drops a nuclear bomb on Vegas—as a final effort to end the zombie wars that took place inside those walls.[7]

The narrative of *The Professionals*, filmed fifty-five years before in a desert only fifty miles away from Las Vegas, presents similar conventions. While the film was shot in the Nevada desert, that desert represents the Chihuahuan Desert, which forms a large part of the border between Texas and Mexico. While a destroyed Vegas teeming with uncivilized zombies creates a premodern condition in *Army of the Dead*, within *The Professionals*, the post-Revolution borderlands of Mexico in the early 1920s reveals a setting far from the civilization of the early industrial United States. In lieu of zombies, the savage desert space in *The Professionals* is occupied by Mexican guerillas, disaffected soldiers from the continual efforts toward a Mexican Revolution of the working classes. Like those characters from *Army of the Dead*, the protagonists in *The Professionals* are skilled veterans who once fought in the desert in a futile war, though these "professionals" fought *with* the guerillas as revolutionaries—further complicating the arbitrary lines between the good and bad guys. In a nod to captivity narratives of older westerns, the men are hired to complete a mission, to rescue the kidnapped wife of a wealthy oil tycoon from the uncivilized lands and peoples of Mexico—paralleling the zombie hordes of *Army of the Dead*. Yet as the leader of the group, Fardan (Lee Marvin), explains, these professionals also have a primary mission of monetary gain; they're going back to Mexico not for the Revolution but "this time, strictly for cash." In these parallel narratives surrounding commissioned robbery, one of money and another of a woman, both films find their place within the genre of the heist.[8]

Despite the difficulty of identifying the genre of the heist due to its evolving and adaptable nature, Lee defines the genre through the presence of a "team" of individuals consisting of specific character types such as "the gang leader," "the mentor," and other individuals who possess specific skills with little social value.[9] According to Lee, the group often consists of "social misfits" with specific skills, including those of safecrackers and mechanics such as Dieter (Matthias Schweighöfer) and Peters (Tig Notaro) in *Army of the Dead*, as well as demolitions experts such as Dolworth (Burt Lancaster) in *The Professionals*. Beyond character types, the narrative trajectory defines the heist film, and at the "heart of the heist film" lies a plot in which there exists an "extraordinary robbery of a formidable institution that requires careful planning and the skills of specialists."[10] The broad possibilities of such a plot allow the subgenre to exist across different genres ranging from noir to comedy to western, and yes, in the case of *Army of the Dead*, even zombie western. As Sintumuang writes in his introduction to an interview with Snyder, "*Army of the Dead . . .* pushes the zombie movie into heist territory. Think *Ocean's Eleven*, with zombies." The parallel character types in *The Professionals* and *Army of the Dead* and the narrative trajectory of the films invite us to "participate in the interrogation" of the subgenre of the heist itself, to examine the implications of its breaks from and adherence to conventions.

Keeping this goal in mind, *The Professionals* and *Army of the Dead* both clearly orient themselves as part of this semantic definition of the heist, but they also share what Lee refers to as the shared purpose of heist films and what he argues are the two specific *social* functions of the heist. First they "provide a critique of the socio-economic order through mostly likeable characters achieving something extraordinary from marginalized social positions" and second, through the metaphor of the heist they "reflect on the *raison d'etre* and condition of the film artist in a commercial medium from within a commercial genre."[11] Furthermore, Lee speaks to the way that the overarching social functions remain static despite the fact that the specific social message of the films may change over time based on the particular politics of the age.[12] Fittingly with both of these films, we see such a critique of their respective "socio-economic order," as the attempts to transfer wealth into the hands of the "marginalized" hired guns reveal the inhumanity of the wealthy men who hire them, as well as the systems through which these men have acquired wealth.[13] Within *The Professionals*, a film set at the turn of the century but shot in the 1960s, the socioeconomic critique develops among the political upheavals of the civil rights era, the Vietnam War, and second-wave feminism, whereas the more contemporary *Army of the Dead* escalates its critique of twenty-first-century global capitalism, particularly surrounding two seemingly disperse subjects: the military-industrial complex and sexual consumption.[14]

In such a critique of socioeconomic systems, the heist film makes a natural generic companion for both the western and the zombie film, and perhaps keeping such layered generic coding in mind allows us to further narrow down the shared purpose of the two films. According to David Lusted, *The Professionals* belongs to an era of postwar period westerns, which often critique instead of assume the previously perpetrated ideas of American exceptionalism and Manifest Destiny. Here the setting of the U.S.-Mexican border may serve as a metaphor for the U.S.-occupied Vietnam—the violence in each space leaving one to question the ethical imperative of the capitalistic United States as heroic defender of the good.[15] In *The Professionals*, this ethical imperative becomes particularly problematic when the site of this power negotiation is the female body of the kidnapped wife. *Army of the Dead* similarly invokes contemporary scrutiny of globalization, particularly that of the military-industrial complex, in that the initiator of the heist, the man who hires this team, hails from Japan, and is portrayed early on in the film as being in cahoots with the U.S. military leadership. Furthermore, *Army of the Dead*'s setting of Vegas, with its architectural artifices from Venice, Paris, Egypt, and Rome, serves to critique global consumerism. Such a critique runs particularly true for audiences familiar with generic conventions of twentieth-century zombie films, which since Romero's *Dawn of the Dead* have come "to represent the kind of mindless consumers produced by late-capitalist culture."[16] Finally, Snyder's choice of Vegas as setting emphasizes contemporary concerns over not just consumption of artifice and man-made creations of late capitalist culture but also the consumption linked to sexual hedonism, which Vegas is known for, and the not unrelated commodification of marriage.

Both films accomplish such critiques of sexuality, marriage, and capitalism through their subversion of the dichotomy between civilization and the savage on their respective "frontiers." In the case of *The Professionals* we see the socioeconomic order in the civilizing forces of the U.S. settlement of the West, which in this film is embodied by the oil tycoon Joe Grant (Ralph Bellamy), who for the sum of $100,000 hires the protagonists to save his wife from Jesus Raza (Jack Palance), "the bloodiest cutthroat in Mexico," a place he deems "the desert, a hellhole." While Grant's socioeconomic status denotes his participation in the civilizing mission of the West, his belief that such status allows him to treat his wife as object and personal possession eventually subverts his assumed space as the "civilized" within the social order. *Army of the Dead* explores a similar frontier, or at least it appears to in the beginning of the film as the shipping container wall delineates the space between the soon-to-be-nuked zombie wastelands and the human world. However, early on in the film, the existence of the "quarantine camp" between the zombie savagery and human civilization, a space in which guards sexually harass and assault disempowered refugees in tents, suggests that savagery exists in both human and zombie worlds. In *Army of the Dead*, the zombies inhabit the same "hellhole desert," but their savage space sits on the destroyed shells of the human effort to civilize that space. In contrast to their world, within *Army of the Dead* we see a modern-day Joe Grant, embodied by the well-dressed Tanaka (Hiroyuki Sanada), the wealthy Japanese businessman with a relationship with the U.S. military, who hires the team to go into that uncivilized space of violence for $200 million. However, in a way even more condemnatory than in *The Professionals*, from the moment the audience arrives on the other side of that border, the lines between civilization and savagery fall apart with dire consequences, particularly when Tanaka's man on the inside, Martin (Garret Dillahunt), takes possession of an autonomous female (zombie) body.

Capitalism and Commodification of Women's Bodies

Like *Army of the Dead*, *The Professionals* opens with a montage, introducing us to each of these "professionals" prior to the job with Grant. In our introduction to the Dolworth character, the lens through which we will see much of the commodification of the female body, we see him not working like his cohorts but having sex with a married woman. The husband beats down the door, and the wife tries to cover for Dolworth, who leaps through the window in his long johns. The scene works for comedy, but it also establishes the film's uneven assessment of sex and marriage. In this scene, the woman, clearly complicit and consenting to the act, tries to cover for her lover at the expense of herself, as her husband throws his hat at her in chastisement; as wife she belongs to him. The scene is short, and overall forgettable, unless viewed in contrast to the larger picture. The philandering Dolworth and his cohorts are hired by a husband (Grant) to go into Mexico to save his wife, but long after the men discover that the captivity narrative is false, for she does not want to be "saved" from the Mexican "cutthroat" revealed to be her lover, they attempt to honor their contract and reap their monetary reward. In doing so they supersede her desire—her bodily autonomy—and enforce an institution that they, based upon the establishing scene at least, have little allegiance to.[17] When we see Dolworth again another early scene reinforces that relationship between sex and capital commodity. Fardan asks Dolworth how he lost his pants, and he responds, "In a lady's bedroom trying to raise the cash." While the comment again is clearly meant to be humorous, perhaps even suggesting a metaphorical link between male sexuality and capital gain (both of which require something to be raised), it is worth noting the ways in which sexuality even in this brief scene becomes transactional, part of what Smith discusses as the oft-ignored political economy of sexuality.

The transactional nature of sexuality in the film, and the female characters' subjugation and objectification as part of these transactions, reflects societal realities critiqued by 1970s feminist scholars such as Gayle Rubin and Luce Irigaray, who spoke to the lack of autonomy implied by what Rubin identifies as sexual systems of power that determine the "exchange of women" in society and what Irigaray critiques as the designation of woman as "commodity" in patriarchal society. The two women of the film, Chiquita (Marie Gomez), the soldier, and María (Claudia Cardinale), the wife, both women of color, are continually seen through the male gaze—which both objectifies and monetizes their being. In one scene, Dolworth spies on a topless Chiquita bathing from above and says, "Now there's a woman worth a ransom. She never says no." In another scene, the camera angle emphasizes his gaze down María's loose-fitting deeply V-necked dress.[18] When she looks up, they have an exchange and he asks, "What makes you worth $100,000?" In both cases, his statement in combination with his objectifying gaze reinforces the assumption that a woman's value as commodity lies in her sexuality. Despite Dolworth's objectification, both women demonstrate limited agency as they weaponize the assumptions and desires that come with that gaze; they, like Snyder's zombie strippers, attempt to disrupt the power dynamic between consumer and consumed.[19] In the case of Chiquita, she recognizes Dolworth's desire for her body and decides to ride out first across the canyon he is protecting; when Raza, her commander, tells her to go to the back, she refuses. When he adds, "Do as I say woman," she demonstrates her agency but also the weaponization of her status as woman when she argues, "A woman he will not shoot." While her plan fails, as she is shot, she again weaponizes her sexuality when after being fatally wounded, she uses an exchange about her "fine times" together with Dolworth as an opportunity to pull a gun on him one more time "for the Revolution." Unfortunately, the gun is empty and she dies. In a parallel scene, we see María utilize these same assumptions against Dolworth, yet in her exchange the commodification of the female body becomes even more explicit. She first offers Dolworth money to aid in her escape, and then realizing she has a more valuable asset, she begins to undress and asks, "You want me? My price is high." While Dolworth negates the offer, she, like Chiquita, doubles down on her efforts and begins to kiss him in order to steal his gun. She, like Chiquita, is thwarted. Released just a year after *Griswold v. Connecticut* declared that *married* couples could use contraception, these women's weaponization of their sexuality disrupts the notion of woman as mere object; they possess agency. Yet ironically such scenes are accomplished through objectifying shots that reinforce the male gaze, and in their failure, such limited agency embodies the limits to women's autonomy within the larger system.

While this weaponization of their sexuality can be read as an attempt to disarm the socioeconomic hegemony (quite literally since they are doing it for the Revolution), within the dialogue surrounding the heist we see more explicit critiques of existing patriarchal power structures within a capitalistic society. María tells the story of her marriage with Grant to the group, and within it highlights the link between marriage, ownership, and capitalism. She explains how "Mr. Joe Grant" bought the hacienda from her father, and how upon his deathbed her father, in an effort to raise the status of the family through marriage, gave her to Grant to be his wife. María narrates, "Mr. Joe Grant wants you for his wife. You will become Doña Grande a fine lady. That is my wish. Here a wish is a command." Through her voice, and the disdain with which María talks about this exchange, the film critiques the institution of marriage as transactional, as part of the capitalist world of monetary exchange. María is not the captive of Raza but of her husband through the institution of marriage; yet our heroes continue their efforts to return her to her husband, implying their loyalty not to the protection of the captive but to this power structure.

Later, when María tells Fardan that he is a man loyal to the Revolution like Raza, he retorts that Raza "is a thief" and she is a "whore cheating on her husband." His degrading usage of the word "whore" in this context recalls Foucault's insistence that the need to control sexualities is most often an exercise to maintain economic power. The irony of Fardan's utterance also mirrors Federici's critique of feminists who degrade sex work and fails to recognize that in capitalist societies "women have always had to sell their bodies and not only in brothels and on the streets" but also "in marriage."[20] Due to his own investment in the power structure within the heist, Fardan cannot see the irony of his condemnation; only María understands that whore and wife in this context are one and the same—and she emphasizes such connections when she explains that her husband "stole millions from the land" and states that to get any of it back, she will "steal, and cheat, and yes, whore" for the Revolution.[21]

Despite their reservations throughout the film, by the conclusion, Fardan and the others set María free to be with Raza and fight for the Revolution, but only after reaching Grant. David Lusted describes the professionals as cynical and disillusioned with a world based on "self-interest."[22] In the final scene, Grant tells his man to shoot Raza for what we can assume is the transgression of having sex with María, but perhaps more importantly for disrupting his hegemonic assumptions of power. When the professionals disrupt Grant's efforts, he turns his anger toward María. Grant states to María, "You belong to me," and when María objects to his possession, he grabs and hits her, only to have the professionals respond by setting her free to return with Raza to the Revolution and her own sexual autonomy. Shortly thereafter Grant says to Fardan, "You bastard." Fardan responds, "In my case, an accident of birth. But you, sir, you're a self-made man." Lusted sees this humor and cynicism of the characters as part of "the social and political mood at the time of the film's production," yet within this last usage of the word "bastard" and Fardan's casual acceptance of it, the film also recognizes the limits of marriage to assign status.[23] In this moment Fardan subverts Grant's power and condemns Grant's transactional treatment of his wife. Smith explains the need to deconstruct and interrogate heteronormative power relations that reinforce "political-economic" order through "distinctions between the public/private and moral/immoral that prop up marriage and the nuclear family as economic, political, and cultural institutions."²⁴ In the end, this casual utterance of the word "bastard" does just that, and our ambivalent heroes ride off into an ambiguous sunset, as Grant's humiliation reveals a small step toward accountability for the violation of María's autonomy.

By the time we reach these same questions in the near-future setting of *Army of the Dead*, we see the relationship between marriage, sex, and commodity treated even more explicitly and more ambivalently. The apocalyptic oral sex between newlyweds, the zombie showgirls, and the bachelorette zombies and strippers of the opening sequence imply what Steve Jones identifies as the zombie metaphor of "consumerist greed akin to hedonistic gluttony" and the disruption of the hegemonic distribution in power between consumer and consumed.²⁵ As the film progresses, the human women in the film, like those of *The Professionals*, more consciously recognize the power to be gained through manipulating that greed and gluttony. In a mode quite similar to María and Chiquita in *The Professionals*, early within *Army of the Dead*, we see a woman weaponizing her sexuality in relation to the male gaze in order to gain power, and interestingly also a gun. In this early scene, Lily (Nora Arnezeder), the Coyote, who serves as scout for the mission, asks Cummings (Theo Rossi), a predatory police officer from the quarantined area surrounding Vegas, for his gun. Through the exchange, we see Lily utilize his desire for her body, but we also see her own autonomy as perpetrator of the gaze, as if she has weaponized the gaze of the oppressor to make her appear to be the sexual aggressor, and thus to make her even more sexually desirable. She looks down at him in the shot, her eyes scanning him up and down, and they have a sexually charged exchange regarding the gun as the two get closer and the shot tightens:

> LILY: It's beautiful.
> CUMMINGS: It's reliable too.
> LILY: Oh yeah?
> CUMMINGS: Yeah.
> LILY: Can I touch it?
> CUMMINGS: You wanna touch it?
> LILY: Yeah.
> CUMMINGS: Just for a second.
> LILY: Just for a second [whispered].

In order to arm herself, Lily implies her own sexuality as a commodity for exchange but also utilizes objectifying language for the gun, in a playful gun as penis metaphor. However, unlike the female characters of *The Professionals*, Lily succeeds in her exchange, takes power with the gun, and shoots Cummings in the leg as a sacrifice to the zombies. When he begs for compassion, she clarifies her justification to the group as she reminds Cummings that within the quarantine zone he raped and "lorded power" over the women in his charge. Lily's act and her justification situate this film within the #MeToo era of feminism that, as Nussbaum points out, "has helped win accountability," but primarily social accountability rather than legal. Nussbaum argues that this "ironically turned a movement that started as a movement against objectification [into] one that can lead to reverse objectification" in the form of retribution.[26] We see such "reverse objectification" as the rapist is offered as a commodity of exchange to the female zombie as a part of retribution. Within these walls, justice is brutal and retributional. Here for his violation of female autonomy, Cummings, no longer protected by his previously empowered status, loses autonomy, as he becomes the victim of the captivity narrative. His "abject terror" then, parallels the women whom he tormented in the zone, even as they both are held captive in different rooms at the home of Zeus, the zombie King, at "Olympus." For Cummings, of course, the experience is shown as emasculating karma for his own lorded power in the camps. And he now is shown experiencing the familiar captivity narrative of both western and horror films, which revel in the female terror when captured by the savage.[27] However, unlike the female captives, the audience is not meant to feel sympathy, and no hero will try to save him, for they have deemed him expendable due to his participation in the victimization of women.

While such scenes imply Snyder's efforts to explore explicitly feminist ideas within the zombie film, the stronger statement about the problematic commodification of the female body within capitalist society, like that of *The Professionals*, lies in the heist itself.[28] In *Army of the Dead*, the audience only discovers the true nature of the heist 127 minutes into the film, keeping the dramatic irony alive, as most of our heroes have yet to find out. Through an exchange between Martin and Lily, we learn that the point of the mission was not to extract the money for Tanaka but to extract biological material from one of the Alpha zombies—the ones who are, as Lily explains early on, "smarter, faster, and organized" and were bitten by Zeus, the original Alpha zombie. At this point, the earlier shot of Tanaka nodding to the U.S. military generals in the film starts to make sense, as the audience realizes the heist's value to the military-industrial complex. Martin explains this value to Lily just after decapitating the Alpha Queen: "Do you know how much this is worth to my boss, to the government. In the right hands, we have the power to make more. . . . That's the ultimate WMD." In the team's failure to understand the true mission, this film finds parallels within original critiques of capitalism in that the workers, or here the team, do not have full knowledge of the product of their labor; yet the critique here also situates itself within a specific horror of global twenty-first-century capitalism, specifically the military-industrial complex.[29] Despite their belief that they risked their life for an individualistic desire for money, the reality of their heist, like that in *The Professionals*, lies in the exchange of a female body, or in this case a female without a body.

What makes this commodification of the female zombie body more damning in the narrative of *Army of the Dead* is how her sexuality folds into the narrative. According to Steven Gerrard, Samantha Holland, and Robert Shail in their discussion of Craig Engler and Karl Schaefer's television series *Z Nation* (2014–18), "The political purpose of zombies [is] as metaphors for processes of Othering; as a stand-in for all those who have to be rejected in favour of a very specifically gendered, racialized, and sexualized normative body(-politic)."[30] Within *Army of the Dead*, while such themes of othering occur, particularly in the discussions of the quarantine area, the sexualized and gendered nature of the Alpha zombies makes them not entirely separate from the "normative body-politic." The sexuality of the Other has been the norm within U.S. film, including western narratives. Just look at the demonstrative sexuality of the Mexican women María and Chiquita of *The Professionals* for an example; however, within zombie narratives, such sexuality of the zombie Other has not been the case.[31] While recent "zom-com" genres have begun to explore the sexuality of the zombie in modes that, according to Ian Olney, show "the patriarchy as living death" and demonstrate "a concern with the status of women in Western culture that could be broadly defined as feminist," zombies in horror films have largely been seen as rapacious only for human flesh.³² With our introduction of the Alpha Queen, when she comes for the offering of Cummings, we see a new type of zombie. Snyder has made the sexuality of these Alpha zombies part of their makeup, part of their humanity, and part of their effort toward creating a civilization—thus making her "death" at the hands of Martin more meaningful.

While the introduction of a "sexy" zombie wearing a translucent dress and bikini does not immediately scream feminist zombie film, her cognizance in the early scene challenges objectification.³³ The humanity of the Alpha Queen, her non-thingness, is emphasized when we see her response to the gaze of the humans occupying the zone she has been charged to protect. When she arrives, despite Cummings's dehumanizing language of "what is it?" her agency clearly designates her from the hordes of zombies the audience was introduced to in the opening montage. The group that has violated her sanctuary gaze upon her. This gaze is emphasized by Martin's removal of his glasses—his effort to take in the object he sees before him—but she gazes back, and all but Martin look away. The long camera angles emphasize this reciprocal gaze; unlike María from *The Professionals*, the Queen, while clearly sexualized in her defiance, is shown as not object but equal subject as she meets Martin's gaze and gazes back from above. While Martin stares at her as an object, as subhuman, she stares at him to warn him that she is anything but. Unfortunately for humanity, he still assesses her value as an object, a commodity—the extent to which neither the audience nor the other characters in the film fully understand until later. Olney suggests, "Zombie culture functions like a funhouse mirror, reflecting our dominant social order—white, Capitalist, and patriarchal—as a kind of living death: insatiably rapacious and perversely enduring."³⁴ Within this scene, as the Alpha Queen's gaze is placed back upon the "white," "Capitalist," "patriarchal," and "rapacious" Martin, we see her attempt to disrupt his social order; however, despite her attempt, through his initial gaze, the film implies that *she* becomes the zombie Martin wants. Silvia Federici argues, within and because of capitalistic society, female bodies exist as "the main targets, the privileged sites, for the deployment of power-techniques and power relations."³⁵ In part due to her proximity to Zeus as Queen but equally in that Martin sees in her status as *female* and challenger, he feels the need to conquer and objectify her.

When the Alpha Queen returns to her fellow Alpha zombies' home base at the fallen Olympus, the Alpha General pulls Cummings along as sacrifice, and we see the Alpha Queen interact beyond her earlier role as protector, negotiator, and warrior of the zombies. Instead here we see her as lover. As Zeus enters, she does not throng in subservience like the other Alphas at the ceremony but stands separate, back arched and gazing at her partner in wait. Her gaze is returned and importance emphasized as Zeus turns to address his Queen before even looking upon the sacrifice that she has brought. While their screeching sounds are horrifying to the audience (and poor rapist Cummings on the ground), their response to one another—her arched back and the evolution of their snarls into softer near moans as they bite at one another's face—all emphasize sexual tension and longing. It is not a human display but familiar enough for a human audience to recognize the sexuality as the camera shots cut from Zeus's face resting between the Queen's hips, to her face expressing pleasure that alludes to orgasm. While the full significance of this scene cannot be understood until later, the allusion to oral sex and fulfillment exists within this first viewing—and the parallels between oral fixation of both zombies and the sexual consumer from the earliest moments of the film only heighten viewers' sensitivity to such references. As Snyder explains, "I believe that some sweet zombie love happened, some sweet zombie lovemaking. I don't know if it was sweet. It was probably pretty aggressive."[36] In this scene, the Queen as zombie Other is not the sexualized object seen through Martin's gaze but a conscious being with sexual desires. Cantor draws a parallel between the zombies of *The Walking Dead* and the Other in the old western: "The zombies play the stereotypical role traditionally assigned to Indians in Westerns—the barbarian hordes lurking on the borders of the civilized community and threatening to annihilate it. Just like the Indians in many Westerns, the zombies are nameless and virtually faceless, they never speak, and they may be killed indiscriminately."[37] Like María, the lover of Raza from *The Professionals*, the Alpha Queen chooses to be the lover of the barbarous Other, and in her choice she demonstrates the flaw in assumptions regarding the civilized and savage in *her* world. Like Jesus and María in their love of both one another and the Revolution, the Alpha zombies in their demonstrative affection and adherence to societal structures are not these dehumanized Others. Their murder therefore is not indiscriminate—and like the Mexican Guerillas of *The Professionals*, who were depicted in a similar manner, these zombies are not nameless barbarians.

Another way in which the zombies demonstrate their level of civilization in the film is that unlike the humans, these zombies play by a set of rules; they possess an ethical standard.[38] Just before that scene in which the audience discovers the true nature of the heist, we see Lily explain to Martin the corruption in the camps. In contrast, she clarifies, "Within these walls, the rules are clear. You don't see them fucking each other over," and without missing a beat, she threatens Martin if he "screws" her over. Her dialogue reveals that she trusts the Alpha zombies' adherence to rules more so than the human whom she fights beside. While we find Lily's agreement was to help him capture the Queen so he could extract a vial of blood, a vial will not satisfy Martin's greed, hedonistic desire, or cruelty. Instead, once the Queen is captured, he takes her head, for its value is greater than merely blood. Martin, not the zombies, embodies that which Romero's early zombies, the zombie predecessors of Snyder's, represented, the unlimited greed of consumerism: "They don't eat for sustenance. Instead, they eat simply for the sake of eating. They desire to have more."[39] Martin does not need the higher dollar amount that will be gained by the removal of her head, but his desire for "more" transcends need, and thus he ensures not only his own end in the jaws of Siegfried and Roy's zombie tiger but that of civilization itself—embodying what Olney identifies as that primary metaphor of the zombie film, the cannibalistic nature of the late capitalistic appetite to consume, until "we are our-selves consumed by the capitalist appetite that drives us."[40] Yet here the human embodiment of capitalism in Martin, not the zombie, embodies that cannibalistic drive; for the zombies are not the real monsters of this film. Like Mr. Joe Grant in *The Professionals* before him, in Martin, the capitalistic forces of "progress and civilization" themselves prove less civilized and more monstrous than the barbarous hordes.

Martin's status as monster and an arm of the military-industrial complex reveals itself in the moments before the Queen's beheading, in which the audience sees that capitalism, cruelty, greed, and the commodification of the female body effectively ensure the apocalypse. The connection between his need to dominate and his own dehumanization of her as sexual object occurs shortly after he captures her. In these moments during which he mimics a rape scene, he embodies what Martha Nussbaum sees as the U.S. culture's "entrenched male privilege that defines females as subordinate," as "commodities or objects for male use."[41] These objectifying attitudes allow, if not encourage, the violation of female autonomy in sexual assault and harassment. In his own assault, Martin gazes at the Queen's thrashing body, calls her "gorgeous," flips her over, and mounts her, while jokingly saying, "oh yeah." In Nussbaum's discussion of violations of female autonomy, she cites the gender pride and greed endemic of U.S. culture to be the key culprits that inhibit legal accountability for sexual assault on women. Martin in his actions demonstrates both, but he also suffers from what Nussbaum calls the "visual impairment" that comes with each.[42] Much like Mr. Joe Grant, who fails to anticipate his hired help's offense at his abuse of María at the end of *The Professionals*, Martin's inhumane behavior, motivated by greed and enabled through his pride and innate sense of superiority over the object in his possession, inhibits him from seeing the eventuality of accountability for his actions. He becomes the embodiment of rape culture.

Less blinded by gender pride and greed, Lily anticipates that they might be held accountable, that there will be an Alpha response as a result of Zeus hearing his Queen's "death cry."[43] The Queen's decapitation has left her body dead, and as Zeus comes to mourn her body's death, we see the extent to which Martin has violated both the Queen's autonomous body and the civilization of the zombies. Zeus, aboard his zombie horse, humanely proceeds with a funeral for his Queen. The symbolic act of burial again draws parallels between the Alphas and early human (and humanoid) societies, emphasizing their evolution. Such evolution is made more apparent, as well as more biological in nature, when Zeus, in his grief, reaches into the Queen and pulls out a zombie fetus, which outside of its mother's womb immediately expires. The audience sees Zeus's grief over the tied fate of mother and child, echoing the grief the audience feels over the "Soccer Mom" of the opening sequence. In this moment, a greater understanding of the audience's first observation of Zeus and the Queen emerges. What had been first viewed as sexual desire can now be understood as reverence for the procreation that occurs as a result of that desire, implicating that motherhood exists as a separate yet related aspect of female autonomy.

Feminist critics such as Federici and Smith point to capitalist society's dependence upon control of the female body, which acts as a producer of both labor and surplus demand; such dependence, they argue, encourages the devaluation of women's autonomy.[44] In preventing the Alpha zombie's birth, Martin violates the autonomous control of reproduction of the Queen but also of her society, a society rebuilding in the ashes of the ultimate capitalistic indulgence embodied by Las Vegas.[45] Ironically, Martin's failure to recognize this autonomy prevents the zombie civilization from evolving beyond violence as a mode of reproduction. Snyder explains that "zombies in [this] movie are working toward not needing a human host to procreate their species. . . . That's the ultimate evolution."[46] Through the murder of the Queen and her child, Martin has effectively put human hosts back on the menu.

In her book that focuses on the "reclaiming of the body in contemporary capitalism," Federici predicts the frightening possibilities of attempts to control women's reproduction: "If capitalism is an unjust exploitative social system, it's worrisome to think that in the future capitalistic planners might be able to produce the kind of human beings that they need."[47] Snyder's film imagines just that, as the military-industrial complex first creates Zeus and indirectly, through Martin, destroys nonlethal autonomous zombie procreation due to the greed and pride such an industry propagates. Olney proposes that the prevalence of zombie movies in the twenty-first century and the way they serve as critiques of consumption might be a sign that "we are rapidly approaching capitalism's apocalyptic limit."[48] In the end, the capitalist need to control procreation in order to create the ultimate labor for war, coupled with Martin's violation of the Queen's autonomy, provides the catalyst for such an apocalypse. As *Army of the Dead* comes to a close, the heist fails, most characters die, and Tanaka is shown disappointed.[49] With the narrative seemingly concluded, the screen goes black. Then from the darkness, the apocalyptic ruins of Vegas become visible, and Vanderohe (Omari Hardwick), a surviving member of the group, emerges, cash in hand, from the vault. And for a few moments, the audience believes he alone has survived and thrived—slighting Tanaka's power as he keeps the money and books himself a private plane. But in the last moments, the audience discovers that he has not really survived but has been bitten by Zeus. The film ends ambiguously with Vanderohe, now destined to be the next Alpha King, en route aboard a private plane flying to Mexico. The implied global infection and spread reveals a world that may well be held accountable for Martin's violation of the Queen; all of human society may pay the price for such capitalist greed. It seems that in the twenty-first century, our ambivalent heroes do not get to ride into the sunset like those in *The Professionals*.

Conclusion

Even genre films attempting to break new territory cannot help but to adhere to some of those same conventions they push against. The film industry itself is predicated upon consumption, for without a paying audience, the films cannot get made, so it is important to acknowledge that while both of these films do work to push against narratives that objectify women, and against contemporary socioeconomic systems of power, their creation also requires that they participate in those systems they critique. And thus, *The Professionals*, in part as a western and in part as a commodity, engages in its own gaze, its own objectification of women, even as it promotes the contemporary trends of second-wave feminism and counterculture antimaterialism. Likewise, *Army of the Dead* relies upon the conventions of the genre, upon our interpretation and understanding of the gaze and the sexual objectification of women—even as it pushes against those systems with an awareness and a context of #MeToo and global critiques of the military-industrial complex. In both films, such complexities find resonance in Lee's discussion of the heist as genre, the purpose of which is to serve "as a vehicle for exploring aesthetic value and artistic creation as problematic in which capitalistic economics, labour, and pure aesthetic value face off against each other, or at least appear to."[50] Through their engagement with the problem of women's autonomy within the capitalist system, Brooks's and Snyder's critiques do just that. But it is worth noting that Snyder's critiques push harder and, in so doing, reveal that dissent and accountability in film have evolved.

Late into postproduction of *Army of the Dead*, Chris D'Elia, who was originally cast and filmed in the role of the skilled helicopter pilot and mechanic, was accused of "pursuing multiple teenage girls."[51] With filming complete, and with the nation in a pandemic, Snyder chose to recast the role. Tig Notaro, the lesbian female comedian who steals each scene she is in with dry humor and cigar chomping near open flames, replaced the other actor. Each scene, carefully shot in green screen, was eventually integrated into the film for a cost of an undisclosed amount that was apparently less than the cost of the CGI zombie tiger. While not encumberingly expensive in the scope of such a large production, Snyder's choice to cast Notaro, whose attire and behavior in the film contrast the stereotyped sexualized femininity seen in zombie films (including this one), pushes against a narrative of woman as object, a narrative that Chris D'Elia's pursuit arguably embraced. The fearless cigar chomping, perhaps just a happy accident, might also be viewed as a biting commentary on accountability and presumptions regarding phallic power, particularly in light of the film's motifs of oral consumption, though this time such accountability transcends the film itself. Perhaps such a move and others like this are a sign that narratives of accountability for violations of female autonomy might appear in the western, in the zombie movie, and in the weird zombie western, but slowly also in the industry as well. Maybe if this latest stage of capitalism can incorporate some degree of accountability, we will be able to not quite ride off into the sunset but at least avoid the apocalypse.

Notes

1. Smith, *Capitalism's Sexual History*, 5.
2. Cantor, *Pop Culture*, 148.
3. Johnson, Lush, and Spurgeon, "Westworld(s)," 2.
4. Johnson, Lush, and Spurgeon. "Westworld(s)," 11.
5. Sintumuang, "Zack Snyder Tells Us."
6. In classic western texts, oftentimes the protagonist is a Confederate soldier seeking redemption in the West after fighting on the losing side of the war.
7. Notably, this rescue mission is secondary and only performed after the protagonist hero, Scott Ward, is coerced by his daughter, who threatens to rescue them on her own if her dad doesn't help—because, as pointed out by the Soccer Mom in the earlier scenes, the good parents in this film want to protect their children.
8. In his landmark study of the western as genre, *Sixguns & Society: A Structural Study of the Western*, Will Wright extensively discusses the deconstruction of the good/bad dichotomy in *The Professionals*, coming to the conclusion that Raza

may be a villain in that he's trying to kill the heroes, but despite this, in no way could he be considered the bad guy.
9. Wright places *The Professionals* within the subgenre of the "professional" western. Within his definition he lays out common plot points, establishing norms parallel to those of Lee's "heist" films: heroes consist of a skilled group of societal misfit fighters hired for money, not justice; they take on a fight that traditional forces can't handle against a very strong villain; they demonstrate their bonds in the fight; they win (at least a little, and often in opposition to societal or capitalist powers that be); and they live or die together. But interestingly, Wright also mentions that the motivations or buildup for the fight take second place to the extended battle itself and the relationships that develop through the battle, thus creating a genre of western in which the plots vary more so than other plots. The heist plot then, I'd argue, is just one such variation.
10. Lee, *The Heist Film*, 5.
11. Lee, *The Heist Film*, 5.
12. Lee, *The Heist Film*, 10.
13. In *Gunfighter Nation: The Myth of the Frontier in Twentieth-Century America*, Richard Slotkin discusses *The Professionals* at length and points to this ideology of capitalist critique when he explains that "as American heroes, they [Rico and his crew] ought to have known that their 'side' was that of 'the people,' not the side of the corporation."
14. Slotkin points to the connection between the revolutionary Raza and the Chicanos linked to Chavez's farmworkers movement, designated by the term La Raza.
15. Slotkin extensively discusses the Vietnam War as context for *The Professionals*, particularly in regard to its engagement with the "Special Forces or 'commando raid' concept." Slotkin, *Gunfighter Nation*, 567–74.
16. Olney, *Zombie Cinema*, 55.
17. Here, I am working with Nussbaum's definition of autonomy based on humans being able to "make certain important life defining choices for themselves, rather than having their lives dictated to them by others." Such "life defining choices," including things like marriage, reveal humans' ability to define their role in larger systemic socioeconomic contexts.
18. I am using "the gaze" from Laura Mulvey, who identifies the verisimilitude accomplished when camera angles and male protagonist simultaneously view the female as "erotic object" for both spectator and character. The concept of object combined with the context emphasizes the ways in which the woman becomes both a commodity in the film and in the audience's eyes.
19. When I speak to agency here, it differs from autonomy in that agency merely speaks to her ability to exert power, to act of her own volition, while autonomy refers to self-government within the context of larger societal institutions.

20. Federici, *Beyond the Periphery of the Skin*, 29.
21. In regard to this exchange, Slotkin points out how María's role as "whore" for both the Revolution and Raza proves her ethics of professionalism on par with Rico's own.
22. Lusted, *The Western*, 207.
23. Lusted, *The Western*, 207.
24. Smith, *Capitalism's Sexual History*, 30.
25. Jones, "xxxZombies," 198.
26. Nussbaum, *Citadels of Pride*, xv.
27. Lusted discusses the western's use of the captivity narrative in which the female might be subject to horrors "worse than death," implying rape and torture, at the hands of the uncivilized Native Americans; similarly, Gerrard, Holland, and Shail speak of the ways captivity narratives in horror act to emphasize the abject (and objectified) horror of the female characters.
28. The explicitly feminist nature of Snyder's text, while problematic at times, is quite explicit when it comes to his choices, such as when Ana de la Reguera (Maria Cruz), shown as a successful mechanic/businesswoman wearing a familiar red bandana on the cover of a magazine in her previous life, wears a t-shirt that reads "The Future Is Female Ejaculation" while obliterating zombies with a .50-caliber machine gun.
29. In *Das Capital*, one of Marx's fundamental critiques of capitalism, is its reliance on separating the laborer from the product. Such separation results in workers' disengagement from their work and their eventual dehumanization.
30. Gerrard, Holland, and Shail, *Gender and Contemporary Horror in Television*, 26.
31. Molina-Guzmán and Valdivia describe this sexualization as commodity in U.S. culture: "Dominant representations of Latinas and African American women are predominately characterized by an emphasis on the breasts, hips, and buttocks. These body parts function as mixed signifiers of sexual desire and fertility as well as bodily waste and racial contamination."
32. Zom-coms or zom-rom-coms are a hybrid of romantic comedies and zombie films, which oftentimes play up the lack of seriousness in both genres in order to parody certain aspects of human life, including marriage. Olney, *Zombie Cinema*, 84–85.
33. The Alpha Queen's ensemble resembles Leia's in the Jabba the Hutt scene from *Return of the Jedi*, and while such an ensemble definitely promotes the gaze, particularly given the iconic nature of Leia's outfit, as a friend pointed out, at least this female is not in chains.
34. Olney, *Zombie Cinema*, 11.
35. Federici, *Beyond the Periphery of the Skin*, 29.
36. Sintumuang, "Zack Snyder Tells Us."

37. Cantor, *Pop Culture*, 149.
38. The allusions to classical Rome throughout the film seem to parallel many ways that this society works, for while the ethics of Rome were not those of classical Greece, they were a brutal simulacrum.
39. Bishop, *American Zombie Gothic*, 140.
40. Olney, *Zombie Cinema*, 53.
41. Nussbaum, *Citadels of Pride*, 3.
42. Nussbaum, *Citadels of Pride*, 32.
43. In using this language, I should note that this *is* a zombie movie, so while they call it her death cry, and her partner responds to it as such, *she*, or rather her head, does survive this mostly alive and unhappy in a bag being held by Martin. Such an image of the disposable female body reliably aligns with feminist readings of the film.
44. Nowhere is such a reality more apparent than in the experience of female slaves in the ultimate dehumanizing capitalistic project of slavery, upon which the United States is built.
45. It is also worth noting here, of course, that the conversation of female reproductive autonomy occurs within this film released just one year prior to the Supreme Court's reversal of its stance on such autonomy in *Dobbs v. Jackson*.
46. Sintumuang, "Zack Snyder Tells Us."
47. Federici, *Beyond the Periphery of the Skin*, 21.
48. Olney, *Zombie Cinema*, 53.
49. The apocalypse notwithstanding, the leader of the heist, Scott Ward's daughter, escapes and survives, only after shooting her zombie father. This emphasizes again the humanity of the parent-child bond but also hearkens back to the earlier western heroes, as she, not the mercenary professionals, is motivated by a just cause, so only she is deemed worthy of survival.
50. Lee, *The Heist Film*, 10.
51. Reilly, "How to Un-cast an Actor."

Bibliography

Bishop, Kyle William. *American Zombie Gothic: The Rise and Fall (and Rise) of The Walking Dead in Popular Culture*. London: McFarland, 2010.

Brooks, Richard. *The Professionals*. Pax Enterprises, 1966.

Cantor, Paul A. *Pop Culture and the Dark Side of the American Dream: Con Men, Gangsters, Drug Lords, and Zombies*. Lexington: University Press of Kentucky, 2019.

Federici, Silvia. *Beyond the Periphery of the Skin: Rethinking, Remaking, and Reclaiming the Body in Contemporary Capitalism*. Oakland: PM Press, 2020.

Foucault, Michel. *The History of Sexuality: An Introduction*. New York: Random House, 1978.

Gerrard, Steven, Samantha Holland, and Robert Shail. *Gender and Contemporary Horror in Television*. Bingley, UK: Emerald, 2019.

Irigaray, Luce. "Women on the Market: A Selection from *This Sex*." In *Literary Theory: An Anthology*, 2nd ed., edited by Julie Rivkin and Michael Ryan, 795–811. Hoboken NJ: Blackwell, 2004.

Johnson, Michael K., Rebecca M. Lush, and Sara L. Spurgeon. "Westworld(s); Race, Gender, Genre in the Weird Western." Introduction to *Weird Westerns: Race, Gender, Genre*, edited by Kerry Fine, Michael K. Johnson, Rebecca M. Lush, and Sara L. Spurgeon, 1–36. Lincoln: University of Nebraska Press, 2020.

Jones, Steve. "XXX Zombies: Economies of Desire and Disgust." In *Thinking Dead: What the Zombie Apocalypse Means*, edited by Murali Balaji, 197–214. Lanham MD: Lexington Books, 2013.

Lee, Daryl. *The Heist Film: Stealing with Style*. New York: Columbia University Press, 2014.

Lusted, David. *The Western*. Abingdon, UK: Routledge, 2014.

Marx, Karl, and Friedrich Engels. *Capital: A Critique of Political Economy*. New York: International Publishers, 1967.

Molina-Guzmán, Isabel, and Angharad N. Valdivia. "Brain, Brow, and Booty: Latina Iconicity in U.S. Popular Culture." *Communication Review* 7 (2004): 205–21.

Mulvey, Laura. "Visual Pleasure and Narrative Cinema." In *The Critical Tradition: Classic Texts and Contemporary Trends*, edited by David H. Richter, 1444–53. New York: Bedford Books, 1998.

Nussbaum, Martha. *Citadels of Pride: Sexual Abuse, Accountability, and Reconciliation*. New York: W. W. Norton, 2021.

Olney, Ian. *Zombie Cinema*. New Brunswick NJ: Rutgers University Press, 2017.

Reilly, Dan. "How to Un-cast an Actor: When an *Army of the Dead* Star Got Called Out, Zack Snyder Called on Tig Notaro to Save a Role." *Vulture*, May 11, 2021. https://www.vulture.com/2021/05/zack-snyder-tig-notaro-army-of-the-dead.html.

Romero, George A., dir. *Dawn of the Dead*. Laurel Entertainment, 2004.

Rubin, Gayle. "The Traffic in Women." In *Literary Theory: An Anthology*, 2nd ed., edited by Julie Rivkin and Michael Ryan, 770–95. Hoboken NJ: Blackwell, 2004.

Sintumuang, Kevin. "Zack Snyder Tells Us Where Zombie Babies Come from in *Army of the Dead*." *Esquire*, May 21, 2021. https://www.esquire.com/entertainment/movies/a36505010/zack-snyder-army-of-the-dead-nudity-zombie-baby-sequel-interview/.

Slotkin, Richard. *Gunfighter Nation: The Myth of the Frontier in Twentieth-Century America*. New York: Atheneum, 1992.

Smith, Nicola J. *Capitalism's Sexual History*. New York: Oxford University Press, 2020. https://doi.org/10.1093/oso/9780197530276.001.0001.

Snyder, Zack, dir. *Army of the Dead*. The Stone Quarry, 2021.

Wright, Will. *Sixguns & Society: A Structural Study of the Western*. Kindle edition. Berkeley: University of California Press, 2023.

PART 5

The Woman in Room 237

Western Domesticity and Oedipal Conflict in *The Shining*

JEFFREY CHISUM

Deep into *The Shining* (1980), as Jack Torrance (played by Jack Nicholson) begins to unravel mentally, he finds his way to the grand ballroom of the haunted Overlook Hotel, where he finds a large, Roaring Twenties–style party in full swing. The ghostly bartender, Lloyd, pours him a drink, and as he gets up to join in the revelries, he bumps into a waiter carrying a tray of cocktails, which spill onto Torrance's jacket. It's a pivotal moment in the movie because afterward, the two retreat to an eerily red men's room where the waiter (who turns out to be Delbert Grady, the former Overlook Hotel caretaker who murdered his family) begins to clean the spill off of Jack's coat and proceeds to instruct Jack to kill his own family. What viewers might miss is the song that plays in the background during this sequence. It's an old tune by Henry Hall called "Home," the lyrics of which (in part) go: "Night covers all and . . . sweet dreams will never take me home." "Home"—as both a place and a concept—is crucial to understanding *The Shining* and the peculiar way that the film sits astride both the western and horror genres or, rather, the way it represents a "mash-up" of classic horror and western tropes. Supposedly a place of safety and domestic reassurance, "home" in *The Shining* turns out to be a source of haunting violence, deeply inscribed oedipal conflicts, and perhaps most unsettling of all, a disturbing sexuality that sits squarely at the center of the narrative.

Part of what stands out about *The Shining* is its indelible imagery: the identically dressed girls beckoning to young Danny Torrance; Jack Nicholson hacking through a bathroom door with an axe while his wife, played by Shelley Duvall, screams in terror; Danny pedaling his tricycle across the patterned carpet of the Overlook Hotel; the elevators that unleash a slow-motion tsunami of blood. And then there is the woman in room 237: first a tall, stately, and completely nude woman who emerges out of the bathtub;

and then, in Jack Torrance's embrace, an old woman with rotting skin and teeth, cackling at Torrance as he reels away in terror. The scene stands out amid the many memorable moments from the film for several reasons. It's a moment of frankly grotesque supernatural terror, for one thing. The full-frontal nudity—unusual for 1980—is also unsettling as it occurs in the midst of a movie that is otherwise almost entirely devoid of sexuality and icy in its overall tone. And it's clearly meant to be disturbing—both to Jack Torrance and his status as a patriarch and married man, and to the viewer—even before the woman transforms into a decaying hag. Perhaps more importantly, the scene offers a way of understanding *The Shining* as a narrative that combines elements of the western and horror genres at the same time that it infuses them with menacing sexuality and an unraveling of the idea of "home" as a place of domestic safety and stability.

On the surface, *The Shining* seems simple enough: it's a story about a haunted hotel and the troubled father who finally snaps amid the psychic pressures the hotel exerts on him. Hotels are "transitional" spaces, though—temporary "homes" that offer respite as people move from one space to another. Similarly, the American West was also, from a mythological standpoint, a new "home" during colonialist westward expansion—an idea that is touched upon both in dialogue and in some of the set design of the film. Meanwhile, as a director, Stanley Kubrick was known for steering genre films in new directions (*2001: A Space Odyssey* and *Full Metal Jacket*, for example, are good examples of the way that Kubrick tweaked the science fiction and war story genres respectively). Still, the majority of critics and probably most viewers tend to think of *The Shining* primarily as a horror film. It routinely shows up on lists of the greatest horror films of all time, and it was featured prominently on the "Ghost Stories" episode of Eli Roth's AMC television series, *History of Horror* (2018).

The Shining clearly has elements of the western genre, too, from its isolated and lonesome setting to the décor of the Overlook Hotel to the references to Native American artifacts and history. But the way that these elements are handled represents a "weirding" of western location rather than a remix of the "classic" westerns that are exemplified by films like *The Searchers* or *Unforgiven*, or the novels of Louis L'Amour and Zane Grey. Western narratives can be divided into at least two categories: genre westerns, which usually take place in the Old West and feature familiar tropes like cowboys and Indians, six-shooters, horses, and wide-open landscapes, and western stories, which maintain a western setting while departing from the most obvious genre conventions. *The Shining* fits into the latter of these two categories. The west in *The Shining* is a fractured and mixed-up place. For example, the movie opens with a panoramic shot of a yellow Volkswagen Beetle driving through the mountains of the American West. This isn't Colorado, though, where the story supposedly takes place—the images were actually filmed along Going-to-the-Sun Road in Glacier National Park in northern Montana. Shortly afterward, we see the exterior of the Overlook Hotel, though again, this isn't Colorado; it's actually the Timberline Lodge, located on Mt. Hood in Oregon. Meanwhile, the interior of the hotel was apparently modeled after the Ahwahnee Hotel in Yosemite, including the eerie red elevator doors, and the bulk of the movie itself was filmed on a set in England. The West in *The Shining* is a fractured, jumbled West, created out of scraps of real western locations, and also international in its genesis.

The film is weirdly and undeniably "western" in other ways, too. As Jack Torrance is being given a guided tour of the hotel grounds, the manager, Stuart Ullman, tells him, "Construction [on the hotel] began in 1907. It was finished in 1909. The site is supposed to be on an Indian burial ground, and I believe they actually had to repel a few Indian attacks as they were building." The hotel and its location, then—assembled out of bits and pieces of both the real and the symbolic West—also represent a corrupted "home," a new sort of domicile constructed on the deaths of the Native American predecessors. As Ullman leads Jack and Wendy through the interior of the Overlook, Wendy asks, "Are all these Indian designs authentic?" And Ullman replies, "Yeah, I believe so. Mainly based on Navajo and Apache motifs." In their review of the movie in *Film Quarterly*, Jeffress and Liebowitz expound at some length on the movie's "western" qualities, referring to Jack as "a would-be cowboy with a typewriter . . . doing his duty, writing the Great American Novel that will insure his rightful place among the successful."[1] They note, "The Indian motifs cannot be merely accidental, there are just too many of them" and helpfully direct our attention to "the image of Jack at work in the cavernous lobby, backed by an American flag but surrounded on three sides by Indian designs."[2] Native American history both surrounds the narrative and is buried by it. Or, perhaps more accurately, it is given a discordant stillness—or a ghostly, quiet presence—that works to underscore the thematic horror of the film. These details also serve as reminders and reinforcement of the idea of the American West as a constant yet shifting "home," where people and cultures are displaced to make way for new "tenants," even if ghosts and memories remain.

There is at least one more way in which the movie is "western": namely, the way by which it reproduces a noticeably gendered sense of sexuality and violence. In his conversations with the male ghosts in the Overlook, there is a clear annoyance and hostility toward women that's common in western movies: "Can't live with 'em, can't live without 'em," as Lloyd the bartender says. Or consider Jack himself, who refers to his wife, Wendy, as "the old sperm bank upstairs." So much of the conflict in the film stems from Jack's determination to prove himself as a lone "cowboy" figure amid the loneliness and isolation of the Overlook—in this regard, he feels burdened by his family. Without Wendy and Danny's "bothersome" interruptions, he'd be free to write unencumbered, to resume drinking again, and to do whatever he'd like. But the "freedom" so often represented in western narratives is seldom as it seems, and in *The Shining*, this western "freedom" is directly linked to the hauntings and horror that punctuate the rhythms of the narrative.

In that sense, the weird western "home" that *The Shining* presents is as puzzling and byzantine as the hedge maze that sits beside the hotel—a pastiche western home-space made out of real and actual places, but one that's also a fractured, uncertain, and arguably menacing West. Stuart Ullman "*believes*" but does not know whether the Indian "motifs" are "authentic," for example. (And does "authentic" in this instance mean that the items were handmade by Apache and Navajo people? Or merely that the designs were appropriated from them?) It is also very much a haunted west: the death of the Indians lingers ghostlike in the minds of the whites who own and operate the hotel. And there are other western deaths that haunt the film as well. As the Torrances are driving up to the Overlook, Wendy asks about the Donner Party, "Hey, wasn't it around here that the Donner Party got snowbound?" Jack replies, "I think that was further west in the Sierras," before explaining to Danny, with apparent relish, that the Donners had to resort to cannibalism. And during his interview, Stuart

Ullman tells Jack about Delbert Grady: "From what I've been told he seemed like a completely normal individual. But at some point during the winter, he must have suffered some kind of complete mental breakdown. He ran amok and"—he pauses as he's saying this, smirking or grimacing slightly—"he killed his family with an axe. Stacked them neatly in one of the rooms in the West Wing, and then he put both barrels of a shotgun in his mouth." Jack responds by assuring Ullman that "that's not gonna happen with me," and he adds that Wendy will "be absolutely fascinated when I tell her about it. She's a confirmed ghost story and horror film addict."

The Shining's West is permeated with and haunted by this unstable violence. It does not matter where the Torrances go—dead Indians lay beneath their feet; the dead members of the Donner party, located hundreds of miles away, resurface in the present in Colorado, in the Torrances' conversation. The Torrances cannot escape the history of the place—which is to say, the history of the West—even as they do their best to treat the Overlook Hotel as their "home" for the winter. During their initial tour, Wendy marvels at all the food and equipment stored in the kitchen, and as they are shown their main living quarters, Jack notes that the extra bedroom is "perfect for a child." Ullman replies, "Yes, very cozy for a family!" Indeed, that may be what defines *The Shining*'s status as a weird western—the way that it successfully fuses together notions that are crucial to understanding the West, such as Native American genocide, the harshness of nature, "regeneration through violence," isolation amid an indifferent landscape, and perhaps most importantly, the attempt to carve out a new "home" in a "savage" countryside. But this "home" is corrupt and haunted, and ultimately threatened by a monstrous female sexuality. During his conversation with Mr. Hallorann about the Overlook early in the movie, Danny Torrance asks, "Is there something bad here?" It's a question we could equally ask about the West.

Indeed, there most certainly *is* something bad lurking in the Torrances' adopted western home, and it surfaces prominently at roughly the midway point of the movie, a point that Roger Luckhurst, in his excellent book-length study of the film, calls "the navel of the film."[3] Jack is quarreling with Wendy over an incident involving Danny, whose clairvoyant abilities have gotten him into trouble; he appears with bruises on his neck. Despite having been warned to stay away from room 237, Danny is nonetheless lured to the room, and off-screen, he's assaulted by some unknown presence. Wendy accuses Jack of hurting Danny (something that has happened in the past), which sends Jack into a rage, and he storms off angrily. He finds his way to the empty bar in the ballroom of the Overlook, and he bemoans his sobriety, only to look up to see Lloyd the bartender ready to pour him a drink and lend a friendly ear as Jack complains about his wife. His reverie is interrupted by Wendy, though, who tells him there's a "woman" in the hotel who tried to strangle Danny. "Which room?" Jack demands, and the film cuts and we see Mr. Hallorann—the psychic, African American cook of the Overlook Hotel—lying in his bed on the other side of the country, and a stricken expression comes across his face; he can see something in his mind. On the soundtrack, we hear a high-pitched ringing, and then a heart begins to beat. We are meant to understand that something has come alive, that some malignant force has woken up. What is it, though? Next, we see Danny in his room, trembling, a foamy gob of drool dangling from his lip, caught in the grip of a psychic seizure. This really is a remarkable passage. Through the editing, the movie connects all of the film's main four characters (Danny, Jack, Wendy, and Mr. Hallorann)—one of whom is on the other side of the country—and turns the tension up to a fever pitch as the camera places us in a first-person point of view. *We* are meant to witness whatever it is that's at the heart of the Overlook Hotel's evil.

In his book, Luckhurst wonders if the throbbing heartbeat belongs to the hotel, and more specifically, whether it is connected to the hotel's status as a domestic space: "Is the womb, the lost home, the unhomely site of horror? Is that the mother's heartbeat?"[4] Perhaps so, if we decide to think of the domestic home-space of the Overlook as feminine, and there are several reasons why this interpretation makes sense. First, Danny is lured away from playing with his toy cars when a curiously pink tennis ball rolls into the frame. Danny looks up to where it apparently came from, but no one's there. Later, as Danny approaches room 237, he calls out, "Mom, are you in there?" There is indeed a woman in room 237, but it isn't Wendy Torrance. Instead, it's an apparition who later appears to Jack as a lithe, stately woman but who later transforms, in his embrace, into a decaying, cackling hag. The main evil "pull" in the narrative, then, is feminine, and the woman in room 237 is the catalyst for the horror that unfolds in the movie's second half. Luckhurst writes that a common feature of horror movies involves "a progressive unveiling of domestic physical space that defies rational order and instead shows wrinkles and tears in the space-time continuum."[5] Here, the "wrinkles and tears" are literally on the old, decaying woman's body, and there is a strange, brief cut that shows her silent and still, submerged in the bathtub, with her eyes vacant and open. The "unveiling of domestic physical space" comes about via the young/old woman in room 237, who terrifies Jack and sets off Danny and Mr. Hallorann's psychic alarms. Interestingly, Jack later lies to Wendy, telling her that there was nobody in room 237, which raises a question: Is the horrific feminine sexuality in room 237 a *threat* to Jack Torrance's status as "patriarch" in the Overlook, as some critics have suggested? And yet another question lingers: Why would Danny assume that his mother is in room 237? He has plenty of good reasons to be fearful of his parents—of his father's violent anger and of his mother's seeming inability to keep him safe. And due to his clairvoyant abilities, he knows there is something haunted about room 237. Why would he associate that with his mother, though? Does he assume that Wendy would be drawn to the evil that he has psychically sensed?

Interestingly, a lot of the scholarship dealing with *The Shining* takes a Freudian, psychoanalytical approach—often drawing upon works by writers ranging from Julia Kristeva (especially *Powers of Horror*) to Jacques Lacan and Barbara Creed. For example, in a *Literature/Film Quarterly* article from 1984, Christopher Hoile notes a Freudian interpretation of the movie is appropriate because of "two books Kubrick and Diane Johnson reportedly read while writing the script—Freud's essay 'The Uncanny' (1919) and Bruno Bettelheim's *The Uses of Enchantment* (1976)."[6] Hoile reads the film as a dramatization of "the ever-present oedipal tensions between father, mother, and child" and he observes that the "horror in *The Shining* does not lie in the ghosts but in the inescapability of the oedipal tensions in the family of which they are an expression."[7] Hoile also adroitly points out that for both Danny, who is told by Hallorann to stay away from room 237, and Jack Torrance, who is lured in by the malignant forces of the hotel, the room "explicitly represent[s] sexual knowledge."[8]

Hoile's views are reinforced by Ya-huei Wang in "Archetypal Anxieties in Stanley Kubrick's *The Shining*," from 2011. Wang writes, "For Jack, the woman in the bathtub—seductive, beautiful, dangerous—symbolizes his latent wish to have a substitute for Wendy," whereas for Danny, "it represents psychic and sexual awakening."⁹ Also referencing Freud and Bettelheim, Wang continues: "According to Bettelheim (1977), a locked room often refers to the female sexual organs, and turning the lock of the door symbolizes intercourse" but points out, "Danny's painful sexual initiation in Room 237 is reminiscent of Freud's theory that a child must see the sexual act as disgusting as long as his sexual desire is attached to his parents in order to not violate the incest taboo and destabilize the family." Whatever happens to Danny in room 237 occurs off-screen, though; when he reappears in front of his parents, his clothing is slightly disheveled, with a rip near the neckline of his sweater, and with bruises on his neck, and he's sucking his thumb. Is it a "painful sexual initiation," then, as Wang suggests? Perhaps in a symbolic or Freudian sense.

Echoing Wang and drawing upon Lacanian ideas, Robert Kilker writes that "it is well within reason to consider shining an especially maternal power. Lacanian psychoanalytic theory generally regards preverbal communication as a special province of the mother-child relationship" and that "American patriarchal culture insists on such separation ... encouraging children to grow into adults and 'cut the apron strings,' a domestic metaphor for the umbilical cord."[10] And recall that Luckhurst, in his book, describes the scene with room 237 as the "navel" of the film. Thus the movie—for Kilker and other critics—represents a deep Freudian blend of patriarchal anxieties fused to terrors related to what Kilker, referencing Barbara Creed, calls "the monstrous feminine," which he connects to "a fear of the abject, that which defies boundaries of separation from the self."[11] Drawing upon the work of Kristeva, he elaborates on this idea:

> Abject body fluids such as blood, vomit, feces, pus, mucus, and others are things that our culture teaches us to see as foul and therefore wish to conceal in shame. Since such fluids are traditionally horrifying, the feminine body that produces one of them (blood) every month is especially monstrous. Birthing is perhaps the most terrible abjection of all, as a feminine body produces amid blood and amniotic fluid a child connected to its mother via the umbilical cord. With all these signifiers of abject horror culturally constructed around motherhood, failure to "cut the apron strings" is not merely a sign of immaturity; it is a sign of certain doom.[12]

While Kilker acknowledges that "*The Shining* is ultimately a movie about a male monster"—Jack Torrance—he argues that the film "also codes the feminine as monstrous, and equally threatening as the patriarchal forces that would try to contain it."[13] This interpretation dovetails with the repeated imagery of the elevators spewing blood in *The Shining*, and may also remind horror fans of another classic film where blood and menstruation—along with feminine psychic power—figure prominently in the story: Brian De Palma's 1976 film, *Carrie*, where, similarly, the title character's initiation into a new stage of life is linked to psychic abilities, violence, and (in more ways than one) "the monstrous feminine."

In *Camera Obscura: The Politics and Ideology of Contemporary Hollywood Film*, Ryan and Kellner suggest that horror movies often serve as a critique of "the normal operations of a social system run on principles of aggressivity, competition, domination, and the survival of the fittest."[14] They argue that *The Shining* "examines the psychopathology of right-wing disciplinarianism and primitivism," with Jack Torrance and the other white male characters in the film (Grady, Ullman, Lloyd, etc.) being the chief representatives of this ideology.[15] The authors suggest that, ironically, the movie presents a scenario in which "conservatism evidence[s] a desire ultimately to escape from conservatism," and they cite the scene in room 237 as one of the key examples.[16] In their reading, the scene is a "descent into the unconscious [that] permits a liberation from restraint, but [is] also represented as a potentially dangerous pathway that unleashes repressed horrors—in this case, the fear of woman's sexuality."[17] As the "ulcerous woman" lurches toward Jack, he stumbles backward, reeling, and her cackling laughter is reminiscent of what Helene Cixous calls "the Medusa's Laughter": a humiliation of the patriarchy that Jack Torrance represents— "her shameful sickness is that she resists death, that she makes trouble," Cixous writes.[18] It may be worth pointing out that the three characters who react to the woman in room 237 are all male—Danny, Mr. Hallorann, and Jack. Danny is apparently assaulted by her; Jack is terrorized by her; and so is Mr. Hallorann, who lays in his bed in a kind of terrified psychic stupor. Wendy, meanwhile, only *hears* about the woman via Danny. The woman in room 237, then, is strictly a threat to the males in the film.

Meanwhile, that disquieting heartbeat, overlaid with discordant music from Penderecki, continues to throb on the soundtrack. There can be no doubt that it's the rotten heart of some malignant force, but does it belong to the woman? To the hotel? To some collective, timeless, and genderless evil? Luckhurst wonders if it's "the mother's heartbeat," but what if we interpret the heartbeat as belonging to western history itself? A rhythmic heartbeat pulsing on and on, luring us into madness. In his book, Luckhurst writes that the fact of the Overlook being located on the site of "an Indian burial ground" is "an echo of the foundational violence at the origin of the American Republic," which is to say, the history of the West. Luckhurst adds, "The utopia of the American Republic was meant to escape from the ghosts of fallen Europe, but the Puritans only dragged these spectres with them, or conjured new ones out of the shadows."[19] Perhaps what is so frightening about *The Shining* is the sheer persistence of the hauntings and violence.

Later in his book, Luckhurst argues that the "dominant symbol" of the movie is the maze, both the actual hedge maze outside the hotel (where Jack will eventually lose himself and freeze to death) and the model replica of the maze inside the Overlook. Pauline Kael, in her terrific *New Yorker* review of the movie, supports Luckhurst's view: "Even the methodical use of tracking patterns is thematic—a visual representation of the repetitive, cyclical nature of experience. Probably Kubrick meant to draw us into the swirling movement from the start and make the evil palpable—and then, as we gradually became disoriented in time, we were supposed to accept the mystic inevitability of the ugly theme (the timelessness of murder)." Isn't this one of the ways we are meant to understand the West more generally—as a place where a "mystically" inevitable Manifest Destiny is fused with violence? I can't help but be reminded of Judge Holden's remark in Cormac McCarthy's novel *Blood Meridian* that "war is god," a remark that's meant to justify the horrific bloodshed that punctuates that novel. The Judge explains that war and violence, due to the high stakes, represent the ultimate "game," and "every child knows that play is nobler than work," he says.[20] It's easy enough to reformulate his statement, which is exactly what *The Shining* does: "All work and no play makes Jack a dull boy."

In the movie, the hedge maze is meant to be an area for "play"—Danny and Wendy go strolling through it, laughing and having fun over getting lost, while Jack seemingly watches them as he stares menacingly and vacantly at the model replica of the maze in the hotel's lobby. But the maze is also where Jack dies—fooled by a clever Danny who tricks Jack into losing his way. If the maze can be read as a metaphor for *The Shining*, for the West, and perhaps for sexuality and patriarchy, then it represents a kind of "forced" pathway that nonetheless creates the illusion of choice. And as Kael rightly points out, the "mystic inevitability" of violence and evil is one of the major themes of the narrative, and there are multiple points where events are foretold or presaged by premonitions, such as Danny's visions of the bloody elevator, or of room 237, or the murdered twin girls—all violent events that either *have* or *will* come to pass. Perhaps the most notable instance of malevolent "mystic inevitability" comes when Jack Torrance is instructed to "correct" his family by the "spirit" of the hotel. In a sense, *The Shining* is a reiteration of one of the oldest stories about a man being commanded by God to kill—that is, the story in the Old Testament about Abraham and Isaac. In chapter 22 of Genesis, Abraham is commanded by God to "go to the land of Moriah, and offer him [Isaac] there as a burnt offering on one of the mountains that I shall show you." Despite the obvious depravity of the Abraham story, critics have often interpreted it as having significance due to the way that Abraham's faith is tested. After all, what greater test of one's loyalty is there than being asked to kill one's own child? Soren Kierkegaard, in his long essay examining the Abraham story, *Fear and Trembling*, writes, "The ethical expression for what Abraham did is that he meant to murder Isaac; the religious expression is that he meant to sacrifice Isaac—but precisely in this contradiction is the anxiety that can make a person sleepless."[21] Jack Torrance—who is shown to have sleeping problems in the film—fails at the task he was instructed to do, but there is no reprieve from "God" in *The Shining*, no fulfillment of "Manifest Destiny." Instead, Kubrick sends us into the twists and turns of the maze, where Jack loses sight of Danny and eventually freezes to death.

But the idea of being instructed or guided by a higher power seems fundamentally "western" in its relation to the idea of Manifest Destiny, or the notion that one is "entitled" to settle "new" lands. Delbert Grady tells Jack Torrance in the bathroom that he "corrected" his own wife and daughters, which is yet another way that *The Shining* can be seen as an examination of the ways that the patriarchal order can be upset or challenged—or twisted. As Jeffress and Liebowitz put it: "Jack's sense of self and of his relation to others in his often fantasized world shows him to be animated by a patriarchal authoritarianism," which he views as being undermined by Danny and Wendy.[22] Elizabeth Jean Hornbeck, in a 2016 *Feminist Studies* article, extends this idea: "Danny's story recapitulates Freud's oedipal myth through which the male subject grows into (hetero) sexual maturity, [and] Wendy's story enacts its female counterpart."[23] Hornbeck interprets the movie as an example of gothic horror and notes, "In keeping with Gothic conventions, secrets concerning sexuality and violence emerge in the film's frenetic climax."[24] Arguably, one of the most disturbing moments in the entire film comes toward the end, as Wendy attempts to flee the Overlook. As she's running, she catches a glimpse of two men in one of the rooms, apparently engaged in a sexual act, and one of them is wearing a mask. Hornbeck writes that this man is "dressed as something like a tusked teddy bear . . . performing fellatio on a tuxedo-clad man," and she argues that the scene "reveals a frightening but ambiguous truth, which could be the hotel's threat to its human occupants, the castrating threat Jack poses to Danny, the oedipal threat Danny presents to his father, or even a sexual abuse narrative."[25] But Hornbeck's reading of this scene is also interesting in part because she interprets it as "*upholding the patriarchal social order*" (emphasis added).[26] Hornbeck argues, "The blade [that Wendy] holds erect symbolizes the phallic power she needs in order to take action; Danny/Tony, in giving her the blade, acted to restore phallic qualities to his mother vis-à-vis the fetish object, thus restoring the boy's relationship with the phallic, pre-oedipal mother. Wendy as phallic mother restores the mother-child bond, and at the same time she restores the heterosexual narrative order."[27] To a certain extent, the conclusion of *The Shining* is a relief, with Wendy and Danny escaping to safety, and with a semblance of "order" restored to the narrative, but Hornbeck's analysis points to a basic problem. If we view *The Shining* as a "weird western"— and I think it very clearly fits within that hybrid genre—then isn't it simply reinforcing many of the problematic elements (patriarchy, repression of sexuality, settler colonialism) of traditional westerns? Perhaps. And it's worth noting that the film doesn't end with Danny and Wendy's escape.

    The final shot of *The Shining*, famously, is a slow dolly in on a black-and-white photograph hanging on one of the walls of the Overlook. A caption on the photo reads, "July 4th, 1921," and we can clearly see a tuxedo-clad

Jack Torrance beaming at the head of the crowd. "You've always been the caretaker," Grady tells Jack in an earlier scene, and indeed, the image of Jack in the photo seems to imply that he has always been present at the hotel. His violence, his rage, and the hauntings that are embodied in him persist. Luckhurst quotes from Nietzsche's *The Gay Science*: "What if a demon crept after you one day or night in your loneliest solitude and said to you: 'This life, as you live it now and have lived it, you will have to live again and again, times without number.'" Or, as Kierkegaard writes in *Fear and Trembling*, "If a human being did not have an eternal consciousness, if underlying everything there were only a wild, fermenting power that writhing in dark passions produced everything, be it significant or insignificant, if a vast, never appeased emptiness hid beneath everything, what would life be then but despair?"

Isolation, the terrible thrill of violence, and promptings from angry spirits—these are threads that run not just through *The Shining* but through so many texts dealing with the West, from *Blood Meridian* and Edward Abbey's *Desert Solitaire* to Stephen King's *Desperation*, Brian Evenson's *The Open Curtain*, or other western-set horror films like *Poltergeist* and *Hereditary*. One of the classic images of western progress is John Gast's 1872 painting *American Progress*, which depicts a gigantic white woman dressed in flowing white finery, floating westward, closing in on the buffalo, Indians, and wild animals that are fleeing into the darkening western horizon. Considering what she represents, it's not too difficult to reimagine her as rotting and diseased—not unlike the crone who lurches after Jack in room 237. I wonder, too, if it's fair to think of the bleeding elevators in *The Shining* as an appropriate counter to "American Progress"—gallons of blood gushing from elevators in a place where time has ceased to have meaning. The bloodshed is unending and persistent, all in a domestic western space that was constructed atop an Indian burial ground.

In a piece written in the early 1980s for the journal *Social Text*, Fredric Jameson wrote, "The Jack Nicholson of *The Shining* is possessed neither by evil as such nor by the 'devil' or some analogous occult force, but rather simply History, by the American past as it has left its sedimented traces in the corridors and dismembered suites of this monumental rabbit warren."[28] This "monumental rabbit warren" is, in other words, a home, a gigantic home—the Overlook Hotel, or the West itself—an enormous, corrupted home. Or even—to refer back to Luckhurst—a "womb," the original feminine home to which, in Freudian terms, the psyche forever longs to return. "I wish we could stay here forever . . . and ever . . . and ever," Jack tells Danny, and at the end of the movie, he seems to get his wish, beaming eternally in a photo dated 1921. But he isn't alone in that photo; he's merely at the front of what looks to be quite an extensive crowd. If the ghost of Jack Torrance persists at the Overlook, then, presumably, so do the spirits of the Indians buried beneath the hotel's foundation. So does the ghost of Delbert Grady and his murdered family, and so does the woman in room 237—decaying, with her arms outstretched and cackling with laughter . . . forever . . . and ever . . . and ever.

Notes

1. Jeffress and Liebowitz, "*The Shining* by Stanley Kubrick," 46.
2. Jeffress and Liebowitz, "*The Shining* by Stanley Kubrick," 46.
3. Luckhurst, *The Shining*, 65.
4. Luckhurst, *The Shining*, 65.
5. Luckhurst, *The Shining*, 20.
6. Hoile, "The Uncanny and the Fairly Tale," 5.
7. Hoile, "The Uncanny and the Fairly Tale," 7.
8. Hoile, "The Uncanny and the Fairly Tale," 9–10.
9. Wang, "Archetypal Anxieties," 115.
10. Kilker, "All Roads Lead to the Abject," 57.
11. Kilker, "All Roads Lead to the Abject," 57.
12. Kilker, "All Roads Lead to the Abject," 58.
13. Kilker, "All Roads Lead to the Abject," 54, 56.
14. Ryan and Kellner, *Camera Politica*, 168.
15. Ryan and Kellner, *Camera Politica*, 177.
16. Ryan and Kellner, *Camera Politica*, 177.
17. Ryan and Kellner, *Camera Politica*, 173.
18. Cixous, "The Laugh of the Medusa," 876.
19. Luckhurst, *The Shining*, 18.
20. McCarthy, *Blood Meridian*, 249.
21. Kierkegaard, *Fear and Trembling*, 30.
22. Jeffress and Liebowitz, "*The Shining* by Stanley Kubrick," 46.
23. Hornbeck, "Who's Afraid of the Big Bad Wolf?," 715.
24. Hornbeck, "Who's Afraid of the Big Bad Wolf?," 716.
25. Hornbeck, "Who's Afraid of the Big Bad Wolf?," 716.

26. Hornbeck, "Who's Afraid of the Big Bad Wolf?," 717.
27. Hornbeck, "Who's Afraid of the Big Bad Wolf?," 717.
28. Jameson, "The Shining," 119–20.

Bibliography

Cixous, Helene. "The Laugh of the Medusa." Translated by Keith Cohen and Paula Cohen. *Signs* 1, no. 4 (Summer 1976): 875–93.

Hoile, Christopher. "The Uncanny and the Fairly Tale in Kubrick's *The Shining*." *Literature/Film Quarterly* 12, no. 1 (January 1, 1984): 5–12.

Hornbeck, Elizabeth Jean. "Who's Afraid of the Big Bad Wolf? Domestic Violence in *The Shining*." *Feminist Studies* 42, no. 3 (2016): 689–719, 769–70.

Jameson, Fredric. "The Shining." *Social Text*, no. 4 (Autumn 1981): 114–25.

Jeffress, Lynn, and Flo Liebowitz. "*The Shining* by Stanley Kubrick." *Film Quarterly* 34, no. 3 (Spring 1981): 45–51.

Kael, Pauline. "The Shining: Devolution." *New Yorker*, June 9, 1980, 130.

Kierkegaard, Soren. *Fear and Trembling*. Edited and translated by Howard V. Hong and Edna H. Hong. Princeton NJ: Princeton University Press, 1983.

Kilker, Robert. "All Roads Lead to the Abject: The Monstrous Feminine and Gender Boundaries in Stanley Kubrick's *The Shining*." *Literature/Film Quarterly* 34, no. 1 (2006): 54–63.

Kristeva, Julia. *Powers of Horror: An Essay on Abjection*. New York: Columbia University Press, 1982.

Kubrick, Stanley, dir. *The Shining*. Warner Brothers Pictures, 1980.

Luckhurst, Roger. *The Shining*. New York: Palgrave Macmillan, 2013.

McCarthy, Cormac. *Blood Meridian*. New York: Vintage International, 1985.

Ryan, Michael, and Douglas Kellner. *Camera Politica: The Politics and Ideology of Contemporary Hollywood Film*. Bloomington: Indiana University Press, 1987.

Sayenga, Kurt, dir. *Eli Roth's History of Horror*. Season 1, episode 7, "Ghost Stories." Aired November 18, 2018, on AMC.

Wang, Ya-huei, "Archetypal Anxieties in Stanley Kubrick's *The Shining*." *Surabaya* 13, no. 1 (June 2011): 112–22.

Transgression on the Frontier   12

The Ludicity of Incest in
Bioshock Infinite   CHRISTINA FAWCETT AND
                                                  MARC A. OUELLETTE

Set in 1912, *Bioshock Infinite*, the third game in the *Bioshock* series, plays at the edge of the frontier by framing the flying city of Columbia as a new American West. Combining the end of the western era with the quintessential science fiction "what if?" scenario, the imagined world of the game looks both back and ahead. Evoking the year when the last western territories joined the Union, *Infinite*'s hero, Booker DeWitt, travels to Columbia, which seceded from the United States in 1902 under the leadership of theocrat Father Comstock. Booker's goal and, by proxy, the player's, is to kidnap/rescue a young woman, Elizabeth, to erase his debts. Elizabeth, whose history forms the narrative core, becomes Booker's focus and, as an effective AI character, draws the player into the world of Columbia. As we connect with Booker, he becomes more drawn to his captive and ally Elizabeth, who gradually appears more sexualized in her speech and dress. Concurrent with Elizabeth's maturation is her increase in power and mastery over "tears"—rips between Booker's world and other realities. These provide mechanical benefit to Booker but also center the game's engagement with time: the tears introduce the many-worlds theory of quantum mechanics and establish the logical framework for the game's final revelation. The climactic reveal—that Elizabeth is Booker's kidnapped daughter Anna and Booker is Father Comstock in another world-line—positions Elizabeth as both the mechanism and object of the game's revelation of taboo. Booker is both Elizabeth's father and her rescuer; thus, his growing affection for Elizabeth is incestuous.

Columbia initially appears an oppressive space of religious zealotry and racial segregation but gradually reveals an underlying battle: a rebellion against the theocracy to assert the citizens' freedom. The Vox Populi, in resisting Father Comstock's rule, push to make Columbia a truly free space and achieve what Lee Clark Mitchell identifies as the goal of the West in the western: "the opportunity for renewal, for self-transformation, for release from constraints associated with an urbanized East. Whatever else the West may be, in whatever form it is represented, it always signals freedom to achieve some truer state of humanity."[1] Columbia offers a different form of frontier, so while *Infinite* appears a simple first-person shooter, its political complexity belies a more intricate set of ideas at work. *Infinite* deploys a complex relationship with time, history, American imperialism, the language of Manifest Destiny, and the segregationist and self-loathing of the American past. Lizardi argues that the alternate history of *Infinite* emphasizes the cultural norms and political violence of the end of western expansionism, which situates *Infinite* in a science fiction framework and shows contention with its western roots.[2] The steampunk pastiche keeps focus on the western genre in the speculative space, reflecting what Johnson, Lush, and Spurgeon describe in the introduction to *Weird Westerns* as "inviting us to recognize genre conventions as conventions and actively participate in their interrogation."[3] For players, the function of the western frontier in the narrative keeps us aware of the constant pull between law and freedom, the Manifest Destiny that drove exploration and the many lives and communities steamrolled in that inevitable march.

These elements, showing the dystopia underpinning Columbia, reflect American myths at the end of the western expansion. More importantly, playing the game affords an opportunity to witness and enact the relationship between masculinity and the western—and the revision of both. *Infinite* invites us to consider the many problems of the western, as Booker struggles with honor, justice, and most importantly, masculinity. Reading Booker through the western lens situates him in familiar tropes of the lone gunslinger: a strong, stoic figure of masculinity who must contend with issues of justice and freedom. The narrative locates Booker at the end of the Wild West as a soldier who fought at the Battle of Wounded Knee and a former Pinkerton, the national detective agency that chased down outlaws from the West, among other functions. *Infinite* offers a variation on the western formula through the player's enactment and the prominent role of Elizabeth, yet Booker echoes the problems with which Mitchell opens his study of the western genre: "The problem of progress, envisioned as a passing of frontiers; the problem of honor, defined in a context of social expediency; the problem of law or justice, enacted in a conflict of vengeance and social control; the problem of violence, in acknowledging its value yet honoring occasions when it can be controlled; and subsuming all, the problem of what it means to be a man, as aging victim of progress, embodiment of honor, champion of justice in an unjust world."[4] These problems are also issues of masculinity; we engage with Booker as avatar but also as character. His stoicism offers a space for the player to expand and invest, as his sketchy past and equally sketchy memory produce what Warner calls "a version of the fable of self and system which dichotomizes fictional space into two positions. The self, often associated with nature and the erotic, becomes the locus for the expression of every positive human value, most especially 'freedom.' Opposite the self is the System, which in its colorless, mechanical operations, is anathematized as a faceless monster using its insidious powers to bend all human effort to its own service."[5] For Warner, these elements of the western play out in succeeding genres that invoke the same mythos. The father figure is frequently split into two, as it appears here with Booker and Comstock: the same man from different versions of reality. The game's end revelation—that Booker is Comstock from another reality—means both men are Elizabeth's father. While not enacted, the game suggests a growing romance between Booker and Elizabeth; the player, engaging with Booker as avatar, is drawn into that emotional investment as well. As the game progresses through the alternate realities, Elizabeth becomes more flirtatious and her clothing becomes more sexualized while Booker grows more dependent on her for resources and healing. Simultaneously, she shows increasing jealousy toward Daisy, head of the Vox Populi, further setting up the key reveal. As the revelation is the climactic moment, the threat of incest denies the player time to work through the idea within the gameworld. The interplay of the frontier with the underlying narrative of incestual romance creates a simultaneous danger and potential of the threshold.

Experiencing Columbia

The player arrives in Columbia to discover a preexisting conflict between Father Comstock—a religious and political leader called the Prophet by his followers—and the Vox Populi. Comstock's ethical and political values are the law of the land, as his self-centered evangelism maps Christian tropes to the Founding Fathers and celebrates the revolutionary independence that Columbia itself claimed from the United States. Booker enters Columbia through a baptismal chapel full of religious declarations, including "And though we deserved not his mercy, / He has led us to this new Eden."[6] In challenging the trope of the western revival, *Infinite* parodies the character type of the evangelical preacher whose self-aggrandizing myths demand loyalty of his citizenry.

Standing in opposition to Comstock are the Vox Populi, a secular group under the leadership of Daisy Fitzroy, a Black woman who is the visible antithesis of Comstock's white theocratic patriarchy. The politics of the game highlight the boundaries and frontiers that Columbia represents, as the Vox violently opposes the economic and racial injustices central to the operation of Columbia and running through the game. Players can find Voxophone recordings by Black men brought to Columbia as slave labor explaining their near invisibility and Jeremiah Fink's descriptions of importing nonwhites to Columbia as a workforce.[7] Columbia's cosmology, then, not only establishes the frontier of the American West but, in so doing, also ties the racism and imperialist politics of its expansion to its patriarchal and evangelical Christian roots. The game establishes clear systemic racial brutalities from the outset, and Booker meets Daisy Fitzroy when she takes the airship he is trying to steal: "There's already a fight, DeWitt. Only question is, which side you on? Comstock is the god of the white man, the rich man, the pitiless man. But if you believe in common folk, then join the Vox. If you believe in the righteous folk, then join the Vox." Her appeal to justice and freedom points to the inherent contradictions of Columbia, which map onto Booker's relationship with Elizabeth.

Infinite engages the western genre with the science fiction trope of "what if?" This alternate history narrative offers a counterfactual history, which MacCallum-Stewart and Parsler describe as "tak[ing] our own world and in some way chang[ing] it through the alteration of an event in our known past. The resultant story portrays a world which is still clearly identifiable to the reader, yet changed by this occurrence."[8] The play of the counterfactual—in the gameworld and through its tears—enables *Infinite* to explore and to challenge simultaneously the ideologies of the western era in American history and our modern understanding of those conceptions. Moreover, Booker's past makes him an embodiment of that history so that the player's experiences in Columbia are bound to tropes of the western frontier: honor, justice, and violence. Each, however, relates to Booker's performance of masculinity and the incest taboo.

In extending figures of the western, McCluskey cites Smith's typology of the hero's "three-stage shift from objectification to masochism to empowerment"; from the beginning, Booker oscillates between and among these positions.[9] He is the object of Elizabeth's gaze, as well as Comstock's, and frequently submits to painful acts and processes to achieve his goals—taking on the role of the beaten hero.[10] Moreover, the player participates in the process through the various choices and options available, as the emphasis on the male body precludes or obscures an analysis of performativity while simultaneously applying a unifocal lens to the gaze. Games, then, offer the simulation and enactment of these performances, asking us to participate in the tropes and transgressions of masculinity.

As Conway observes, games place the player "in the game dynamic's reification of a specific performance of masculinity."[11] Indeed, as Ouellette and Conway note, "It becomes clear that the building of masculinity and the empowerment of the character become one and the same. . . . Games become a ritual of traditional masculinity, in which the player . . . reclaims manhood."[12] Here, they take their cue from Connell's germinal work, which argues that masculinity is bound in discourses, performances, and power relations.[13] Games, then, offer the simulation and enactment of these performances. *Infinite* deploys multivalent ideologies that make up the American identity, so playing as Booker problematizes the usual outcomes and depictions of frontier masculinity. The player enters the world as an outsider, seeing through Booker's eyes, and thus the game can unfold information gradually. We are immersed in the stoic figure, filling in the emotional gaps and engaging in the issues of justice, honor, and romantic interest. The trope of the western gunslinger is disrupted, challenged, and reiterated through the floating city of Columbia.

Booker goes to Columbia to fulfill a bargain: find and bring Elizabeth to New York to erase his debt. The player is offered prompts like "Go to Monument Island to find the girl" and "Escape the Statue with Elizabeth," while load screens feature Booker's first-person reflections: "I've been told to tell the girl whatever she wants, so long as she comes along."[14] We are thus situated between our position as player and our performance as Booker. Because

Booker's speech acts are scripted, the player can read his abrupt responses or silence as part of his role as western hero: we have no control over his dialogue or disclosure. When asked about his work with the Pinkertons, Booker's response is terse and sparing: "I'll tell you this: sometimes there's precious need for folks like Fitzroy. . . . Cause of folks like me."[15] The power of this moment lies in what is unsaid, as Booker only answers Elizabeth's questions with vague or brief responses, if he answers at all. Booker's silence takes on a kind of authority but also offers a complication for the player. As Corneau notes, silence is a key means of enforcing masculinity, which builds on Tompkins's assertion that the deployment of silence is a means of maintaining men's dominance over women: "Talk dissipates presence, takes away the mystery of an ineffable self which silence preserves."[16] A hero's stoic silence in film offers the audience a chance to project and presume the character's emotional inner life. Here the player provides the emotional work as the game enacts it. Booker's speech is sparing compared to Elizabeth, who is quite expressive throughout the game, so Booker-as-avatar invites us to project the emotions behind his silence, assuming its affective intentionality. This emotional entangling makes the narrative reveal more powerful, as the silent hero drives our emotional participation in a sexual taboo.

To consider Booker as a gunslinger is to focus on how the narrative articulates his masculinity. His flashbacks and recollections establish him as the spectacle and the beaten male who will eventually triumph: sitting at a desk, passed out from alcohol and hearing loud banging on the door, while his hands, which bear a branding of the initials A.D., serve as an omnipresent reminder of his need for recuperation and rehabilitation. However, the performance and enactment of masculinity in a game affords an alteration of the identifications because it produces what Conway calls an "oscillation between grandiose displays of masochism (illustrating endurance of unbelievable pain) and sadism (infliction of overwhelming suffering)."[17] The effect is that we are invited to not feel with and for Booker. Our projections fill the motivations of our avatar, collapsing the distance between the two, particularly through the game's reward structures and its partial basis on video shorts that fill in part of the game's riddle so that Booker and the player become aware simultaneously.

The emotional involvement, particularly with Elizabeth, engages the player in more than just the mechanical interplay of discovery and game directives, as the rich environment and complex characters give the player something to invest in. Järvinen's discussion of emotional experiences in games argues that "as long as the player is willing to care enough about the goals of the game and the social situation in order to 'play along,' games arguably set up conditions for eliciting emotions."[18] *Infinite* provides space for positive emotional investment but reminds the player of Booker's guilt and dishonesty. Through declarative in-game goals and the load screens' personal pronouns, the player is pulled into Booker and his internal conflicts. Despite this linguistic separation, the player operates in a complex relationship described by Rehak: "Players experience games through the exclusive intermediary of another—the avatar—the 'eyes,' 'ears,' and 'body' of which are components of a complex technological and psychological apparatus. . . . To blur the distinction between players and their game-generated subjectivities is to bypass pressing questions of ideological mystification and positioning inherent to interactive technologies of the imaginary."[19] Booker defines the player's movement and field of view; he is our mechanism of experience in Columbia but also a kind of filter. The game's emotional impact comes from Booker's identity, making him what Mateas calls a "subjective avatar" who manipulates the "viewer's subjective position within the virtual world. These avatars have an autonomous personality model which reacts to events in the world and maintains an emotional state and narrative context relative to these events."[20] Moreover, Booker's backstory and motivations shape the way we experience the story; we engage with his motivations and the process of emotional justification.

The game goes beyond the avatar as simple input mechanism; we are drawn into Booker's body by cuing our senses. Booker's hands create a visual awareness of our embodiment. One hand is always visible holding a gun in the frame and the other rises into the field of view to highlight the current equipped vigor. We are tied to the actions of an idealized form of frontier masculinity—the gunslinger—who pervades American myth and popular imagination. Booker's physicality and violence bring us into his experience and lie alongside his emotional conflicts and our investment in them. This cognitive and affective response reinforces the western's capacity to "*narrat[e]* all those contradictions involved in what it means to be a man, in a way that makes them seem less troubling than they are."[21] Since the game includes the player in the process, we are invited to participate in this contradiction, learning to care about Elizabeth while engaging in brutality and violence, and embodying the actions the hero undertakes.

Conflicting with our embodiment is the rigid narrative line. While the player moves Booker, his story moves us. The player can exercise limited choices, but the game's major events are set. Conway defines ludicity as "the degree to which digital games allow play, 'play' here being defined as the possibility to act and have an effect upon the gameworld."[22] *Infinite* varies in its levels of ludicity, as the story can limit the player's ability to influence Booker's movement, exploration, and combat. How Booker treats and speaks to Elizabeth or whether he moves into interdimensional tears are set elements. While the player controls the view, direction, and pace of movement, and the discovery of secondary information, many aspects of the game function similarly to film, as short video clips provide a host of information and teach the player how to behave, how to move, and how to interact with Elizabeth and the gameworld.

The conflict between embodiment and distantiation is important in a game that draws the player into the character's emotional exchanges and then suggests taboo. The primary driver of our emotional engagement is, of course, the narrative focus: Elizabeth. As Booker is rowed to the Lighthouse in the opening sequence, he is handed a box with his name on it; it contains, among other things, a photo of Elizabeth with the instruction "Bring to New York Unharmed" written across the back. The mantra of "Deliver the girl and wipe away the debt" appears throughout the game, reiterating that Elizabeth is the key motivation; thus, the mechanics of involvement have greater impact in *Infinite* than the standard first-person shooter game. The player's attachment to Elizabeth, enhanced through Booker's stoic silence and space for emotional projection, determines the impact of the end reveal.

The Virtual Gaze

Elizabeth is a visually attractive character. The game mechanically returns the eye to her, while her character is designed to appeal to the player. Elizabeth's traits highlight emotional expression, as her large eyes and cartoonish face shape separate her from the other characters populating Columbia. She is called the Lamb and the child, terms of infantilization, which match the visual cues her facial features provide. Shawn Robertson, animation director for *Bioshock Infinite*, explains that to develop "a companion you want to elicit an emotional connection to, you really need to be able to see what she's thinking at all times. . . . First we wanted Elizabeth to not have human proportions, even if you look at her face it's obvious we've given her larger eyes, a larger mouth. . . . I mean, if you saw a real person walking around looking like her you'd think she was odd!"[23] The focus on Elizabeth's face as a mechanism of emotional expression is a tool to encourage player investment. Elizabeth's emotions need to be visible across great distance, as her body language and facial reactions shape the player's experience. The result is a companion who fosters an emotional connection between player and Elizabeth via Booker: "We wanted her to share that journey with the player. We wanted a relationship the player could emotionally buy into."[24] The embodiment, emotional cuing, and Elizabeth's design and mechanics all bring the player into the relationship between Elizabeth and Booker. The strong emotional connection makes the taboo both possible and impactful.

Elizabeth's changing fashion becomes a cue for the player's attention. Booker's first sight of Elizabeth shows her in a rather simple and young state of dress: she wears a calf-length blue skirt, white blouse, and blue tie. Her outfit is reminiscent of a schoolgirl's uniform, highlighting her childlike traits. This ensemble becomes disheveled as Elizabeth and Booker attempt to escape Columbia and as Elizabeth attempts to escape Booker. The shoulder rips, the tie loosens, and the skirt looks the worse for wear. Eventually, she undoes her tie and her shirt is more open at the neck, showing cleavage that was previously concealed. The final iteration of Elizabeth's costume change is a more visible cue to the complex relationship between fathers and daughters, as she dons the outfit of her adopted mother, Lady Comstock. When she wears the borrowed clothing, becoming a reflection of her mother, Elizabeth does not know Lady Comstock is not her biological parent. The outfit, consisting of a white corset with a flowing blue skirt, maintains her color palate while appearing more adult, a signal of Elizabeth's maturity. In an act of frustration, she cuts off her ponytail, leaving her hair short and loose; her ponytail, and its visible ribbon bow, lays at her feet in the scene, showing her casting off the trappings of childhood. This change is disruptive, as Booker's companion now looks like an adult instead of a child, with more attention drawn to her décolletage and slender waist. Donning Lady Comstock's clothing, she becomes more visually appealing to both Booker and potentially Comstock, her father(s). Stepping into the dress of one father's lover suggests that she is potentially inhabiting that role to the other.

One of the more unsettling scenes occurs when the player observes Elizabeth for the first time. The girl lives in captivity, inside the statue of Columbia—the personification of Comstock's floating Eden. The captivity narrative, which dominated the frontier narratives of the late seventeenth century, often features the faithful being held hostage by the so-called savage Natives as a test of faith. Slotkin notes the power of the captivity narrative to "serv[e] (often simultaneously) as literary entertainment, material for revival sermons, vehicle for political diatribes, and 'experimental' evidence in philosophical and theological works."[25] *Infinite* flips this convention, having Elizabeth held by the religious leader. She is both captive and test subject, surrounded by various directories, observation rooms, and movie cameras, constructed for the gaze, for what Laura Mulvey calls her "to-be-looked-atness." This positioning produces an instant reminder that "the pleasure in looking has been split between active/male and passive/female."[26] In Mulvey's formulation, the look of the male onscreen aligns with the male off-screen, for whom the gaze is ultimately created. Mulvey sets up what she calls the two contradictory aspects of the pleasurable structures of looking in film. Crucially, both parts of what Mulvey calls the contradictory pleasures of looking apply. First, scopophilia, the pleasure of using another person as an erotic object "implies a separation of the erotic identity from the object on the screen."[27] We do not look at Booker looking at Elizabeth but instead look directly; Elizabeth is the object of the gaze of the men studying her in her prison inside the statue of Columbia while she is the object of the gaze of the player. She is held captive in the tower and held captive in our gaze. She becomes increasingly sexualized and produced for the gaze, abandoning her infantile framing and clothing to become more adult as the player gets closer to the moment of discovery. Mulvey notes that narcissistic identification occurs through "the spectator's fascination with and recognition of his like."[28] Being interjected into the body of Booker brings the player's worldview and experience of the game to the position of the gazer.

The player's identification with Booker is not a simple collapse of subjective spaces; rather, it offers the potential for multiple and simultaneous modes of viewing. However, Schleiner highlights the ways that the ludic apparatus of video games "allows for a multiplicity of sometimes quite contrary positions and subjectivities."[29] She concludes these identifications are particularly important because of the pedagogical possibility afforded by individual potential for critical reading and interpretation: a female player in a male avatar gazing at a female non-player character (NPC) opens spaces of ironic complexity. Similarly, Fantone writes that a game involves a "process [that] opens possibilities for a resisting oppositional gaze and subversive practices, beyond the commercial aims of the games' designers."[30] In this way, the game works out the problematic incest taboo in and through the instantiation of it. *Infinite* quite literally performs and plays with the proverbial question, "What if it were your daughter?" Mulvey notes that scopophilia is already sexual: the gaze from Booker and the implied gaze by Comstock, the Lutèce twins, and any workers in the complex, is a fetishized—or at least a fascinated—form of looking. Elizabeth lives in a cage behind the one-way glass *and* is being filmed for future looking. Ultimately, she is constructed as the object of multiple simultaneous gazes. Her relationship with Booker exemplifies the "femme fatale" and the "mentor" roles Schleiner enumerates as occurring in and through gameplay.[31] She occupies these roles simultaneously, as a woman trapped in the proverbial inescapable situation who possesses seemingly magical powers and manipulates Booker through flirting and random gifts while offering just enough hints about how to navigate the gameworld and solve the mystery. Both these sexualized roles are occluded by Mulvey's framework but realized in the game.

The Gaze and Gameplay

The player's power increases concurrently with the sexualization of Elizabeth and Booker's developing relationship with her. Conway offers the term "hyper-ludicity" to describe the ways in which games bestow powers and possibilities upon the player and especially "broaden a game's learning curve [through] use and implications of these features."[32] Elizabeth's frequent contributions of salt, health, ammunition, and coins—along with the occasional use of dimensional tears to escape harm or summon relief—point to the hyper-ludic rewards gained from the process. The game fosters the relationship and the incest taboo as the player moves from gazing at Elizabeth to relying on her. While the player can search for clues, coins, lockpicks, Voxophones, and codes, the reliance on Elizabeth has the counterintuitive effect of reducing player agency and ability to play. Conway describes "hypo-ludic" features as those that remove "control and agency so necessary to the experience."[33] Conway's third formulation, "contra-ludicity," or moments when the game resists the player, and hypo-ludicity work in concert to show how Elizabeth provides the missing element, as periodic prompts to push a button and the camera swivel focus the player back on her.[34] Both are induced by Elizabeth's gifts, which place the player in a position of submission and acquiescence to her offering but also to their effects. The game limits the player's inputs to reinforce the centrality of a relationship with Elizabeth. *Infinite*, through the carefully crafted Elizabeth AI, guides the player to negotiate between what Booker can do (*ludus*) and what he is compelled to do (*paidia*) in the game. As such, the ludic structure draws the player into Booker's desirous gaze at Elizabeth—we want to be prompted to look at her—offering both scopophilic and ludic reward. As a player, we seek her for help, and as Booker, we seek her for the promise of salvation, so we are not just implicated but are also part of the discovery and Elizabeth's objectification.

Elizabeth is a powerful character in her complexity and in her control of interdimensional tears; she can travel frontiers in a way that Booker cannot. While she starts as the captive subject—"a single individual, usually a woman, stand[ing] passively under the strokes of evil, awaiting rescue by the grace of God"—she shifts her role to be an agentive figure seeking her own escape.[35] While we control Booker, making him our protagonist, Elizabeth is a heroic figure in her own right. She is the center of the game from the very first moments, as Booker's goal is to get Elizabeth. The game also highlights her centrality by having the player seek Elizabeth and her attentions, but she does not remain the object of the search narrative. She becomes a temptress: unlike many passive non-player character AIs, Elizabeth runs ahead and actively engages with the space, drawing the player along the intended path and doling out trinkets, hints, and potions. For example, Elizabeth will make a sound of interest when a player is near an interactive item, luring the player and encouraging greater attention to the details of Columbia. As Mateas notes, "Within a performative space the [AI] expresses the author's ideas. The [AI] is both a messenger for and a message from the author."[36] Elizabeth is the author's mode of interaction with the player. As narrative center, ludic center, and source of rewards, Elizabeth encourages player investment.

While she occasionally needs rescue, Elizabeth is far from a damsel in distress. The game highlights this after Booker and Elizabeth escape her tower. When leaving Battlefield Bay, the game screen features the text, "You don't need to protect Elizabeth in combat. She can take care of herself."[37] This message has two effects. The first is mechanical: the player need not adjust the style of combat based on the NPC. While many games with a rescue component enact penalties for the target getting hurt, *Infinite* does not: the player can engage in combat with hesitation or reckless abandon. The second effect is narrative: Booker needs to recognize Elizabeth's power and self-efficacy. This pivot away from the captive female to the self-sufficient figure sets up the later progression of her power surpassing Booker's. He may have liberated her from the tower, but her power to manipulate quantum tears far outshines his ability to fire a gun or use a vigor. She is a frighteningly powerful figure and a rescuer. When the player is overwhelmed in combat, no Game Over screen appears; instead, the screen goes black before showing brief flashes of Elizabeth tapping a large needle over Booker and bringing him back to life. She sustains Booker and reinvigorates him when he collapses, so we know she gazes at the spectacle of the gunslinger's beaten body. While we do not see as Elizabeth, this moment evokes the trope of "the Western's focus of our gaze on the male body—a body that must . . . be beaten, distorted, and pressed out of shape."[38] The beaten body and Elizabeth's ministrations to Booker remind us that westerns focus on the attractiveness of the masculine body and "invok[e] violence only to show how the restrained, fetish-laden body is not to be deprived of life but made to stand as a desirable emblem of masculinity. . . . Beating the hero can thus be thought of as a kind of artificial respiration, raising his temperature and bringing a bloom to his cheek."[39] Elizabeth bringing Booker back through dramatic medical intervention shows her concern and fear at losing him, and her fixation on his beaten state. This support is significant in both play and the building of romantic incest through the ongoing discovery of the family relationship between and among Elizabeth, Comstock, and Booker. Elizabeth engages Booker, particularly through the interplay of temptation and rewards, the latter mapping onto the ludic structure. With a single button press, "Catch coin," the player's focus snaps to Elizabeth, who throws Booker money. She will smile or respond to Booker before the screen returns to whatever the player was pursuing. Recentering the player's focus to Elizabeth means that even when the player looks at other elements of Columbia, we must return to Elizabeth. When Booker is rewarded for exploring the world, the player is rewarded with a view of an increasingly sexualized Elizabeth.

Elizabeth can pick locks, further enabling Booker to access places otherwise beyond reach. Indeed, Elizabeth is frequently an agent of hyper-ludicity, giving the player additional power-ups and varied means of solving problems. Her powers enable her to move through spaces and across frontiers; we can ask for her to pick a lock, but her doing so actually blocks the lock from view. She protects the privileged skill, yet only picks locks to enable Booker's movement. So, while she is a powerful figure, she is framed as helper, not hero. The female NPC powering up the male avatar positions the female as a mechanism of male assistance. Elizabeth enables Booker to be stronger, last longer in combat, and purchase more upgrades from vending machines. She heightens the player's abilities and changes the combat experience, influencing the player's ludic capability. Yet those power-ups always draw the player to look at Elizabeth, refocusing on her even mid-combat. Origitano notes that Elizabeth's hyper-ludic abilities are explicitly tied to her oppression: "Elizabeth learned code-breaking and lock-picking while in her tower. Booker asks her about both, to which she responds, 'You put someone in a cage, they develop interests in such things.' Elizabeth's abilities, then, are a direct result of her oppression."[40] The player's experience of hyper-ludicity is therefore framed through Elizabeth's abuse; her objectification is a means of empowerment for Booker as well as for the player. Again, the fact that these are enacted adds another layer of complexity, for these skills are not necessary for completion. Instead, they offer in-game rewards. The hyper-ludic elements build the experience, enriching Columbia and adding to discovery and exploration. Elizabeth heightens play and becomes an object of augmentation and pleasure.

The Experience of Taboo

In *Erotic Innocence*, James Kincaid emphasizes the ways popular culture portrayals eroticize children and deny its occurrence. The dominant tropes tend to sanction the behavior by shifting the blame onto the children themselves. While Kincaid does not specifically address how video games contribute to the reinscription, reconfiguration, or reconciliation of the cultural processes involved, he provides a framework for considering tales of eroticized children and the associated taboos, including incestuous desires. Video games offer the potential to make more obvious and explicit the subtle processes Kincaid identifies in literature and film through player engagement and participation. Rather than a series of individual stories about "victims" or "survivors," Kincaid sees the same kernel story from our "cultural storehouse" being repeated: "Our preoccupations and the stories that give them power are not necessarily individualized, and, more important, . . . the relentless individualizing we engage in draws our attention away from cultural analysis."[41] Thus, the tendency to stress the uniqueness of each case tends to obscure the persistent sameness; moreover, it prevents an analysis on these grounds. The narrative sets up the incestuous frame through Booker's memory loss, the time traveling, and Elizabeth's kidnapping by Comstock. Her sexualization, both in the story and in the player's visual frame, occurs notably when Booker sees the observation chambers, and as Elizabeth changes into Lady Comstock's clothing. However, the player and Booker must repeatedly chase and mollify Elizabeth; after all, she, not Booker, is the victim—of Comstock, of Booker, and of the player.

The game offers multiple and simultaneous means for experiencing and negotiating the various directions of sexualization. As much as the ubiquitous Freudian tale centers on the child's desires for the adult, Kincaid's work points to a contingent and incumbent sexualization of the child. *Infinite* contributes to conversations about the reconciliation of these taboos as the player moves and gazes as Booker, the parent. Notably, Elizabeth is an adult positioned as child. While dressed and styled as a juvenile, the greater issue is her relationship with her parent. Kincaid asserts that considerations of form are insufficient because tales of the eroticized child have an "outside, where those of us who tell it can stand,

and an inside, occupied by those about whom it is told.... Those inside are enmeshed in a script with nothing but bad parts.... There are two main roles, monster and victim."[42] Not only do video games highlight how these roles tend to become interchangeable, they facilitate the imbrication into the means and methods through which children are eroticized in popular culture. As much as Elizabeth is a victim, she also has several moments of monstrosity, not least of which is her ability to tear open portals. Her severed fingertip—and the thimble covering it—remind us of her power; as she lost her finger in a tear, we see the thimble as a seeming affectation. Instead, her ability to control tears is bound up in her split existence; the tip of her finger was left behind when she was stolen as a baby, so she is perpetually simultaneously split. She exists between spaces and controls the tears from her liminality. Indeed, one of Booker's load-screen reflections notes that part of his job entails staying on the good side of Elizabeth's temper. She manipulates him and the player and, in the process, resists victimization even as she draws Booker's eye.

As Elizabeth becomes more sexualized in terms of her figure and her dress, she becomes more inquisitive about Booker's past. After Booker wakes in Battleship Bay, Elizabeth states, in the form of a question, "You kept repeating a woman's name, 'Anna,'" having already asked him several times about a "woman in your life."[43] Booker calling out for Anna does seem reminiscent of a lover calling for a lost beloved, and the player can fall into the same assumptions as Elizabeth. He shuts down this line of questioning with a simple dismissal: "I don't want to talk about that."[44] His stoic silence compounds his gunslinger role but also delays important information: Anna is the name of Booker's daughter who was kidnapped. While we read his unconscious calls as romantic, he is calling for the very daughter expressing interest in his romantic life. Elizabeth's interest balances his terse, silent masculinity and ensures the player makes contingent assumptions. We fill that emotional space: the game prompts the player's interest in Elizabeth while showing her growing interest in Booker. Elizabeth's frustration at her helplessness and need for more information and control culminates in Elizabeth killing Daisy Fitzroy while Booker watches helplessly. Ironically, to reach Daisy, Elizabeth must be boosted up by Booker, and he lifts her to reach a small passage—a reversal of her bolstering activities throughout the game. Conway claims that such moments "kill play" because they remove the player's agency and ability to effect change.[45] Yet the move has several important effects relating to the player's ultimate imbrication, as player and bystander, in the eroticization of Elizabeth. As Elizabeth becomes more and more of a sexualized object, Booker and the player draw closer to discovering Elizabeth is Booker's daughter.

Conclusion

Infinite confirms Espen Aarseth's axiom that the "gameworld is its own reward."[46] Aarseth arrives at such a position because what "makes such games playable at all, and indeed attractive, is the sequence of shifting, exotic, often fascinating settings (levels), where you explore the topography and master the virtual environment."[47] While Aarseth overstates the centrality of the mastery aspects of play, *Infinite*'s gameworld is its own reward on multiple, simultaneous levels. The relationship with and eroticization of Elizabeth form a key component of her status as player-reward. Her function is emphasized through her frequent gifting, reminders of Booker's debt, and the revelation of her erstwhile adoption by Comstock. She is a reward for all the major figures, including the player.

The frontier of the western, at the edge of civilization and exploration, order and lawlessness, is also a frontier between the masculine and feminine. The focus on the masculine, and the masculine as a complex and multivalent process of dominance and restraint, informs our reading of Booker and emotional projection into our avatar's stoic silence. We play an echo of the frontier, coming to a city where defiance of the law is defiance of religious ideals. Father Comstock's theocracy frames lawlessness as godlessness, creating an opening for Booker to engage in immoral actions in the name of justice. Elizabeth—the helper, the narrative center, the reward, and the threat—is a figure of great allure and also great danger. Elizabeth, in her position as a manipulator of quantum tears, is a point of disruption and an embodiment of the frontier.

The player is pulled into Columbia, the body of Booker DeWitt, and the complex relationship between Elizabeth and her father, Zachary Hale Comstock. The game's mechanisms of investment center on Booker's—and the player's—interest in Elizabeth. The character design, the AI, the world of Columbia, and the player's sense of embodiment all attract the player, and Elizabeth's shift from childlike Lamb to adult partner to formidable frontier-traveler is emotionally important. Elizabeth becomes more mature and more powerful as the game progresses, as Booker becomes more entangled in her escape from Columbia. The building relationship grounds the player emotionally and provides investment in the end reveal. Elizabeth and Booker's relationship, their growing dependence on one another, makes her forced revelation all the more powerful. Elizabeth knows what is happening before Booker does, bringing him into his past, into moments he has forgotten. The child leads the parent to discover the truth of his past, and leads the player to discover the truth of her experience. The mechanisms of player involvement and emotional imbrication complicate the rendering of taboo, as crossing over frontiers and thresholds makes the taboo possible.

Notes

1. Mitchell, *Westerns*, 5.
2. Lizardi, "Bioshock: Complex."
3. Johnson, Lush, and Spurgeon, "Westworld(s)," 11.
4. Mitchell, *Westerns*, 3.
5. Warner, "Spectacular Action," 676.
6. Levine, *Bioshock Infinite*.
7. Voxophones are recording devices that, in appearance, resemble a classic AM radio. They are tools for recording brief messages, and they appear around Columbia to enrich the political setting. Fink is the primary industrialist in Columbia and owner of Fink Industries, which makes the vending machines and vigors the player finds in Columbia.
8. MacCallum-Stewart and Parsler, "Alternative History," 21.
9. McCluskey, "'Rough! Tough!,'" 81.
10. Booker's viewed position inverts Mulvey's (1989) conception of the gaze as inexorably male; however, it does reify how gaze is bound to gender.
11. Conway, "Poisonous Pantheons," 946.
12. Ouellette and Conway, "He Scores," 122.
13. Connell, *Masculinities*.
14. Levine, *Bioshock Infinite*.
15. Levine, *Bioshock Infinite*.
16. Corneau, *Absent Fathers*; Tompkins, "Women and the Language of Men," 60.
17. Conway, "Poisonous Pantheons," 950.
18. Järvinen, "Video Games as Emotional Experiences," 87.
19. Rehak, "Playing at Being," 104.

20. Mateas, "Expressive AI," 147.
21. Mitchell, *Westerns*, 27 (emphasis in original).
22. Conway, "Hyper-ludicity," 135.
23. Robertson quoted in Gera, "*Bioshock Infinite*'s Original Elizabeth."
24. Robertson quoted in Corriea, "Animating *Bioshock*."
25. Slotkin, "Captivity Narratives," 95.
26. Mulvey, *Visual and Other Pleasures*, 19.
27. Mulvey, *Visual and Other Pleasures*, 18.
28. Mulvey, *Visual and Other Pleasures*, 18.
29. Schleiner, "Fake Polygons," 222.
30. Fantone, "Final Fantasies," 51.
31. Schleiner, "Fake Polygons," 224.
32. Conway, "Hyper-ludicity," 136.
33. Conway, "We Used to Win," 38.
34. Conway, "Hyper-ludicity," 135.
35. Slotkin, "Captivity Narratives," 94.
36. Mateas, "Expressive AI," 150.
37. Levine, *Bioshock Infinite*.
38. Mitchell, *Westerns*, 160.
39. Mitchell, *Westerns*, 172.
40. Origitano, "'The Cage Is Somber,'" 41–42.
41. Kincaid, *Erotic Innocence*, 242.
42. Kincaid, *Erotic Innocence*, 30.
43. Levine, *Bioshock Infinite*.
44. Levine, *Bioshock Infinite*.
45. Conway, "We Used to Win."
46. Aarseth, "Genre Trouble," 51.
47. Aarseth, "Genre Trouble," 51.

Bibliography

Aarseth, Espen. "Genre Trouble: Narrativism and the Art of Simulation." In *First Person: New Media as Story, Performance, and Game*, edited by Noah Wardrip-Fruin and Pat Harrigan, 45–55. Cambridge MA: MIT Press, 2004.

Connell, R. W. *Masculinities: Knowledge, Power and Social Change*. 2nd ed. Berkeley: University of California Press, 2005.

Conway, Steven. "Hyper-ludicity, Contra-ludicity, and the Digital Game." *Eludamos: Journal for Computer Game Culture* 4, no. 2 (2010): 135–47.

———. "Poisonous Pantheons: God of War and Toxic Masculinity." *Games and Culture* 15, no. 8 (2020): 943–61.

———. "We Used to Win, We Used to Lose, We Used to Play: Simulacra, Hypo-Ludicity and the Lost Art of Losing." *Westminster Papers in Communication and Culture* 9, no. 1 (2012): 28–46.

Corneau, Guy. *Absent Fathers, Lost Sons: The Search for Masculine Identity*. 2nd ed. Boston: Shambhala Publications, 2018.

Corriea, Alexa Ray. "Animating *Bioshock Infinite*'s Elizabeth to Foster Emotional Connections." *Polygon*, March 21, 2014. http://www.polygon.com/2014/3/21/5530892/animating-bioshock-infinite-elizabeth-to-foster-emotional-connections.

Fantone, Laura. "Final Fantasies Virtual Women's Bodies." *Feminist Theory* 4, no. 1 (2003): 51–72.

Gera, Emily. "*Bioshock Infinite*'s Original Elizabeth Character Model Wasn't 'Attractive Enough,' Says Designer." *Polygon*, March 20, 2013. http://www.polygon.com/2013/3/20/4126766/bioshock-infinite-initial-elizabeth-character-design-wasnt-attractive.

Järvinen, Aki. "Video Games as Emotional Experiences." In *The Video Game Theory Reader 2*, edited by Bernard Perron and Mark J. P. Wolf, 85–108. New York: Routledge, 2009.

Johnson, Michael K., Rebecca M. Lush, and Sara L. Spurgeon. "Westworld(s): Race, Gender, Genre in the Weird Western." Introduction to *Weird Westerns: Race, Gender, Genre*, edited by Kerry Fine, Michael K. Johnson, Rebecca M. Lush, and Sara L. Spurgeon, 1–36. Lincoln: University of Nebraska Press, 2020.

Kincaid, James. *Erotic Innocence: The Culture of Child Molesting*. Durham NC: Duke University Press, 1998.

Levine, Kevin, dir. *Bioshock Infinite*. Novato CA: 2K Games, 2016. PS4.

Lizardi, Ryan. "Bioshock: Complex and Alternate Histories." *Game Studies* 14, no. 1 (2014). http://gamestudies.org/1401/articles/lizardi?utm_source=dlvr.it.

MacCallum-Stewart, Esther, and Justin Parsler. "Alternative History." In *The Greenwood Encyclopedia of Science Fiction*. Westport CT: Greenwood Press, 2007.

Mateas, Michael. "Expressive AI: A Hybrid Art and Science Practice." *Leonardo: Journal of the International Society for Arts, Sciences, and Technology* 34, no. 2 (2001): 147–53.

McCluskey, John Michael. "'Rough! Tough! Real Stuff!': Music, Militarism, and Masculinity in American College Football." *American Music* 37, no. 1 (2019): 29–57.

Mitchell, Lee Clark. *Westerns: Making the Man in Fiction and Film*. Chicago: University of Chicago, 1996.

Mulvey, Laura. *Visual and Other Pleasures*. Bloomington: Indiana University Press, 1989.

Origitano, Catlyn. "'The Cage Is Somber': A Feminist Understanding of Elizabeth." In *Bioshock and Philosophy: Irrational Game, Rational Game*, edited by

Luke Cuddy, 38–48. Blackwell Philosophy and Pop Culture Series. Malden MA: Wiley/Blackwell, 2015.

Ouellette, Marc, and Steven Conway. "He Scores Through a Screen: Mediating Masculinities Through Hockey Video Games." In *Masculinities in Play*, edited by Nicholas Taylor and Gerald Voorhees, 109–26. New York: Palgrave Macmillan, 2018.

Rehak, Bob. "Playing at Being: Psychoanalysis and the Avatar." In *The Video Game Theory Reader*, edited by Mark J. P. Wolf and Bernard Perron, 103–27. New York: Routledge, 2003.

Schleiner, Anne-Marie. "Does Lara Croft Wear Fake Polygons? Gender and Gender-Role Subversion in Computer Adventure Games." *Leonardo* 34, no. 3 (2001): 221–26.

Slotkin, Richard. "Israel in Babylon: The Archetype of the Captivity Narratives (1682–1700)." In *Regeneration Through Violence: The Mythology of the American Frontier, 1600–1860*. Norman: University of Oklahoma Press, 1973.

Tompkins, Jane. "Women and the Language of Men." In *West of Everything: The Inner Life of Westerns*, 47–67. New York: Oxford University Press, 1993.

Warner, William. "Spectacular Action: Rambo and the Popular Pleasures of Pain." In *Cultural Studies*, edited by Lawrence Grossberg, Cary Nelson, and Paula Treichler, 672–88. New York: Routledge, 1992.

13

Dead Fathers and Monstrous Daughters in *The Last of Us II*

SARA HUMPHREYS

The modern western and video games have been ideological partners in the production, performance, and control of sex and gender for decades. In the early 1980s, for example, the atrocious *Custer's Revenge* featured the historical figure of General Armstrong Custer with a pixelated erection repeatedly raping an Indigenous woman tied to a pole.[1] In the 1990s, side-scrolling, arcade-style video games with western iconography were popular, such as *Billy the Kid Returns*, which featured "Deadly Senoritas" and "Ambush Apaches" that Billy, as the rugged outlaw cowboy, had to defeat to collect points and rewards.[2] As computational processing and technology improved, so did the capacity of video games to not only feature complex storylines and more realistic roleplay in expansive fictional worlds (or gameworlds) but also to replicate gender conventions and stereotypes. Games like *Red Dead Revolver* (2005), *Gun* (2006), and *Red Dead Redemption* (2010) gave the player the opportunity to perform as a cowboy who rescues damsels in distress, shoots bad guys, and performs rugged masculinity via his swagger, lithe body, and mannerisms. That is, when a player picks up a video game controller and presses the buttons necessary to make a player-character (or the character the player can control) fight a duel, jump on a horse, or skin a bear, the player is immersed within the sex and gender norms and values that character embodies. In other words, "while print texts and film can only desire to represent," computational processes replicate gestures, movements, clothing, body shape, and sex positions that constitute the expected conventional sex and gender performances found in and popularized by the western (or whatever genre comprises that particular gameworld).[3] Most popular gameworld westerns follow the conventions first mapped out by Owen Wister's *The Virginian* (1902), which means that sex and gender performance is harnessed to a very specific form of heteronormative, brute masculine nation-building.[4]

And then there is the revisionist weird western gameworld *The Last of Us II* (2020) that both critiques and queers the rugged masculinity of the cowboy figure.[5] I use the word "queer" here carefully, framing it via Lauren Berlant's and Michael Warner's loose and baggy definition of queer theory as a means to interrogate "the full range of power-ridden normativities of sex."[6] In this sense, *The Last of Us II* is a queer game that attempts to redraw the boundaries that define sexuality and gender in gameworld westerns. *The Last of Us II* writers Halley Gross and Neil Druckmann challenge how gender and sexuality are understood in third-person action games by creating moral quandaries concerning the ethical choices made by the main characters in the first game, aptly titled *The Last of Us*.[7] They achieve this effect through two main narrative conduits: first through the gothic doubling of a revenge cycle performed by the ostensible protagonist, Ellie Williams, and second through the apparent antagonist, Abby Anderson. This doubling, in turn, blurs binary understandings of sex, love, gender, heroism, and villainy.

The revenge cycle starts with Abby murdering the main player-character, Joel Miller, a postapocalyptic cowboy, by beating him to death for murdering her father, Dr. Jerry Anderson. Player attachment to Joel is not simply based on playing as this character for hours and hours, collecting the necessary items to increase his abilities and weaponry. It's also that his brand of masculinity, exuding folksy charm, preternatural knowledge, and other frontier attributes, is familiar territory for those who play popular console games. Whether players enjoy the game or not is immaterial; by playing a game, reading a book, watching a film, or engaging with narrative in other mediums, players/readers/viewers enter into a negotiation with the characters, setting, and gameplay that in turn helps to shape their worldview.[8] Wayne Booth called this form of negotiation "coduction," a process by which characters and their players/readers/viewers interact. While Booth was referring to fictional worlds in print, his description of this negotiation is a useful means to think through the connection between players and player-characters in gameworlds:

> If . . . I am not an individual self at all, but a character, a social self, a being-in-process many of whose established dispositions or habits belong to others—some of them even to all human kind—then I need

have no anxiety about finding and preserving a unique core for the various characters that in a sense have colonized me and continue to do so. I should be able to embrace the unquestioned ethical power of narratives, in order to try on for size the [player] character roles offered to me. I can hold a fitting of various "habits," to see if they enhance or diminish how I/we appear to myself/ourselves. And I should then be able to talk with my selves . . . about the strengths and weaknesses I have found—found in one sense in the narrative but in another sense in me/us. Some of the roles opened to me as I move through the field of selves that my cultural moment provides will be good for "me/us," some not so good, some literally fatal. It will be the chief and most difficult business of my life to grope my way along dimly lit paths, hoping to build a life-"plot" that will be in one of the better genres.[9]

In complex gameworlds, players perform the dispositions and habits of the character they are playing, thereby making the "dimly lit paths" Booth refers to not just more well-lit but perhaps difficult to refuse. Put another way, the performative aspect of player-characters renders them even more influential than print or film characters, as evidenced by the extreme reactions from fans regarding the death of Joel and, in turn, the necessity of playing as Abby for at least fourteen hours of gameplay.[10] Therefore, it was no small feat for Gross and Druckmann to upend player expectations and create characters with a variety of habits and dispositions for players to "try on for size." This gameworld challenges players to assess the choices both Abby and Ellie make as queer characters who wield the dispositions of brute masculinity to enact vengeance. That is, no matter what sex or sexuality Abby and Ellie identify as, these qualities of brute masculinity are performative. This is not to say that such performances can be turned on and off like a video game; rather, this gameworld makes clear that the expectations of conventional brute masculinity are pathological, in part due to the durability of the western genre and its cowboy figure.

In contrast to its sequel, *The Last of Us* is largely an example of the status quo in popular console gaming. This gameworld adheres to the convention of a straight white male player-character, Joel, who protects the damsel in distress, Ellie.[11] Under attack from zombies, aliens, monsters, and in the case of *The Last of Us* franchise, those infected by the cordyceps brain virus, the "white male savior . . . plays out the classic narrative of save the world and rescue the girl."[12] Of course, this default identity "has a literary origin story" in the form of frontier narratives, such as the frontier romance and the modern western.[13] Joel is the sole playable character in all chapters of the game save one, and therefore, his worldview and embodied experience is the key point of view players can invest in, but he does not begin the game as the rugged cowboy hero.[14] He grows into this identity as he traverses the postapocalyptic frontier as Ellie's protector. We first meet Joel in the early days of the pandemic as he tries to escape Austin, Texas, with his brother Tommy, who survives, and Joel's twelve-year-old daughter, Sarah, who dies tragically. The game jumps ahead twenty years to Boston, where Joel is a smuggler living in a quarantined area of the city controlled by the remnants of the U.S. government, the Federal Disaster Response Agency or FEDRA. He works with Tess, a no-nonsense, hardy non-player character (NPC) who sacrifices herself to ensure Joel's and Ellie's survival.

Tess and Joel are betrayed by another smuggler who sells their guns and supplies to a rebel group (or terrorist group, depending on the rhetorical context) called the Fireflies. They end up making a deal with the Firefly's leader, Marlene, who agrees to return their guns with more supplies if they deliver Ellie, who is fourteen in *The Last of Us*, to the Firefly enclave out west.[15] Ellie is immune from the virus and, therefore, is humanity's last hope (ergo Joel is her white male savior). Joel, Tess, and Ellie head out on a postapocalyptic frontier (largely comprising ruins as opposed to wilderness) where outposts are under constant threat from the "infected." Tess ultimately sacrifices herself to save Joel and Ellie but not before extracting a deathbed promise from Joel to deliver Ellie to Firefly headquarters. Ashley Dressel calls these types of promises "directed obligations," some of which can be fulfilled prior to death and some after.[16] In this case, Tess, who had been bitten by one of the infected while protecting Ellie, deploys a direct obligation requiring Joel to become Ellie's guardian from "savages," which are stock frontier NPCs.

These savages are not simply the infected but also survivors who have "turned savage" from the loss of "civilization" on this playable frontier. Killing these savages provides rewards, such as ammunition and supplies, encouraging players to kill as many savages as possible, paradoxically casting heroes as *needing* to be savage but for a greater good. In this way, the game follows the frontiersman paradigm set forth by early nineteenth-century frontier romances such as James Fenimore Cooper's *The Last of the Mohicans* (1826) or Catharine Sedgwick's *Hope Leslie* (1827). Like other popular depictions of a neo-frontier, perhaps most notably Joss Whedon's cult favorite space western *Firefly* (2002), sci-fi westerns invest in a common trope Meredith Harvey locates as a form of deracialized indigeneity that "operate[s] at an allegorical level to present the continuity and eventuality of the United States as a settler colonial state."[17] Following this paradigm, *The Last of Us* comprises a deracialized frontier with settler colonies intent on culling "savages," thus perpetuating the myth that "savages" do not cultivate, can't learn, and need to be removed.

Tess cements Joel's obligation to protect Ellie from the "savages" and savagery of this postapocalyptic frontier by sacrificing what little life she has left fending off FEDRA soldiers so Joel and Ellie can escape. Doubly trapped by Tess's directed obligation and sacrifice, Joel reluctantly agrees to be Ellie's protector, thus beginning his transformation into a frontiersman and eventually a cowboy who plays guitar, creates art inspired by Frederic Remington, and protects the burgeoning civilization emerging from what was Jackson, Wyoming. The nagging question of why Tess couldn't take up the mantle of protector begs the first game but certainly speaks to the durability of the straight white male savior in gaming. After Joel delivers Ellie to the Fireflies, Marlene tells him that Ellie will not survive the procedure to create a vaccine. An enraged Joel rescues Ellie and murders the doctor about to perform the procedure, Jerry Anderson, who is Abby's father. And so, as mentioned earlier, this act initiates the revenge cycle that informs the sequel.

Where the first game is largely a postapocalyptic western-horror, the sequel is a revenge western structured by gothic conventions.[18] This weird narrative remix challenges players to rethink the binary pairs so common to the western, such as civilization/wilderness, east/west, and cowboys/savages.[19] But that's what weird westerns do, don't they? They form "unexpected combinations with other genres."[20] They challenge the ways in which durable genres enable readers, viewers, and players to group symbols in rhetorical contexts (to make sense of the world) by remixing conventions;

however, in complex gameworlds like *The Last of Us II*, this kind of remixing is not weird but commonplace.[21] In this chapter, for example, I had to limit the number of durable genres I can discuss, despite the fact that such genres shape this gameworld and guide gameplay. For example, Amy Green convincingly argues that the *Last of Us* is underpinned by the conventions of naturalism, of which the most prevalent is humankind against nature (the virus) or humankind against itself (survivors brutalizing survivors).[22] Further, the sequel has a war story embedded within it that follows many of the conventions of antiwar narratives and even postwar noir. Abby is a soldier, first and foremost, and her dark, harrowing storyline follows the antiwar convention of the disillusioned soldier who comes to see the enemy as fully human. There is an antihuman zombie narrative that plays in the background of this revenge western as well. This multivalent ability to remix copious genre elements has to do with the expansive nature of complex video games, explains Green. *The Last of Us* takes an average of twenty-five to hours to play through (it took me twenty-eight hours), which equates to an entire season of a television series, for example.[23] Yet, this remixing doesn't necessarily challenge hidebound ideologies concerning gender and sexuality in the ways that weird westerns often do. Weird westerns invite X factors or unexpected narrative variables that change the formula of durable genres in ways that challenge conventions and norms. .

Revenge tragedies combined with westerns (or revenge westerns) perform different cultural work than classic revenge narratives. Whereas revenge tragedies highlight and attempt to correct deficiencies in juridical systems, the western changes the game by deploying revenge to reaffirm "the public's sense of right and wrong."[24] Of course, the words "right" and "wrong" are loaded. Christine Bold has made clear that this form of revenge in the name of justice largely originates from Owen Wister's *The Virginian* (1902) and was fueled by the ethos of The Frontier Club, a term coined by Bold to describe a group of patrician eastern magnates (e.g., Henry Cabot Lodge), politicians (e.g., Teddy Roosevelt), and scions (e.g., Owen Wister) who headed west to recuperate from the trials and travails of their urban existences.[25] Club members' exploits informed Wister's remediation of the dime western into canon-worthy literature, but it's Wister's revision of the Johnson County War that deeply influenced the conventions and, in turn, the perception of frontier justice. Wister recasts the small ranch owners who fought eastern corporate ranch interests in the late nineteenth century as rustlers and the corporate ranch owners as victims who are defended by the Virginian's sense of "natural" vigilante justice. Therefore, revenge westerns do reaffirm public perceptions of right and wrong, but that perception is often from a privileged point of view that positions those with wealth, property, and power as marginalized victims under threat. This paradigm very likely influenced the development of the straight white male hero convention in video games or at least works well within "gameworlds where white men are the 'persecuted' minority" who are "humanity's only hope."[26] The *Last of Us II* challenges these patriarchal paradigms common to popular console gaming, the western, and the revenge tragedy by creating player-characters who traverse uncannily similar timelines, doubling the gameplay and characters, thus disrupting the easy transmission of conventions that reinforce the status quo.

Making Good Genre Trouble

Gothic motifs have a history of disrupting the more static conventions of the western, explains Tara Penry.[27] Jack Halberstam describes the gothic as a "technology of subjectivity" that "produces deviant subjectivities" in order to define that which is normal and natural.[28] Modern gothic motifs and monstrosities in queer narratives follow a similar trajectory critiquing the ways in which social norms render queer sexualities and bodies as monstrous and uncanny.[29] In this gameworld, the gothic excess of doubling is used to trouble the hidebound, static, and ultimately fantastical abilities of the cowboy figure to dictate the fates of others. The cowboy enacts a form of social control, explains Lee Clark Mitchell, with his preternatural linguistic and physical talents used in the service of policing social, cultural, sexual, and gendered performances. More broadly, the western sustains "frontier values in a post-frontier world," bringing the past into the present and reaffirming a normative trajectory of U.S. history that defines static gender binaries as a necessary part of attaining the good life.[30] The gothic troubles these nostalgic values by "creating proximities between the past and the present, as though one reflects, echoes, or repeats the other."[31] The gothic narrative structure Abby and Ellie navigate unsettles and even ruptures the player's relationship with these player-characters and, by extension, the events that unfold in the story.

The Last of Us II opens in postapocalyptic Jackson, Wyoming, where a nineteen-year-old Ellie wakes up with a hangover compounded by anxiety over a kiss she shared with Dina at a barn dance, which causes Seth, a local, to make trouble over the appropriateness of this kiss in a "family" setting. Joel comes to Ellie's defense, but Ellie is angered at Joel's interference in her life, particularly her love life. Later that day, Ellie comes out to Joel, who, to Ellie's surprise, supports her. He not only supports her but makes it clear that he does not have a say in her life. He does so by simply noting that Dina would be lucky to have Ellie as a partner. In other words, he does not need to say he "approves" or "gives permission." This scene is so pivotal that it is replayed in flashbacks, but most importantly at the end of the game—more on this particular iteration later in the chapter. For now, it's enough to know that this conversation is crucial to mending their broken relationship. Their estrangement began after Ellie learned that Joel had lied to her about the day he murdered Dr. Jerry Anderson. She was not conscious during her rescue, and when she asked Joel what happened, he told her that a vaccine wasn't possible. In yet another flashback, Ellie discovered the truth: Joel killed Dr. Anderson to stop him from using her brain tissue to make a vaccine to cure the cordyceps virus. Joel's lie seems reasonable because "the cowboy liar can legitimately lie . . . to certain groups or social members within specific contexts, thus defining those who either possess or lack the cultural capital to demand honesty."[32] Ellie's ethos is largely defined by Joel's love for her in the first game, and so his lies are not ideal but also not fatal to his ethos. In the second game, Joel's lie has consequences that complicate his cowboy/frontiersman status. Ellie's refusal to accept Joel's control of her body and life choices initiates his transformation from rugged, brute, frontier masculinity to a nurturing and supportive father figure *and cowboy* who loves his queer daughter.

Ellie is rightfully furious with Joel for not giving her a say in her own fate, but Joel was simply doing what was right according to his cowboy code of honor. The cowboy is the exemplar of "ultragendered, outwardly violent hyper-masculinity" because he is the product of the frontier, which "is the source of rough and rugged American character and manhood."[33] Shortly after Ellie comes out to Joel and they begin to mend their broken relationship, Joel is murdered in front of Ellie by the remnants of the core Firefly group: Abby, Owen (Abby's ex-boyfriend), Mel (Jerry's former grad student), Manny, Nora, and Danny. Abby beats Joel to death with a golf club while Ellie begs her to stop. His death isn't simply heartbreaking because of the storyline but also the many hours players haptically performed as Joel. As a classic frontiersman/cowboy, Joel gives players the opportunity to both gaze upon and kinesthetically (through pushing buttons on the controller) connect with his sign-laden body through his "sonic stillness."[34] Through Joel, players can shoot enemies expertly, ride horses, play the guitar, defend Ellie (and other innocents), feel grief for the loss of his family, and trust in his heteronormative choices. The graphic display of Joel's mutilated body frustrated player expectations regarding conventional revenge tragedies. Grotesque displays of bodily mutilation have been most often enacted on the female body in revenge tragedies (and sister genres of horror), explains Stevie Simkin, in order to work through the "anxieties and fantasies of a society that clings to patriarchy."[35] While cowboys are often battered and beaten over the course of a western, they also often recuperate, gaining "not only firmer muscle tone but also firmer emotional tone."[36] In this case, Joel's "tall, handsome . . . broad-shouldered body" that both articulates and celebrates white cisgender male privilege via the western is silenced in a "spectacle of death."[37]

Shortly after Joel's death, Ellie's revenge cycle begins, replicating Abby's quest for frontier justice. Female revengers are rare and rarer still for female avengers to survive their vengeance cycle.[38] The doubling of these paternal revenge cycles is a form of procedural rhetoric that encourages players to feel empathy for Joel's murderer and contempt or even disgust with Ellie's tactics. If procedurality "refers to the practice of encapsulating specific real-world behaviors in programmatic representations," then procedural rhetoric pertains to the ways in which these computational processes persuade players of particular ideological or rhetorical stances.[39] Ellie's quest for vengeance has an exceptionally high body count of innocent victims that counters the gunslinger's disciplined form of vigilante justice.[40] Both Ellie's ventriloquizing of Joel's frontier violence (shoot first, ask questions later) and Abby's ultimately redemptive character ask players to reassess their allegiance to the ultraviolent, rugged masculinity that's commonplace in western gameworlds.

The performative connection between player and player-character is one of the conventions that renders video games arguably more influential and persuasive than other forms of narrative media, such as film and print. Bryan Behrenshausen challenges the idea that a player can be reduced to a "set of eyes fixed on a screen," because the experience of playing a game is so "powerfully performative" that an intersubjective experience occurs between player and player-character.[41] Petri Lankoski argues that if players sympathize with player-characters' motives and actions, these characters will earn players' allegiance.[42] Of course, this allegiance is informed by the durable genres that rhetorically enable players to make sense of rhetorical situations and contexts.[43] Joel is a player-character with earned allegiance, because he is encoded as a frontiersman and cowboy, both stock characters that fit well within the commonplace of white cisgender male saviors in popular gaming culture. Abby does not fit this bill; she is a unique character constructed from genre elements drawn from war and action narratives. Both her gender and body do not have much, if any, precedence in gameworlds. Her deviation from gaming norms caused a great deal of genre and gender trouble.

It's not simply her physique that caused an uproar, although certainly her female masculinity incited numerous derogatory comments in *Last of Us II* subreddits and Twitter feeds.[44] One such rant on Reddit that was upvoted over a thousand times proclaims:

> Midway through you are fucking Abby. Sorry. You're she-hulk now. They purposefully obscured this fact not as a "stunning and brave subversion of expectations," but because they fucking KNEW people wouldn't want to play as anyone other than Ellie, Joel or possibly Tommy. . . . Naughty Dog, you've tarnished your brand, legacy, and have deeply damaged my faith in your company. You spat in the faces of your customers by allowing personalities like Druckman[n] to dominate the company culture. You do nothing but wallow in the controversy and call foul on any dissenters as the SJW bucks roll. You're clowns. You should be ashamed.[45]

On Twitter, fans sent the developers, writers, and the voice actor who played Abby, Laura Bailey, death threats filled with homophobic, transphobic, and antisemitic hate.[46] It's an understatement, then, to say that players with allegiance to Joel and Ellie found it odious to play as Abby.[47] But this resistance to Abby is crucial to one of the central arguments this gameworld wants to make: Abby's rejection of patriarchal norms and values counters the hypermasculinity that informs many durable genres and popular console gaming alike (one often informs the other). This transformation of Abby from villain to antihero begins with a narrative structure haunted by the kills players make as Ellie. In other words, players speak to dead people (and their dead pets) when playing as Abby and the effect is unsettling, to say the least.

There are two sets of identically titled chapters that temporally run parallel for both Abby and Ellie: Seattle Day One, Seattle Day Two, and Seattle Day Three. Much like a three-act play, these are the timelines where Ellie and Abby traverse similar territory, sometimes just hours apart. I am going to call this narrative spectacle "procedural prolepsis" because future events, namely the deaths of the NPCs Abby interacts with, have already happened. Usually, narrative prolepsis occurs when a narrator narrates events out of sequence, but in a video game, the sequence of events is executed via missions with playable goals. Put another way, all forms of expressive media, including print and film, have "fungible unit operations," which means that any form of cultural narrative has procedures readers/viewers/players can understand and follow.[48] Procedural prolepsis, then, is the rendering of narrative prolepsis through the rules and processes of gameplay; the future is not simply "already written" but has already been played, meaning players are, in part, responsible for the deaths of Abby's friends and colleagues. This form of dramatic irony means that players already know that Abby's circle of friends has been brutally murdered, rendering her a figure of empathy rather than derision (or both). More importantly, this procedural prolepsis reanimates the socially destructive consequences of Ellie's vengeance.[49] This doubling of gameplay casts doubt on the validity of Ellie's ultraviolent choices, which were instilled via Joel's (and Tommy's) lessons in the ways of brute masculinity in both gameworlds.

Abby loses most of her friends not just to Ellie's monstrous rage but also because of Abby's brutal beating of Joel. One of her former friends, Mel, calls Abby a "piece of shit" in reference to the brutality of the attack on Joel. The doubled plot lines of these female revengers suggest that redemption does not lie in the heteronormative trajectories of marriage, motherhood, and accumulation but in reciprocal relationships built through shared goals and community building. Abby's position in the discourse time of this gameworld renders her as both an object lesson for Ellie and a queer character in her own right.

Abby's timeline in Seattle begins as she wakes from a recurring nightmare in which she finds her father's body in a pool of blood on the operating room floor in Salt Lake City, where the climactic ending of the first game is set. Abby is a member of the Washington Liberation Front (WLF) along with the other members of the defunct Salt Lake City Firefly group she and her father joined. The WLF are at war with an ultrareligious group called the Seraphites who ritualistically cut their faces and, as a result, are called Scars. Abby and Manny are ordered to the front by the WLF leader Isaac.[50] Subsequently, Abby is caught by the Seraphites who ritualistically disembowel and then hang prisoners of war and those they deem criminals or sinners. Just before Abby is disemboweled and hung, two Seraphite prisoners, Yara and Lev, arrive for punishment as sinners. Abby's execution is delayed when Yara's arm is broken to "clip her wings," and Lev in turn uses his bow to kill the Seraphite torturers. A seasoned soldier, Abby takes advantage of the chaos and all three escape.

When Abby asks what their crime was, Yara says Lev shaved his head, which leaves Abby confused. She doesn't pursue the conversation further, but later we discover that Lev is transgender, and by shaving his head, he was committing a sin punishable by death. The three bond over their mutual escape and near death experience, and of course, Abby now owes Lev and Yara her life (yet another "directed obligation"). Abby decides to help Yara by bringing her back to the abandoned Seattle Aquarium where her former friends and Fireflies Owen and Mel live. Mel reluctantly agrees to treat Yara, and upon examination, she tells Abby that Yara's arm is so badly damaged, it needs to be amputated. From the Aquarium, Abby and Lev set out to find the necessary medical equipment, and so Abby begins her trek through Ellie's proleptic swath of destruction.

This "swath of destruction" includes Mel, who is pregnant with Owen's child and dies by Ellie's hand in a gruesome scene. While Ellie does not know Mel is pregnant, she does not hesitate to kill any WLF member, which seems reasonable via action game conventions. They are the enemy, and enemies must be killed and rewards gathered. However, when playing as Abby, players pass by a daycare filled with WLF children, some of whom are sure to be orphaned by Ellie's rampage. She also kills WLF dogs, which are also pets, including Owen and Mel's dog Alice. During Ellie's hunt for Abby at the Aquarium, Alice attacks her and a quicktime event is engaged.[51] The square button on the controller has to be pushed rapidly to ensure Alice dies so the game story can continue. These grotesque acts are not simply part of violent gameplay to collect rewards or an attempt to humanize WLF members but an integral function of the frontier setting. Reminiscent of Cooper's frontier in *The Last of the Mohicans*, women and children on the postapocalyptic frontier are classified as burdens ripe for slaughter.[52] On this type of frontier "[these deaths] mark a conflict of what makes up a person, or how persons are made," explains Samuels.[53] Ellie takes up the mantle of the frontiersman who can dictate who lives, who dies, and who has value. When her girlfriend, Dina, confesses that she is pregnant, Ellie explodes in anger and says her pregnancy is a liability. In Abby's timeline, a visibly pregnant Mel is cleared for active duty with Abby and is an asset to their missions. Druckmann and Gross write Mel as a pregnant woman who is a formidable fighting force rather than a metaphorical representation of land, weakness, or nationhood common to Cooperesque fantasies of the American frontier. Abby, Mel, and Owen all gather at the Aquarium, which is a liminal queer space or counterfrontier until Ellie destroys it in her quest for frontier justice.

The Aquarium is infiltrated by Ellie in Seattle Day Three, near the end of her play cycle. She breaks through one area after another until she opens a door that triggers a quicktime event, a dog attacks her, and as mentioned earlier, this dog is Alice, who is stabbed to death by Ellie. Subsequently, she stumbles upon Owen and Mel arguing, and after a brief confrontation, she shoots Owen, and in another quicktime event, the player presses the square button on the controller, causing Ellie to slit Mel's throat. This requirement to participate in such a brutal death is part and parcel of the game's argument that the performance of brute masculinity is socially destructive, no matter who is playing the role. Upon discovering Mel is pregnant, Ellie falls to her knees retching (indicating she is not evil, just terribly misguided). Tommy and Jesse enter the room under pursuit and all three flee the scene after turning the Aquarium from a bastion of queer community into a barren space destroyed by frontier hypermasculine individualism.

Abby's next visit to the Aquarium occurs in a flashback when she visits Owen and Mel, who are celebrating Christmas complete with stockings, tree, and carols. Each visit gives more information to the player about Owen and Mel (and Alice), who are clearly likable and honorable characters. The Aquarium is where Owen and Mel try to build a life. It's also where Yara receives treatment for her injury. Lev befriends Alice despite his fear of dogs. The Aquarium is a space of performance, spectacle, and apparent safety, enacting Michael Warner's theory of fluid publics, where folks can interact across the boundaries of their "publics" or constituent groups without retaliation and violence.[54] Publics who usually hate each other on the postapocalyptic frontier comprising WLF, Fireflies and Seraphites, exist peacefully and even intimately in this liminal undersea space. Water tropes are common forms of imagery in queer narratives, illustrating the fluidity and intimacy of this homebase.[55] The Aquarium is also a metadramatic environment that comments on performativity itself. Once a space where captive sea creatures performed for humans, it is now a fishbowl where survivors hide from the social destruction of brute masculinity, enacting the socially constructive rituals of home and hearth, including holiday celebrations and playing with pets. In one scene, Abby teaches a fearful Yara to play with Alice. The player uses the controller to throw a squeaky toy, which Alice fetches and returns. Presumably, a player could spend the rest of the game in this scene of domestic intimacy. Gameplay like this immerses the player in classic sentimentality, creating an emotional connection between player and characters that is made pathetic by the knowledge that Alice will soon be slaughtered by Ellie's hunger for frontier justice.

Abby often leaves the Aquarium to help others, as opposed to Ellie, who seeks blood-soaked vengeance. After Mel tells Abby she needs specific medical instruments to finish Yara's amputation, Abby and Lev head to the hospital, crossing zones of war populated by the infected, the Seraphites, and the WLF. By helping Yara and Lev, Abby is disobeying direct orders from the WLF leader, so she, like Ellie, is not welcome by the WLF at the hospital. Before her former WLF compatriots learn of her defection, she is able to ask where her former Firefly and partner in vengeance Nora is so Abby can gather the medical instruments she needs. The folks we chat with as Abby, the dog we pet as Abby (an optional action), and our conversation with Nora, whom Ellie tortures and murders, are uncanny.

These interactions with soon-to-be-dead characters are a form of gothic defamiliarization enacted via game mechanics. Shira Chess explains that game mechanics in gothic gameworlds not only defamiliarize by having players revisit environments repeatedly but also engage a type of liminality that enables players to "embody the mechanics of the gothic [narrative]."[56]

Perhaps nowhere is this queer embodiment of the gothic more apparent than when Abby goes deep into the bowels of the hospital to retrieve the necessary medical equipment to save Yara's life. She leaves the uncannily familiar environment Ellie traversed and enters a claustrophobic setting reminiscent of Ridley Scott's sets in the *Alien* franchise. Along the way, I certainly built my skills, improved my weaponry, and stopped as often as possible to add to my inventory. In other words, the game mechanics gave the player (me) agency to give Abby a fighting chance in a genre that often positions the "traditional gothic heroine . . . at the mercy of patriarchal forces."[57] Once Abby has gathered the surgical equipment, the game unleashes a horrifying monster for Abby to fight. The developers named this monstrosity "The Rat King" in reference to the tangled tails of many rats forming a writhing mass of rodent bodies. An amalgamation of almost every type of infected undead, this hideous multiarmed, multimouthed monster chases Abby relentlessly, until she shoots enough rounds to kill it. By naming any monstrous phenomenon a "king," that phenomenon is therefore defined as powerful. Yet, the gothic subverts, explains Chess, and by defeating this king, Abby is her own liberator, saving Yara after Yara saved her.[58] There are no damsels in distress here; the gaming commonplace of the white male savior is subverted and replaced with a gender-nonconforming antihero.

While Yara recovers, Abby tracks Owen to the sailboat moored in one of the pools at the Aquarium. He tells her he plans on sailing to Santa Barbara with Mel. There is a rumor the last of the Fireflies have gathered in that final stop on the western trail: California. He wants her to join them, but she knows Mel does not want her there. Passions rise and they briefly kiss, initiating a sex scene. Abby allows Owen to enter her from behind, giving players a full view of her naked, muscular body. The camera is angled just below Abby, as if players, now engaging in classic scopophilia, are peeking over the table she is bent over. This scene challenges gamers to gaze at a female player-character that is not hypersexualized.

This sex scene highlights Abby's control of her sexuality and performance of both masculinity and femininity. She is a gender-nonconforming character that confused (primarily cisgender male) gamers who angrily tried to pin down her gender and sexuality.[59] Even though Leo Bersani argues that gay men "gnaw at the roots of male heterosexuality" by engaging in penetrative sex, Abby's queering of heteronormative sex performs similar work.[60] Gay sex violates the very core of stereotypical male heterosexuality, which defines penetrative sex as a form of dominance, a myth that Abby dismantles. Abby's masculinity also counters the myth that broad-chested, muscular, or "jacked" bodies define rugged masculinity. Her muscles are on full display as she guides Owen's penis into her from behind. For a man to be penetrated, argues Bersani, "*is to abdicate power*" in a heteronormative world.[61] As a gender-nonconforming character, Abby defies the heteronormative topography that rigidly maps out the performance of sex and gender. Owen is a kind and gentle man who wants a heteronormative relationship; Abby wants sex and nothing else. She has no allegiance to patriarchal, heteronormative conventions of behavior, power, sex, and control. In the bowels of the hospital, she slayed the Rat King—a metaphorical representation of patriarchal power—to save two Seraphite children, Yara and her transgender brother Lev. She defies Isaac, the leader of her community, to protect them. She listens to Lev when he asks her not to enact frontier justice. These are choices outside of gaming and western genre norms. Abby claims the power of resistance rather than the subjectivity of compliance.

The graphic nature of Abby's and Owen's encounter stands in stark contrast to the more intimate and implied sex that occurs between Dina and Ellie earlier in the game narrative. On patrol just outside of Jackson, Dina and Ellie stumble upon a former Firefly's hideout that includes a room filled with long dead marijuana plants; they get high, tease each other, kiss, and the scene fades out. The heterosexual sex scene between Owen and Abby lacks this warmth and love. Dina and Ellie kiss passionately and lovingly, clearly enjoying each other. Was it prudishness on the part of the developers to not show Dina and Ellie having sex or was it a refusal to engage in the more pornographic and power-laden norms of sex often found in popular console gaming? This scene rhetorically not only frames lesbian sex as outside of the scopophilic gaze of gameplay but also refuses to represent lesbian sex. Representation creates meaning, and that's crucial in certain contexts, but in this case, lesbian sex has so often been co-opted in heterosexual pornography that implied meaning gives more freedom and range to imagine what sex can be. However, Ellie's lust for frontier justice destroys her relationship with Dina.

Choose Life

The final chapters of the game return to a more linear narrative order as Abby and Ellie's timelines intersect. Ellie is visited by Tommy (Joel's brother), who begs Ellie to continue hunting Abby after he is given information on her whereabouts. She agrees, leaving behind Dina, their child, and a thriving farm set in a pastoral landscape. Ellie eschews life for the barren code of frontier justice. These missions are among the most violent in the game with the addition of an almost comically hypermasculine gang of slavers named The Rattlers. The members of this gang are laden with the signs of stereotypical villainous hypermasculinity, including dark sunglasses, tattoos, bulging muscles, leather, and loaded guns (pun intended). Despite their impressive display of brute masculinity, Ellie largely destroys their base on her quest for Abby, eventually discovering that Abby (along with Lev) was enslaved by them and then crucified on a beach. Ellie ironically saves Abby so she can murder her. Once cut from her ties, Abby immediately saves Lev and they head to a boat launch. Abby has no intention of revenge, despite Ellie murdering all of Abby's former friends. Ellie demands that she and Abby finish their revenge cycle with a final battle. Abby refuses—she has psychically escaped the dead-end cycle of patriarchal aggression and domination. However, Ellie has not, and she threatens an unconscious Lev with death unless Abby complies.

Both Ellie and Abby are shadows of their former selves, wounded and malnourished; neither are in fighting shape. Both Ellie and Abby swing at each other, exhausted and weak, until Ellie holds Abby underwater, choking her. In that moment, Ellie has a brief flashback to Joel strumming his guitar, just before she comes out to him. As mentioned earlier, Joel's performance of masculinity in this scene is not informed by his hypermasculine cowboy persona but by a more nurturing masculine performance of parental love. In a sense, Ellie realizes that Joel came out to her in that moment as a loving parent intent on recognizing and supporting his daughter's gendered and sexual identity. Gross and Druckmann frame Joel as much more than his ruggedly masculine, white-savior game persona: instead of dictating how Ellie should behave, he accepts her for who she is. Ellie understands in that moment that her fealty to Joel is not as a revenger but as a grieving daughter. She lets Abby go, and then sits in the water sobbing. In that scene, she, like Abby earlier in the game, is freed from the cycle of frontier justice. She no longer has to perform hypermasculinity to show her loyalty to Joel.

To highlight this freedom, in the final scenes of the game, Ellie returns to the deserted farm. She finds Joel's guitar and strums the tune Joel wrote for her but then rests it against the windowsill. The player watches Ellie leave the farm, walking across the field and out of view. She can't be controlled further in this game environment, perhaps further indicating her freedom from her violent narrative. The poignancy of an earlier flashback is brought to mind here: Joel hands the guitar to Ellie and says, "I promised to teach you how to play," and Ellie says meaningfully, "You did." He taught her how to perform or "play" brute masculinity, but in the end, he also accepted her for who she is, asking her to live her life with her partner. Ellie leaves behind the guitar, that conventional symbol of the cowboy, signaling that, like Abby and Joel, she chooses life.

Notes

1. Wikipedia, "Custer's Revenge," last modified February 27, 2022, https://en.wikipedia.org/wiki/Custer%27s_Revenge.
2. Note that PlayDosGames has a catalogue of games from the 1980s and 1990s for view, including *Billy the Kid Returns*. PlayDosGames, "Billy the Kid Returns," https://www.playdosgames.com/online/billy-the-kid-returns/.
3. Humphreys, *Manifest Destiny 2.0*, 94.
4. For the remainder of the chapter, I will refer to video game westerns with complex storylines steeped in realism as gameworld westerns.
5. Gross and Druckmann, *The Last of Us II*.
6. Berlant and Warner, "Guest Column," 345.
7. Druckmann is also the game's director and copresident of Naughty Dog, the company that developed the game.
8. Booth, *The Company We Keep*, 227.
9. Booth, *The Company We Keep*, 268.
10. There are numerous subreddit threads ranting about Abby as a terrible character. One example of many is THATONEGUY69699, "Last of Us 2 Abby Is a Terrible Person," February 1, 2021, https://www.reddit.com/r/CharacterRant/comments/la5lmf/last_of_us_2_abby_is_a_terrible_person/.

11. Salter and Blodgett, *Toxic Geek Masculinity in Media*, 75.
12. Salter and Blodgett, *Toxic Geek Masculinity in Media*, 77.
13. Humphreys, *Manifest Destiny 2.0*, 75.
14. Ellie is a player-character in a chapter called "Winter" and then in an expansion pack (expansion of the gameworld) released on February 14, 2014, titled *Left Behind*. This chapter contains several mission episodes in which Ellie needs to find medicine to save Joel. She is chased by a pedophile and attacked ruthlessly by an all-male gang called The Hunters (which both Joel and his brother Tommy belonged to at one time). She is a fourteen-year-old girl who is brutalized and often killed (if the player fails) in ultraviolent ways. Do these missions highlight her strength, or do they make clear that a woman on the frontier is not safe from rape, violence, and captivity?
15. Marlene is a Black NPC who remains unplayable even in the sequel. There are no playable Indigenous or BPOC characters in either game.
16. Dressel, "Directed Obligations."
17. Harvey, "Shining the Light of Civilization," 247.
18. In 2023 HBO released a highly successful remediation of *The Last of Us* cowritten by Neil Druckmann and Craig Mazin. The series maintains much of the original plotline but emphasizes the queer aspects of the game, including an episode that unpacks Bill and Frank's love story. In the game, their relationship is largely implied but not fully fleshed out.
19. Numerous scholars have noted the binary pairs that compose and are generated by the modern western, including Meredith Harvey, Christine Bold, Victoria Lamont, Richard Slotkin, and Jim Kitses, to name a few.
20. Johnson, Lush, and Spurgeon, "Westworld(s)," 2.
21. Devitt, *Writing Genres*.
22. Green, "The Reconstruction of Morality."
23. Green, "The Reconstruction of Morality"; Barker, "*The Last of Us 2*."
24. Joyce, *Gunslinging Justice*, 33.
25. Bold, *The Frontier Club*.
26. Salter and Blodgett, *Toxic Geek Masculinity in Media*, 75.
27. Penry, "Attack of the Monstrous Vegetable," 39.
28. Halberstam, *Skin Shows*, 2.
29. Palmer, *The Queer Uncanny*.
30. Mitchell, *Westerns*, 374.
31. Kirkland, *Videogames and the Gothic*, 3.
32. Humphreys, "'Truer 'N Hell,'" 32.
33. Pettegrew, *Brutes in Suits*, 21.
34. Mitchell, *Westerns*, 165.
35. Simkin, *Early Modern Tragedy*, 212.

36. Mitchell, *Westerns*, 177.
37. Simkin, *Early Modern Tragedy*, 212; Mitchell, *Westerns*, 161.
38. Simkin, *Early Modern Tragedy*, 213–21.
39. Bogost, *Unit Operations*, 13.
40. Joyce, *Gunslinging Justice*, 38.
41. Behrenshausen, "Toward a (Kin)Aesthetic of Video Gaming," 336.
42. Lankoski, "Player Character Engagement in Computer Games."
43. Humphreys, *Manifest Destiny 2.0*.
44. Hernandez, "*Last of Us 2* Proves Gaming Doesn't Know."
45. [Username deleted], "You really play ½ the game as Abby. I'm finished. Not continuing," June 21, 2020, https://www.reddit.com/r/TheLastOfUs2/comments/hd53bn/you_really_play_12_the_game_as_abby_im_finished/. SJW stands for Social Justice Warrior.
46. Hernandez, "*Last of Us 2* Dev Naughty Dog Condemns Harassment."
47. Erb, Lee, and Doh, "Player-Character Relationship."
48. Bogost, *Unit Operations*, 14, 15.
49. Ellie's swath of destruction also echoes Abby's brutal choices during her revenge cycle.
50. Isaac is a brutal authoritarian leader played by Jeffrey Wright. There are rumors of a third installment of *The Last of Us* series, and hopefully Firefly leaders Marlene and Isaac, who are Black NPCs, will become playable characters.
51. A quicktime event is a filmic sequence with interactive elements accessed via the controller.
52. Samuels, *Generation through Violence*, 109.
53. Samuels, *Generation through Violence*, 109.
54. Warner, "Publics and Counterpublics."
55. Berns, "Water and Queer Intimacy."
56. Chess, "Uncanny Gaming."
57. Chess, "Uncanny Gaming."
58. Chess, "Uncanny Gaming."
59. Glennon, Johnston, and Francisco, "The Rest of Us."
60. Bersani, "Is the Rectum a Grave?," 209.
61. Bersani, "Is the Rectum a Grave?," 212.

Bibliography

Barker, Sammy. "*The Last of Us 2*: How Long Does It Take to Beat?" *Push Square*, May 6, 2021. https://www.pushsquare.com/guides/the-last-of-us-2-how-long-does-it-take-to-beat.

Behrenshausen, Bryan G. "Toward a (Kin)Aesthetic of Video Gaming: The Case of Dance Dance Revolution." *Games and Culture* 2, no. 4 (2007): 335–54.

Berlant, Lauren, and Michael Warner. "Guest Column: What Does Queer Theory Teach Us about X?" *PMLA* 110, no. 3 (1995): 343–49. http://www.jstor.org/stable/462930.

Berns, Fernando G. Pagnoni. "Water and Queer Intimacy." In *Space and Subjectivity in Contemporary Brazilian Cinema*, 185–200. Springer International, 2017.

Bersani, Leo. "Is the Rectum a Grave?" *October* 43 (1987): 197–222. https://doi.org/10.2307/3397574.

Bogost, Ian. *Unit Operations: An Approach to Videogame Criticism*. Cambridge MA: MIT Press, 2006.

Bold, Christine. *The Frontier Club: Popular Westerns and Cultural Power, 1880–1924*. New York: Oxford University Press, 2013.

Booth, Wayne. *The Company We Keep: An Ethics of Fiction*. Berkeley: University of California Press, 1988.

Chess, Shira. "Uncanny Gaming: The Ravenhearst Video Games and Gothic Appropriation." *Feminist Media Studies* 15, no. 3 (2015): 382–96.

Devitt, Amy J. *Writing Genres*. Carbondale: Southern Illinois University Press, 2004.

Dressel, Ashley. "Directed Obligations and the Trouble with Deathbed Promises." *Ethical Theory and Moral Practice* 18, no. 2 (2015; 2014): 323–35.

Erb, Valérie, Seyeon Lee, and Young Yim Doh. "Player-Character Relationship and Game Satisfaction in Narrative Game: Focus on Player Experience of Character Switch in the Last of Us Part II." *Frontiers in Psychology* 12 (2021). https://doi.org/10.3389/fpsyg.2021.709926.

Fine, Kerry, Michael K. Johnson, Rebecca M. Lush, and Sara L. Spurgeon, eds. *Weird Westerns: Race, Gender, Genre*. Lincoln: University of Nebraska Press, 2020.

Glennon, Jen, Dais Johnston, and Eric Francisco. "The Rest of Us: The Last of Us Trans Controversy, Explained." *Inverse: Gaming*, May 14, 2020. https://www.inverse.com/gaming/last-of-us-2-trans-controversy-explained-abby-tlou.

Green, Amy M. "The Reconstruction of Morality and the Evolution of Naturalism in the Last of Us." *Games and Culture* 11, no. 7–8 (2016): 745–63. https://doi.org/10.1177/1555412015579489.

Gross, Halley, and Neil Druckmann. *The Last of Us II*. Naughty Dog. Sony Interactive Entertainment. Playstation, 2020.

Halberstam, Jack. *Skin Shows: Gothic Horror and the Technology of Monsters*. Durham NC: Duke University Press Books, 2012.

Harvey, Meredith. "Shining the Light of Civilization: The Savage Other of the Frontier in *Firefly* and *Serenity*." In *Weird Westerns: Race, Gender, Genre*, edited by Kerry Fine, Michael K. Johnson, Rebecca M. Lush, and Sara L. Spurgeon, 231–54. Lincoln: University of Nebraska Press, 2020.

Hernandez, Patricia. "Last of Us 2 Dev Naughty Dog Condemns Harassment, Death Threats." *Polygon*, July 6, 2020. https://www.polygon.com/2020/7/6/21314543

/the-last-of-us-2-harassment-neil-druckmann-laura-bailey-naughty-dog-abby-death-threats-ps4.

———. "*Last of Us 2* Proves Gaming Doesn't Know How to Deal with Muscular Women: Welcome to the Gun Show." *Polygon*, July 1, 2020. https://www.polygon.com/2020/7/1/21309926/the-last-of-us-part-2-abby-body-actor-naughty-dog-ps4-playstation-sony-body-diversity.

Humphreys, Sara. *Manifest Destiny 2.0: Genre Trouble in Video Games*. Postwestern Horizons. Lincoln: University of Nebraska Press, 2021.

———. "'Truer 'N Hell': Lies, Capitalism, and Cultural Imperialism in Owen Wister's 'The Virginian,' B. M. Bower's 'The Happy Family,' and Mourning Dove's 'Cogewea.'" *Western American Literature* 45, no. 1 (2010): 30–52.

Johnson, Michael K., Rebecca M. Lush, and Sara L. Spurgeon. "Westworld(s): Race, Gender, Genre in the Weird Western." Introduction to *Weird Westerns: Race, Gender, Genre*, edited by Kerry Fine, Michael K. Johnson, Rebecca M. Lush, and Sara L. Spurgeon, 1–36. Lincoln: University of Nebraska Press, 2020.

Joyce, Justin A. *Gunslinging Justice: The American Culture of Gun Violence in Westerns and the Law*. Manchester, UK: Manchester University Press, 2018.

Kirkland, Ewan. *Videogames and the Gothic*. New York: Routledge, 2022.

Lankoski, Petri. "Player Character Engagement in Computer Games." *Games and Culture* 6, no. 4 (2011): 291–311.

Mitchell, Lee Clark. *Westerns: Making the Man in Fiction and Film*. Chicago: University of Chicago Press, 1996.

Palmer, Paulina. *The Queer Uncanny: New Perspectives on the Gothic*. Cardiff: University of Wales Press, 2012.

Penry, Tara. "Attack of the Monstrous Vegetable: Bret Harte's Pioneer Nightmare and 'Miscegenation' Dream." In *Weird Westerns: Race, Gender, Genre*, edited by Kerry Fine, Michael K. Johnson, Rebecca M. Lush, and Sara L. Spurgeon, 39–66. Lincoln: University of Nebraska Press, 2020.

Pettegrew, John. *Brutes in Suits: Male Sensibility in America, 1890–1920*. Baltimore: Johns Hopkins University Press, 2007.

Salter, Anastasia, and Bridget Blodgett. *Toxic Geek Masculinity in Media: Sexism, Trolling, and Identity Policing*. New York: Palgrave Macmillan, 2017. https://doi.org/10.1007/978-3-319-66077-6.

Samuels, Shirley. *Generation through Violence: Cooper and the Making of Americans*. In *New Essays on The Last of the Mohicans*, edited by H. Daniel Peck, 87–114. Cambridge, UK: Cambridge University Press, 1992.

Simkin, Stevie. *Early Modern Tragedy and the Cinema of Violence*. New York: Palgrave Macmillan, 2006.

Warner, Michael. "Publics and Counterpublics." *Public Culture* 14, no. 1 (2002): 49–90.

14

"Do I Bring My Own Leash, or Do I Pick One Up at the Door?"

Kink, Camp, and Queer Masculinity in CBS's *The Wild Wild West*

SARA L. SPURGEON

It has become something of a cliché by now to point out the (barely) hidden homoerotics of the western, from the narrator's breathless admiration of the eponymous Virginian's muscled shoulders to Tess's futile offering of heterosexual cuddles to Matt in *Red River* as he lies in her arms obsessing about John Wayne's Dunson, to the male love triangle of Pat Garrett, Doc, and Billy in *The Outlaw* in which Jane Russell, as the voluptuous Rio, is of less interest to the men than a horse. Indeed, many gallons of ink have been spilled describing the erotically charged homosocial partnerings of cowboy bromances lurking beneath the heterosexual cover of guns, sweat, and cattle.[1]

However, not all offerings in the genre have aimed for subtlety in their queer subtexts. CBS's popular series *The Wild Wild West* (1965–69), for example, was "the 1960s' gayest show" according to critic Louis Bayard.[2] In a flamboyantly campy decade that gave the world *Batman* and Liberace, that's quite a claim. It turns out, however, that not only was *The Wild Wild West* the 1960s' gayest show, but it may also have been the kinkiest.[3] The series is perhaps most remembered today for the skintight wardrobe of its star, Robert Conrad, who was outfitted with specially tailored pants and snug-fitting bolero jackets designed to show off his muscled physique as he performed many of his own stunts for the show's deservedly famous fight scenes. Both Conrad's stunt work and trousers remained iconic enough to be referenced in Quentin Tarantino's *Once Upon a Time in Hollywood* (2019) when Leonardo DiCaprio, playing an actor named Rick Dalton, discusses his stuntman (Brad Pitt) with Al Pacino's Marvin Schwarz, who snarks, "The next week it's Bob Conrad, wearing his tight pants, kicking your ass."[4]

The Wild Wild West's success and subversions, however, rest on more than just the sexualization of Robert Conrad's butt cheeks. Like many previous westerns, it revolves around a homoerotic relationship between two men, albeit not an especially sublimated one. The male-marriage at the center of the series between Conrad's James West and his partner, Artemus Gordon (Ross Martin), features the two men living together in a specially fitted-out train car to which they regularly retire for chilled champagne, romantic dinners cooked by Artie, and games of billiards complete with ample fondling of balls and stroking of pool sticks. The campy fun the series has with the two men obviously invites queer readings, but even more intriguing, I argue, is the show's regular use of BDSM play centered on its male lead. In fact, *The Wild Wild West*'s exuberantly genderqueer camp at once sugarcoats and amplifies the repetitive bondage and disciplining of its supposedly straight male hero. This combination of kink, camp, and queer masculinity reveals not just the homoerotic heart beating beneath the cowboy's broad, manly chest but the profoundly kinky and genderqueer nature of the genre's laboriously constructed version of American manhood.

The bondage in *The Wild Wild West*, extending across its four-year run, mainly involves James West, helpless until his inevitable escape at the hands of various evildoers. In "The Night of the Poisonous Posey," James is captured by the villain and bound, spread eagle, with a massive block of ice positioned between his legs, threatening a very cold castration.[5] In "The Night of the Deadly Bed," James is captured by the villain and bound, upright and spread eagle, in front of the bronze disk of a massive gong with a phallic, log-sized striker pointed at his groin.[6] In "The Night of a Thousand Eyes," James is captured by the villain and bound, nude from the waist up, in a suspended cage.[7] In "The Night of the Burning Diamonds," James is captured by the villain and hung upside down from the ceiling while the villain's lovely assistant delicately wipes his sweaty brow with her lace handkerchief, winkingly reifying the consensual, mutually pleasurable nature of the relationship between dom and sub, but also reminding us of Gilles Deleuze's contention that the figure being beaten in the BDSM scene is not the Freudian embodiment of feminine passivity prostrate before the law of the phallic father but rather the Lacanian law of the father himself—in this case, as in many westerns, a literal *lawman*.[8]

As these BDSM scenarios suggest, the series, while clearly a western, was also unapologetically queer from the start. Series creator Michael Garrison was well known in Hollywood as a mostly out gay man, uncomfortably out for some CBS executives, who killed a treatment Garrison sent them near the end of season 1 pitching an episode that would guest star Liberace, even though Liberace, who had already agreed to do the spot, was one of the most famous entertainers in the world at the time.[9] The reason behind this decision, according to John Kneubuhl, a regular writer for *The Wild Wild West* who worked on the treatment, was that "CBS was very nervous about Michael [Garrison] playing around with any material that would bring that association up in the front office."[10] Presumably without bringing "that association up," Garrison had earlier successfully pitched *The Wild Wild West* to CBS as a kind of "James Bond on horseback," roping the popularity of the emerging Bond franchise to Garrison's personal love of westerns, which by the mid-1960s were fading from their previous domination of American television.[11] The series' two main characters are Secret Service agents working undercover in the post–Civil War West on behalf of the administration of President Ulysses S. Grant.

Beyond the unexpected mash-up of western and government espionage, the show is even weirder in its presentation of itself as a western. As Johnson et al. argue in *Weird Westerns: Race, Gender, Genre*, the western, despite a reputation for gritty realism, "is often deeply rooted in fantasy and has always shared many elements with its historical sibling, science fiction."[12] *The Wild Wild West*'s cross-genre embrace of science fiction is immediately visible in the series' fascination with imaginary, futuristic, Victorian-era technology. Commonly known as steampunk today, *The Wild Wild West* was among the first television series to embrace the retrofuturistic aesthetic.[13] It was known for its Bond-like gadgets such as James West's sleeve-gun (a Remington Double Derringer that drops conveniently out of his coat sleeve and into his hand); the knife blade that pops out of the pointed toe of his perfectly polished black cowboy boot, allowing him to cut through the many ropes that bind him over the course of the series' run; and the train car living quarters fitted out with spring-loaded weapons compartments and exploding billiard balls. It also featured the outlandish inventions of its several mad-scientist villains—everything from robot assassins, a device that causes earthquakes, a sonic stimulator that allows paintings to be used as portals to other dimensions, a steam-powered wheelchair with rockets, and a computer dating machine designed to guarantee happy marriages. While this last item may not seem like an especially villainous device, it is emblematic of the surprising levels of engagement the series had with contemporary issues such as the civil rights movement, the Cold War, and second-wave feminism, not to mention its fascination with the genderqueering potentials of BDSM.

The steampunk elements clearly mark the series as what Johnson et al. identify as a "weird western," that is, a text that utilizes "a hybrid genre format, blending canonical elements of the western with either science fiction, fantasy, horror, or some other component of speculative literature."[14] While that definition suggests what weird westerns are, what weird westerns *do*, they argue, is invite us "to recognize genre conventions as conventions and actively participate in their interrogation."[15] Such interrogations, they posit, can draw attention to the ways in which weird westerns work to subvert or uphold, to queer or retrench assumptions about American history, frontiers, and the contested terrain of racialized, gendered, and sexual identities. While many conventional and weird westerns are obsessed with the policing of race, especially as imagined within narratives of settler colonialism, *The Wild Wild West* is most concerned with gender identity, specifically with masculinity. What sets it apart from other westerns is the series' interrogation of masculinity through the lens of camp, an aesthetic as well as a genre not typically associated with westerns, even weird ones. Or is it?

While camp and BDSM are not the same in terms of what they are, they are surprisingly similar in terms of what they *do*. As with drag, camp and BDSM practices function to destabilize assumptions of "natural" categories of sex and gender identity (and the relations of power assumed to reside in each), deliberately drawing attention to their performative, rather than essential, natures. The theatricality and costuming each kind of performance demands helps to reveal the fluidity of the multiple roles any performer may inhabit. In the 1960s the spectacle of unironic BDSM scenes would have been too outré or outright frightening (not to mention probably illegal) to be broadcast on primetime American television. Camp, however, could make the scariness go away by allowing the subversive nature of BDSM to hide in plain sight. The playful irony of camp functioned as a form of sugarcoating of both the violence of the BDSM acts themselves and the slippage such acts revealed in the supposedly stable categories of sexuality and gender. Camp television in the 1960s, Wyatt Phillips and Isabel Pinedo argue, frequently "pointed to ruptures emerging in normative culture but did so within the confines of a playful diegesis. The purposeful malleability of gender representation that was associated with camp generally, and recognizable specifically within a number of Camp TV shows of the 1960s," they maintain, smoothed over the otherwise sharp or frightening edges that practices like drag, and I argue BDSM, could reveal.[16]

While Susan Sontag maintained that camp is disengaged, depoliticized, or at least apolitical, many critics have since countered this description, most specifically regarding the political role of camp for LGBTQIA+ communities and queer critiques of heteronormativity.[17] Although the aesthetics of camp date back at least as far as vaudeville, as a mainstream phenomenon, camp comes into its own in the mid-twentieth century, emerging from mostly gay male communities into primetime visibility. Phillips and Pinedo identify "a televisual genre cycle comprised of a relatively cohesive group of programmes, all of which premiered on American television in the mid-1960s" that they call "Camp TV," that is, series that "contained in most, if not all, of their episodes, camp elements such as irony, farce, performativity and theatricality."[18] They explain that camp TV immediately fused with the disruptive vogueishness of pop art (its intense color schemes newly visible to viewers through the emerging technology of color television) and that both "were applied in an intertwined and—to a degree—subversive form to American television in this period in a manner that altered the historical trajectory of camp by effectively, if never fully, commercializing it for the masses."[19] Among other popular 1960s camp TV series, they identify *Batman, Bewitched, Get Smart, The Man From U.N.C.L.E., Gilligan's Island*, and *The Monkees. The Wild Wild West* is not among those they discuss, but it is immediately recognizable as camp TV and is identified as camp by at least one of its writers.[20] As Phillips and Pinedo contend, the mainstreaming and commercialization of camp and its pop art visual aesthetic in 1960s primetime television diluted the potential for open political or social critique. Nevertheless, they insist the popularity of camp TV opened "a space for second-level meanings to emerge. And it is here that we can recognize the importance of camp as a concomitant movement that engaged

Pop Art's bold colour schemes and similarly foregrounded its ironic and satiric treatment of mainstream culture."[21]

And in the mid-twentieth century, nothing was more mainstream in American culture than the western. The campiness of *The Wild Wild West* exaggerates the conventional western subtext of the cowboy as anxious hetero constantly trying to bury his gay by presenting instead a full-blown, fluidly gendered queer in drag as a straight arrow. Unlike *Batman*, where Robin the Boy Wonder (Burt Ward) is the character most frequently captured by the villains and who must therefore be rescued by the square-jawed leading man (Adam West's Bruce Wayne/Batman), in *The Wild Wild West*, scenes involving the capture, bondage, and disciplining of James West's square-jawed (and arguably rather square) lead far outnumber those of his less hypermasculine partner, Artie. The reason for this, I argue, is the show's deliberate subversion of the conventions of the mainstream western, specifically the western's insistence on its hero's rigid heterosexuality. The series' camp presentation of BDSM, in other words, makes the western's subtext the *text*, offering, as Phillips and Pinedo suggest, a place where second-level meanings can emerge. The repeated bondage and disciplining of James West acts as a kind of kinky, weird western striptease, with the grim, silent manliness of the genre western's male hero given the full monty treatment. Within the safely ironic and playful confines of camp, the conventional gender identity of the western's John Wayne–style leading man is performed as a kind of tear-away drag costume revealing a sexy, nicely muscled queer underneath.

Judith Butler, of course, has long argued that the notion of a stable gender identity is an illusion retroactively created by our performance of it. "In opposition to theatrical or phenomenological models which take the gendered self to be prior to its acts," they explain, "I will understand constituting acts not only as constituting the identity of the actor, but as constituting that identity as a compelling illusion, an object of *belief*."[22] Practices such as drag, they suggest, can destabilize belief in the "truth" of sexual and gender identity through parodic performance of it, especially in the realm of camp. Considered in this light, it is possible that the western always had not only a secret, homoerotic heart but a kinky, campy queer lurking underneath the stoic, taciturn machismo of the cowboy like a reverse form of drag.

Lee Clark Mitchell writes about the two most common presentations of the western hero and his masculinity—the strong, silent cowboy who must grimly endure physical punishment to reaffirm the indestructibility of his male body, and the handsome, sexy young cowboy presented for our viewing pleasure—without ever fully reconciling them, or recognizing the potential camp lurking beneath their stern, manly surface. In his chapter "A Man Is Being Beaten," Mitchell notes the masochistic requirements of masculinity the western genre demands, pointing out that the "frequency with which the body is celebrated, then physically punished, only to convalesce, suggests something of the paradox involved in making true men out of biological men."[23] Not only does the paradoxical making of a "true" man who is supposedly always/already biologically male require him to be shot, stabbed, beaten, or tortured into unconsciousness, but often his convalescence is made possible by the tender nursing of a pretty female love interest. This triangulating feminine presence aids in what the genre western must do to disguise the kinkiness of its BDSM fetish and the queer gender it reveals. After all, Mitchell contends, "ever since [James Fenimore] Cooper, putting the male body in an object position has required evasive narrative strategies, as if in overcompensation for making that body not appear female."[24] The conundrum, of course, is that ever since Freud, masochism has traditionally been defined as "feminine," and the position of sub in the dom-sub relationship has generally been assumed to be feminizing by its very nature. Mitchell muses that "countless novels and films attest to the central importance of beating scenarios in the western's construction of masculinity. . . . Even so, it is far from apparent why the genre takes such pleasure in punishment."[25]

I argue that the playful, campy BDSM of *The Wild Wild West*, heightened by its steampunk weirdness, makes quite apparent why the genre takes pleasure in punishment. It is not, as Mitchell correctly intuits, that this violence against the male body is the director's punishment of the homoeroticism westerns cannot allow themselves to admit to; rather, it is a kinky celebration of it.[26] To put it bluntly, James West gets tied up and likes it. And presumably many American television viewers did too, since the show had an average audience share in the midthirties.[27] But while the weirdness of this 1960s western puts BDSM front and center, in reality, cowboys were campy and kinky from the start. Mitchell admits that even in mainstream westerns, the eye is trapped and held up by fetish items associated with parts of the body, as our gaze is directed from . . . chests, legs, and various muscle groups to articles instead that either cover or exaggerate them . . . ornate buckles, gun belts worn low . . . chaps (with the groin area duly uncovered and framed), and tight-fitting . . . leather pants in the only genre that allows men to wear them . . . all the way up and down, the cowboy's costume invites and deflects our gaze, doing so in a characteristic moment . . . of nervous distortion that seems ever attached to the scandal of aimlessly gazing at men.[28]

In *The Wild Wild West*, however, any sense of nervousness or scandal is gleefully discarded, and the male body is presented as unambiguously sexualized and queer. Bayard notes that although the series regularly pairs James West with a string of pretty young women in need of rescue and/or reform, the character is "more than heterosexual, Jim West is truly sexual. . . . See how snugly his clothes are tailored to his form—the bolero jacket, the extra-tight trousers (not to mention Season 4's leather chaps, which would not be out of place in a gay pride parade). And see how readily he takes those garments off at the slightest incentive. See how he carries that fine body of his. Jim West is a man who enjoys being desired."[29]

Enjoyment in being desired, as well as in being bound and beaten, is emphatically genderqueer in the series. The characters who tie up, desire, discipline, and endlessly gaze at Jim West's "fine body" include both women and men, often guest stars who were well known for playing queer roles in other popular camp TV series. One such guest star was Victor Buono, who also regularly portrayed the flamboyantly campy King Tut on *Batman* (apparently less queer in the eyes of CBS executives than Liberace). Cast as the evil magician Count Carlos Mario Vincenzo Robespierre Manzeppi, who may or may not possess actual magic powers indicated by his uncanny ability to vanish in a puff of hot pink smoke, Buono first appears in the role of Count Manzeppi in an episode produced by Michael Garrison, "The Night of the Eccentrics."[30] This episode, which also features a very young Richard Pryor as Manzeppi's protégé, Villar the Ventriloquist (one of Manzeppi's band of assassins), is particularly illustrative of the genderqueering work done by campified BDSM. Originally the eighth episode shot for season 1, "The Night of the Eccentrics," was deemed so colorful it was used instead as the opening episode for season 2, the first season broadcast in color.

Introducing himself to James West as a "lover of all that is corrupt, forbidden, and blasphemous," Count Manzeppi, garbed in an embroidered pink waistcoat, yellow cravat, and crimson velvet opera cape, watches avidly as James is forced to wrestle Titan (Michael Masters), the count's circus strongman/assassin, clad only in baby blue tights and a pair of tiny pink satin swim trunks. To highlight the theatricality of the scene, they battle on the raised outdoor stage at an eerily deserted Mexican amusement park. When James finally flings the strongman off the stage and onto the dusty ground below, Titan is so unmanned at his defeat that he hastily crawls on his hands and knees like an enormous baby to hide under the stage. The camera, in a high angle shot from the stage above, looks down at Titan's wiggling bottom in its pink satin underwear as it disappears directly between West's legs.

This performance lacks even the veiled triangulation of a female character. The objectifying male gaze evoked by the camera is most frequently that of Count Manzeppi, clearly titillated at the spectacle of attractive male bodies he has arranged for his (and the audience's) viewing pleasure. In this and many similar scenes in *The Wild Wild West*, it is the body of a man, not a showgirl or other female performer as Laura Mulvey suggests is most common in Hollywood cinema, displayed as a fetishistic object for the erotic gaze of the viewer. Mulvey distinguishes between fetishistic scopophilia (pleasure in looking) and voyeurism, explaining that "fetishistic scopophilia builds up the physical beauty of the object, transforming it into something satisfying in itself. . . . Voyeurism, on the contrary, has associations with sadism: pleasure lies in ascertaining guilt . . . , asserting control and subjugating the guilty person through punishment or forgiveness."[31] We can see both these avenues of visual pleasure—fetishistic scopophilia and voyeurism—deployed in this episode, although the beautiful body being objectified and gazed at is always male. This scene, in which the count forces James West to wrestle his strongman, is fetishistic, inviting us to enjoy the surface-level pleasure of gazing at two taut, muscular men straining in each other's arms. Narratively, the sadistic pleasure of voyeurism with its need to discover, then punish, guilt is not yet in play. The genderqueering that emerges from this male-on-male spectacle eagerly watched by a queer male character who becomes, at least temporarily, the audience surrogate in directing our gaze at the two men performing for him, is profoundly, comically, destabilizing to the western's conventions of heteromasculinity. The expansive, good-natured camp of Buono's performance throws a safe veneer onto this startlingly queer moment of fetishistic scopophilia through, as Phillips and Pinedo term it, a "playful diegesis" that will be even more important later in the episode when voyeurism, with its sadistic scopophilia, becomes the primary narrative driver of the elaborate BDSM scene the count sets up in his dungeon.

When James refuses Count Manzeppi's offer to join his band of assassins who are to be paid $1 million to kill Mexican president Benito Juarez, the count declares that West has made him lose his temper and must be taught "a most salutatory and highly corrective lesson." With Jim's guilt established, Pryor's Villar the Ventriloquist, anticipating the punishment to come, gestures at the whip-wielding assassin Miranda (played by actress Legrand Mellon), who is costumed as a harem girl, and eagerly asks Count Manzeppi, "Now can Miranda take a turn with the whip? She does it so well!"[32] A smiling Buono shakes his head and declares, "As the old saying goes, 'This one's on me.'" James is brought down into the count's dungeon, where the count, effectively framing and doubling the voyeuristic gaze of the camera, watches him through an instrument resembling a sextant, highlighting a trope the series employs throughout its 104 episodes—steampunk gadgets that also perform a genderqueering function, both distracting from and drawing attention to the materiality of the BDSM performance taking place on camera.

After lowering his sextant-like instrument, the count directs his henchmen to back West up against a tall metal pole affixed to a small platform. Two giant robotic metal hands extend from the pole and, at the count's direction, clamp themselves around West's chest and groin, pinning him against the pole. The hands are what Quinlan Miller terms "a tertiary sex characteristic," which he defines as "transgendered signifiers capable of replacing primary and secondary traits in the cis-sexist paradigm of perceiving gender truth in anatomical sex," something like Liberace's trademark candelabra.[33] In this case, the hands are visually transgendered—they have red-painted fingernails, suggesting a woman's hands, but the right discharge of sexual tension, becomes vital as the promised death and its resolution of tension must be symbolically replaced, while still maintaining the heightened anxiety of the masochistic scene and the pleasure it affords to all parties. This tension is resolved through the reintroduction of the whip-wielding Miranda.

As soon as the count leaves, Miranda, still dressed as a harem girl, slips into the dungeon and proposes a bargain: she will free James West, the two of them will betray Manzeppi and the other assassins by saving President Juarez, and then they will split the reward. West agrees to her terms. To free him, Miranda must use her whip to disconnect the anachronistic electric cables supplying power to the electrified platform below. This move emphasizes the materiality necessary to perform the BDSM scene, pointing to the ways the steampunk technology of this weird western is utilized in surprisingly erotic ways. As in many other episodes, the tertiary sex characteristic (in this case, the Amorous Amanda) at once diverts our attention from the voyeuristic violence of the BDSM scenes while playfully exaggerating the genderqueer action taking place within them.

The series frequently leans into such instances of queer materiality to further other important aspects of BDSM. For example, Miranda must sever the electric cables before the rope breaks and drops James onto the electrified platform below, but as the minutes tick by, she protests that the wires are too close to the rope; she is afraid she might miss and break the rope instead. "That's where the fun comes in," West insists. His response here following the bargaining of the previous moments illustrates the importance of another characteristic of masochism identified by Deleuze—the contract—and the surprisingly subversive ways in which it destabilizes conventions of masculinity. Deleuze argues that "the masochist appears to be held by real chains, but in fact he is bound by his word alone," pointing to a central "problem" of the masochistic aesthetic, that of a male character acting in a "feminine" way by willingly receiving pleasure from masochism.[37] Deleuze understands masochism as a structure similar to language in the Lacanian sense, arguing that unlike the functioning of the law and its contract in patriarchy, which normally figures the woman as object, the contract in masochism reverses this state of affairs and figures the woman as the one with whom the contract is entered into by the masochist.

In other words, contrary to Freud's assumption that masochism is an inherently feminine expression of a girl's pleasure in witnessing her father beating another child, which then slips into the fantasy of the father beating her, Deleuze contends that "what is being beaten is the image of the father."[38] This is why, according to Deleuze, "the master/torturer must be, symbolically, a woman.... A contract is drawn up between the subject and torturer.... The masochistic contract implies not only the necessity of the victim's consent," Deleuze continues, but also, importantly, "his ability to persuade, and his pedagogical and judicial efforts to train his torturer."[39] In this scene in *The Wild Wild West*, the torturer is actually and symbolically a woman. James West, the image of the law of the father and Miranda's eager sub, must persuade her to use her whip, albeit in a safely deflected, family-friendly way, near but not on his body, with the threat of death by electrocution providing slim cover for his consensual agreement to this negotiated contract.

After James insists the agony of not knowing whether Miranda's whip will sever the electrical cables or the rope is "fun," Miranda draws out the suspense even further. "I'm nervous, I can't," this professional assassin implausibly demurs. West begs her to use her whip, imploring, "Miranda! Right now!" Miranda finally complies, cracking her whip repeatedly inches away from West's face. Her whip snaps the electrical cables in the nick of time, allowing for Jim's release from the metallic embrace of Amorous Amanda's genderqueer hands in a shower of sparks. Deleuze's idea that what is being beaten in the masochistic scene is not a child or a woman but the image of the father emphasizes why westerns can't help but take pleasure in punishing men, and why the playful, campified BDSM of *The Wild Wild West* so easily parodies the hypermasculinity of the male hero, exemplar of the law in both the Lacanian and the frontier justice sense of the term. As Deleuze's argument suggests, the queerness at the heart of the western is *persuasive*. The camp of the series' presentation of BDSM allows it to slyly, rhetorically train its torturer to pleasure itself and its audience in violently ripping off the outer costume of the law of the father, laying bare the hollow image of "natural" heteromasculinity and "true men" the western has worked so hard to establish and defend. Punishing the guilty image of the father in an ironic and playful way that is also contractual, consensual, and erotically enjoyed by the dom and her sub, queers the male hero rather than buttressing his supposedly unassailable heteromasculinity.

The role of women as symbolic and actual torturers in the many BDSM scenes like the one in "The Night of the Eccentrics" should not be read as reflecting an especially progressive view of women in the series overall. *The Wild Wild West*'s concern with gender is focused almost entirely on the masculinity of its male lead, but its engagement with emerging second-wave feminism is occasionally addressed, most obviously in "The Night of the Vicious Valentine."[40] Once again, this is an episode featuring a guest star famous for a role in another popular camp TV series, in this case actress Agnes Moorehead, who also played Endora, the flamboyant, acid-tongued mother of pretty witch Samantha on ABC's *Bewitched* (1964–72), where Moorehead's character regularly bemoaned the drudgery of the life of the nonmagical American housewife that her daughter has inexplicably (in her view) chosen through her marriage to bumbling mortal Darrin. In "The Night of the Vicious Valentine" Moorehead (who garnered *The Wild Wild West* its only Emmy for her role) plays Emma Valentine, a charming Washington hostess who is secretly training beautiful but poor young women to seduce the West's wealthiest tycoons into marrying them, after which the men are mysteriously murdered and their fortunes disappear. President Grant explains the Secret Service must investigate because the fortunes involved are so massive that, should they be concentrated in the hands of a single individual, the financial power could "jolt the national economy."

The connection between patriarchy and capitalism as twinned systems structuring power relations, especially between genders, is made even more apparent after James's inevitable capture, when he awakens in Emma Valentine's hyperfeminine bedroom, featuring a massive pink heart-shaped bed perched on a pedestal bookended by life-size cupids and backed by a heart-shaped headboard and lavender floor-to-ceiling draperies. This is the alluring, dangerous heart of stereotypical mainstream femininity, but rather than simply a campy version of a vagina dentata, Moorehead's Valentine is a feminist avenger with a sympathetic mission she explains in detail to James West as he lies bound to the elaborately tufted Victorian fainting couch at the foot of her bed.

Similar to the Amorous Amanda, Emma Valentine's bondage device is a tertiary sex characteristic involving appendages, this time on the ends of lifelike pairs of women's arms, clad in frilly, ruffled sleeves, that emerge from the back of the fainting couch and clamp their manicured and bejeweled hands to West's chest and thighs. Moorehead's Emma, dressed in a pink satin gown and ropes of pearls, her signature red hair elaborately coiffed, swishes delightedly around her immobilized captive, explaining that she can tighten the "dainty hands of the harem" via a remote-control device. She demonstrates her power to punish West by activating the hands, noting with amusement that it is precisely what most men fantasize about. She laughs softly as West writhes and groans, then loosens the hands' painful grasp and says, "My dear Mr. West, I regard myself not as a criminal but as a savior of all womankind."

"Interesting," James replies. "And what do women have to be saved from?"

Valentine responds while circling the immobilized West, first passing left to right behind him, then passing right to left, crossing in front of the camera, and pausing at the left side of the shot to gaze down at his prone body: "From domination of the spirit," she declares, "economic exploitation, annihilation of the mind. . . . In brief, all the injustices wrought by men."

Valentine clearly acts here as the imagined spokeswoman of feminism, while also being a villainous mastermind responsible for a string of murders. Unlike the episodes with villains who are former Confederates, however, all of whom are presented as unambiguously evil, Emma Valentine's presentation is nuanced through the formal elements of the scene, her anger at patriarchy obliquely acknowledged in James's refusal to deny or defend the unjust oppression of women Valentine aims to reverse. As Egizii et al. demonstrate, in Hollywood cinema, antagonists typically move laterally from the right to the left side of the screen and generally occupy the left side in a shot-counter shot sequence, while protagonists do the opposite.[41] Valentine, however, continuously circles James, first moving left to right, then crossing the screen in the opposite direction. She pauses several times during their extended conversation, alternating her placement on both the left and right sides, so that about half the time James West is screen left, the side generally assigned to the villain, while Emma Valentine is screen right, the side generally associated with the sympathetic protagonist.

And just as the formal placement of Valentine within the scene disrupts our assumptions about "good" and "bad" characters, the BDSM play disrupts assumptions about gender, power, and pleasure. Alba Nabusi explains, "Domination and submission go beyond the physical dimension—no phallic penetration is needed to achieve pleasure—while they assume power's circulation as fundamental. Foucault has always criticised the conception of power as something static, exclusively owned by institutions or political figures—power circulates, he says."[42]

Specifically, Foucault says, "S/M is the eroticization of power, the eroticization of strategic relationships."[43] Foucault continues: "Power is characterized by the fact that it constitutes a strategic relationship that has stabilized in institutions. Within power relations, mobility is therefore limited. . . . This means that the strategic relationships between individuals are characterized by rigidity. In this regard, S/M play is very interesting because, although it is strategic, it is always fluid. . . . It is a staging of power structures through a strategic game capable of providing sexual or physical pleasure."[44]

The fluid destabilization of relationships between individuals, presumed to be stabilized in institutions such as capitalism and patriarchy, is performed in this scene through the circulation of pleasure and power via BDSM, their intertwined natures made visible in the back-and-forth play of the question-and-answer game that weaves its way through the bondage and punishment of the male lead by the overdefined female torturer who quite literally circulates through the room and around his immobilized body.

Again, establishing the consensual contract Deleuze confirms as characteristic of the masochistic scene, West agrees to Valentine's request that he answer her questions by offering to do so freely if she will in turn answer questions from him. With the terms of the contract agreed upon, Valentine crosses from the left to the right side of the screen and retrieves a piece of red construction paper and a pair of scissors that she uses to cut variously sized heart shapes into the paper in response to James's answers to her seemingly innocuous personal queries, such as "Question! What is your favorite wine?" or "Question! Do you prefer blondes, brunettes, or [obviously referencing her own scarlet tresses] . . . *redheads?*"

"Yes!" West immediately declares. It is clear that Valentine, like nearly all the female characters in the series (and more than a few of the males), openly desires her handsome captive. Moorehead, sixty-five years old at the time the scene was shooting, is considerably senior to Conrad, who was thirty, but she is never presented as ridiculous. The sexual tension between them in this bondage scene is initially established earlier in the episode in the scene in which they first meet. Moorehead's Valentine, still posing as a simple society hostess, gazes at West, her eyes moving approvingly up and down his body before she declares he must be her next "offering" to "those silly dressed-up sheep that come to my parties," for whom James will be as a wolf among them, albeit a wolf she intends to control like a tame dog. She proposes he act as the exciting spectacle she will introduce at her upcoming fête, the reception following the wedding of her next victim, the "biggest beef tycoon of Kansas City." Their verbal sparring in this scene is witty, ironic, and spiked with kinky innuendo, as James accepts both Valentine's party invitation and her implicit promise to tame him by giving her a slow smile, then deadpanning, "Do I bring my own leash, or do I pick one up at the door?"

The circulation of power and pleasure through this episode, both in the initial meeting and in the later scene in Valentine's bedroom, is the opposite of what audiences might expect, with an older, experienced woman in complete physical control of a younger man. The pleasure of release in the masochistic scene, which comes from the promised punishment of the willing sub, plays out via the question-and-answer game, illustrating, as Foucault suggests, the ease with which supposedly rigid positions of power can be disrupted by the pleasurable, strategic play of BDSM. "Question!" Valentine declares, as James, still pinned to the fainting couch, watches her. "Do you think a woman should know how to cook and sew?"

"Only if they intend to be cooks or seamstresses," he responds.

Then, because Valentine has earlier explained she plans to use the fortune she is amassing to take control of the U.S. economy and make herself queen of America, for his turn West asks, "You mentioned a temporary monarchy?"

"Oh yes, I should not like to rule forever, only long enough to secure total independence for women. Then after a time I shall release this country into a democracy. . . . Under my scientific reign, this country will flourish as never before. . . . A prosperous country is composed of happy people and happy people are made by happy marriages." She uses her remote-control device to spin the fainting couch 180 degrees so West, again on the left side of the shot, faces Valentine standing screen right in front of a wall of knobs and lights representing a Victorian-era steampunk version of a computer. "And happy marriages," she declares, "are made by the Love Eternal Machine."

She unfolds the piece of red construction paper she has been snipping and says that when she feeds it into the machine it will produce a card that can be matched with another individual whose personality will supposedly guarantee them both marital bliss. "Dear me, Mr. West," she muses, as she examines his card. "On the basis of your answers, it seems your ideal mate is a combination of Aphrodite, Helen of Troy, and Lola Montez!"[45] West smirks, and Valentine laughingly insists, "It can't be done!" even as she runs her hand suggestively down her own waist and hips. She clicks off the whirring machine and saunters back to where West is still bound to the fainting couch by the dainty hands of her mechanical harem. The camera cuts to a low-angle over-the-shoulder shot from West's point of view, looking up at Emma Valentine, still screen right as she leans over him. She grasps his chin and in a reverse shot, gazes down at her captive, purring, "You understand, don't you, Mr. West?" stroking his face as he stares up at her. She then moves her fingers to his lips, whispering throatily, "Ahhh, Mr. West." The sexual tension built throughout this scene by withholding the longed-for release is finally provoked, as Deleuze suggests, by the sub, not the dom. West rejects Valentine's overture, replying, "If I have a choice, may we go back to questions and answers?" In another low-angle shot we see Valentine draw her hand back from caressing West's face to give him two sharp, back-and-forth slaps. West shudders, releases a long-drawn-out breath, then after a pause to compose himself asks, "Whose turn was it, Miss Valentine?"

Pleasure and power in this scene circulate in much the same way Emma Valentine circles the bound body of James West, destabilizing heteropatriarchal gender expectations of control and compliance, mobility, and stasis through the disruptive play of BDSM. Ostensibly, West is imprisoned by Valentine's bondage device/tertiary sex characteristic, placing her in the position of power, but as Deleuze argues, the masochist is really bound by the bargain he has freely entered into, complying with or deliberately violating its rules. West rhetorically persuades his dom to punish him and provide the pleasurable release of sexual tension both characters have been maneuvering toward since their first meeting early in the episode, strategically manipulating the relationships of power Foucault argues are not at all the stable ones popularly imagined from within the structures of patriarchy, capitalism, or the repressed gender conventions of the genre western.

Margot Weiss, however, cautions against overestimating the subversive power of representations of BDSM, which she claims in "Mainstreaming Kink" "allow the mainstream audience to flirt with danger and excitement, but ultimately reinforce boundaries between protected and privileged normal sexuality, and policed and pathological not-normal sexuality. These mechanisms solidify the ideological dichotomies that animate American understandings of sexuality, where normal is heterosexual, monogamous, romantic, private, married, and suburban, while abnormal is nonheterosexual, nonmonogamous, unromantic, public, unmarried, and urban."[46]

While Weiss's point is well taken, I think, in more straightforward and nonwestern representations of BDSM, I would argue that *The Wild Wild West* mainstreams its kink through camp in such a way that the solidification of ideological dichotomies Weiss points out are subverted in the series, which positions its male lead as anything but heterosexual, monogamous, romantic, private, married, or suburban. In fact, the conventions of even the standard western already disrupt this neat dichotomy, as the cowboy hero traditionally fits none of these categories except (supposedly) heterosexual, and of course decades of scholarship have examined the subversions of this last category in westerns to the point of banality, suggesting again that the western has always been far less vanilla than it pretends. *The Wild Wild West*, a weird steampunk western fixated on campy, theatrical BDSM play, queers these ideological dichotomies even further, with mainstream notions of heteronormativity flung off like a cheap drag costume every time the manly Jim West bargains for a beating.

It is important to stress as well that the series does not present just the occasional episode featuring kinky bondage but repeats the scenario so often throughout its four-year run it becomes "a ritualized process," as Butler argues gender performativity must be.[47] All of this suggests the second-level meanings exposed by *The Wild Wild West*'s BDSM play are quite political, after all. In *The Politics and Poetics of Camp*, Moe Meyer claims not only that camp can be read as a critique of ideology but that in contrast to interpretations by critics like Sontag or Andrew Ross, what emerges from camp "is a suppressed and denied oppositional critique embodied in the signifying practices that processually constitute queer identity."[48] Meyer identifies several important constructions of camp, beginning with his insistence that "Camp is political," followed by his contention that "Camp is a solely queer (and/or sometimes gay and lesbian) discourse; and Camp embodies a specifically queer cultural critique."[49] In other words, Meyer concludes that in many ways mainstream camp is a genre in drag. While camp is always playful, he argues, underneath, it is always serious.[50]

Considered in this light, then, the subversiveness of a gay man's weird western involving the regular bondage and disciplining of its straight male hero is openly—hilariously—political, an extended social critique parodying, mocking, and queering mainstream, primetime ideals of what Weiss terms "normal sexuality." The genre of the western, presumably the primary producer of red-blooded all-American manhood, is revealed by the series' BDSM play to be queer as hell, with James West performing a campy, kinky dragging of the genre's fondest imaginings of sexuality and gender. While camp, as Meyer argues, is playful on the surface but serious underneath, *The Wild Wild West* represents the western and its hero as the opposite, with rigid heteronormativity just a playful costume donned by a cowboy even queerer than we imagined. *The Wild Wild West* is wild indeed.

Notes

1. For more on the homoerotics of the western, see Vito Russo's *The Celluloid Closet: Homosexuality in the Movies* (1987); Lee Clark Mitchell's *Westerns: Making the Man in Fiction and Film* (1998); Robert Lang's *Masculine Interests: Homoerotics in Hollywood Films* (2002); Le Coney and Trodd's chapter "Sonnet Subtexts and Palatable Stories: Gay Cowboys and the Heterotopian Frontier of Modern-Classic Westerns" from Paul Varner's edited collection *Westerns: Paperback Novels and Movies from Hollywood* (2007); William Handley's edited collection *The Brokeback Book: From Story to Cultural Phenomenon* (2011); Barbara Mennel's *Queer Cinema: Schoolgirls, Vampires, and Gay Cowboys* (2012); and Hiram Pérez's *A Taste for Brown Bodies: Gay Modernity and Cosmopolitan Desire* (2015), among others.
2. Bayard, "The 1960s' Gayest Show."

3. *Batman* (1966–68) was certainly a close second but ran for only three seasons, and not even Adam West's Batsuit was as ass-huggingly tight as Robert Conrad's specially tailored pants.
4. Tarantino, *Once Upon a Time in Hollywood*.
5. Crosland, "The Night of the Poisonous Posey."
6. Witney, "The Night of the Deadly Bed."
7. Sarafian, "The Night of a Thousand Eyes."
8. Moore, "The Night of the Burning Diamonds"; Deleuze, *Masochism*, 75.
9. Liberace, already a star by the 1950s, became even more famous in the 1960s when he began performing regular shows in Las Vegas, which allowed him to add chorus girls, cars, and live animals to his act. He also guest starred in many 1960s TV series, including a two-part *Batman* episode in 1966 directed by Larry Peerce, "The Devil's Fingers" and "The Devil's Ringers," in which he played both a concert pianist and his own evil twin.
10. Kesler, *The Wild Wild West: The Series*, 79.
11. Kesler, *The Wild Wild West: The Series*, 8.
12. Fine et al., *Weird Westerns*, 2.
13. The series' use of these anachronistic technologies predates even the term "steampunk," coined by science fiction writer K. W. Jeter in 1987.
14. Johnson, Lush, and Spurgeon, "Westworld(s)," 2.
15. Johnson, Lush, and Spurgeon, "Westworld(s)," 11.
16. Phillips and Pinedo, "Gilligan and Captain Kirk," 35.
17. Sontag, *Notes on Camp*, 7.
18. Phillips and Pinedo, "Gilligan and Captain Kirk," 21.
19. Phillips and Pinedo, "Gilligan and Captain Kirk," 23.
20. Kesler, *The Wild Wild West: The Series*, 79.
21. Phillips and Pinedo, "Gilligan and Captain Kirk," 24.
22. Butler, "Performative Acts," 271.
23. Mitchell, *Westerns*, 155.
24. Mitchell, *Westerns*, 162.
25. Mitchell, *Westerns*, 170.
26. Mitchell, *Westerns*, 174.
27. Kesler, *The Wild Wild West: The Series*, v. "Audience share" refers to the percentage of viewing households tuned in to a particular station at a particular time and date.
28. Mitchell, *Westerns*, 165.
29. Bayard, "The 1960s' Gayest Show."
30. Sparr, "The Night of the Eccentrics."
31. Mulvey, "Visual Pleasure," 60.

32. Actress and singer Legrand Council Mellon is most well known for supporting roles on *The Wild Wild West*, in the short-lived 1966 series *Kraft Summer Music Hall*, and for a trio of singles she recorded with Columbia in the 1960s. In 1991 she married Herbert Sargent, television writer and producer for *The Steve Allen Show*, *The Tonight Show*, and *Saturday Night Live*, where he famously created, along with Chevy Chase, the "Weekend Update."
33. Miller, *Camp TV*, 44.
34. Deleuze, *Masochism*, 74–75.
35. Deleuze, *Masochism*, 75.
36. Deleuze, *Masochism*, 70–71.
37. Deleuze, *Masochism*, 75.
38. Deleuze, *Masochism*, 75.
39. Deleuze, *Masochism*, 75.
40. Moore, "The Night of the Vicious Valentine."
41. Egizii, "Which Way Did He Go?," 226.
42. Nabusi, "Erotics of the Extreme," 32.
43. Foucault, "Sex, Power, and the Politics of Identity," 165.
44. Foucault, "Sex, Power, and the Politics of Identity," 173.
45. Lola Montez was the stage name of Eliza Rosanna Gilbert, Countess of Landsfeld (1821–61). Born in Ireland, she became a courtesan and mistress of King Ludwig I of Bavaria before reinventing herself as a "Spanish" dancer and actress. From 1851 to 1857 she toured the world, from Australia to the U.S. West. Performing her scandalously erotic "Spider Dance," in which she pretended to shake and swat a spider out of her voluminous skirts, which she would lift so high the audience could see she was naked beneath them as she energetically slapped her bare thighs and buttocks in futile search of the spider. She later settled in San Francisco, where she delivered public lectures on women's rights.
46. Weiss, "Mainstreaming Kink," 105.
47. Butler, "Performative Acts," 60.
48. Meyer, introduction to *The Politics and Poetics of Camp*, 1.
49. Meyer, introduction to *The Politics and Poetics of Camp*, 1.
50. Meyer, introduction to *The Politics and Poetics of Camp*, 10.

Bibliography

Bayard, Louis. "The 1960s' Gayest Show." *Salon*, August 12, 2008. https://www.salon.com/2008/08/12/wild_wild_west/.

Butler, Judith. "Performative Acts and Gender Constitution: An Essay in Phenomenology and Feminist Theory." In *Performing Feminisms: Feminist Critical Theory and Theatre*, edited by Sue-Ellen Case, 270–82. Baltimore: Johns Hopkins University Press, 1990.

Crosland, Alan, dir. *The Wild Wild West*. Season 2, episode 7, "The Night of the Poisonous Posey." Aired October 28, 1966, on CBS.

Deleuze, Gilles. *Masochism: Coldness and Cruelty & Venus in Furs*. Reprint ed. New York: Zone Books, 1991.

Egizii, Matthew L., Kimberly A. Neuendorf, James Denny, Paul D. Skalski, and Rachel Campbell. "Which Way Did He Go? Film Lateral Movement and Spectator Interpretation." *Visual Communication* 17, no. 2 (2018): 221–43.

Fine, Kerry, Michael K. Johnson, Rebecca M. Lush, and Sara L. Spurgeon, eds. *Weird Westerns: Race, Gender, Genre*. Lincoln: University of Nebraska Press, 2020.

Foucault, Michel. "Sex, Power, and the Politics of Identity." In *Ethics: Subjectivity, and Truth*, edited by Paul Rabinow, 163–73. New York: New Press, 1997.

Freud, Sigmund. "'A Child Is Being Beaten': A Contribution to the Study of the Origin of Sexual Perversions." In *The Standard Edition of the Complete Psychological Works of Sigmund Freud, Volume XVII (1917–1919): An Infantile Neurosis and Other Works*, 175–204. London: Hogarth Press, 1955.

Jeter, K. W. "Letter to the Editor." *Locus* 20, no. 4 (April 1987): 57.

Johnson, Michael K., Rebecca M. Lush, and Sara L. Spurgeon. "Westworld(s): Race, Gender, Genre in the Weird Western." Introduction to *Weird Westerns: Race, Gender, Genre*, edited by Kerry Fine, Michael K. Johnson, Rebecca M. Lush, and Sara L. Spurgeon, 1–36. Lincoln: University of Nebraska Press. 2020.

Kesler, Susan A. *The Wild Wild West: The Series*. Downey CA: Arnett Press, 1988.

Meyer, Moe. Introduction to *The Politics and Poetics of Camp*, edited by Moe Meyer. New York: Routledge, 1994.

Miller, Quinlan. *Camp TV: Trans Gender Queer Sitcom History*. Durham NC: Duke University Press, 2019.

Mitchell, Lee Clark. *Westerns: Making the Man in Fiction and Film*. Chicago: University of Chicago Press, 1996.

Moore, Irving J., dir. *The Wild Wild West*. Season 1, episode 26, "The Night of the Burning Diamonds." Aired April 8, 1966, on CBS.

———. *The Wild Wild West*. Season 2, episode 20, "The Night of the Vicious Valentine." Aired February 10, 1967, on CBS.

Mulvey, Laura. "Visual Pleasure and Narrative Cinema." In *Feminism and Film Theory*, edited by Constance Penley, 57–68. New York: Routledge, 2013.

Nabusi, Alba. "Erotics of the Extreme, a Philosophical Perspective: Foucault's Understanding of BDSM." In *Desire, Performance, and Classification: Critical Perspectives on the Erotic*, edited by Jessica Pfeffer, 27–36. Oxford: Interdisciplinary Press, 2013.

Peerce, Larry, dir. *Batman*. Season 2, episodes 15 and 16, "The Devil's Fingers" and "The Devil's Ringers." Aired October 26 and 27, 1966, on ABC.

Phillips, Wyatt, and Isabel Pinedo. "Gilligan and Captain Kirk Have More in Common Than You Think: 1960s Camp TV as an Alternative Genealogy for Cult TV." *Journal of Popular Television* 6, no. 1 (2018): 19–40.

Ross, Andrew. "The Uses of Camp." In *Queer Aesthetics and the Performing Subject: A Reader*, edited by Fabio Cleto, 308–29. Ann Arbor: University of Michigan Press, 1999.

Sarafian, Richard, dir. *The Wild Wild West*. Season 1, episode 6, "The Night of a Thousand Eyes." Aired October 22, 1965, on CBS.

Sontag, Susan. *Notes on Camp*. London: Penguin Classics, 2018.

Sparr, Robert, dir. *The Wild Wild West*. Season 2, episode 1, "The Night of the Eccentrics." Aired September 16, 1966, on CBS.

Tarantino, Quentin, dir. *Once Upon a Time in Hollywood*. Sony Pictures, 2021.

Weiss, Margot. "Mainstreaming Kink." *Journal of Homosexuality* 50, no. 2 (2006): 103–32.

Witney, William, dir. *The Wild Wild West*. Season 1, episode 2, "The Night of the Deadly Bed." Aired September 24, 1965, on CBS.

Contributors

Elizabeth Abele is an American studies scholar and professor. She has published on the intersections of American culture with history, gender, and race. Her work has appeared in *American Studies*, *Journal of Transnational American Studies*, and *College Literature*, and in edited anthologies on works of Kurt Vonnegut, Ridley Scott, Annie Proulx, and M. Night Shyamalan. She is the author of *Home Front Hero: The Rise of a New Hollywood Archetype, 1988–1999* (2014) and coeditor of *Screening Images of American Masculinity in the Age of Postfeminism* (2015).

Joshua T. Anderson is the conservation director for the Walsh County Three Rivers Soil Conservation District in rural North Dakota. His scholarship includes essays in *Inks: The Journal of the Comics Studies Society* and *Weird Westerns: Race, Gender, Genre*. His creative writing appears in *North American Review*, *Essay Daily*, *Bourbon Penn*, and Mary Swander's Emerging Voices series. He is currently the host of *Common Ground: A Prairie Podcast*, available on Spotify, YouTube, and walshcounty1938.com.

Miriam Brown Spiers is an associate professor of English and American studies at Kennesaw State University, where she serves as the director of the MA in American studies. Her research and teaching interests include contemporary Native American and Indigenous literatures, science fiction, and comics. She is the author of *Encountering the Sovereign Other: Indigenous Science Fiction* (Michigan State University Press, 2021). Her work has also appeared in *Studies in American Literature*, *Transmotion*, and *Native South*.

Jeffrey Chisum is a professor of writing at USC, where he teaches writing courses centered on aesthetics. His scholarship focuses on the stories of the American West, with a more recent research emphasis on the horror genre. Some of his more recent publications include an article on the TV show *Breaking Bad* as a "western tragedy" and a book chapter on the novels of the Reno-born author/songwriter Willy Vlautin.

Micah Donohue is an associate professor of English at Eastern New Mexico University. His teaching and research focus on speculative literature and film in borderlands, Latinx, and hemispheric American contexts. His work has been published in *Science Fiction Studies*, *Utopian Studies*, *Western American Literature*, MELUS, ASAP/*Journal*, *Hispanófila*, *Chiricú*, *Comparative American Studies*, and *Adaptation*, among other journals.

Christina Fawcett is a genre, media, and monster theorist in the Department of English at the University of Winnipeg, Canada; she studies villainous and monstrous spaces in video games, media, and young people's texts. Her research addresses genre and cultural studies, monstrosity and trauma, and the affect and emotion of digital participation, embodiment, and identification.

Kerry Fine is an instructor in the English Department at Arizona State University. She is the author of "She Hits Like a Man, but She Kisses Like a Girl: TV Heroines, Femininity, Violence, and Intimacy" in *Western American Literature*, and coeditor (with Michael Johnson, Rebecca Lush, and Sara Spurgeon) of *Weird Westerns: Race, Gender, Genre* (University of Nebraska Press).

Katie Googe earned a PhD in English from the University of Southern California in 2024 with a dissertation that focuses on the relationship between temporality and colonialism in late nineteenth- and early twentieth-century speculative fiction in the United States. Other research interests include early pulp magazines, the history of queerness in fiction, and science fiction's visions of personhood as considered through lenses of race, gender, and technology.

Meredith Harvey is an associate professor at Aurora University, where she teaches English courses, many of which focus on issues of gender, ethnicity, and culture. Her research looks at the intersections of place, gender, and ethnicity, with an eye toward postcolonial landscapes. Within this scope, she has published a paper in *Humanities* looking at African identities in Caribbean literatures and contributed an essay to *Weird Westerns: Race, Gender, Genre*.

Jennessa Hester is a transgender scholar and poet working out of Texas Tech University. Her research focuses on embodiment, identity, and various forms of media, both classical and cutting edge. Beyond her own writing, Jennessa serves as a managing editor for the *Iron Horse Literary Review*, assistant editor for the *Journal of Cinema and Media Studies*, poetry editor for *Wrong Publishing*, and member of the *International Journal of Disney Studies*' editorial board.

Sara Humphreys is an associate teaching professor at the University of Victoria in Canada. She teaches courses in game studies, rhetoric, and writing. Her next project investigates how many popular console games are rhetorical platforms for debate over pressing social and cultural issues.

Anne Mai Yee Jansen is a lifelong lover of weird and disturbing stories who teaches literature and ethnic studies at California Polytechnic State University, San Luis Obispo. Before this, she earned her PhD in English from the Ohio State University and worked as an associate professor of interdisciplinary studies and English at the University of North Carolina at Asheville. Her research centers on the relationship between race and genre in contemporary U.S. ethnic literatures.

Michael K. Johnson is a professor of American literature at the University of Maine at Farmington. He is the author of *Black Masculinity and the Frontier Myth in American Literature* (University of Oklahoma) and *Speculative Wests: Popular Representations of a Region and Genre* (University of Nebraska Press). He is also coeditor (with Kerry Fine, Rebecca Lush, and Sara Spurgeon) of *Weird Westerns: Race, Gender, Genre* (University of Nebraska Press).

Jana Koehler currently works in the Writers' Studio at Arizona State University. In 2019 she graduated from the University of New Mexico with a PhD in American literary studies with a focus on southwestern and western ethnic literature. She lives in New Mexico with her three cats.

Rebecca M. Lush is a professor in the Literature and Writing Studies Department and Faculty Center director at California State University San Marcos. She coedited *Weird Westerns: Race, Gender, Genre* (University of Nebraska Press, 2020) and Margaret Fell's Women's Speaking Justified *and Other Pamphlets* (Iter Press, 2018). She has published articles in *Horror Studies, Studies in American Indian Literature*, and others. Her current research interests include horror, popular culture, and performance studies.

Marc A. Ouellette teaches gender and cultural studies at Old Dominion University. He is an award-winning educator, including the 2023 ODU award for outstanding graduate mentorship. Marc is the author of *Playing with the Guys: Masculinity and Relationships in Video Games* (McFarland, 2021), and he is widely published on gender, sex, and sexuality in video games, including several chapters in forthcoming handbooks.

Scott Pearce, PhD, is the author of two novels, *Faded Yellow by the Winter* (2019) and *The Rider on the Bridge* (2022). His academic research has been published in edited collections and academic journals. He writes about the western film genre, horror, New Hollywood, and colonialism. He teaches at Alia College in Victoria, Australia.

Sara L. Spurgeon works on literatures of the U.S. West at Texas Tech University, where she directs the Literature, Social Justice, and Environment program. She is coauthor of *Writing the Southwest*, author of *Exploding the Western: Myths of Empire on the Postmodern Frontier*, editor of a collection on Cormac McCarthy, and coeditor of *Weird Westerns: Race, Gender, Genre*. Her articles have appeared in *Western American Literature*, *ISLE*, *American Quarterly*, and *Transnational American Studies*.

hand sports a massive replica of the ruby ring Count Manzeppi wears on his own right hand.

The bondage device consisting of the pole and metal appendages, the count explains, is named the "Amorous Amanda," and James smilingly promises to get used to her "hot little hands." The Amorous Amanda as a tertiary sex characteristic carries a female-gendered name while being coded as an animated extension of the count's body, acting as a transgendered signifier that both caresses and restrains the male hero. In "Coldness and Cruelty," Deleuze creates a list of characteristics of masochism, which he defines as far more than simply the enjoyment of pain. The first characteristic is the elaborate setup, the highly stylized "form of the fantasy . . . the scene which is dreamed, dramatized, ritualized," always played for campy, theatrical effect in *The Wild Wild West*.[34] The second characteristic, especially important in this portion of the scene, is the "suspense factor," or "the waiting, the delay, the expressing the way in which anxiety affects sexual tension and inhibits its discharge."[35]

The Amorous Amanda, the count's tertiary sex characteristic, is connected at the top of her pole to a pulley that raises James, still clamped to the pole by Amanda's metal hands, into the air as Manzeppi explains the pulley's rope will break in fourteen minutes, dropping James onto an electrified platform below. "Oh, I *wish* I could stay and watch!" the count proclaims dramatically, having already spent much of the episode watching James West, but he and the other assassins must catch up to President Benito Juarez in order to carry out their assassination. In a medium close-up, we see the broadly smiling count gaze at West suspended above him. He spreads his arms in a wide embrace and declares, "Mr. West, enjoy!" West, the hypermasculine epitome of a two-fisted western hero, willingly complies with this important component of masochism.

Leopold von Sacher-Masoch emphasizes the state of waiting as pleasurable and indispensable to masochism, and in his chapter on "The Art of Masoch," Deleuze argues that "ritual scenes of hanging, crucifixion, and other forms of physical suspension," along with other types of suspense, such as the excruciating pleasure of waiting, are also important.[36] Because the audience knows that the hero will not, in fact, be killed in a show like *The Wild Wild West*, the temporal suspense factor, the holding off of the

Index

Aarseth, Elizabeth, 284
Abbey, Edward, 265
Abele, Elizabeth, 195n19
abject, 247n27, 260–61
The Aeneid (poem), 191
African Americans, 152–68. *See also* Black cowboys
Ambler, Marge, 164
Ambush (film), 80
American Progress (painting), 265
American Psycho (film), 208
Anderson, Paul W. S., 177
Anzaldúa, Gloria, 141
Army of the Dead (film), xxi, xxiii, 226–48
Arnezeder, Nora, 236
Autonomous (Newitz), ix–xiii

Bailey, Laura, 298
Batman (TV series), 311, 316, 318, 331n3, 331n9
Bayard, Louis, 311, 318
BDSM, 31–32, 54, 202, 312–16, 320, 326–29
Behrenshausen, Bryan, 298
Bellamy, Ralph, 231
Berlant, Lauren, 290
Berliner, Todd, 201
Bersani, Leo, 304
Bettelheim, Bruno, 259–60
Between Men (Sedgwick), 180

Bewitched (TV series), 315, 324
Beyoncé, xv–xvi, xxvnn30–31
Billy the Kid Returns (video game), 289
Bioshock (video game), xxii, 268–85
Bioshock Infinite (video game), 268
The Bird Is Gone (Jones), xxivn11
Bitter Springs (film), 81
Black Arts movement, 152
"Black Canaan" (Howard), 152–55, 158–60
Black Christmas (film), 222n27
Black cowboys, xvi, 152, 156
Black Mirror (TV series), xix, 22–49
Blade Runner (film), 178–79, 184
Blodgett, Bridget, 292, 295
Blood Meridian (McCarthy), 262, 265
Bloom, John. *See* Briggs, Joe Bob
Blue Oyster Cult, 217
Bogost, Ian, 297
Bohannon, Mary, 153
Bold, Christine, 130, 294
Booth, Wayne, 290–91
Bordo, Susan, 159
Branch, Michael, 213
Briggs, Joe Bob, 206, 218, 222n28
Brokeback Mountain (film), xiii, xiv
Brooks, Richard, 228, 244
brute masculinity. *See* hypermasculinity
Buffy the Vampire Slayer (TV series), 111
Buono, Victor, 318, 320
Burns, Marilyn, 203

339

Butch Cassidy and the Sundance Kid (film), 91, 165
Butler, Judith, 316, 329

Cadillac Desert (Reisner), 55, 58
Camera Obscura (Ryan and Kellner), 261
camp, xv–xvi, 311, 314–15, 320, 323, 324, 329–30
Campbell, Neil, 115, 132, 149n34
Campbell, Neve, 199
Campbell, Owen, 216
Candyman (film), 218
Cantor, Paul A., 227, 240
captivity narrative, 55, 60, 213, 229, 233, 237, 247n27, 277
Cardinale, Claudia, 233
Carpenter, John, 220n2, 222n27
Carrie (film), 261
Cash, Johnny, 196n31
Chapman, Erin, 159
Chess, Shira, 303
Chinatown (film), 55
Cities of the Plain (McCarthy), 56, 67
civilization and savagery opposition. See frontier myth
Cixous, Helene, 261
The Clone Wars (TV series). See *The Mandalorian* (TV series)
Clover, Carol, 198–200, 213. See also final girl; final grandma
Connell, R. W., 272
Conrad, Robert, 311–12, 331n3
Conway, Steven, 272, 273, 275, 278–79, 283–84
Cooper, Gary, 96, 211
Cooper, James Fenimore, xi, 118, 180, 293, 301, 317
Corneau, Guy, 272
Cowan, Douglas, 219

cowboy archetype, xiii, xiv–xv, 8, 14, 28, 39, 76, 83–84, 130, 136–37, 140, 145, 153, 157, 162, 165–66, 256, 289–90, 295–96, 305, 312, 316, 329
Cowboy Carter (album), xxv
"Cowboys Are Frequently, Secretly Fond of Each Other" (song), xvii, xxvin38
Creed, Barbara, 259, 260
cross-dressing, 166, 171n84, 210. See also drag
Curtis, Jamie Lee, 199, 222n27
Custer, George Armstrong, 171n84, 289
Custer's Revenge (video game), 289
"A Cyborg Manifesto" (Haraway), 178
cyborgs, 177–94

Danzinger, Allen, 203
Das Capital (Marx), 247n29
Davis, Arabella, 153
Davis, Robert, 164
Dawn of the Dead (film), xxi, 227, 231
Dead by Daylight (video game), 207
"Dear Final Girls" (Jones), 218
"Dear John Wayne" (Alexie), 9
"Dear John Wayne" (Erdrich), 129
Deep Throat (film), 204
Deleuze, Gilles, 312, 321–23, 326, 328
D'Elia, Chris, 244, 245
Deloria, Philip J., 210
Deloria, Vine, Jr., 121, 124
Del Toro, Guillermo, 195n27
De Palma, Brian, 261
Desert Solitaire (Abbey), 265
Desperation (King), 265
The Devil's Rejects (film), 208
DiCaprio, Leonardo, 311
Dillahunt, Garret, 232
Dirty Harry (film), 99
Dobbs v. Jackson, 198, 248n45

domesticity, xiii, xxivn12, 28, 39, 166, 202, 205, 207–11, 220, 253–59, 265–66, 302
dom-sub (dom/little), 15–17, 317, 324
Donner Party, 256
Dracula (Stoker), 203, 223n29
drag, 166, 210, 314
Dressel, Ashley, 292
Druckmann, Neil, 290–91, 301, 305–6
Duvall, Shelley, 253

Eastwood, Clint, 9, 10, 91, 95, 97, 99, 177, 207, 211; and *High Plains Drifter* (film), 177; and *Pale Rider* (film), 177
Egizii, Matthew, 325
Ellison, Ralph, 157
Erotic Innocence (Kincaid), 282
Evenson, Brian, 265
Everett, Percival, 171n84
Evil Dead II (film), 208
Eye Killers (Carr), xx, 111–27

Face / Off (film), 184
Faludi, Susan, 183
Fantone, Laura, 278
Federici, Silvia, 235, 243
The Female Man (Russ), xi
female masculinity, 147, 298
Fernbach, Amanda, 181
Fiedler, Leslie, xi, 179–80, 183
final girl, 198–202, 213, 216
final grandma, 200–202, 207, 208, 216, 220
Firefly (TV series), 24, 293
Fisher, Carrie, 4, 5, 6
For a Few Dollars More (film), 10–11
Ford, Harrison, 4, 5
Ford, John, 4, 76, 91, 93, 97
Forgetting the Alamo, or, Blood Memory (Pérez), xx, 129–50

Foucault, Michel, 235, 326, 327, 329
Fox, Robert Elliot, 156
Frankenstein (film), 203
Freud, Sigmund, 259–60, 264, 266, 282, 312, 323
Friday the 13th (film), 218, 220n2
Frontier Club, 294
frontier myth, 64, 212; and civilization and savagery opposition, 118, 229, 231–32, 240, 292–93; and regeneration through violence, xiii, 161, 212, 257. *See also* Slotkin, Richard
"Frontier Thesis." *See* Turner, Frederick Jackson
Full Metal Jacket (film), 254

Garrison, Michael, 313, 318
Gast, John, 265
Gattaca (film), 184
gaze, xiv, 39, 59, 89, 139, 187, 233, 236, 239, 275–83. *See also* Mulvey, Laura
Gerrard, Steven, 238, 247n27
The Getaway (film), 91
Gilman, Charlotte Perkins, 214
Godey's Lady's Book (periodical), 202, 210
God's Country (Everett), 171n84
Gomez, Marie, 233
Gone with the Wind (film), 202
Goth, Mia, 210
gothic, 153, 293, 295
Grant, Ulysses S., 313
Green, Amy, 294
Green, Paul, 152
Grey, Zane, x, 254
Griswold v. Connecticut, 234
Gross, Halley, 290–91, 301, 305–6
Gun (video game), 289
Gunfight at the OK Corral (film), 96
gunslinger, 4, 10, 12, 13, 15, 22, 136, 163, 228

Index 341

Halberstam, Jack, 170n45, 170n52, 203, 213, 295
Hale, Sarah Josepha, 210
Hall, Henry, 253
Halloween (film), 199, 218, 220n2
Halloween H20: Twenty Years Later (film), 222n27
Halloween Kills (film), 199
Hamlet (play), 205
Hansen, Gunnar, 203
Hardwick, Omari, 243
Harraway, Donna, 178–79, 181, 184–85, 187–88, 192
Harvey, Merdith, 293
Hauer, Rutger, 184
Heflin, Van, 178
heist genre, 229–30, 244, 246n9
Hereditary (film), 265
hero archetype, xiii, 8, 61, 76, 80, 83, 95–97, 114, 153, 159, 161–62, 164–65, 167, 177, 180, 183, 194, 211, 244n13, 279, 292–93, 295, 316, 329
heteronormativity (heteronormative), 44, 45, 55, 59, 61, 77, 79, 82–83, 87, 89, 95, 136, 143, 182, 200, 211, 235, 289, 297, 304, 315, 329
High Noon (film), 80, 96, 182, 211
High Plains Drifter (film), 177, 211
Hinkel, Kim, 204
Histoire de l'oeil (Bataille), 54, 56, 66, 68
Histoire d'O (Desclos), 54, 56, 62, 67
History of Horror (TV series), 254
Hitchcock, Alfred, 208, 220n2
Holland, Samantha, 238, 247n27
home. *See* domesticity
"Home" (song), 253
homoerotic (homoeroticism), viii, xii, xiv, xxiii, xxvn25, 6, 42, 94, 171n84, 311
homophobia, xiii, 39, 44, 84, 171n84

homosexuality, 164–66, 180, 296, 307n18
homosocial, 8, 180, 188
Hood, Gavin, 190
hoodoo (voodoo, vodun), 152, 156–57
Hooper, Tobe, 198, 202, 204, 217
Hope Leslie (Sedgwick), 293
Hornbeck, Elizabeth Jean, 264
horses, 167
Hour of the Gun (film), 98
House of 1000 Corpses (film), 208
Howard, Robert E., 152–55, 158–60, 165–66, 168
How Much of These Hills Is Gold (Zhang), xx, 129–50
Humphreys, Sara, 296
Hunt, Alex, 162
hypermasculinity, 181, 192–93, 211, 289, 291, 296, 297, 299–302, 305–6, 316

I Am Legend (Matheson), 115
Indigenous knowledge, 120–21
Interview with the Vampire (film), 111, 115
Irigaray, Luce, 233
Isaacs, Jason, 186

Jackman, Hugh, 177
Jackson, Samuel L., 177
Jameson, Fredric, 64, 265
Jansen, Famke, 190
Jeffress, Lynn, 255, 263
Johnson, Michael K., 54, 57, 59, 115–17, 131, 157, 163, 227, 269, 313–14
Jones, Stephen Graham, 218–19
Jones, Steve, 236
Joyce, Justin, 294
Julius Caesar (play), 191
Justine (Sade), 56, 62

Kael, Pauline, 262, 263

Kaplan, Amy, 207, 210
Karen Memory (Bear), 58
Keen, Dafne, 191
Kennedy, Jamie, 212
Kierkegaard, Soren, 263, 265
Kilker, Robert, 260, 261
Kincaid, James, 282–83
King, Stephen, 265
Kirkland, Ewan, 295
Klock, Geoff, 190, 191
Kneubuhl, John, 313
Kolodny, Annette, 134, 144
Kristeva, Julia, 259
Kubrick, Stanley, 254

Lacan, Jacques, 259, 260, 312, 322, 323
Ladd, Alan, 178, 179
Laguna Woman (film), 111
L'Amour, Louis, 254
Lancaster, Burt, 230
Lankoski, Petri, 298
Lanza, Joseph, 207
LaSalle, Eriq, 192
The Last of the Mohicans (Cooper), 293, 301
The Last of Us (TV series), xxivn12, 307n18
The Last of Us (video game), 290, 292, 294
The Last of Us II (video game), xxiii, 290–306
"The Lavender Cowboy" (poem), xiv–xv
Lawrence, D. H., 179
Lee, Daryl, 228, 229–30, 244
Le Guin, Ursula K., xviii, 53, 67
Lehman, Peter, 194
Leigh, Janet, 222n27
Leone, Sergio, 10, 66
Liberace, 311, 313, 318, 320, 331n9

Liebowitz, Flo, 255, 263
The Life and Adventures of Joaquin Murieta (Ridge), 129
L'Image (Berg), 54, 56, 62, 65
Little House on the Prairie (TV series), 206
Lizardi, Ryan, 269
Logan (film), xxi, 177, 179, 181, 189–94
Lonely Are the Brave (film), 76
Lone Women (LaValle), 129–30
The Lost Boys (film), 22, 42–43
Love, Nat, 156
Love and Death in the American Novel (Fiedler), 179
Lovecraft, H. P., 153
Luckhurst, Roger, 257, 258, 260, 262, 265, 266
Lush, Rebecca M., 54, 57, 59, 115–17, 131, 227, 269, 313–14
Lusted, David, 231, 247n27

MacCallum-Stewart, Esther, 271
Mad Max (film), xx, xxiii, 75–104
Mad Max Beyond Thunderdome (film), 78
Mad Max: Fury Road (film), 78)
Mad Max 2 (film), 78
The Mandalorian (TV series), xix, xxiii, 3–19
Mangold, James, 177, 190
Manifest Destiny, 111, 116–18, 123, 231, 262, 263
"Manifest Domesticity" (Kaplan), 207
The Man Who Shot Liberty Valance (film), 76, 97
Martin, Ross, 312
Marvin, Lee, 229
Marx, Karl, 247n29
masochistic (masochism, sadomasochism), 8, 15, 17, 59, 62, 273. *See also* BDSM
Masters, Michael, 319

Mateas, Michael, 274, 280
McCabe & Mrs. Miller (film), 80
McCarthy, Cormac, 262
McCluskey, John, 272
McDormand, Frances, 204
McGee, Patrick, 161
McMinn, Terri, 203
McVeigh, Stephen, 156, 162
Meljac, Eric, 162
Mellon, Legrand, 320, 332n32
Men, Women, and Chain Saws (Clover), 199
Mescudi, Scott, 215
Meyer, Moe, 329–30
Miller, Michael Vincent, 214
Miller, Quinlan, 320
Miner, Steve, 222
Missing and Murdered Indigenous Women (MMIW), 112–13, 125
Mitchell, Lee Clark, xiv, 66, 136, 186–87, 269, 274, 280, 295, 297, 317–18
Mitchell, S. Weir, 214
Molina-Guzmán, Isabel, 247n31
monstrous feminine, 260–61
Montez, Lola, 328, 332n45
Montgomery, Mitch, 190, 191
Moorehead, Agnes, 324–27
Mulvey, Laura, 246n18, 277–78, 285n10, 319. See also gaze
My Darling Clementine (film), 93

Nabusi, Alba, 326
Native Americans, 164, 204, 210, 247n27, 255–56, 266, 293
Neal, Ed, 203
The Negotiator (film), 177
Nelson, Connie, 186
Niccol, Andrew, 184
Nicholson, Jack, 253, 265
A Nightmare on Elm Street (film), 218

Nomadland (film), 204, 213
Nosferatu (film), 111
Notaro, Tig, 229, 245
"Nude Ranch" (performance), xvii
Nussbaum, Martha, 237, 242, 246n17

Ocean's Eleven (film), 230
Oedipal conflict, 253, 259–61, 264, 266
Okamoto, Tao, 196n30
Olney, Ian, 238–39, 241, 243
Once Upon a Time in Hollywood (film), 311
The Open Curtain (Evenson), 265
Origitano, Catlyn, 281
Ortega, Jenna, 216
Ouellette, Marc, 272
The Outlaw (film), 311
The Outlaw Josey Wales (film), 91, 97

Pacino, Al, 311
Palance, Jack, 231
Paquin, Anna, 190
parody, 152
Parsler, Justin, 271
Partain, Paul, 203
partnership, 8, 11, 164
Pascal, Pedro, 9, 12, 14
Peck, Orville, xvi, xxvi
Peckinpah, Sam, 66, 91
Penry, Tara, 295
Peoples, David Webb, 178
Pertwee, Sean, 186
Pettegrew, John, 296
phallocentrism, 59, 61
Phillips, Wyatt, 315
Pilgrim, David, 159
Pinedo, Isabel, 315
Pitt, Brad, 311
The Politics and Poetics of Camp (Meyer), 329
Poltergeist (film), 265

Poole, W. Scott, 201–2
Powers of Horror (Kristeva), 259
Prast, Simon, 216
The Professionals (film), xxi, 226–28, 229, 231–38, 240–44
Pryor, Richard, 318
Psycho (film), 208, 218, 220n2, 222nn26–27

queer, xi, xv, 166, 167, 200, 290, 291, 300, 301–2, 304, 315–16, 317, 320, 330

Raimi, Sam, 208
Red Dead Redemption (video game), 289
Red Dead Revolver (video game), 289
Red River (film), xi, 311
Reed, Ishmael, 152–73; and neo-hoodoo, 156; and stereotypes, 160–61
regeneration through violence. *See* frontier myth
Rehak, Bob, 274
Remington, Frederic, 214, 293
Return of the Jedi (film), 247n33
revenge western, 290, 293–95
Riders of the Purple Sage (Grey), x, xiii
Rifkin, Mark, 203
Rio Bravo (film), 80
The Road (McCarthy), 67
Robertson, Shawn, 276
RoboCop (film), 184, 190, 195n19
Robopocalypse (Wilson), 123
Roe, Jane, 205
Roe v. Wade, 198, 205
Romero, George A., 227, 231, 241
Roosevelt, Teddy, xv, 214, 294
Ross, Andrew, 329
Rossi, Theo, 236
Roth, Eli, 254
Rowlandson, Mary, 213

Rubin, Gayle
Russell, Jayne, 311
Russell, Kurt, 177, 181

Sacher-Masoch, Leopold von, 321
Salter, Anastasia, 292, 295
Samuels, Shirley, 301
Sanada, Hiroyuki, 232
Saturn Devouring His Son (Goya), 206
Schleiner, Anne-Marie, 278
scopophilia, 277–79, 303, 304, 319
Scott, Ridley, 178, 303
Scream (film), 199, 208, 212, 222n27
The Searchers (film), 91, 99, 182, 254
Sedgwick, Catharine, 293
Sedgwick, Eve Kosofsky, 14, 180, 182
sex: and consumption, 226, 230, 231, 237, 240, 245; and monstrosity, 257–59, 261, 264; and otherness, xviii; and women's sexuality and capitalism, 228, 232–35
Shail, Robert, 238, 247n27
Shane (film), viii, xxi, 83–84, 177–94
The Shining (film), xxii, 253–66
The Ship Who Sang (McCaffrey), xxiv
"The Significance of the Frontier in American History" (Turner), 204, 210
The Silence of the Lambs (film), 208
Simkin, Stevie, 297
Singer, Bryan, 184
Sintumuang, Kevin, 230
Skin Shows (Halberstam), 203
Slotkin, Richard, 26, 38, 137, 212, 246nn13–15, 247n21, 277, 279. *See also* frontier myth
Smith, Joshua, 152
Smith, Nicola, 226, 235, 243
Snow, Brittany, 215
Snyder, Zack, 226–28, 240, 244, 247n28
Soldier (film), xxi, 177–94

Sontag, Susan, xix, 53–71, 315, 329
Spacey, Kevin, 177
Spears, Britney, 219, 223n43
Spurgeon, Sara L., 54, 57, 59, 115–17, 131, 227, 269, 313–14
Star Trek (TV series), xi–xii, 24
Star Wars (film). See *The Mandalorian* (TV series)
steampunk, 313–14, 317, 320, 322, 328, 329, 331n13
stereotypes: of African Americans, 153, 155, 159, 160; of homosexuality, 153, 155, 159, 160–62, 165–66, 168; of Native Americans, 164, 210, 240
Stevens, George, 177
Stewart, Patrick, 190

Tarantino, Quentin, 311
technomasculinity, 181
The Texas Chain Saw Massacre (film), xxi, 198–223
Texas Chainsaw 3D (film), 207
Texas Heartbeat Act (Senate Bill 8), 198
They Died with Their Boots On (film), 80
Thorne, Jared, 187
The Thousand Crimes of Ming Tsu (Lin), 130
Tietchen, Todd, 157, 167, 168
Tompkins, Jane, 14, 60, 95, 99, 167, 183, 273
Total Recall (film), 184
Trail of Lightning (Roanhorse), 62–64
transexual, 211
transphobia, 211
tricksters, 152, 168
True Grit (film), 83, 93
Turner, Frederick Jackson, 24, 32, 37, 64, 90, 156, 204, 210, 217, 219
Twilight (Meyer), 111, 115
2001: A Space Odyssey (film), 254

Ulmer, Jesse Gerlach, 183, 184
"The Uncanny" (Freud), 259
Under the Glacier (Laxness), 56
Unforgiven (film), 254
Ure, Stephen, 212
The Uses of Enchantment (Bettelheim), 259

Valdivia, Angharad N., 247n31
Vampires of El Norte (Cañas), 130
Verhoeven, Paul, 184
The Virginian (Wister), xiii, xiv, 184, 289, 294–95, 341
"Viva Las Vegas" (song), 226
Vizenor, Gerald, 63
Von Teese, Dita, xvi–xvii

The Walking Dead (TV series), 93, 96, 240
Wang, Ya-huei, 259–60
War Code (film), 111
Ward, Burt, 316
Warner, Michael, 290, 301
Warner, William, 270
Washington, Booker T., 164
The Water Knife (Bacigalupi), xix–xx, xxiii, 53–71
Wayne, John, 8–9, 10, 11, 14, 41, 76, 84, 91, 93, 95, 97, 99, 211, 311, 313
Weird Tales (periodical), 153, 154
weird western, definition of, vii, xxivn2, 3, 55, 77, 152, 227
Weird Westerns (Fine et al.), 269, 313
Weiss, Margot, 329
Wells, Ida B., 170n65
West, Adam, 316, 331n3
West, Ty, 198, 202, 204, 217, 218
Westworld (TV series), xiii, 11, 14, 41
Whedon, Joss, 293
The Wild Bunch (film), 91
The Wild Wild West (TV series), xxiii, xiv, 311–22; and "The Night of

the Eccentrics," 318–24; and "The Night of the Vicious Valentine," 324–28
Winter in the Blood (Welch), 129
Wister, Owen, 214, 289, 294–95
The Wolverine (film), 190
Woo, John, 184
Worden, Daniel, 183
Wright, Will, 245n8, 246n9

X (film), xxi, 198–202, 204, 206–12, 215–20
X-Men (film), 184, 190

X-Men Origins (film), 190

Yellow Back Radio Broke-Down (Reed), xx–xxi, 129, 152–71

Z Nation (TV series), 238
Zombie, Rob, 208
zombie apocalypse, 228
zombies, 226–48; and consumption, 236, 241; and frontier myth, 232; and Native Americans, 240; and westerns, 227, 230; and zom-coms, 238, 247n32

In the Postwestern Horizons series

The Places of Modernity in Early Mexican American Literature, 1848–1948
José F. Aranda Jr.

Dirty Wars: Landscape, Power, and Waste in Western American Literature
John Beck

Post-Westerns: Cinema, Region, West
Neil Campbell

The Rhizomatic West: Representing the American West in a Transnational, Global, Media Age
Neil Campbell

The Comic Book Western: New Perspectives on a Global Genre
Edited by Christopher Conway and Antoinette Sol

Hell-Bent for Leather: Sex and Sexuality in the Weird Western
Edited by Kerry Fine, Michael K. Johnson, Rebecca M. Lush, and Sara L. Spurgeon

Weird Westerns: Race, Gender, Genre
Edited by Kerry Fine, Michael K. Johnson, Rebecca M. Lush, and Sara L. Spurgeon

Positive Pollutions and Cultural Toxins: Waste and Contamination in Contemporary U.S. Ethnic Literatures
John Blair Gamber

A Planetary Lens: The Photo-Poetics of Western Women's Writing
Audrey Goodman

Dirty Words in Deadwood: *Literature and the Postwestern*
Edited by Melody Graulich and Nicolas Witschi

True West: Authenticity and the American West
Edited by William R. Handley and Nathaniel Lewis

Teaching Western American Literature
Edited by Brady Harrison and Randi Lynn Tanglen

Manifest Destiny 2.0: Genre Trouble in Game Worlds
Sara Humphreys

Speculative Wests: Popular Representations of a Region and Genre
Michael K. Johnson

We Who Work the West: Class, Labor, and Space in Western American Literature
Kiara Kharpertian
Edited by Carlo Rotella and Christopher P. Wilson

Captivating Westerns: The Middle East in the American West
Susan Kollin

*Postwestern Cultures:
Literature, Theory, Space*
Edited by Susan Kollin

Westerns: A Women's History
Victoria Lamont

*Manifest and Other Destinies:
Territorial Fictions of the
Nineteenth-Century United States*
Stephanie LeMenager

*Unsettling the Literary West:
Authenticity and Authorship*
Nathaniel Lewis

Morta Las Vegas: CSI *and
the Problem of the West*
Nathaniel Lewis and Stephen Tatum

*Late Westerns: The
Persistence of a Genre*
Lee Clark Mitchell

*María Amparo Ruiz de Burton:
Critical and Pedagogical Perspectives*
Edited by Amelia María de la
Luz Montes and Anne
Elizabeth Goldman

*In the Mean Time: Temporal
Colonization and the Mexican
American Literary Tradition*
Erin Murrah-Mandril

Unhomely Wests: Essays from A to Z
Stephen Tatum

To order or obtain more information on these or other University of Nebraska Press titles, visit nebraskapress.unl.edu.

www.ingramcontent.com/pod-product-compliance
Lightning Source LLC
Chambersburg PA
CBHW030603230426
43661CB00053B/1821